HAR...
20
WOORDEN

BASISWOORDENBOEK
ENGELS-NEDERLANDS

HARRAP'S
2000
WOORDEN
BASISWOORDENBOEK
ENGELS-NEDERLANDS

P. H. Collin
Ron Helsloot
Eva Reichling

HARRAP
London

First published in Great Britain 1983
by Harrap Limited
19–23 Ludgate Hill, London EC4M 7PD

© Harrap Limited, 1983
Reprinted 1985

ISBN 0–245–53944–1

Typeset in Monophoto Times and Univers
and printed in Great Britain by
Richard Clay (The Chaucer Press) Ltd,
Bungay, Suffolk

Voorwoord

Dit woordenboek bevat de 2000 meest gebruikte Engelse woorden. Daarnaast zult u er echter veel woorden in aantreffen die met die hoofdwoorden zijn samengesteld of ervan zijn afgeleid. Het totaal aantal opgenomen woorden komt zo op 4000.

Het woordenboek zal u op verschillende manieren tot steun kunnen zijn bij het leren van de Engelse taal. Ten eerste worden de woorden die erin voorkomen gebruikt in de eerste jaren van Engelse cursussen. Vervolgens is ieder hoofdwoord vertaald en achter de vertaling volgen voorbeelden van hoe het in zinnen kan worden gebruikt. Waar de betekenis van een zin niet direct duidelijk is, is bovendien een vertaling van die hele zin of van een gedeelte daarvan gegeven. Van elk woord is daarnaast aangegeven hoe het moet worden uitgesproken. En verder zijn aan het eind van veel trefwoorden op een grijze strip grammaticale opmerkingen toegevoegd.

Het laatste gedeelte van het boek bevat tenslotte oefeningen die u zelf of in klasseverband kunt doen. Het geeft niet als u een antwoord fout heeft—de juiste antwoorden treft u achterin het boek aan.

Uitspraak

In het woordenboek worden onderstaande tekens gebruikt om aan te geven hoe een woord wordt uitgesproken.

Ook wordt het teken (′) gebruikt om aan te geven waar in een woord de klemtoon komt te liggen, maar denk erom dat het hierbij slechts om algemene aanwijzingen gaat en dat de uitspraak van een woord kan veranderen al naar gelang de plaats die het in de zin inneemt.

æ	back	ə	afraid	ð	then	r	round
ɑː	farm	əʊ	boat	dʒ	just	s	some
ɒ	top	əʊə	lower	f	fog	ʃ	short
aɪ	pipe	ɜː	word	g	go	t	too
aʊ	how	iː	heap	h	hand	tʃ	chop
aɪə	fire	ɪ	hit	j	yes	θ	thing
aʊə	flower	ɪə	hear	k	catch	v	voice
ɔː	bought	uː	school	l	last	w	was
ɔɪ	toy	ʊ	book	m	mix	z	zoo
e	fed	ʌ	but	n	nut	ʒ	treasure
eə	hair	b	back	ŋ	sing		
eɪ	take	d	dog	p	penny		

Alfabet

Dit zijn de letters van het Engelse alfabet, de uitspraak is ernaast aangegeven.

Aa	eɪ	**Hh**	eɪtʃ	**Oo**	əʊ	**Vv**	viː
Bb	biː	**Ii**	aɪ	**Pp**	piː	**Ww**	′dʌbljuː
Cc	siː	**Jj**	dʒeɪ	**Qq**	kjuː	**Xx**	eks
Dd	diː	**Kk**	keɪ	**Rr**	ɑː	**Yy**	waɪ
Ee	iː	**Ll**	el	**Ss**	es	**Zz**	zed
Ff	ef	**Mm**	em	**Tt**	tiː		
Gg	dʒiː	**Nn**	en	**Uu**	juː		

Aa

a, an [eɪ, æn *of* ə, ən] *lw*
(a) een; I want a glass of water; a big car; he has a good job; an empty house; a useful knife.
(b) per; these oranges cost 50p a kilo; the car was doing 30 kilometres an hour.
Let op: **an** *wordt gebruikt voor woorden beginnend met* **a, e, i, o, u** *en met* **h** *als de* **h** *niet wordt uitgesproken* (**an apple; an hour**); **a** *wordt voor de overige letters gebruikt en ook voor de* **u** *wanneer deze als* **ju** (**a university**) *wordt uitgesproken.*

able [ˈeɪbl] *bn*
he wasn't able to breathe = hij kon niet ademen; will you be able to come to the party? = kunt u op het feest komen? he wasn't able to find the house.
Let op: **able** *wordt met* **to** *en een werkwoord gebruikt.*
ability [əˈbɪlɪtɪ] *zn*
vermogen; bekwaamheid; I'll do it to the best of my ability = zo goed mogelijk.

about [əˈbaʊt] *bw & vz*
(a) over; tell me about your holiday; what do you want to speak to me about? he is worried about his health.
(b) ongeveer; the room is about three metres square; the next train leaves at about four o'clock; she's about twenty years old; the town is about ten kilometres from here.
(c) in het rond; he left his papers lying about on the floor.
(d) to be about to do something = op het punt staan iets te doen; I was just about to go out when you phoned.

above [əˈbʌv] *bw & vz*
boven; the plane flew above the clouds; the temperature was above 40°.

abroad [əˈbrɔːd] *bw*
in/naar het buitenland; he lives abroad; they are going abroad on holiday.

absence [ˈæbsəns] *zn*
afwezigheid; in the absence of Mr Smith = als Mr Smith afwezig is.
absent [ˈæbsənt] *bn*
afwezig; three children are absent because they are ill.

absolutely [ˈæbsəluːtlɪ] *bw*
volkomen/absoluut; you're absolutely right; the weather was absolutely awful.

accent [ˈæksənt] *zn*
accent; uitspraak; he speaks English with an Irish accent; she has a southern accent.

accept [əkˈsept] *ww*
(a) aannemen/accepteren; will you accept this little present?
(b) toestemmen; I invited her to the party and she accepted.
accepts—accepting—accepted— has accepted

accident [ˈæksɪdənt] *zn*
(a) toeval; I met her by accident at the bus stop.
(b) ongeluk; she had an accident and had to go to hospital; three people were killed in the accident on the motorway.
accidentally [æksɪˈdentəlɪ] *bw*
(a) toevallig; I found the missing watch accidentally.
(b) bij een ongeval; he was killed accidentally.

accompany [əˈkʌmpnɪ] *ww*
(a) vergezellen; he accompanied his wife to hospital; roast beef accompanied by boiled potatoes.
(b) begeleiden; he was accompanying the

singer on the piano; she accompanied herself on the piano.

accompanies—accompanying—accompanied—has accompanied

according to [ə'kɔːdɪŋ tʊ] *bw*
volgens; **according to the newspaper, today is a public holiday; according to the TV, it will be fine tomorrow.**

account [ə'kaʊnt] *zn*
(*a*) (bank)rekening; **how much money do you have in your account? he put £10 into his bank account.**
(*b*) **on account of** = vanwege; **the trains are late on account of the fog.**

ache [eɪk] *zn*
pijn; (*wordt samen met andere woorden gebruikt om aan te geven waar de pijn zit: zie* **headache, toothache**)

across [ə'krɒs] *bw & vz*
(*a*) over; **he swam across the river; don't run across the road; the river is 50 metres across** = breed.
(*b*) aan de overkant; **he lives across the street; their house is across the street from ours** = recht tegenover.

act [ækt] *ww*
(*a*) (film/toneel etc.) spelen; **she's acted on TV many times; he acted the part of Hamlet in the film.**
(*b*) handelen; **he had to act quickly to save his sister.**

acts—acting—acted—has acted

action ['ækʃn] *zn*
daad; **he regretted his action** = hij had spijt van wat hij gedaan had.

active ['æktɪv] *bn*
levendig/actief; **although he is over eighty, he is still very active.**

actor ['æktə] *zn*
acteur.

actress ['æktrəs] *zn*
actrice.

meervoud **actresses**

act upon, *ww*
handelen naar aanleiding van; **he acted upon your suggestion.**

actual ['æktjʊəl] *bn*
werkelijk/feitelijk; **what are the actual figures for the number of children in school?**

actually, *bw*
werkelijk/echt; **is he actually going to sell his shop?**

ad [æd] *zie* **advertisement**

add [æd] *ww*
(*a*) optellen; **if you add ten and fifteen you get twenty-five.**
(*b*) toevoegen; **if your coffee isn't sweet enough, add some more sugar** = doe er dan nog een beetje suiker bij; **she added a few words at the end of the letter.**

adds—adding—added—has added

addition [ə'dɪʃn] *zn*
optelling; **she is good at addition, but not at multiplication.**

add up, *ww*
(bij elkaar) optellen; **if you add up all these figures, the answer should be a thousand.**
Let op: **add the numbers up** *of* **add up the numbers,** *maar alleen* **add them up**

add up to, *ww*
opleveren; **the sums of money we have spent add up to over £100** = komen bij elkaar op £100.

address [ə'dres] **1.** *zn*
adres; **what is the address of the new bookshop? write all their addresses on a piece of paper; her address is: 15 High Street, Bradford, Yorkshire.**
meervoud **addresses**
2. *ww*
adresseren; **the letter is addressed to your father.**
addresses—addressing—addressed—has addressed

adjective ['ædʒɪktɪv] *zn*
bijvoeglijk naamwoord; **in the phrase 'a big green door', 'big' and 'green' are both adjectives.**

admire [əd'maɪə] *ww*
bewonderen; **he was admiring my new car.**
admires—admiring—admired—has admired

admiration [ædmə'reɪʃn] *zn*
bewondering; I have a great admiration for his work.

admit [əd'mɪt] *ww*
(*a*) toelaten; this ticket admits one person; children are admitted free.
(*b*) toegeven; he admitted he was the person who broke the window/he admitted to having broken the window.
admits—admitting—admitted— has admitted

adult ['ædʌlt, ə'dʌlt] *zn & bn*
volwassen(e); the price for adults is £1; an adult elephant.

advantage [əd'vɑ:ntɪdʒ] *zn*
(*a*) voordeel; it will be an advantage if you can speak Italian.
(*b*) to take advantage of = profiteren van; we took advantage of the fine weather and went on a picnic.

adventure [əd'ventʃə] *zn*
avontuur; he told us of his adventures while he was crossing the desert.

adverb ['ædvɜ:b] *zn*
bijwoord; in the sentence 'he drives quickly', the word 'quickly' is an adverb.

advert ['ædvɜ:t] *zie* **advertisement**

advertise ['ædvətaɪz] *ww*
adverteren; he advertised his car in the newspaper; the company is advertising for new secretaries; jobs are advertised in the local paper.
advertises—advertising— advertised—has advertised

advertisement [æd'vɜ:tɪzmənt], **advert** ['ædvɜ:t], **ad** [æd] *zn*
advertentie; if you want to sell the carpet, put an ad in the paper; I sold the carpet through an advert in the paper; she answered an advertisement in the paper and got a better job.
Let op: advert *en* ad *worden wel in de spreektaal gebruikt, maar zelden geschreven*

advice [əd'vaɪs] *zn*
advies; he went to the teacher for advice on how to do his homework; she would not listen to my advice; my advice to you is that you should take a long holiday; the doctor's advice was to stay in bed; he took the doctor's advice and went to bed. *geen meervoud:* some advice; a piece of advice

advise [əd'vaɪz] *ww*
adviseren/aanraden; the doctor advised him to stay in bed; she advised me to sell my car; I would advise you to drive slowly.
advises—advising—advised—has advised

advise against, *ww*
afraden; I wanted to learn to fly, but she advised against it; the doctor advised against going to bed late.

aeroplane ['eərəpleɪn] *zn* (*Amer.* **airplane**)
vliegtuig; the passengers got into the aeroplane.

afford [ə'fɔ:d] *ww*
zich (kunnen) veroorloven/permitteren; I can't afford a new pair of shoes; how can you afford two holidays a year?
affords—affording—afforded— has afforded

afraid [ə'freɪd] *bn*
(*a*) to be afraid (of) = bang zijn (voor); I am afraid of snakes; she's afraid of the dark; he's afraid to climb on to the roof.
(*b*) I'm afraid (that) = het spijt me (dat); I'm afraid we have no seats left; I'm afraid she's ill; have you got a watch?— no, I'm afraid not.
Let op: afraid *kan niet voor een zelfstandig naamwoord gebruikt worden:* she's afraid *maar* a frightened girl

after ['ɑ:ftə] **1.** *vz*
(*a*) na; if today is Monday, the day after tomorrow is Wednesday = overmorgen; he arrived after me; I must go to bed— it's after midnight; they came in one after the other.
(*b*) to be after = achterna zitten; the police are after him; if you eat all the cake, your mother will be after you;

what's he after? = wat wil/moet hij eigenlijk?
2. *vw*
nadat; **after the rain came the grass started to grow; after the driver got in, the bus set off; phone me after you get home.**
Let op: **after** *wordt met allerlei werkwoorden gebruikt:* **look after; take after,** *etc.*

after all, *bw*
(*a*) toch; **he changed his mind and decided to go to the party after all.**
(*b*) tenslotte; **I think I shall stay at home—after all, I have no work to do at the office and it's a fine day.**

afternoon [ɑːftə'nuːn] *zn*
middag; **I always have a little sleep in the afternoon; she doesn't work on Tuesday afternoons; we met at 3 o'clock in the afternoon;** = **'s middags; I will try to catch the afternoon train; can you come to see me this afternoon or tomorrow afternoon?** = vanmiddag of morgenmiddag?

afterwards ['ɑːftəwədz] *bw*
later/naderhand; **we'll go shopping first, and visit the museum afterwards; he was very well before lunch, but felt ill afterwards.**

again [ə'geɪn *of* ə'gen] *bw*
opnieuw/weer; **he sang the song again; you must come to see us again.**
once again = weer (een keer); **once again, the car refused to start.**
yet again = weer (eens); **he is back in hospital yet again.**

against [ə'genst] *vz*
(*a*) tegen; **the ladder is leaning against the wall; he hit his head against a low branch.**
(*b*) **against the rules/against the law** = tegen de regels/de wet; **it's against the law to open the shop on a Sunday; you can't hold the football in your hands— it's against the rules; have you anything against my going out this evening?** = vindt u het goed als ik uitga? **she was against the idea of going to the cinema.**
(*c*) tegen; **our school is playing against**

the girls' school at football; it's hard cycling against the wind.

age [eɪdʒ] *zn*
(*a*) leeftijd; **what's your age on your next birthday?** = hoe oud word je etc.; **he was sixty years of age; she looks younger than her age; old age** =(op) hoge leeftijd.
(*b*) **for ages** = eindeloos; **I've been waiting here for ages.**
aged, *bn*
(*a*) [eɪdʒd] oud; **a boy aged twelve; he died last year, aged 64.**
(*b*) ['eɪdʒɪd] bejaard; **an aged man.**

agent ['eɪdʒnt] *zn*
agent/vertegenwoordiger; **he is the agent for Japanese cars; Mr Smith is our agent in Australia.**

ago [ə'gəʊ] *bw*
geleden; **I saw him five minutes ago; she left home two years ago; it all happened a long time ago** = lang geleden.

agree [ə'griː] *ww*
het eens zijn; toestemmen; **I agree with you that we need a new car; we asked her to come with us and she agreed.**
agrees—agreeing—agreed—has agreed

agreement, *zn*
instemming; **he nodded to show his agreement; they are in agreement with our plan** = ze zijn het ermee eens.

ahead [ə'hed] *bw*
voor; **our team was losing, but now we are ahead; ahead of us was a big old house; he has a lot of work ahead of him; we walked on ahead of the others** = vooruit; **run on ahead and keep some seats for us.**

aim [eɪm] *ww*
(*a*) richten/mikken; **he aimed his gun at the policeman.**
(*b*) streven; **we aim to save enough money to go on holiday.**
aims—aiming—aimed—has aimed

air [eə] *zn*
lucht; **the air felt cold; he kicked the ball up into the air.**

by air = per vliegtuig; per luchtpost;
**we are travelling to France by air; I must
send this letter by air.**
aircraft, *zn*
vliegtuig; **the pilot got into the aircraft.**
Let op: het meervoud is **aircraft: one
aircraft, six aircraft**

air force, *zn*
luchtmacht; **he's joining the air force.**
air hostess, *zn*
stewardess.
meervoud: **air hostesses**

airplane, *zn*
(*Amerikaans voor* **aircraft**) vliegtuig.
airport, *zn*
vliegveld; **we are due to leave London
Airport at five o'clock; you can take a
bus to the airport.**

alcohol ['ælkəhɒl] *zn*
alcohol.
alcoholic [ælkə'hɒlık] *bn*
alcoholisch; **an alcoholic drink.**

alike [ə'laık] *bn*
gelijk; **the two brothers are very alike** =
lijken veel op elkaar.
Let op: **alike** *wordt alleen na een
werkwoord gebuikt*

alive [ə'laıv] *bn*
levend/in leven; **the fish is still alive, even
though it was caught an hour ago; my
grandfather was alive when the first aero-
planes flew.**
Let op: **alive** *kan niet voor een zelfstandig naamwoord gebruikt worden:*
the fish is alive *maar* **a live fish**

all [ɔ:l] **1.** *bn & vz*
alle; allemaal; **all the tomatoes are red;
are all the children here? we all like
chocolate; let's sing the song all together**
= allemaal tegelijk.
2. *bw*
helemaal; **the ground was all white after
the snow fell; I forgot all about her
birthday.**
all at once = plotseling; **all at once
the telephone rang.**
not at all = helemaal niet; **do you
mind waiting for ten minutes?—not at
all!**

all by yourself = helemaal alleen;
**he was all by himself; I'm all by myself;
she did it all by herself** = helemaal zelf.
all over = (*a*) overal; **there was sugar
all over the cake** = over de hele cake;
she poured water all over the table.
(*b*) voorbij; **when it was all over we went
home.**
all right, *bn*
(*a*) in orde; **I was sick yesterday, but I'm
all right now.**
(*b*) **will you answer the telephone for
me?—all right** = goed!
all the same, *bw*
toch; **I don't like parties, but I shall come
to yours all the same.**

allow [ə'laʊ] *ww*
toestaan; **you are not allowed to walk on
the grass; he allowed me to see his stamp
collection; are we allowed to sit down?** =
mogen we gaan zitten?
**allows—allowing—allowed—has
allowed**

almost ['ɔ:lməʊst] *bw*
bijna; **he is almost as tall as I am; hurry
up, it's almost time for the train to leave.**

alone [ə'ləʊn] *bn*
alleen; **she was all alone in the house; I
want to talk to you alone** = onder vier
ogen.

along [ə'lɒŋ] **1.** *vz*
langs; **there are trees along both
sides of the road; he was walking along
the bank of the river.**
2. *bw*
to go along/to come along = mee gaan/
komen; **come along with us; he went
along to the police station to report the
accident.**

aloud [ə'laʊd] *bw*
hardop/luidop; **he was reading the
newspaper aloud; I was just thinking
aloud** = ik dacht alleen hardop.

alphabet ['ælfəbet] *zn*
alfabet; **A is the first letter of the alphabet.**
alphabetical [ælfə'betıkl] *bn*
alfabetisch; **the telephone book has all**

the names in alphabetical order = in
alfabetische volgorde.

already [ɔːl′redɪ] *bw*
al; **it is already past ten o'clock; has he
finished work already?** = nu al; **I've seen
that film already** = al eerder/al een
keer.

also [′ɔːlsəʊ] *bw*
ook/eveneens; **he sings and can also play
the piano; she came to dinner, and her
son also came.**

although [ɔːl′ðəʊ] *vw*
hoewel; **although it was snowing, it was
not very cold; although he is eighty, he
still goes running every morning;** *zie ook*
though.

altogether [ɔːltə′geðə] *bw*
(*a*) samen/bij elkaar; **the shirt is £10 and
the tie is £5, that makes £15 altogether.**
(*b*) helemaal/volledig; **he forgot about it
altogether.**

always [′ɔːlweɪz] *bw*
altijd/steeds; **he is always late; it always
rains when we want to go for a walk; in
tropical countries it is always hot; she's
always in a hurry.**

am [æm] *zie* **be**

a.m. [′eɪ ′em] *bw*
's morgens/'s ochtends; **I have to get up
at 6 a.m. every day; she's going to catch
the 10 a.m. train to Edinburgh.**
Let op: met **a.m.** *wordt meestal het
hele uur aangeduid en het woord—
wordt dan weggelaten.*

ambulance [′æmbjʊləns] *zn*
ambulance/ziekenauto; **the injured man
was taken away in an ambulance.**

America [ə′merɪkə] *zn*
(*a*) Amerika (Noord- en Zuid-).
(*b*) de Verenigde Staten; **we're going
to America on holiday; they live in
America.**
*Let op: terwille van de duidelijkheid
kan het land zelf het beste* **the
United States** *of the* **US** *genoemd
worden*

American, 1. *bn*
Amerikaans; **the American President;
she drives an American car.**
2. *zn*
Amerikaan(se); **Americans make very
good ice cream.**

among [ə′mʌŋ] *vz*
(*a*) tussen; onder; **the birds built their
nests among the leaves; among the people
at the party was a man who reads the
news on TV.**
(*b*) onder; **the cake was divided among
the children.**

amount [ə′maʊnt] **1.** *zn*
hoeveelheid; bedrag; **she drinks a large
amount of tea; he gave away his money
in large amounts.**
2. *ww*
bedragen; **the bill amounted to £100.**
amounts—amounting—
amounted—has amounted

amuse [ə′mjuːz] *ww*
vermaken/amuseren; **they amused themselves playing football; the teacher
amused the children by showing them a
film.**
amuses—amusing—amused—has
amused

amusement, *zn*
vermaak; **he poured a bucket of water
over his head to the great amusement of
the children.**
amusing, *bn*
amusant/leuk; **the film was very
amusing; I didn't find the book very
amusing.**

an [æn *of* ən] *zie* **a**

and [ænd *of* ənd] *vw*
en; **my mother and father; he likes apples
and milk; he was running and singing at
the same time; come and sit down.**
*Let op: spreek getallen boven de 100
uit met* **seven hundred and two
(702)**

and so on, *bw*
enzovoort; **he talked about gardens,
flowers, and so on** = en meer van dergelijke dingen.

anger [ˈæŋgə] *zn*
boosheid; **he showed his anger by banging on the table.**
angry [ˈæŋgrɪ] *bn*
boos; **he's angry with his children because they broke a window; she gets angry if the trains are late; everyone is angry about the price of petrol.**
angry—angrier—angriest
angrily, *bw*
boos.

animal [ˈænɪməl] *zn*
dier; **dogs and cats are animals, and man is also an animal; we went to see the animals in the zoo.**

ankle [ˈæŋkl] *zn*
enkel; **he twisted his ankle** = hij heeft zijn enkel verstuikt.

annoy [əˈnɔɪ] *ww*
ergeren; **it annoys me to have to go out in the rain.**
annoys—annoying—annoyed—has annoyed
annoyed, *bn*
kwaad; **he's annoyed because we all forgot his birthday; she's annoyed with the dog because it ate her chocolates.**
annoying, *bn*
vervelend; **it's annoying to have to wait for a bus.**

another [əˈnʌðə] *bn & vnw*
(a) nog een; **would you like another cup of tea?**
(b) een ander(e); **she fell down and made her dress dirty, so she had to change into another one;** *zie ook* **each other, one another.**

answer [ˈɑːnsə] **1.** *zn*
antwoord; **I phoned the office, but there was no answer; have you had an answer to your letter yet?**
2. *ww*
(be)antwoorden; **he hasn't answered my letter; when he asked them if they had enjoyed the book, they all answered 'no'; to answer the telephone** = aannemen.
answers—answering—answered—has answered

answer back, *ww*
brutaal wat terugzeggen; **if you answer back like that the teacher will be angry with you.**

anxious [ˈæŋʃəs] *bn*
(a) angstig/bezorgd; **my sister is still ill—I am anxious about her.**
(b) iets erg graag willen; **she was anxious to get home; I was anxious to see him.**

any [ˈenɪ] **1.** *bn & vnw*
(a) welk(e) je maar wilt; ieder; **take any one you like; come any day next week.**
(b) enig(e), wat; **have you any salt? is there any cake left? would you like any more coffee?**
(c) not ... any = geen (meer/over); **there aren't any cakes left; give me your money—I haven't got any** = niets.
2. *bw*
not ... any + *vergrotende trap* = (helemaal) niet; **I can't sing any louder; the car won't go any faster.**
anybody [ˈenɪbɒdɪ], **anyone** [ˈenɪwʌn] *vnw*
(a) iedereen; **anybody can learn to ride a bicycle; anybody can do it, can't they?**
(b) iemand; **can anybody lend me ten pounds? I didn't meet anybody** = niemand.
anyhow [ˈenɪhaʊ] *bw*
toch; in ieder geval; **it was raining, but I didn't want to go out anyhow.**
anyone [ˈenɪwʌn] *zie* **anybody**
anything [ˈenɪθɪŋ] *vnw*
(a) alles (wat); **you can take anything you want; our dog will eat anything.**
(b) iets; **did anything happen during the night? has anything made you ill? do you want anything more to drink? he didn't eat anything** = niets.
anyway [ˈenɪweɪ] *bw*
toch; in ieder geval; **it was raining but I didn't want to go out anyway; the doctor told me to stay in bed, but I'm still going to the party anyway.**
anywhere [ˈenɪweə] *bw*
(a) ergens/overal; **put the book down anywhere.**
(b) ergens; **is there anywhere where I can put this box? I haven't seen it anywhere** = nergens.

apart [ə'pɑ:t] *bw*
apart/uit elkaar; **the two towns are very far apart; the watch came apart in my hands** = is uit elkaar gevallen; **they live apart now** = ze wonen nu gescheiden.
apart from = behalve; **they all wore black hats, apart from me.**

apartment [ə'pɑ:tmənt] *zn*
Amerikaans voor **flat**

appear [ə'pɪə] *ww*
(*a*) verschijnen; **a ship suddenly appeared in the distance** = opdoemen; **a man appeared at the door.**
(*b*) schijnen; **he appears to be ill; it appears to be raining.**
appears—appearing—appeared—has appeared

appearance [ə'pɪərəns] *zn*
verschijning; **you could tell from her appearance that she had been climbing trees; he put in an appearance at the meeting** = hij is even geweest

apple ['æpl] *zn*
appel; **apple pie; don't eat that green apple—it isn't ripe yet.**
apple tree, *zn*
appelboom.

apply [ə'plaɪ] *ww*
(*a*) solliciteren; zich aanmelden; **she applied for a job as a teacher; he applied to join the police force.**
(*b*) betrekking hebben (op); **this applies to all of you; the rule applies to visitors only.**
applies—applying—applied—has applied

application [æplɪ'keɪʃn] *zn*
sollicitatie; **if you are applying for the job, you must fill in an application form** = aanmeldingsformulier.

appoint [ə'pɔɪnt] *ww*
benoemen/aanstellen; **he was appointed headmaster.**
appoints—appointing—appointed—has appointed

appointment, *zn*
(*a*) benoeming/aanstelling; **on his appointment as headmaster** = bij zijn benoeming.
(*b*) afspraak; **I have an appointment with the doctor/to see the doctor on Tuesday; can I make an appointment to see Dr Jones? I'm very busy—I've got appointments all day.**

appreciate [ə'pri:ʃɪeɪt] *ww*
waarderen; **he always appreciates good food.**
appreciates—appreciating—appreciated—has appreciated

approach [ə'prəʊtʃ] *ww*
naderen; **as the policeman approached, all the children ran away; the time is approaching when we will have to decide what to do.**
approaches—approaching—approached—has approached

approve [ə'pru:v] *ww*
to approve of something = goedkeuren; **I don't approve of noisy children; the police don't approve of fast cars; he approves of staying in bed.**
approves—approving—approved—has approved

April ['eɪprəl] *zn*
april; **his birthday is in April; she died on April 20th; we went on holiday last April; today is April 5th.**
Let op: **April 5th:** *zeg* 'the fifth of April' *of* 'April the fifth'
Let op: **April** *wordt altijd met een hoofdletter geschreven*

apron ['eɪprən] *zn*
schort; **put on an apron if you are going to do the washing up.**

are [ɑ:] *zie* **be**

area ['eərɪə] *zn*
(*a*) oppervlakte; **to measure the area of a room you must multiply the length by the width; the area of the garden is 250 square metres.**
(*b*) gebied; terrein; **the houses in this area are very expensive; the police are searching the area round the school.**

aren't [ɑ:nt] *zie* **be**

argue [ˈɑːgjuː] *ww*
(rede)twisten; ruzie hebben; she argued with the waiter about the bill.
argues—arguing—argued—has argued

argument [ˈɑːgjʊmənt] *zn*
woordenwisseling; ruzie; they got into an argument about money.

arithmetic [əˈrɪθmətɪk] *zn*
(het) rekenen, rekenkunde.

arm [ɑːm] *zn*
(a) arm; his arm hurt after he fell down; she broke her arm skiing; lift your arms up above your head.
(b) (arm) leuning; he sat on the arm of my chair.
(c) **arms** = wapens.
armchair, *zn*
leunstoel.
armed, *bn*
gewapend/bewapend; the soldiers were armed with knives; are the policemen all armed? the armed forces = de strijdkrachten.

army [ˈɑːmɪ] *zn*
leger; the British army; he left school and joined the army.
meervoud **armies**

around [əˈraʊnd] *vz*
(a) om . . . heen; rond; the water was all around the house.
(b) ongeveer; the car costs around £4,000.

arrange [əˈreɪndʒ] *ww*
(a) ordenen/rangschikken; she arranged the books in rows; the books are arranged in alphabetical order.
(b) afspreken; we arranged to meet at 6 o'clock.
arranges—arranging— arranged—has arranged

arrangement, *zn*
regeling; afspraak; all the arrangements have been made for the wedding.

arrest [əˈrest] *ww*
arresteren; the policeman arrested the

burglar; he was arrested as he was climbing out of the window.
arrests—arresting—arrested— has arrested

arrive [əˈraɪv] *ww*
aankomen; the plane arrives in London at 4 o'clock; we arrived at the cinema after the film had started; she arrived home tired out.
arrives—arriving—arrived—has arrived
Let op: you arrive in a town, *maar* arrive at a place

arrival, *zn*
(a) aankomst; the time of arrival is 4 o'clock.
(b) (pas) aangekomene; he's a new arrival.
(c) (*vliegveld*) arrivals = aankomsthal.

art [ɑːt] *zn*
kunst.
art gallery, *zn*
(kunst)museum/(kunst)galerie.

article [ˈɑːtɪkl] *zn*
(a) ding/artikel; article of clothing = kledingstuk.
(b) lidwoord (a *house*, the *tree*).
(c) artikel; did you read the article about/on Germany in yesterday's paper?

artificial [ɑːtɪˈfɪʃl] *bn*
kunstmatig; namaak; artificial wood; he has an artificial leg = kunstbeen.

artist [ˈɑːtɪst] *zn*
artiest/kunstenaar.

as [æz *of* əz] *vw*
(a) aangezien; as you can't drive you must go by bus.
(b) terwijl; as he was opening the door, the telephone rang.
(c) zoals; leave it as it is; you must do as the policeman tells you = je moet doen wat je gezegd wordt etc.
as for = wat betreft; as for you—you must stay here.
as from = vanaf; as from tomorrow = vanaf morgen.
as if = alsof; he walks very slowly, as if he had hurt his leg; she looks as if she's

going to cry; it looks as if it's going to rain.

as ... as = even ... als; he is as tall as me; as green as grass.

as though = as if

as well = ook/eveneens; he ate his piece of cake and mine as well; we visited the castle and the old church as well.

as well as = zowel ... als; he has a house in the country as well as a house in town; as well as teaching English, he also teaches football.

ash [aʃ] *zn*
as; he dropped cigarette ash on to the carpet.

geen meervoud: **ashes** *betekent* stukjes as

ashamed [ə'ʃeɪmd] *bn*
beschaamd (over/voor); he was ashamed of what he had done; don't be ashamed of making mistakes; she was ashamed of her old clothes; I'm ashamed of you!

ask [ɑːsk] *ww*
(*a*) vragen; ask someone to teach you how to swim; he asked the policeman the way to the post office; she went to the railway station to ask about cheap tickets to London.
(*b*) uitnodigen, we asked them in for a cup of tea; don't ask her out—she always wants expensive meals.

asks—asking—asked—has asked

ask for, *ww*
vragen om; he asked for more money; someone knocked at the door and asked for my father; he asked for his pencil back = hij vroeg zijn pen terug.

asleep [ə'sliːp] *bn*
in slaap; he was asleep and didn't hear the telephone ring = hij sliep; she fell asleep in front of the TV = ze is in slaap gevallen.

Let op: **asleep** *voor een zelfstandig naamwoord komt niet voor;* **the cat is asleep** *maar* **a sleeping cat**

assistant [ə'sɪstənt] *zn*
assistent; my assistant will come to meet you; shop assistant = winkelbediende.

astonish [ə'stɒnɪʃ] *ww*
verbazen; I was astonished to see that she had got married.

astonishes—astonishing— astonished—has astonished

astonishing, *bn*
verbazingwekkend/opmerkelijk; it's astonishing how many people speak English well; an astonishing number of the students passed their exams.

astonishment, *zn*
(opperste) verbazing; to his astonishment, she suddenly started to sing.

at [æt *of* ət] *vz*
(*a*) (*van tijd*) om; at ten o'clock; at night = 's avonds/'s nachts; at the weekend = tijdens.
(*b*) (*van plaats*) op/in; meet me at the corner of the street; at the top of the mountain; she's not at home = niet thuis; he's at work.
(*c*) (*van snelheid*) met een vaart van; the train was travelling at 50 kilometres an hour.

Let op: **at** *wordt vaak na werkwoorden gebruikt:* **look at; point at,** *etc.*

ate [et] *zie* eat

attach [ə'tætʃ] *ww*
bevestigen/vastmaken; the seat belt is attached to the floor of the car; the boat was attached with a chain.

attaches—attaching—attached— has attached

attack [ə'tæk] **1.** *zn*
(*a*) aanval; they made an attack on the castle.
(*b*) (ziekte) aanval; he had an attack of fever.
2. *ww*
aanvallen; three big men attacked him and stole his money; the old lady was attacked by robbers.

attacks—attacking—attacked— has attacked

attempt [ə'tempt] **1.** *zn*
poging; he made an attempt to break the record for the high jump.
2. *ww*

pogen/proberen; **she attempted to climb the mountain.**

attempts—attempting— attempted—has attempted

attend [əˈtend] *ww*
bijwonen; **will you attend the meeting tomorrow?**

attends—attending—attended— has attended

attend to, *ww*
behandelen; zorgen voor; **the doctor is attending to his patients.**

attention [əˈtenʃn] *zn*
aandacht; **the boy in the back row was not paying attention to what the teacher was saying** = de jongen ... besteedde geen aandacht aan etc.; **attention please!** = opgelet!

attract [əˈtrækt] *ww*
(aan)trekken/(aan)lokken; **bees are attracted by flowers; to attract attention** = de aandacht trekken.

attracts—attracting—attracted— has attracted

attractive [əˈtræktɪv] *bn*
aardig/aantrekkelijk; **an attractive town; she's a very attractive girl.**

August [ˈɔːɡəst] *zn*
augustus; **my birthday is in August; today is August 15th; I start my new job next August.**
Let op: **August 15th:** zeg 'the fifteenth of August' of 'August the fifteenth'
Let op: **August** wordt altijd met een hoofdletter geschreven

aunt [ɑːnt] *zn*
tante; **here is Aunt Mary.**

automatic [ɔːtəˈmætɪk] *bn*
automatisch; **an automatic door** = deur die vanzelf open gaat.
automatically [ɔːtəˈmætɪklɪ] *bw*
automatisch/vanzelf; **the door opens automatically; when smoke comes into the room it automatically makes a bell ring.**

autumn [ˈɔːtəm] *zn* (*Amer.* **fall**)
herfst; **in cold countries, the leaves turn brown and fall off the trees in autumn; we go on holiday in the autumn; the building will be finished next autumn; I started work last autumn.**

average [ˈævrɪdʒ] **1.** *zn*
gemiddelde; **we scored 10, 12 and 17, so our average is 13; to work out an average you must add all the figures together and then divide by the number of figures which you have added.**
2. *bn*
middelmatig; **he gets average marks in school; she is just an average worker.**

avoid [əˈvɔɪd] *ww*
vermijden; ontwijken; **I want to avoid going out in the rain; the car managed to avoid the lamppost.**

avoids—avoiding—avoided—has avoided

awake [əˈweɪk] **1.** *ww*
(*a*) wekken; **he was awoken by the sound of thunder.**
(*b*) wakker worden; **he awoke when he heard the sound of thunder.**

awakes—awaking—awoke—has awoken

2. *bn*
wakker; **he was still awake at 2 o'clock; the baby is wide awake** = klaar wakker.
Let op: **awake** kan niet voor een zelfstandig naamwoord gebruikt worden.

away [əˈweɪ] *bw*
weg; **they went away on holiday; the nearest town is six kilometres away; go away! put that knife away.**

awful [ˈɔːfʊl] *bn*
verschrikkelijk, vreselijk; **what an awful smell! he has an awful cold.**

awkward [ˈɔːkwəd] *bn*
lastig; onhandig; **that cupboard is in a very awkward place; he was in a very awkward situation.**

awoke [əˈwəʊk], **awoken** [əˈwəʊkn] *zie* **awake**

axe [æks] *zn*
bijl; **he chopped the tree down with an axe.**

Bb

baby ['beıbı] *zn*

(*a*) baby; **babies start to walk when they are about 12 months old; I've known Mary since she was a baby; Mrs Smith had her baby last week** = heeft vorige week een baby gekregen.

(*b*) (*dieren*) jong; **baby elephant.**

meervoud **babies**
Let op: een baby waarvan je het geslacht niet weet, mag je met it *aanduiden:* **the baby was sucking its thumb**

back [bæk] **1.** *zn*

(*a*) rug; **he lay down on his back and looked at the sky; she carried her bag on her back; he hurt his back lifting up the sack; he stood with his back to the wall.**

(*b*) achterkant; **he wrote his name on the back of the photograph** = achterop; **she wrote the address on the back of the envelope; he sat in the back of the car and went to sleep; his bedroom is in the back of the house** = achterin; **he put his trousers on back to front** = achterstevoren.

2. *bn*
achter-; **he knocked at the back door; the back tyre of my bicycle is flat.**

3. *bw*
(*a*) naar achteren; achterover; **he stepped back; she leant back against the wall.**

(*b*) terug; **can you pay me back the £10 which you owe me? he went back into the house; she gave me back my book; he only got back home at 10 o'clock.**

4. *ww*
achteruit gaan/rijden; **he backed his car into the garage; she backed away from him** = achteruit weglopen.

backs—backing—backed—has backed
Let op: **back** *wordt vaak na werkwoorden gebruikt:* **to give back; to go back; to pay back,** *etc.*

background ['bækgraʊnd] *zn*
achtergrond; **the picture shows a house with a background of dark trees; her blue dress stands out against the white background; can you see the two ships in the background?**

back up, *ww*
steunen; **nobody would back her up in her argument with the boss.**

backwards, *bw*
achteruit; **he stepped backwards into the lake; 'tab' is 'bat' spelt backwards** = van achter naar voren; **backwards and forwards** = heen en weer; **the policeman walked backwards and forwards in front of the shop.**

bacon ['beıkn] *zn*
spek; bacon; **we had bacon and eggs for breakfast; can I have some more bacon please? he's already eaten three pieces of bacon and two eggs.**

geen meervoud: **some bacon; a slice of bacon/a piece of bacon**

bad [bæd] *bn*
(*a*) slecht; **too much butter is bad for you; this apple's going bad** = rot; **she's good at maths but bad at English.**

(*b*) naar; erg; **she's got a bad cold; he had a bad accident in his car.**

bad—worse—worst

not bad = (heel) niet slecht; **this cake isn't bad; what did you think of the film?—not bad!**

badly, *bw*
slecht; erg; **he did badly in his English exam; your hair badly needs cutting** = nodig geknipt moeten worden.

badly—worse—worst

bad-tempered, *bn*
he's always bad-tempered = slechtgehumeurd.

bag [bæg] *zn*
zak; a bag of potatoes; he put the apples in a paper bag; she carried her clothes in an old bag; string bag = net(je); shopping bag = boodschappentas; sleeping bag = slaapzak.

baggage ['bægɪdʒ] *zn*
bagage; put all the baggage into the back of the car; we have too much baggage—we will have to pay extra.
geen meervoud: some baggage; a lot of baggage

bake [beɪk] *ww*
bakken (in oven); she baked a cake; do you like baked potatoes?
bakes—baking—baked—has baked

baker, *zn*
bakker; the baker's = de (warme) bakker; bakkerij; he bought a loaf of bread at the baker's; the baker's is next door to the butcher's.

balance ['bæləns] **1.** *zn*
evenwicht; he stood on the top of the fence and kept his balance = z'n evenwicht bewaren.
2. *ww*
balanceren; he was balancing on top of the fence; how long can you balance on one foot?
balances—balancing—balanced—has balanced

ball [bɔːl] *zn*
bal; tennis ball; he kicked the ball into the goal; I threw the ball and he caught it.
ball point pen, ball pen, *zn*
balpen.

balloon [bə'luːn] *zn*
ballon; they blew up balloons for the party.

banana [bə'nɑːnə] *zn*
banaan; he was peeling a banana; the children like to eat bananas; banana split = banaan met slagroom, ijs en noten.

band [bænd] *zn*
(*a*) band(je); the papers were held together with a rubber band = elastiekje.

(*b*) band; the soldiers marched after the band; the band played music; a dance band = dansorkest(je).

bandage ['bændɪdʒ] **1.** *zn*
verband; his head was covered in bandages; put a bandage round your knee.
2. *ww*
verbinden; she bandaged his leg; his arm is bandaged up.
bandages—bandaging—bandaged—has bandaged

bang [bæŋ] **1.** *zn*
boem; the gun went bang; there was a bang and the chimney fell down = klap.
2. *ww*
slaan; dreunen; can't you stop the door banging? he banged on the table with his hand.
bangs—banging—banged—has banged

bank [bæŋk] **1.** *zn*
(*a*) oever; he sat on the bank of the river, trying to catch fish.
(*b*) bank; how much money do you have in the bank? he put all his money in the bank; she took all her money out of the bank to buy a car.
2. *ww*
op een (bank)rekening zetten; have you banked the money yet?
banks—banking—banked—has banked

bank account, *zn*
bankrekening; I put all my savings in my bank account; he opened/closed a bank account = hij opende een(bank)rekening/hij hief zijn (bank)rekening op.
bank holiday, *zn*
wettelijke vakantiedag/beursvakantie; Christmas Day is a bank holiday.
bank on, *ww*
ergens op rekenen; don't bank on getting any money from your father; you can bank on the weather being bad for the school sports day.

bar [bɑː] *zn*
(*a*) a bar of soap = stuk; a bar of chocolate = reep.

(*b*) balk; staaf; spijl; **he escaped from the prison by sawing through the bars** = tralies.
(*c*) bar/buffet; **a bar in a hotel.**
(*d*) **sandwich bar** = snackbar; **coffee bar** = koffiebar.

bare [beə] *bn*
(*a*) bloot; onbedekt; **the children had bare feet; her dress left her arms bare.**
(*b*) kaal; **in winter the branches of the trees are bare.**
barely, *bw*
nauwelijks; **he barely had time to sit down before the telephone rang** = nauwelijks . . . of.

bargain [ˈbɑːgɪn] *zn*
koopje; **£50 return to New York is a bargain; you should buy that fur coat—it's a bargain.**

bark [bɑːk] **1.** *zn*
(*a*) schors.
(*b*) blaf.
2. *ww*
(*van een hond*) blaffen; **the dog barked at the postman; I can hear a dog barking.**
barks—barking—barked—has barked

base [beɪs] *zn*
voet(stuk); **a glass with a heavy base.**
baseball, *zn*
honkbal; **do you want to watch the baseball game on TV? he's playing in the school baseball team.**
basic [ˈbeɪsɪk] *bn*
eenvoudig, fundamenteel; **you should know basic maths if you want to work in a shop; a basic dictionary** = basiswoordenboek.

basin [ˈbeɪsn] *zn*
kom; **wash basin** = wasbak.

basket [ˈbɑːskɪt] *zn*
mand; **throw those papers into the waste paper basket; if you're going shopping, don't forget your shopping basket.**

bath [bɑːθ] **1.** *zn*
(*a*) (*het voorwerp*) bad; **is the bath clean? there's a shower and a bath in the bathroom.**

(*b*) (*het baden*) bad; **after you've been playing football you need a hot bath; my father has a cold bath every morning.**
(*c*) (*het badwater*) bad; **I like to lie in a hot bath.**
(*d*) **swimming baths** = zwembad.
Let op: **one bath** [bɑːθ] *maar* **two baths** [bɑːðz]
2. *ww*
baden; in bad gaan/doen; **he's bathing the baby.**
baths [bɑːθs]—**bathing** [ˈbɑːθɪŋ]—**bathed** [bɑːθt]—**has bathed**

bathroom, *zn*
badkamer; **where's the bathroom? can I use your bathroom, please?** = het toilet; **the bathroom scales must be wrong—I'm heavier than I was yesterday.**

bathe [beɪð] *ww*
(*a*) baden/zwemmen; **we were bathing in the sea before breakfast.**
(*b*) betten; **he bathed his knee with boiled water.**
bathes—bathing [ˈbeɪðɪŋ]—**bathed** [beɪðd]—**has bathed**

battery [ˈbætərɪ] *zn*
batterij; (*in auto*) accu; **the torch needs a new battery; you ought to change the batteries in the radio.**
meervoud **batteries**

battle [ˈbætl] *zn*
slag; **the French navy was defeated in the battle of Trafalgar.**

be [biː] **1.** *ww*
(*a*) (*van staat*) zijn; **the sky is blue; he is taller than his father; tomatoes are red; it's cold today; are you hungry?**
(*b*) (*van leef*)*tijd*) zijn; **he's sixteen; she's only two years old; it's nearly six o'clock; it's time to go to bed; it will soon be summer.**
(*c*) (*van prijs*) zijn; **tomatoes are 30p a pound; sandwiches are 25p each.**
(*d*) (*van beroep*) zijn; **his mother is a teacher; she wants to be a doctor.**
(*e*) (*van formaat*) zijn; **he's six foot tall; the table is more than two metres long; the post office is very close to our house.**
(*f*) (*zich bevinden*) zijn; **there's a crowd**

Bathroom *Badkamer*

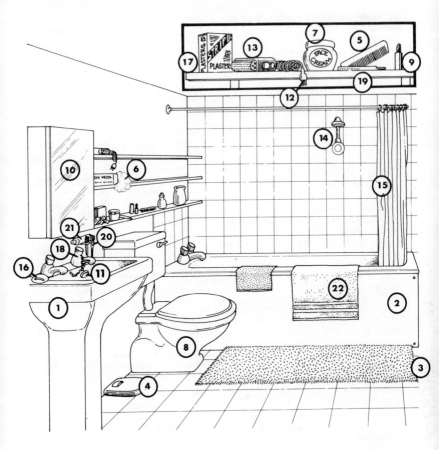

1.	basin	*wasbak*	
2.	bath	*bad*	
3.	bathmat	*badmat*	
4.	bathroom scales	*badkamerweegschaal*	
5.	comb	*kam*	
6.	cotton wool	*watten*	
7.	face cream	*crème*	
8.	lavatory	*w.c.*	
9.	lipstick	*lippenstift*	
10.	mirror	*spiegel*	
11.	plug (in wash-basin)	*stop (voor wasbak)*	

12.	plug (on razor)	*stekker (aan scheer-apparaat)*	
13.	razor	*scheerapparaat*	
14.	shower	*douche*	
15.	shower curtain	*douchegordijn*	
16.	soap	*zeep*	
17.	sticking plaster	*pleister*	
18.	tap	*kraan*	
19.	thermometer	*thermometer*	
20.	toothbrush	*tandenborstel*	
21.	toothpaste	*tandpasta*	
22.	towel	*handdoek*	

of people waiting for the bus; there are only two chocolates left in the box.

(g) (in voltooid tegenwoordige tijd) gaan; **have you ever been to Germany? she has been to see the film three times.**

2. hulpww voor de progressieve vormen van

(a) (de tegenwoordige tijd) **don't talk to him when he's reading; I'm waiting for the bus; they are hoping to go on holiday next week.**

(b) (de verleden tijd) **she was singing in the bath; they were walking in the street when it started to rain.**

(c) (de toekomende tijd) **he will be flying to Paris tomorrow morning.**

(d) (hulpww van de lijdende vorm) **she was knocked down by a bus; the children were told to go home.**

Tegenwoordige tijd: **I am, you are, he is, we are, they are**
Afgekorte vormen: **I'm, you're, he's, we're, they're**
Ontkennende wijs: **I'm not; you're not** of **you aren't; he's not** of **he isn't; we're not** of **we aren't; they're not** of **they aren't**
Toekomende tijd: **I will be/I shall be**
Verleden tijd: **I was, you were, he was, we were, they were**
Ontkennende wijs: **I wasn't, you weren't, he wasn't, we weren't, they weren't**
Voltooid tegenwoordige tijd: **I have been, you have been, he/she/it has been, they have been**

beach [biːtʃ] *zn*
strand; **we sat on the beach and ate our sandwiches; let's go to the beach this afternoon; some of the beaches are covered with oil.**
meervoud **beaches**

bean [biːn] *zn*
boon; **green beans; baked beans** = witte bonen in tomatensaus.

bear [beə] *zn*
beer; **bears like honey; polar bear** = ijsbeer.

beard ['bɪəd] *zn*
baard; **Father Christmas has a long white beard.**

beat [biːt] 1. *zn*
ritme; **the beat of a drum; keep in time with the beat of the music.**
2. *ww*
(a) slaan; **he used to beat his wife with a stick.**
(b) verslaan; **our team beat the Germans 3–0; he was easily beaten in the long jump.**
(c) slaan/kloppen; **his heart was beating fast.**
beats—beating—beat—has beaten

beat up, *ww*
in elkaar slaan; **the old lady was beaten up by the burglars.**
Let op: **they beat the old man up** of **they beat up the old man,** *maar alleen* **they beat him up**

beautiful ['bjuːtɪfəl] *bn*
mooi; **the beautiful colours of the autumn leaves; what beautiful weather! a beautiful Christmas cake.**

became [bɪ'keɪm] *zie* **become**

because [bɪ'kɒz] *vw*
omdat; **I was late because I missed the bus; he's wet because it's raining; she's fat because she eats too much.**
because of = vanwege; **the trains are late because of the fog; we don't use the car because of the price of petrol.**

become [bɪ'kʌm] *ww*
worden; **he wants to become a dentist; the sky became dark and the wind became stronger; they became friends; she's become rather deaf.**
becomes—becoming—became—has become

bed [bed] *zn*
bed; **lie down on the bed if you're tired; she always goes to bed at 9 o'clock; he was sitting in bed drinking a cup of coffee; come on, get out of bed—it's time for breakfast; she's in bed with a cold; have you made your bed?** = heb je je bed opgemaakt?
bed and breakfast, *zn*
kamer met ontbijt; **I only want to have bed and breakfast.**

Bedroom *Slaapkamer*

1. bed	*bed*	10. photograph	*foto*
2. blanket	*deken*	11. pillow	*kussen*
3. chest of drawers	*ladenkast(je)*	12. plant	*plant*
4. curtain	*gordijn*	13. pyjamas	*pyjama*
5. door	*deur*	14. sheet	*laken*
6. drawer	*la(de)*	15. slippers	*sloffen*
7. lamp	*lamp*	16. wardrobe	*hangkast*
8. mattress	*matras*	17. window	*raam*
9. mirror	*spiegel*		

bedclothes, *zn meervoud*
beddegoed; he woke up when all his bedclothes fell off.
bedroom, *zn*
slaapkamer; my bedroom is on the
ground floor; shut your bedroom door if
you want to be quiet.
bedtime, *zn*
bedtijd; 9 o'clock is my bedtime; go to
bed—it's past your bedtime.

bee [biː] *zn*
bij; bees were going from flower to
flower.
beehive, *zn*
bijenkorf.

beef [biːf] *zn*
rundvlees; roast beef and boiled
potatoes; would you like another slice of
beef?
geen meervoud: some beef; a piece
of beef/a slice of beef

been [biːn] *zie* **be.**

beer ['bɪə] *zn*
bier; can I have a glass of
beer? three beers please = drie glazen
pils alstublieft.
het meervoud betekent alleen glasses
of beer

before [bɪ'fɔː] **1.** *bw*
eerder; why didn't you tell me before? I
didn't see him on Tuesday, I saw him the
day before = tevoren.
2. *vz*
voor; he got here before me; make sure
you arrive before 10.30; G comes before
L in the alphabet.
3. *vw*
voordat; before you sit down, can you
pass me the salt? think carefully before
you answer my question; before coming
in, wipe your shoes on the mat.

beg [beg] *ww*
smeken; bedelen; I beg your pardon =
neemt u mij niet kwalijk.
**begs—begging—begged—has
begged**
beggar, *zn*
bedelaar.

began [bɪ'gæn] *zie* **begin**

begin [bɪ'gɪn] *ww*
beginnen; it began to rain; she began to
cry; he's beginning to understand; they
all began talking at once.
**begins—beginning—began—has
begun**
beginner, *zn*
beginner; he can't play well, he's only a
beginner = beginneling.
beginning, *zn*
begin; the beginning of the story is rather
dull; hurry up if you want to see the beginning of the film.

behave [bɪ'heɪv] *ww*
zich gedragen; the children behaved
(themselves) very well when they stayed
with their granny; after she was ill she
began to behave very strangely; if you
don't behave, you'll have to stay in your
bedroom = als je stout bent.
**behaves—behaving—behaved—
has behaved**
behaviour, *zn* (*Amer.* **behavior**)
gedrag; his behaviour was very strange;
the police said that the behaviour of the
young people at the football match was
very bad.

behind [bɪ'haɪnd] **1.** *vz*
achter; they hid behind the curtain; my
pen has fallen behind the sofa; he was
second, only three metres behind the
winner.
2. *bw*
achter; he was second, only three metres
behind; she's left her ticket behind = ze
heeft haar kaartje laten liggen; he stayed
behind to watch TV = hij is achterge-
bleven.
3. *zn*
achterste; he kicked my behind.

being [biːɪŋ] *zie* **human**

Belgian 1. *bn*
Belgisch; a Belgian family has come to
live next door to us; my sister is married
to a Belgian teacher.
2. *zn*
Belg; Belgische; Belgians are fond of

beer; my sister is married to a Belgian.
Let op: **Belgian** *wordt altijd met een hoofdletter geschreven*

Belgium ['beldʒəm] *zn*
België; we went to Belgium on holiday; my sister lives in the north of Belgium; many people from Belgium come to spend their holidays in England.

believe [bɪ'liːv] *ww*
geloven; **people used to believe that the earth was flat; I believe I have seen him before; never believe what he tells you; do you believe in flying saucers?**
believes—believing—believed—has believed

bell [bel] *zn*
klok; bel; **he rang the door bell; you ought to have a bell on your bicycle; they rang the church bells at the wedding.**

belong [bɪ'lɒŋ] *ww*
(*a*) toebehoren/zijn van; **this hat belongs to my sister; who does this house belong to? the old watch used to belong to my mother.**
(*b*) horen (bij)/lid zijn van; **I belong to a youth club.**
belongs—belonging—belonged—has belonged

below [bɪ'ləʊ] **1.** *bw*
beneden/onder; **he looked down from the hill at the town below.**
2. *vz*
beneden/onder; **the temperature was below 60°; can you see below the surface of the water?**

belt [belt] *zn*
riem/ceintuur; **you will have to tighten your belt; seat belt** = veiligheidsgordel.

bend [bend] **1.** *zn*
bocht; **the road is full of bends; he drove too fast round the bend; the pipe under the washbasin has two bends in it.**
2. *ww*
(*a*) (zich) buigen; **he bent the pipe into the shape of an S; the road bends and then goes straight.**
(*b*) zich (voorover) buigen; **he bent down**

to tie up his shoe; she was bending over the table.
bends—bending—bent—has bent

beneath [bɪ'niːθ] **1.** *bw*
onder; beneden; **he looked down from the roof at the people walking beneath.**
2. *vz*
onder; **the ball was stuck beneath the sofa; the ground was soft beneath his feet.**

bent [bent] *bn*
gebogen/krom; **a bent pipe;** *zie ook* **bend**

beside [bɪ'saɪd] *vz*
naast; **he sat down beside me; his house is just beside the post office; put the teapot beside the milk jug.**
besides 1. *vz*
naast/behalve; **he has two other cars besides the red one; besides the football team, our town has a cricket team and a swimming club.**
2. *bw*
(*a*) behalve; ook; **besides managing the shop, he also teaches in the evening.**
(*b*) bovendien; trouwens; **I don't want to go for a picnic—besides, the car won't start.**

best [best] **1.** *bn*
best; **this is the best book I've read this year; what is the best way of cleaning a carpet? he put on his best suit to go to the wedding; she's the best swimmer in the team.**
2. *zn*
het beste; **you must do your best** = je best doen; **he did his best—but he still didn't win.**
3. *bw*
het best(e); **which of the sisters plays the piano best? the engine works best when it's warm; oranges grow best in hot countries.**
best *is de overtreffende trap van* **good** *en* **well**

better ['betə] **1.** *bn*
(*a*) beter (dan); **the weather became better; this book is better than the one I was reading last week; he's better at maths than at history; vegetables are**

better for you than meat = zijn gezon-
der.
(b) beter; hersteld; I had a cold last
week, but now I'm better; I hope you're
better soon.
2. bw
(a) beter (dan); she plays the piano better
than her sister; these scissors cut cloth
better than those ones.
(b) (een stuk) beter/gezonder; he had a
cold but now he's getting better.
had better = er beter aan doen; you
had better hurry up, if you want to catch
the train; she'd better go to bed if she's got
a cold; hadn't you better answer the phone?
better *is de vergrotende trap van*
good *en* **well**

between [bɪ'twi:n] vz
tussen; there's a wall between his office
and mine; the plane flies between London
and Edinburgh; I'm busy between 10
o'clock and 2.30; can you come to see
me between now and next Monday? she
can't tell the difference between butter
and margarine.
in between = tussenin; he had a
meeting at 12.00 and another at 2 p.m.
but managed to play a game of tennis in
between.

beyond [bɪ'jɒnd] vz
voorbij; I can see your house, but I can't
see anything beyond it because of the fog;
to find the post office, you have to go
about 100 metres beyond the traffic
lights.

bicycle ['baɪsɪkl] zn
fiets; he went to school by bicycle; she's
going to do the shopping on her bicycle;
he can drive but he can't ride a bicycle
= hij kan niet fietsen
Let op: wordt vaak **bike** *genoemd*

big [bɪg] bn
groot; I don't want a little piece of
cake—I want a big one; his father has
the biggest car in our street; I'm
not afraid of him—I'm bigger than he is.
big—bigger—biggest

bike [baɪk] zn
(afkorting van **bicycle**) fiets; he came

to school by bike; she fell off her bike;
she's going to the shops on her bike.

bill [bɪl] zn
(a) rekening; she invited me to have a
meal, and then asked me to pay the bill;
I must pay the telephone bill.
(b) snavel; the hen was pulling at the
grass with its bill.
(c) (Amerikaans voor **note**) bankbiljet;
a 5 dollar bill.

bind [baɪnd] ww
(vast)binden; the burglars bound his
hands and feet with string.
binds—binding—bound [baʊnd]—
has bound

bird [bɜːd] ww
vogel; the little birds were learning to fly;
most birds can fly well, but some can't;
the birds were singing in the trees; in the
winter we put a bird table in the garden,
and put food on it for the birds.

birth [bɜːθ] zn
geboorte; **date of birth** = geboorte-
datum.
birthday, zn
verjaardag; my birthday is on June 15th;
her birthday is next week; he's just had
his birthday = hij is net jarig geweest;
he'll be 21 next birthday = hij wordt
21; what do you want for you birthday?
he got a calculator for his birthday;
birthday party = verjaardagsfeestje;
birthday card = verjaardagskaart;
birthday cake = verjaardagstaart.
Happy Birthday = welgefelici-
teerd!

biscuit ['bɪskɪt] zn (Amer. **cookie**)
koekje; biscuitje; I like chocolate biscuits best; cheese and biscuits = crackers
met kaas.

bit [bɪt] zn
(a) stukje; he tied up the parcel with a
bit of string; can I have another bit of
cake, please? = sneetje/plakje; he's
taking my watch to bits = hij is mijn
horloge uit elkaar aan het halen.
(b) **a bit** = een beetje; the photograph is
a bit too dark; let him sleep a bit longer;
have you got a piece of wood a little bit

bigger than this one? wait a bit, I'm not
ready yet = wacht even.
(c) zie **bite**
bit by bit = stukje bij beetje; he
painted the house bit by bit.

bite [baɪt] *ww*
bijten; the dog bit the postman; he bit a
piece out of the apple; she was bitten by
an insect = zij werd gestoken.
bites—biting—bit—has bitten

bitter ['bɪtə] *bn*
bitter; lemons are bitter, but oranges are
sweet.
bitter—more bitter—bitterest

black [blæk] *bn & zn*
zwart; he was wearing a black hat; we
have a black and white TV = zwartwit;
why did you paint your front door black?
black coffee = koffie zonder melk.
black—blacker—blackest

blackbird, *zn*
merel.
blackboard, *zn*
(school)bord

blade [bleɪd] *zn*
lemmet; this knife has a very sharp blade;
my penknife has six blades; the boat's
propeller has three blades = schoep.

blame [bleɪm] **1.** *zn*
schuld; his sister broke the window, but
he got the blame.
2. *ww*
de schuld geven; his father blamed him
for breaking the window; don't blame me
if the car won't start = kwalijk nemen;
I don't blame you for asking for more
money = ik denk dat je er goed aan
doet geld te vragen.
blames—blaming—blamed—has
blamed

blank [blæŋk] *bn*
onbeschreven/wit; a blank cheque =
blanco; write your name in the blank
space =opengelaten ruimte.

blanket ['blæŋkɪt] *zn*
deken; he woke up when his blankets fell
off.

bled [bled] *zie* **bleed**

bleed [bliːd] *ww*
bloeden; his knee is bleeding; my nose
began to bleed; when she cut her finger it
bled.
bleeds—bleeding—bled—has
bled

blew [bluː] *zie* **blow**

blind [blaɪnd] *bn*
blind; a blind man with a white stick;
after her illness she became blind.

block [blɒk] **1.** *zn*
(a) brok; blok; they used blocks of stone
to make the wall; a block of wood fell on
his foot.
(b) blok; go for a walk round the block;
a block of flats = flatgebouw.
2. *ww*
stremmen; the pipe was blocked by a
dead bird; the accident blocked the road
for several hours = versperren.
blocks—blocking—blocked—has
blocked

blood [blʌd] *zn*
bloed; the police followed the spots of
blood to find the wounded man; blood
was pouring from the cut in his hand.

blouse [blaʊz] *zn*
bloes; she wore a skirt and a blouse.

blow [bləʊ] *ww*
blazen; waaien; the wind blew hard all
day; blow on your soup to make it cool;
because she has a cold, she keeps blowing
her nose = ze snuit steeds haar neus.
blows—blowing—blew   [bluː]—
has blown

blow away, *ww*
wegblazen; the wind blew away the
smoke; his hat blew away.
blow down, *ww*
omverblazen; the trees were blown down
by the wind; the fence has blown down.
blow off, *ww*
afblazen; the wind blew off her hat; all
the leaves were blown off the trees.
blow out, *ww*
uitblazen; you must blow out the candles
on your birthday cake; the lamp has

blown out; all my papers blew out of the window.

blow up, *ww*
(*a*) opblazen; oppompen; **to blow up a balloon; your front tyre needs blowing up.**
(*b*) opblazen; **the soldiers blew up the bridge.**
Let op: **the wind blew the smoke away** *of* **blew away the smoke; they blew the bridge up** *of* **they blew up the bridge,** *etc., maar alleen* **the wind blew it away, they blew it up,** *etc.*

blue [blu:] *bn & zn*
blauw; **her car is light blue; they live in the house with the dark blue door; she was dressed all in blue; have you a cloth of a darker blue than this?**
blue—bluer—bluest

blunt [blʌnt] *bn*
stomp; **don't try to cut your meat with a blunt knife; these scissors are blunt— they need sharpening.**
blunt—blunter—bluntest

board [bɔːd] *zn*
plank; **write this sentence on the board** = op het (school)bord.

boast [bəʊst] *ww*
pochen; bluffen; **he was boasting that he had scored three goals; she's always boasting about her new car.**
boasts—boasting—boasted—has boasted

boat [bəʊt] *zn*
boot; **a sailing boat** = zeilboot/zeilschip; **a fishing boat** = vissersboot; **we took the boat across to France; when is the next boat to New York? they went to Australia by boat.**

body [bɒdɪ] *zn*
(*a*) romp.
(*b*) lichaam; lijf; **the dead man's body was found several days later.**
meervoud **bodies**

boil [bɔɪl] *ww*
(*a*) koken; **the soup's boiling; can you boil some water for me to make the tea? the kettle's boiling** = het water kookt.

(*b*) (gaar) koken; **I had a boiled egg for breakfast; I don't like the smell of boiling cabbage; hard-boiled egg** = hardgekookt.
boils—boiling—boiled—has boiled

boil over, *ww*
overkoken; **the milk boiled over and made a mess on the stove.**

bomb [bɒm] **1.** *zn*
bom; **bombs were falling on the town; the enemy dropped bombs on the bridges; his house was destroyed by a bomb.**
2. *ww*
bombarderen; **the enemy tried to bomb the railway lines; they bombed the hospital.**
bombs—bombing—bombed—has bombed

bone [bəʊn] *zn*
been; bot(je); (vis)graat; **he fell over and broke a bone in his ankle; don't try to eat the fish bones.**

book [bʊk] **1.** *zn*
(*a*) boek; **I'm reading a book on gardening; he wrote a book about elephants.**
(*b*) opschrijfboekje; **exercise book** = schrift; **cheque book** = chequeboek; **a book of stamps** = postzegelboekje; **a book of matches** = treklucifers.
2. *ww*
reserveren; boeken; **have you booked a table for the party? I want to book a room for Friday night; I'm sorry the concert is sold out—all the seats have been booked.**
books—booking—booked—has booked

bookcase, *zn*
boekenkast.
book in(to), *ww*
kamer(s) reserveren; **I've booked into the Castle Hotel.**
booking office, *zn*
plaatskaartenbureau.
bookshelf, *zn*
boekenplank.
meervoud **bookshelves**
bookshop, *zn*
boekwinkel.

Body *Lichaam*

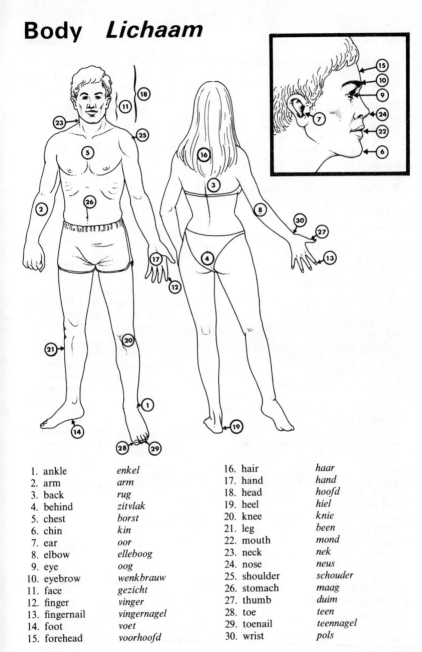

1.	ankle	*enkel*	16.	hair	*haar*
2.	arm	*arm*	17.	hand	*hand*
3.	back	*rug*	18.	head	*hoofd*
4.	behind	*zitvlak*	19.	heel	*hiel*
5.	chest	*borst*	20.	knee	*knie*
6.	chin	*kin*	21.	leg	*been*
7.	ear	*oor*	22.	mouth	*mond*
8.	elbow	*elleboog*	23.	neck	*nek*
9.	eye	*oog*	24.	nose	*neus*
10.	eyebrow	*wenkbrauw*	25.	shoulder	*schouder*
11.	face	*gezicht*	26.	stomach	*maag*
12.	finger	*vinger*	27.	thumb	*duim*
13.	fingernail	*vingernagel*	28.	toe	*teen*
14.	foot	*voet*	29.	toenail	*teennagel*
15.	forehead	*voorhoofd*	30.	wrist	*pols*

book up, *ww*
volboeken; **the hotel is booked up** =
volledig bezet.

boot [bu:t] *zn*
laars; **she was wearing long black boots;
the children wore boots in the rain; football boots** = voetbalschoenen; **ski boots**
= skischoenen/skilaarzen.

border [′bɔ:də] *zn*
grens; **the border between France and
Spain goes along the tops of mountains;
border guards** = grenswacht.

bored [bɔ:d] *bn*
verveeld; **I get bored sitting in the office
all day** = ik verveel me; **she's bored—
ask her to go to the cinema.**
boring, *bn*
saai; vervelend; **he went to sleep watching a boring film on TV; she thinks
cricket is so boring.**

born [bɔ:n] *ww*
to be born = geboren worden; **he was
born in Germany; she was born in 1962.**
Let op: **born** *wordt meestal alleen
gebruikt met* **was** *of* **were**

borrow [′bɒrəʊ] *ww*
lenen; **can I borrow your car to go to the
shops? he borrowed £10 from me, and
never paid it back; she borrowed three
books from the library.**
**borrows—borrowing—
borrowed—has borrowed**
Let op: vergelijk **lend**

boss [bɒs] *zn*
baas; **do you like the new boss? I have
to ask the boss if I can have a holiday.**
meervoud **bosses**

both [bəʊθ] *bn & vnw & vw*
beide(n); allebei; zowel . . . als; **both my
socks have holes in them; you can't eat
both of the cakes; both the children were
ill; hold the handle in both hands; we both
like honey; they both fell down on the
ice; both the teacher and his wife were
ill; he ate both his cake and my cake.**

bother [′bɒðə] **1.** *zn*
last; **he had a lot of bother mending the
car.**

2. *ww*
de moeite nemen; zich zorgen maken;
**she didn't bother to send us a bill; don't
bother about cleaning the room.**
**bothers—bothering—
bothered—has bothered**

bottle [′bɒtl] *zn*
fles; **wine bottle; milk bottle; he drinks a
bottle of milk a day; open another bottle
of orange juice; you can buy beer in
bottles or in cans; he was drinking beer
out of the bottle.**

bottom [′bɒtəm] *zn*
(*a*) bodem; **there was some jam left in
the bottom of the jar** = onderin; **the ship
sank to the bottom of the sea; turn right
at the bottom of the hill** = onderaan;
he's at the bottom of his class = de
slechtste.
(*b*) achterin/achteraan; **the apple tree is
at the bottom of the garden.**
(*c*) achterste; *zie ook* **behind.**

bought [bɔ:t] *zie* **buy**

bound [baʊnd] *zie* **bind**

bowl [bəʊl] *zn*
kom; **a bowl of soup; soup bowl** = soep-
kom; **washing up bowl** = afwasbak.

box [bɒks] *zn*
doos(je); **a box of biscuits/of matches;
put the cakes into a box; she ate boxes
of chocolates.**
meervoud **boxes**

boy [bɔɪ] *zn*
jongen; **they have three children—two
boys and a girl; the boys were
playing in the field; paper boy** = krantenjongen.
meervoud **boys**

brain [breɪn] *zn*
hersenen; brein; **use your brain** =
gebruik je verstand; **he's got brains** =
knap.

brake [breɪk] **1.** *zn*
(hand)rem; **he put on the brakes; he
drove the car with the brake on; you
should use your brakes when you go down
the hill.**

2. *ww*
remmen; **the motorcyclist braked as he turned the corner.**
brakes—braking—braked—has braked

branch [brɑːntʃ] *zn*
(*a*) tak; **the children were swinging in the branches of the trees; they jumped from branch to branch.**
(*b*) bijkantoor; filiaal; **the local branch of the Midland Bank; the bank has branches in all large towns; branch manager** = filiaalhouder.
meervoud **branches**

brave [breɪv] *bn*
dapper; **he's a brave man—he saved the little boy from the burning house.**
brave—braver—bravest

bravely, *bw*
dapper; **he bravely jumped into the water to save the little girl.**

bread [bred] *zn*
brood; **go to the baker's and buy a loaf of bread; cut three slices of bread; the children were eating bread and butter** = boterhammen; **brown bread** = bruinbrood.
geen meervoud: **some bread; a loaf of bread; a slice of bread/a piece of bread**

break [breɪk] **1.** *zn*
(*a*) onderbreking; **he spoke for two hours without a break** = pauze; **the sun came through a break in the clouds** = opening.
(*b*) pauze; **there is a ten minute break in the middle of the morning; the children drink milk during break; coffee break/ tea break** = koffiepauze/theepauze; **we'll have a coffee break now.**
2. *ww*
breken; **he dropped the cup on the floor and broke it; it fell on the floor and broke; I can't use the lift because it's broken** = kapot/defect; **she fell off the wall and broke her leg.**
breaks—breaking—broke—has broken

break down, *ww*
defect raken; **the car broke down and we had to push it.**
breakfast ['brekfəst] *zn*
ontbijt; **I had a boiled egg for breakfast; she didn't have any breakfast because she was in a hurry; we have breakfast at 7.30 every day.**
break in(to), *ww*
inbreken; **burglars broke in during the night; he was caught breaking into the bookshop.**
break off, *ww*
(*a*) afbreken; **he broke the handle off a cup; the branch was broken off the tree.**
(*b*) onderbreken/afbreken; **he broke off in the middle of his story; they broke off the discussion.**
break up, *ww*
(*a*) stukbreken; **the ship was breaking up on the rocks.**
(*b*) uiteengaan, eindigen; **the meeting broke up at 3 p.m.; school breaks up next week** = de (school) vakantie begint etc.

breath [breθ] *zn*
adem; **he ran so fast he was out of breath; stop for a moment to get your breath back; she took a deep breath and dived into the water.**
breathe [briːð] *ww*
ademen/adem halen; **can fish breathe under water? he breathed in the smoke from the fire, and it made him cough.**
breathes—breathing—breathed— has breathed

brick [brɪk] *zn*
baksteen; **a brick house; the wall is built of bricks; he threw a brick through the window.**

bridge [brɪdʒ] *zn*
brug; **the road crosses the river by a very long bridge; the river goes under the bridge; a railway bridge** = spoorbrug.

bright [braɪt] *bn*
(*a*) stralend; helder; **bright sunshine; they have painted their house bright orange.**
(*b*) pienter/knap; **he's a bright little boy; both their children are very bright.**
bright—brighter—brightest

brightly, *bw*
helder; **brightly coloured flags.**

bring [brıŋ] *ww*
brengen; meebrengen; **bring me the money; he brought his father with him; he's bringing his friends along to the party.**
brings—bringing—brought [brɔːt] **—has brought**

bring back, *ww*
terugbrengen; meebrengen; **bring back my book—I want it; he brought back some presents from his visit to France.**

bring down, *ww*
(mee) naar beneden brengen; **can you bring down my coat from the bedroom?**

bring in, *ww*
binnenbrengen; **to come with something or somebody in here; he brought his boots in with him; don't bring your friends in— I've washed the floor.**

bring up, *ww*
grootbrengen; **he was brought up by his uncle; I was brought up in Scotland.**
Let op: **he brought some presents back** *of* **he brought back some presents; she brought the dog in** *of* **she brought in the dog,** *etc.; maar alleen* **he brought them back, she brought it in,** *etc.*

Britain ['brıtn] *zn*
Brittannië/Brittanje; **he's come back to live in Britain; most people in Britain speak English; is this car made in Britain?**
Let op: meestal wordt het land **Great Britain** *genoemd*

British 1. *bn*
Brits; **the British people; the British car industry.**
2. *zn meervoud*
the British = de Britten; **the British make good beer; the Germans fought the British in the Second World War.**

broke, broken [brəʊk, brəʊkn] *zie* **break**

brother ['brʌðə] *zn*
broer; **he's my brother; that girl has three brothers; her brother's a doctor.**

brought [brɔːt] *zie* **bring**

brown [braʊn] *bn & zn*
bruin; **he has brown hair and blue eyes; in autumn the leaves turn brown and fall off the trees** = geel worden; **you're very brown—you must have been sitting in the sun for a long time; I like brown bread better than white; she was wearing dark brown shoes.**
brown—browner—brownest

brush [brʌʃ] **1.** *zn*
borstel; **you must have a stiff brush to get all the mud off your shoes; if you paint with a thin brush you will make fine lines; he was painting white lines on the road with a large brush.**
meervoud **brushes**
2. *ww*
borstelen; **have you brushed your shoes? don't forget to brush your teeth after meals.**
brushes—brushing—brushed— has brushed

brush off, *ww*
afborstelen; **he brushed the mud off his trousers.**

brush up, *ww*
ophalen; **you must brush up your German if you are going to work in Germany.**

bucket ['bʌkıt] *zn*
emmer; **she got a bucket of water from the river; they threw buckets of water on the fire; the children built castles on the sand with their buckets.**

build [bıld] *ww*
bouwen; aanleggen; **the house was built in 1900; we are building a new church; the government is going to build a motorway across this field; he built the model plane out of pieces of wood.**
builds—building—built [bılt] **—has built**

builder, *zn*
aannemer.

building, *zn*
gebouw; **the bomb destroyed several buildings; his office is on the top floor of the building; they will have to knock**

several buildings down to build the new
motorway.

bulb [bʌlb] *zn*
(*a*) (gloei)lampje; **we must get a new
bulb for the light in the kitchen; I can't
use the torch—it hasn't got a bulb.**
(*b*) (bloem)bol.

bump [bʌmp] **1.** *zn*
(*a*) bons; stoot; **the plane landed with a
bump.**
(*b*) bult; **he has a bump on the back of
his head; the car went slowly over the
bumps in the road.**
2. *ww*
opbotsen (tegen); **the car bumped into a
tree; I bumped into her at the bus stop**
= ik trof haar toevallig.
bumps—bumping—bumped—has
bumped

bunch [bʌntʃ] *zn*
bos (bloemen); tros (druiven); **the children picked bunches of flowers; when you
go shopping can you buy a bunch of
grapes?**
meervoud **bunches**

burglar ['bɜːglə] *zn*
inbreker; **burglars broke into the house
and stole our silver; he woke up to find a
burglar in his bedroom.**

buries ['berɪz], **buried** ['berɪd] *zie*
bury

burn [bɜːn] *ww*
branden; in brand staan; **call the firemen—the school is burning! all our
papers were burnt in the fire; she burnt
her hand on the hot frying pan; look,
you've burnt the sausages** = je hebt de
worstjes laten aanbranden.
burns—burning—burnt/burned—
has burnt/burned

burn down, *ww*
(laten) afbranden; **he was playing with
matches and burnt the house down; the
school burnt down before the firemen
arrived.**

burst [bɜːst] *ww*
springen; barsten; **he blew up the balloon
until it burst; she burst all the balloons**

with a pin; don't eat so much or you'll
burst; he burst into tears/she burst out
laughing** = hij/zij barstte in tranen/
lachen uit.
burst—bursting—burst—has
burst

bury ['berɪ] *ww*
begraven; **the dog has buried a bone in
the garden; the path was buried under the
snow; he died on Monday and was buried
on Friday.**
buries—burying—buried—has
buried

bus [bʌs] *zn*
bus; **why do you go by bus?—it's cheaper
than the train; she takes the bus every
morning to go to work; he missed the last
bus and had to walk home; London buses
are red; a school bus takes the children
to school; the number 6 bus goes to
Oxford Street.**
meervoud **buses**

bus stop, *zn*
bushalte; **there was a long queue of
people waiting at the bus stop.**

bush [bʊʃ] *zn*
struik; **a rose bush.**
meervoud **bushes**

bushy, *bn*
(van haar) ruig; **he has bushy eyebrows.**

business ['bɪznɪs] *zn*
zaak; handel; **he runs a secondhand car
business; she's in business selling dresses;
they do business with several European
countries.**
meervoud **businesses**

businessman, *zn*
zakenman.
meervoud **businessmen**

busy ['bɪzɪ] *bn*
(druk) bezig; druk; **he was busy washing
the car; the shop is very busy today** =
het is vandaag erg druk etc.; **she's busy
with her exams; I was too busy to buy
you a present** = ik had het te druk.
busy—busier—busiest

but [bʌt] *vw*
maar; **he is very tall, but his sister is quite**

short; I would like to come, but I am not
free that evening; but you said you would
give me £10!

butcher ['bʊtʃə] *zn*
slager; **the butcher's** = slagerij; **go to the
butcher's and buy some sausages; the
butcher's is closed on Mondays; the butcher is on holiday.**

butter ['bʌtə] *zn*
boter; **he was spreading butter on a piece
of bread; fry the onions in butter.**
geen meervoud: **some butter; a
piece of butter**

butterfly, *zn*
vlinder.
meervoud **butterflies**

button ['bʌtn] **1.** *zn*
(*a*) knoop; **his coat has buttons down the
front; do up the buttons on your coat;
can you sew this button on?**
(*b*) knop; **push the button to open the
doors of the lift; push the top button if
you want a cup of coffee.**
2. *ww*
dichtknopen; **he buttoned up his coat,
because it was cold.**
**buttons—buttoning—buttoned—
has buttoned**
Let op: **button your coat up** *of*
button up your coat, *maar alleen*
button it up

buy [baɪ] *ww*
kopen; **I bought a book on my way home;
he has bought a new car; she's buying a
house; what have you bought her for**

Christmas? **he bought his wife a fur coat;
I've bought myself a new watch; he wants
to buy a car for his sister.**
buys—buying—bought [bɔːt]**—has
bought**

buyer, *zn*
koper.

by [baɪ] **1.** *vz*
(*a*) bij; **the house by the traffic lights; sit
down here by the fire.**
(*b*) tegen; **try to get home by teatime;
you must finish your homework by Friday.**
(*c*) per; door; **send the letter by air; he
goes to school by bus; she made the cake
by mixing eggs and flour; he caught a
cold by standing in the rain.**
(*d*) door; **a play by Shakespeare; now
here is some music by the school band;
the postman was bitten by the dog; I was
knocked down by a bus.**
(*e*) **(all) by yourself** = (helemaal) alleen;
(helemaal) zelf; **she's all by herself all
day; he built his house by himself; you
can find the house by yourself.**
(*f*) met; **fares have been increased by
10%; they beat us by 10 goals to 2.**
2. *bw*
voorbij; **he drove by without stopping.**
by and large = over het algemeen;
**by and large, fat people are happier than
thin ones.**
by the way = tussen twee haakjes; **by
the way, did you see the TV programme
on cars yesterday?**

bye (-bye) [baɪ('baɪ)] *tw*
da-ag! **bye!—see you on Thursday!**

Cc

cabbage ['kæbɪdʒ] *zn*
kool; **we had a salad of raw cabbage and
tomatoes; the kitchen smells of boiled
cabbage; he has a row of cabbages in the
garden.**

Let op: voor **cabbage** *als voedsel
wordt alleen het enkelvoud gebruikt:*
**some cabbage; a spoonful of
cabbage;** *voor de plant ook het
meervoud:* **two cabbages,** *etc.*

cage [keɪdʒ] *zn*
kooi; the little yellow bird was singing in its cage; the white mouse ran across the cage.

cake [keɪk] *zn*
taart; he had a birthday cake with six candles on it; a Christmas cake; would you like some more cake? have a slice of chocolate cake.
Let op: voor **cake** *als voedsel wordt alleen het enkelvoud gebruikt:* **some cake; a piece of cake;** *voor verschillende exemplaren van hetzelfde baksel ook het meervoud:* **she baked ten cakes; there are no cakes left in the shop**

calculate [ˈkælkjʊleɪt] *ww*
berekenen/uitrekenen; he tried to calculate how much he had spent on petrol; can you calculate the distance from London to Amsterdam in kilometres? I calculate that I have spent two hours on the phone to America.
calculates—calculating—calculated—has calculated

calculator, *zn*
rekenmachine; I added up the bill on my pocket calculator.

calendar [ˈkælɪndə] *zn*
kalender; he pinned the calendar on to the wall by his desk; tear off the next page on the calendar—today is November 1st.

calf [kɑːf] *zn*
kalf; a cow and her calf.
meervoud **calves** [kɑːvz]

call [kɔːl] **1.** *zn*
telefoon(gesprek), telefoontje; I want to make a (phone) call to Canada; there were three calls for you while you were out.
2. *ww*
(*a*) roepen; **call the children**—it's time for tea; **call me at 7 o'clock** = wek me om zeven uur; **call a taxi** = houd een taxi aan.
(*b*) noemen; **be called** = heten; **his son is called Peter; his name is James, but everyone calls him Jim; we call our cat**

Natasha; what do you call this machine for spreading glue?
(*c*) (op)bellen, telefoneren; **if he comes, tell him I'll call him when I'm in the office; Mr Smith is out**—shall I ask him to call you back? = zal ik hem vragen u terug te bellen?
(*d*) langskomen; the police called at the house, but there was no one there; he called on me at 10 o'clock can you call at the baker's to get a loaf of bread? = kun je bij de bakker aanlopen etc.
calls—calling—called—has called

callbox, *zn*
telefooncel; I'm phoning from the callbox outside the post office.
meervoud **callboxes**

call off, *ww*
afzeggen, aflasten; he's called off his visit to the USA.

call up, *ww*
oproepen (voor militaire dienst); thousands of men were called up at the beginning of the war.

calm [kɑːm] *bn*
kalm, rustig; the sea is very calm; a calm evening; stay calm—don't lose your temper.
calm—calmer—calmest

calmly, *bw*
kalm, rustig; he calmly walked into the burning house.

calves [kɑːvz] *zie* **calf**

came [keɪm] *zie* **come**

camera [ˈkæmərə] *zn*
camera, fototoestel; he took a picture of the church with his new camera; have you got a film in your camera? cine-camera = filmcamera.

camp [kæmp] *ww*
kamperen; we go camping every summer; a camping holiday; we camped by the side of the lake.
camps—camping—camped—has camped

camping ground, *zn*
kampeerterrein, kampeerplaats.
camping site/camp site, *zn*
kampeerterrein, camping.

can [kæn] **1.** *zn*
blik(je); **he opened a can of beer.**
2. *hulp ww*
(*a*) kunnen; **he can swim, but he can't ride a bicycle; you can't run as fast as I can; can you remember what the policeman said?**
(*b*) mogen; **he says we can go in; the policeman says we can't park here.**
(*c*) (*in beleefde vragen*) kunnen, mogen; **can we come in? can you shut the door, please?**
I can, you can, he can, we can, they can
Ontkennend: **cannot,** *meestal* **can't**
Verleden tijd: **could, could not,** *meestal* **couldn't**
Let op: **can** *en* **could** *worden zonder* **to** *en alleen samen met een ander werkwoord gebruikt*

canal [kə'næl] *zn*
kanaal; gracht; **the Suez Canal.**

candle ['kændl] *zn*
kaars; **there were six candles on her birthday cake; the electricity has gone off—can you light a candle?**

candy ['kændɪ] *zn*
(*Amerikaans voor* **sweet**) snoepje.

canned [kænd] *bn*
in blik, ingeblikt; **canned fruit.**

cannot ['kænɒt] *zie* **can**

can't [kɑːnt] *zie* **can**

cap [kæp] *zn*
(*a*) pet; **he was wearing an old black cap; an officer's cap.**
(*b*) dop; **screw the cap back on the bottle; a silver pen with a black cap.**

capital ['kæpɪtl] *zn*
(*a*) hoofdstad; **Rome is the capital of Italy; what is the capital of the United States?**
(*b*) hoofdletter; **Rome begins with a capital R; write your name in capitals.**
(*c*) kapitaal.
geen meervoud voor (*c*)

captain ['kæptɪn] *zn*
kapitein; gezagvoerder; **go to see the captain.**
Let op: kan met namen gebruikt worden: **Captain Smith,** *etc.*

car [kɑː] *zn*
auto, wagen; **he's bought a new car; her car was stolen last night.**
car park, *zn*
parkeerterrein; **park your car in one of the car parks in the centre of the town.**

caravan ['kærəvæn] *zn*
caravan; **we went on holiday with our caravan to Scotland.**

card [kɑːd] *zn*
(*a*) kaart; **he sent me a card from Italy; how much does it cost to send a card to Canada? birthday card** = verjaardagskaart; **Christmas card** = Kerstkaart; *zie ook* **postcard.**
(*b*) (speel) kaart; **a pack of cards; do you want a game of cards? they were playing cards;** = ze waren aan het kaarten.
cardboard, *zn*
karton; **we put our books into cardboard boxes.**
geen meervoud: **some cardboard; a piece of cardboard**

care ['keə] **1.** *zn*
(*a*) zorg; **take care when you cross the road** = pas op; **he took care to lock the door; take care not to be late** = hij zorgde dat etc.
(*b*) (*op een brief*) **Mr Brown, care of Mrs Green** = Mr Brown p/a Mrs Green.
2. *ww*
geven (om); **he doesn't care if his car is dirty; he couldn't care less** = het kan hem niet schelen.
cares—caring—cared—has cared
care for, *ww*
(*a*) zin hebben in; houden van; **would you care for another piece of cake? I don't care for this music very much.**
(*b*) zorgen voor; **nurses were caring for the injured people.**
careful, *bn*
voorzichtig; **he was careful not to make any noise; be careful, that glass is valu-**

able! she is very careful about what she eats.

carefully, *bw*
voorzichtig; **carry the eggs carefully! drive carefully!**

careless, *bn*
onzorgvuldig, slordig; **he was careless and made mistakes in his homework; she made several careless mistakes.**

cargo ['kɑ:gəʊ] *zn*
vracht; **cargo ship** = vrachtschip.
meervoud **cargoes**

carpet ['kɑ:pɪt] *zn*
tapijt; (vaste) vloerbedekking; **he spilt his coffee on the carpet; we have bought a new carpet for the dining room.**

carriage ['kærɪdʒ] *zn*
wagon; **they got into a 'no smoking' carriage.**

carried ['kærɪd], **carries** ['kærɪz] *zie* **carry**

carrot ['kærət] *zn*
wortel(tje); **boiled carrots; carrot salad; can you go to the greengrocer's and buy two kilos of carrots?**

carry ['kærɪ] *ww*
dragen; **they had to carry the piano up the stairs; the box was too heavy to carry; the bus was carrying sixty passengers** = vervoeren.
carries—carrying—carried—has carried

carry on, *ww*
doorgaan (met); **when the teacher came into the room, the children carried on talking.**

carry out, *ww*
uitvoeren; ondernemen; **they carried out a search for the missing children.**
Let op: **we carried the plan out** *of* **we carried out the plan,** *maar alleen* **we carried it out.**

case [keɪs] *zn*
koffer; **he was packing his case; I lost my cases at the airport; put the gun in its case** = foedraal.
in any case = hoe dan ook; toch;

he's late but **in any case it doesn't matter.**
in case = voor het geval dat; **take your coat in case it is cold; I always carry an umbrella in case it rains.**
in that case = in dat geval.

cash [kæʃ] *zn*
(baar) geld, contanten; **he paid for the car in cash; can I pay by cheque as I haven't very much cash on me?**
geen meervoud: **some cash; a lot of cash**

cassette [kə'set] *zn*
cassette; **a cassette recorder; he played a cassette of Spanish music.**

castle ['kɑ:sl] *zn*
kasteel; **Windsor Castle; the soldiers shut the castle gate.**

cat [kæt] *zn*
kat; **the cat sat in front of the fire; what a beautiful cat! she gave the cat some fish to eat.**

catch [kætʃ] *ww*
(*a*) (op)vangen; **see if you can catch the ball; she caught the ball in her left hand.**
(*b*) vangen; **we caught three fish; he sat by the river all day but didn't catch anything; our cat is good at catching mice.**
(*c*) halen; **you will have to run if you want to catch the 9 o'clock bus; he caught the last plane to Paris** = nemen.
(*d*) (*van ziekte*) oplopen; krijgen; **she caught mumps; he caught a cold from standing in the rain** = hij heeft kou gevat.
(*e*) betrappen; **she caught him stealing apples; the police caught the burglar as he was climbing out of the window.**
(*f*) opvangen, horen; **I didn't quite catch what you said.**
catches—catching—caught [kɔːt] **—has caught**

catch up, *ww*
inhalen; **if you run you will catch the others up/catch up with the others; he walked so slowly that we soon caught him up/soon caught up with him.**

caught [kɔːt] *zie* **catch**

cause [kɔːz] **1.** *zn*
oorzaak; reden; **what was the cause of the accident?**
2. *ww*
veroorzaken; **the accident was caused by thick fog.**
causes—causing—caused—has caused

ceiling [ˈsiːlɪŋ] *zn*
plafond; **each room has four walls, a floor and a ceiling; flies can walk on the ceiling; he painted the bathroom ceiling.**

cellar [ˈselə] *zn*
kelder; **we keep our washing machine in the cellar.**

cement [sɪˈment] *zn*
(*a*) cement; **he bought a bag of cement.**
(*b*) cementlijm.
geen meervoud

cent [sent] *zn*
cent; **this book only costs twenty-five cents (25c).**
in bedragen wordt **cent** meestal geschreven **c: 25c**

centimetre [ˈsentɪmiːtə] *zn* (*Amer.* **centimeter**)
centimeter; **the table is sixty centimetres (60 cm) wide.**
met cijfers wordt **centimetre** meestal geschreven **cm**

centre [ˈsentə] *zn* (*Amer.* **center**)
(*a*) midden; centrum; **a tree was growing in the centre of the field; the centre of the town is very old; this chocolate has coffee cream in the centre** = binnenin.
(*b*) **sports centre** = sportcentrum; **shopping centre** = winkelcentrum.
central, *bn*
centraal; **central heating** = centrale verwarming.

century [ˈsentʃərɪ] *zn*
eeuw; **the nineteenth (19th) century** = de negentiende eeuw; **a 19th century church** = negentiende-eeuws.
meervoud **centuries**

cereal [ˈsɪərɪəl] *zn*
(*a*) graan; **the farmer grows cereals; a cereal crop.**

(*b*) havermout e.d. voor het ontbijt; **he ate a bowl of cereal; you put milk and sugar on your cereal.**

ceremony [ˈserɪmənɪ] *zn*
ceremonie; **the prize-giving ceremony will be held in the school hall** = de prijsuitreiking.
meervoud **ceremonies**

certain [ˈsɜːtn] *bn*
(*a*) zeker; **the police are certain he is the thief; this horse is certain to win the race; he locked the door to make certain that no one could steal his money.**
(*b*) bepaald; **certain plants can make you ill if you eat them; a certain Mr Smith called while you were out.** = een zekere.
(*c*) **a certain amount** = bepaald; zeker; **the storm did a certain amount of damage; painting the house will take a certain amount of time.**
certainly, *bw*
(ja) zeker; natuurlijk; **will you come to the party?—certainly I'll come; please tell him to write to me—certainly, sir.**

chain [tʃeɪn] **1.** *zn*
ketting; **he wore a gold cross on a chain round his neck; that dog should be kept on a chain.**
2. *ww*
ketenen; vastleggen; **the dog was chained to the gate.**
chains—chaining—chained—has chained

chair [tʃeə] *zn*
stoel; **someone has been sitting in my chair; pull up a chair and have some supper; this chair is very hard and not very comfortable.**
chairman, *zn*
voorzitter; **Mr Smith was the chairman at the meeting.**

chalk [tʃɔːk] *zn*
krijt; kalk; **the hills are made of chalk; there are chalk hills along the south coast; he wrote on the blackboard with coloured chalk** = krijtje.

chance [tʃɑːns] *zn*
(*a*) kans, mogelijkheid; **has he any**

chance of winning?—yes, I think he has a good chance of winning; is there any chance of getting a cup of tea? there is no chance of the weather turning cold.

(b) kans, gelegenheid; **I've been waiting for the chance to speak to the manager; he never had the chance to visit the United States.**

(c) toeval; **it was quite by chance that we were travelling on the same bus.**

Let op: **chance of —ing** = mogelijkheid *maar* **chance to** = gelegenheid

change [tʃeɪndʒ] **1.** *zn*
(a) verandering; **we usually go on holiday in August, but this year we're going in July for a change; a cup of tea is a nice change after several cups of coffee; I think it's a change for the better** = verbetering.

(b) **small change** = kleingeld; **I have only got a £5 note, I've no small change at all; have you got change for a £1 note?**

(c) wisselgeld; **the book is £3.50, so you get £1.50 change from £5; you've given me too much change.**

geen meervoud voor (b) *en* (c)

2. *ww*
(a) veranderen; **London has changed a lot in the last few years; he's changed so much since I saw him last, that I didn't recognize him; I've changed my mind** = ik ben van gedachten/mening veranderd.

(b) zich verkleden; **he changed into his old clothes before mending the car; go into my bedroom if you want to change your dress.**

(c) (ver)wisselen; **you ought to change your car tyres; can you change a £5 note?**

(d) overstappen; **to get to London you will have to change at Birmingham.**

changes—changing—changed—has changed

character [ˈkærəktə] *zn*
(a) karakter; **she has a strong character; he's a weak character.**

(b) persoon (in roman/toneelstuk); **at the end of the play all the main characters are dead.**

charge [tʃɑːdʒ] **1.** *zn*
(a) (on)kosten; **there is no charge for service; we will send the parcel free of charge** = gratis.

(b) tenlastelegging; **he was kept in prison on a charge of trying to kill the Prime Minister** = op beschuldiging van.

(c) **in charge** = met de leiding belast; **he is in charge of the department; who's in charge here? he took charge of the class while the teacher was out of the room** = onder zijn hoede nemen.

2. *ww*
(a) rekenen; **they charged me £1 for two glasses of orange juice; how much do you charge for cleaning the car?**

(b) ten laste leggen; **he was charged with stealing the silver.**

charges—charging—charged—has charged

chase [tʃeɪs] *ww*
achtervolgen, nazitten; **the policeman chased the burglar; he was chased by two dogs.**

chases—chasing—chased—has chased

cheap [tʃiːp] *bn*
goedkoop; **this coat is much cheaper than that one; choose the cheapest sort of meat; I bought these books cheap in the market; how much is a cheap return ticket to London?**

cheap—cheaper—cheapest

cheat [tʃiːt] *ww*
bedriegen; vals spelen; spieken; afzetten; **don't play cards with Paul—he cheats; the teacher caught him cheating in the exams; the shopkeeper tried to cheat me out of 50p by giving me the wrong change.**

cheats—cheating—cheated—has cheated

check [tʃek] **1.** *zn*
(a) controle; **the police made a check on everyone who was in the building; the car has to go to the garage for a check** = onderhoudsbeurt.

(b) *Amerikaans voor* **cheque**

2. *ww*
controleren; nagaan; **don't forget to**

check if the doors are all locked; he
checked the times of trains with the
booking office; I asked the garage to
check the brakes.
**checks—checking—checked—
has checked**

check in(to), *ww*
aankomen/zich laten inschrijven (in
een hotel); **they checked in at 10 p.m.;
he's checked into room 15.**
check out, *ww*
(een hotel) verlaten; **they checked out in
the morning; I'm checking out of room
15.**
check up, *ww*
nagaan; nakijken; **can you check up if
the doors are locked? he checked up on
the times of trains to London.**
check-up, *zn*
onderzoek/controle; **I must go to the
dentist for a check-up.**

cheek [tʃiːk] *zn*
wang; **a little girl with red cheeks.**

cheer up [ˈtʃɪərʌp] *ww*
opvrolijken; opmonteren; **this funny film
will soon cheer you up; she cheered up
after we had been to see her.**
**cheers—cheering—cheered—has
cheered**

cheerful [ˈtʃɪəfʊl] *bn*
vrolijk, opgewekt; **he's always cheerful,
even when things go wrong; you must try
to keep cheerful; they sang a cheerful
song as they worked.**
cheerfully, *bw*
vrolijk, blij, opgewekt; **the children
played cheerfully in the garden.**

cheese [tʃiːz] *zn*
kaas; **a piece of cheese; can I have a
pound of cheese, please? at the end of the
meal, we'll have biscuits and cheese;** =
crackers met kaas; **cream cheese** =
room-kaas; **blue cheese** = blauw-gea-
derde kaas.
het meervoud **cheeses** *wordt alleen
gebruikt voor verschillende kazen of
voor verschillende soorten. Meestal
geen meervoud:* **some cheese; a
piece of cheese**

chemist [ˈkemɪst] *zn*
apotheker, drogist; **the chemist's** =
apotheek; drogisterij; **go to the chemist's
to get some cough medicine; the chemist's
is next door to the post office.**

cheque [tʃek] *zn* (*Amer.* **check**)
cheque; **I wrote a cheque for £10; can I
pay by cheque?** *zie ook* **traveller's
cheque**
cheque book, *zn*
chequeboek.

chess [tʃes] *zn*
schaakspel; **would you like a game of
chess? he's no good at chess; she plays
chess very well** = ze schaakt goed.
geen meervoud

chest [tʃest] *zn*
(*a*) kist; **he kept his money in a large
chest.**
(*b*) borst; **he hit me in the chest; she has
a cold on the chest** = ze heeft een kou
op de borst.
chest of drawers, *zn*
ladenkast.

chew [tʃuː] *ww*
kauwen; **he was chewing a piece of meat;
you should chew your food slowly.**
**chews—chewing—chewed—has
chewed**
chewing gum, *zn*
kauwgom

chicken [ˈtʃɪkɪn] *zn*
(*a*) kip, kuiken; **the chickens were running all round the farm.**
(*b*) kip; **we had roast chicken for dinner;
would you like another slice of chicken?
can I have a chicken sandwich?**
geen meervoud voor (*b*)*:* **some chicken; a slice of chicken/a piece of
chicken**

chief [tʃiːf] **1.** *bn*
hoofd-, voornaamste; **what is the chief
cause of traffic accidents? he's the chief
engineer** = eerste machinist.
2. *zn*
chef; leider.
chiefly, *bw*
voornamelijk.

child [tʃaɪld] *zn*
kind; **when I was a child TV didn't exist;
here is a photograph of him as a child;
all the children were playing in the field;
when do the children come out of school?
how many children have they got?**
meervoud **children** [ˈtʃɪldrən]

childhood, *zn*
jeugd; kinderjaren; **he had a happy
childhood in the country; she spent her
childhood in Canada.**

chimney [ˈtʃɪmnɪ] *zn*
schoorsteen; **the smoke poured out of the
chimney; all the smoke went up the
chimney.**
meervoud **chimneys**

chin [tʃɪn] *zn*
kin; **she hit him on the chin; he rested his
chin on his hand while he was thinking.**

china [ˈtʃaɪnə] *zn*
porselein; **a china teacup; put all the
china away in the cupboard.**
geen meervoud: **some china; a piece
of china** = kopje, schoteltje, etc.

chip [tʃɪp] 1. *zn*
(*a*) schilfer(tje); spaan(der); **chips of
stone flew in all directions.**
(*b*) patates frites; **fish and chips; can I
have some more chips?**
2. *ww*
schilferen; **he chipped the old paint off
the door** = hij krabde de oude verf af.
**chips—chipping—chipped—has
chipped**

chipped, *bn*
met een stukje eraf; **a chipped cup; this
plate is chipped.**

chocolate [ˈtʃɒklət] *zn*
(*a*) chocola(de); **can I have a piece of
chocolate? his mother made a chocolate
cake; a bar of chocolate costs 20p; plain
chocolate** = puur; **milk chocolate** =
melk.
(*b*) chocolaatje; bonbon; **a box of
chocolates; John ate six chocolates, and
then felt ill.**
(*c*) chocola; **I always have a cup of hot
chocolate before I go to bed.**

(*d*) chocoladebruin; **we have a chocolate-
coloured carpet in the sitting room.**
geen meervoud voor (a), (c) of (d)

choice [tʃɔɪs] *zn*
keus; keuze; sortering, smaak; **the shop
has a wonderful choice of shoes: I don't
like her choice of music; have you made
your choice yet?**

choose [tʃuːz] *ww*
(uit)kiezen; besluiten; **have you chosen
what you want to eat? in the end, they
chose to go to Germany on holiday; there
are too many tours to choose from—I
can't decide which one to choose; don't
take too long choosing a book to read on
holiday.**
**chooses—choosing—chose
[tʃəʊz]—has chosen [tʃəʊzn]**

chop [tʃɒp] 1. *zn*
karbonade; kotelet; **we had lamb chops
and potatoes; a pork chop.**
2. *ww*
hakken; **he's in the garden chopping up
wood for the fire; chop the onions into
little pieces; they chopped down the tree**
= ze hebben de boom omgehakt.
**chops—chopping—chopped—has
chopped**

Christian [ˈkrɪstʃən] *zn & bn*
Christen; **Christian name** = voornaam;
**I know his name is Smith, but what's his
Christian name?**

Christmas [ˈkrɪsməs] *zn*
Kerstmis; **Christmas Day** = eerste
Kerstdag; **Christmas tree** = kerstboom
Christmas cake/pudding = kerstgebak/
pudding; **what did you get for Christ-
mas?** = wat heb je ... gekregen? **have
you opened your Christmas presents yet?
Christmas card** = kerstkaart; **Father
Christmas** = kerstman(netje).

church [tʃɜːtʃ] *zn*
kerk; **we go to church on Sundays; this is
St Mary's Church.**
meervoud **churches**

cigar [sɪˈɡɑː] *zn*
sigaar; **he was smoking a long cigar.**

cigarette [sɪgə'ret] *zn*
sigaret; **how many cigarettes does he
smoke a day? she went into the shop to
buy a packet of cigarettes.**

cine-camera ['sɪnɪkæmərə] *zn*
filmcamera; **he took a film of the race
with his cine-camera.**

cinema ['sɪnəmə] *zn*
bioskoop; **we went to the cinema on
Saturday night; what's on at the cinema
this week?** = **wat draait er?**

circle ['sɜːkl] *zn*
cirkel; kring; **draw a circle in the middle
of the piece of paper; the children sat in
a circle.**

city ['sɪtɪ] *zn*
stad; **which is the largest city in the
United States? traffic is a big problem in
large cities.**
meervoud **cities**

citizen, *zn*
(staats)burger; **a British citizen; a citizen
of London** = **inwoner.**

claim [kleɪm] *ww*
(*a*) aanspraak maken (op), eisen; **he
claimed the prize.**
(*b*) opeisen; **we found a watch in the
street, but no one has come to claim it.**
(*c*) beweren; **he claimed he was a relative
of mine; she claims that the police
attacked her.**
**claims—claiming—claimed—has
claimed**

clap [klæp] *ww*
klappen; **when the play finished everyone
started clapping; they all clapped the
headmaster when he said the school
would have a day's holiday** = toejuichen.
**claps—clapping—clapped—has
clapped**

class [klɑːs] *zn*
(*a*) klas; les; **the French class; there are
thirty children in Simon's class; we go to
evening classes on Mondays to learn
German** = **we gaan naar Duitse les op
maandagavond.**
(*b*) klasse; stand; **working class** =

arbeidersklasse; **middle class** = middenstand.
(*c*) **first class** = eersterangs; **second class**
= tweederangs.
(*d*) klas(se); **he always travels first class;
first class passengers; the tourist class
fare is much less than the first class.**
meervoud **classes**

classroom, *zn*
klas(lokaal); **when the teacher came into
the classroom all the children stood up.**

clean [kliːn] **1.** *bn*
schoon; **have you got a clean handkerchief? these plates aren't clean; you won't
get any food if your hands aren't clean.**
clean—cleaner—cleanest

2. *ww*
schoonmaken; poetsen; **have you
cleaned your teeth today? don't forget to
clean your shoes; she was cleaning the
bathroom when the telephone rang.**
**cleans—cleaning—cleaned—has
cleaned**

cleaner's, *zn*
stomerij; **I'm taking my suit to the cleaner's.**

clean out, *ww*
een goede beurt geven; **you must clean
out your room; she was cleaning out the
kitchen cupboards.**

clean up, *ww*
opruimen.

clear ['klɪə] **1.** *bn*
(*a*) vrij; helder; **the road is clear now; a
clear blue sky; have you got a clear view
of the TV picture?** = **kunt u het scherm
goed zien?**
(*b*) duidelijk; **he made it clear that he
wanted us to leave; the words on the
medicine bottle are not very clear.**
(*c*) helder; doorschijnend; **clear glass.**
clear—clearer—clearest

2. *ww*
(op)ruimen; schoonmaken; **they cleared
the streets of snow/they cleared the snow
from the streets; he's clearing a blocked
pipe in the kitchen; to clear the table** =
afruimen.
**clears—clearing—cleared—has
cleared**

clear away, *ww*
opruimen/wegruimen; **can you help to clear away the snow from the path?**

clearly, *bw*
kennelijk, duidelijk; **he clearly did not like her dress.**

clear off, *ww*
verdwijnen; wegtrekken; ophoepelen; **clear off!** = smeer 'm!

clear out, *ww*
(*a*) ophoepelen; **clear out! I don't want you here.**
(*b*) leegmaken; **can you clear out the cupboards in your bedroom?**

clear up, *ww*
(*a*) opruimen; **we had to clear up the mess after the party.**
(*b*) ophelderen/oplossen; **the police finally cleared up the mystery.**
(*c*) opklaren; **I hope the weather clears up because tomorrow is our sports day.**
Let op: **clear that mess up** *of* **clear up that mess,** *maar alleen* **clear it up**

clever ['klevə] *bn*
knap; **she's very clever at business; he's clever with his hands** = handig; **she's the cleverest person in the family.**
clever—cleverer—cleverest

climb [klaɪm] *ww*
(be)klimmen; **he climbed up a tree; the children climbed over the wall; she climbed through the window and down the wall by a rope; the car climbed the steep hill with some difficulty; when you have climbed Everest, there is nothing higher to climb; he goes climbing every weekend** = hij beoefent de bergsport.
climbs—climbing—climbed—has climbed

clock [klɒk] *zn*
klok; **the school clock is always right; your clock is five minutes slow; the clock has stopped—it needs winding up;** *zie ook* **o'clock.**

close¹ [kləʊs] *bn & bw*
dichtbij; **our house is close to the post office; keep close by me if you don't want**

to get lost; **go further away—you're too close.**
close—closer—closest

close² [kləʊz] *ww*
sluiten; **please close the window; would you mind closing the door? the shops are closed on Sundays; he closed his book and turned on the TV.**
closes—closing—closed—has closed

close down, *ww*
opheffen, sluiten; **the shop closed down last week; they're going to close down the factory.**

cloth [klɒθ] *zn*
doek; **wipe the floor with a wet cloth; face cloth** = washandje; **dish cloth** = vaatdoek.

clothes [kləʊðz] *zn meervoud*
kleren; **he hasn't any clothes on; the policeman took off his clothes and jumped into the river; you ought to put some clean clothes on; they haven't had any new clothes for years.**
clothing, *zn*
kleding.
geen meervoud: **some clothing; a piece of clothing**

cloud [klaʊd] *zn*
wolk; **I think it is going to rain—look at those clouds; the aircraft flew above the clouds; clouds of smoke poured out of the house** = rookwolk.
cloudy, *bn*
bewolkt; **a dull cloudy day; the weather turned cloudy; when it's cloudy, it isn't easy to take good photographs.**
cloudy—cloudier—cloudiest

club [klʌb] *zn*
(*a*) club; **youth club; I'm joining a swimming club; our town has one of the best football clubs in the country; the sports club is near the police station.**
(*b*) (*kaarten*) klaver; **the ten of clubs.**
(*c*) knots, knuppel.

cm *zie* **centimetre**

Co. *zie* **company**

Clothes *Kleren*

1.	belt	*riem*	16.	pocket	*zak*
2.	boot	*laars*	17.	pullover	*trui*
3.	button	*knoop*	18.	purse	*portemonnaie*
4.	cap	*pet*	19.	raincoat	*regenjas*
5.	collar	*boord; kraag*	20.	sandal	*sandaal*
6.	dress	*jurk*	21.	shirt	*overhemd*
7.	glove	*handschoen*	22.	shoe	*schoen*
8.	handbag	*handtas*	23.	shorts	*short(s)*
9.	handkerchief	*zakdoek*	24.	skirt	*rok*
10.	hat	*hoed*	25.	sleeve	*mouw*
11.	heel	*hak*	26.	sock	*sok*
12.	helmet	*helm*	27.	suit	*pak*
13.	jacket	*jasje, colbert*	28.	tie	*das*
14.	jeans	*jeans*	29.	trousers	*broek*
15.	overalls	*overal(l)*	30.	zip	*ritssluiting*

coach [kəʊtʃ] **1.** *zn*
(*a*) bus, touringcar; **we took the coach**
to Scotland; when does the coach leave for
London? we all went on a coach tour to
France; I get sick on long coach journeys.
(*b*) wagon; **a train with eight coaches.**
(*c*) trainer; **tennis coach; he's a football**
coach.
meervoud **coaches**
2. *ww*
trainen; **he's coaching the England tennis**
team.
coaches—coaching—coached—
has coached

coal [kəʊl] *zn*
(steen)kool; **put some more coal on the**
fire; the electric power station burns
coal.
geen meervoud: **some coal; a bag of**
coal; a lump of coal

coast [kəʊst] *zn*
kust; **after ten days, they saw the coast**
of Africa in the distance; the south coast
is the warmest part of the country.

coat [kəʊt] *zn*
(*a*) jas; **you'll need to put on a coat—it's**
just started to snow; she was wearing a
fur coat.
(*b*) **a coat of paint** = laag; **we gave the**
door two coats of paint = we hebben de
deur twee lagen verf gegeven.

cock [kɒk] *zn*
haan.

cocoa [ˈkəʊkəʊ] *zn*
cacao; **I always have a cup of cocoa in**
the evening; put a spoonful of cocoa into
each cup.

coffee [ˈkɒfɪ] *zn*
(*a*) koffie; **would you like a cup of coffee?**
this coffee is too bitter; black coffee/
white coffee = koffie zonder/met melk.
(*b*) kopje koffie; **three coffees and two**
teas, please.
(*c*) lichtbruin; **we have a coffee-coloured**
carpet in the sitting room.
meervoud alleen voor (*b*)

coffee cup, *zn*
koffiekopje.

coffee pot, *zn*
koffiepot.
coffee table, *zn*
koffietafel.

coin [kɔɪn] *zn*
munt(je); geldstuk/muntstuk; **he gave**
me my change in 10p and 5p coins; this
telephone box takes 10p coins; I've
dropped a coin inside the piano.

cold [kəʊld] **1.** *bn*
koud; **you'll have to wash in cold water;**
the weather is colder than last week; they
say it will be even colder tomorrow; it's
so cold—I think it's going to snow; if
you're cold, come and sit by the fire; my
hands are cold, but my toes are warm;
start eating, or your soup will get cold.
cold—colder—coldest
2. *zn*
verkoudheid; **he caught a cold by stand-**
ing in the rain; she's got a cold, so she
can't go out; mother's in bed with a cold;
don't come near me—I've got a cold.

collar [ˈkɒlə] *zn*
(*a*) boord; kraag(je); **my shirt collar's**
too tight; she turned up her coat collar
because of the wind.
(*b*) halsband; **our dog has his name writ-**
ten on his collar.

collect [kəˈlekt] *ww*
(*a*) afhalen/(op)halen; **my wife collects**
the children from school at 4 o'clock; can
you collect my suit from the cleaner's?
(*b*) verzamelen; **he collects stamps.**
(*c*) collecteren; **I'm collecting for the old**
people's home.
collects—collecting—collected—
has collected
collection [kəˈlekʃn] *zn*
verzameling; collectie; collecte; **he**
showed me his collection of gold coins;
have you seen his stamp collection?

college [ˈkɒlɪdʒ] *zn*
(gedeelte van) universiteit; academie;
I'm going to college to study engineer-
ing.

colour [ˈkʌlə] *zn* (*Amer.* **color**)
kleur; **what colour is your hat?—it's a**

pale blue colour; I don't like the colour
of her dress; all the pictures in the book
are in colour; his socks are the same
colour as his shirt; colour TV/colour film
= kleurentelevisie/kleurenfilm.

colour-blind, *bn*
kleurenblind; **he's colour-blind.**

coloured, *bn*
gekleurd; **a coloured postcard; a book
with coloured pictures.**

comb [kəʊm] **1.** *zn*
kam.
2. *ww*
kammen; **she was combing her hair; have
you combed your hair?**
combs—combing—combed—has
combed

come [kʌm] *ww*
(*a*) komen; aankomen; **come and see me
again soon; he came to see me yesterday;
they came to school by car; hide behind
the door, there's a policeman coming;
come up to my room for a cup of coffee;
the teacher told him to come in.**
(*b*) komen, volgen; **what comes after B
in the alphabet? T comes before U; what
comes next in the programme?**
comes—coming—came [keɪm]—
has come

come across, *ww*
tegenkomen; **I came across this book in
a little shop.**

come along, *ww*
meekomen; **come along with us** = kom
met ons mee; **come along, or you'll miss
the bus!** = schiet op!

come apart, *ww*
uit elkaar vallen; **the watch came apart
in my hands.**

come back, *ww*
terugkomen; he left the house to go to work,
but came back for his newspaper; **come
back here, I want to talk to you.**

come of, *ww*
komen van; **nothing came of his plan** =
er is niets van zijn plan gekomen.

come off, *ww*
(*a*) losgaan; losraken; **the button has
come off my shirt; the handle came off in
my hand.**

(*b*) loskomen; **the ink won't come off the
tablecloth** = de inkt is niet uit het
tafelkleed te krijgen.

come on, *ww*
(*a*) opschieten; **come on, or we'll be late.**
(*b*) naderen; komen opzetten; **there's a
storm coming on; I think I have a cold
coming on.**

come out, *ww*
(*a*) ergens uitgaan; **the ink marks won't
come out.**
(*b*) verschijnen; **the magazine comes out
on Fridays.**

come to, *ww*
komen op/tot; **the bill comes to more
than £10.**

comfortable [ˈkʌmftəbl] *bn*
comfortabel; **what a comfortable bed!
the seats in the cinema aren't very comfortable; make yourself comfortable** =
maak het je gemakkelijk.

command [kəˈmɑːnd] *zn*
(*a*) bevel; **the soldiers were given the
command to stop fighting.**
(*b*) **in command** = het bevel hebben,
voeren (over soldaten); **who is in command here?**

committee [kəˈmɪtɪ] *zn*
comité, bestuur; commissie; **the tennis
club committee organizes the matches;
he's on the committee of the youth club;
would you like to join the committee?
there's a committee meeting at 10
o'clock.**

common [ˈkɒmən] *bn*
(*a*) gewoon; **accidents are quite common
on this part of the motorway; that's a
common mistake** = veelgemaakte fout.
(*b*) **in common** = gemeen; **we have two
things in common—we are all English
and we all have red hair.**
common—commoner—
commonest

common sense, *zn*
gezond verstand; **it's common sense to
lock your car at night.**

companion [kəmˈpænjən] *zn*
(met)gezel.

company ['kʌmpnɪ] *zn*
(*a*) firma; zaak; **the company is doing well; John Smith and Company.**
(*b*) gezelschap; **will you keep me company?**
meervoud **companies** *maar geen meervoud voor* (*b*)
Let op: **Company** *wordt als* **Co.** *geschreven in een firmanaam:* **John Smith & Co.**

compare [kəm'peə] *ww*
vergelijken; **try on the two pairs of shoes to compare them; you can't compare tinned fruit to/with fresh fruit; compared with/to his father, he is not very tall.**
compares—comparing— compared—has compared

comparative [kəm'pærətɪv] *zn*
vergrotende trap/comparatief; **'fatter' is the comparative of 'fat'; 'faster' is the comparative of 'fast'.**
comparison, *zn*
vergelijking; **you can't make a comparison between the two men.**

competition [kɒmpə'tɪʃn] *zn*
competitie; **a crossword competition; she entered a competition to win a holiday in Spain.**

complain [kəm'pleɪn] *ww*
klagen; **she complained about the food; he is complaining of pains in his legs; we will complain to the police about the noise from the restaurant.**
complains—complaining—com plained—has complained

complaint, *zn*
klacht; **the manager wouldn't listen to the complaints from the customers.**

complete [kəm'pliːt] **1.** *bn*
volledig; **I have a complete set of the new stamps; he has read the complete works of Shakespeare.**
2. *ww*
afmaken; **he completed the whole job in two days.**
completes—completing— completed—has completed

completely, *bw*
volledig; **the house was completely de**

stroyed; **I completely forgot about her birthday.**

concern [kən'sɜːn] **1.** *zn*
(*a*) bedrijf; **a large industrial concern.**
(*b*) bezorgdheid; **concern for poor people; his health is giving cause for con cern.**
2. *ww*
te maken hebben met, betreffen; **it doesn't concern you** = het gaat jou niet aan; **as far as food is concerned** = wat voedsel betreft; **as far as I'm concerned** = wat mij betreft.
concerns—concerning— concerned—has concerned

concerned, *bn*
bezorgd; **I really am concerned about your health.**
concerning, *vz*
over; aangaande; **I want to talk to you concerning your son's behaviour.**

concert ['kɒnsət] *zn*
concert; **we went to a Beethoven concert last night.**

concrete ['kɒŋkriːt] *zn*
beton; **a concrete pavement; they made a path out of concrete.**
geen meervoud

condition [kən'dɪʃn] *zn*
(*a*) staat, conditie; **the old car is in very good condition; he is ill, and his condition is getting worse; living conditions are very bad** = omstandigheden.
(*b*) voorwaarde; **I will come on condition that you pay me** = onder/op voor waarde dat etc; **I don't agree with some of the conditions in the contract.**

conduct 1. *zn* ['kɒndʌkt]
gedrag; **the teacher sent him out of the classroom because his conduct was so bad; she got a prize for good con duct.**
2. *ww* [kən'dʌkt]
dirigeren;
conducts—conducting— conducted—has conducted

conductor [kən'dʌktə] *zn*
(*a*) dirigent.
(*b*) conducteur.

confuse [kən'fju:z] *ww*
verwarren; in de war brengen; **if you all
ask questions at the same time, you will
only confuse the teacher; there was a
confusing noise of voices.**
confuses—confusing—
confused—has confused

congratulate [kən'grætjʊleɪt] *ww*
feliciteren; **we want to congratulate you
on winning the prize.**
congratulates—congratulating—
congratulated—
has congratulated

congratulations [kəngrætjʊ'leɪʃnz]
zn meervoud
felicitatie(s); **congratulations on your success!/on your 21st birthday!**

conjunction [kən'dʒʌŋkʃn]
voegwoord (zoals **and** of **but**).

connect [kə'nekt] *ww*
aansluiten; **the cooker is connected to the
gas pipe; have you connected the electric
wires to the mains?**
connects—connecting—
connected—has connected

connection [kə'nekʃn] *zn*
verband; aansluiting; **what is the connection between the dead man and the
murderer? is there any connection between the bombs and the election?**
in connection with = in verband
met; **I want to speak to you in connection
with your letter.**

conscience ['kɒnʃəns] *zn*
geweten; **he has a guilty conscience** =
slecht geweten.

conscious ['kɒnʃəs] *bn*
bewust; **he became conscious of two red
eyes looking at him in the dark; it was
two days after the accident before she
became conscious** = ze kwam pas twee
dagen na het ongeluk weer tot be-
wustzijn.

consider [kən'sɪdə] *ww*
overwegen; **he is considering going on
holiday to Spain; have you considered
complaining to the manager?**
considers—considering—
considered—has considered

considerable, *bn*
aanzienlijk; **he lost a considerable
amount of money; she has put a considerable amount of effort into her shop.**
considerably, *bw*
aanzienlijk; **he's considerably thinner
than he was last year.**

consist of [kən'sɪstɒv] *ww*
bestaan uit; **our English class consists of
twenty girls and two boys; he had a snack
consisting of an apple and a glass of
milk.**
consists—consisting—
consisted—has consisted

contain [kən'teɪn] *ww*
bevatten; **this bottle contains two litres
of milk; he had a box containing a knife,
a piece of thread and some buttons.**
contains—containing—
contained—has contained

container, *zn*
doos(je), bak(je), vat, etc. **have you a
container for this soft cheese? the container cracked, and all the contents
spilled out into the road.**

contents ['kɒntents] *zn meervoud*
(*a*) inhoud; **he turned the box upside
down and the contents fell out on to the
floor; the police were inspecting the contents of her suitcases.**
(*b*) inhoud; **she wouldn't tell me the contents of the letter.**

continue [kən'tɪnju:] *ww*
doorgaan; voortzetten; **the talks continued for three days; the snow continued
to fall for 24 hours; they continued their
conversation; they continued eating as if
nothing had happened.**
continues—continuing—
continued—has continued

continual, *bn*
voortdurend; herhaald; **there were continual interruptions.**
continuous, *bn*
onafgebroken; **a continuous performance
in a cinema** = doorlopend.

control [kən'trəʊl] **1.** *zn*
controle; bedwang; **he has no control**

over his children; the fireman brought the
fire under control = de brandweerman
is de brand meester geworden; the fire
got out of control = het vuur greep om
zich heen.
2. *ww*
beheersen, controleren; the police were
controlling the traffic; we can't control
the sales of foreign cars; the government
controls the price of bread.
controls—controlling—
controlled—has controlled

control tower, *zn*
verkeerstoren

convenient [kən'viːnjənt] *bn*
geschikt; handig; the house is convenient
for the shops = dichtbij; let's find a
convenient spot for a picnic; when is the
most convenient time for us to meet?

conversation [kɒnvə'seɪʃn] *zn*
conversatie, gesprek; they had a long
conversation about their holidays; he
suddenly changed the subject of the conversation.

cook [kʊk] **1.** *zn*
kok; she's a very good cook.
2. *ww*
(*a*) koken; you should learn how to
cook—it's quite easy; I'm cooking
breakfast; how do you cook cabbage?
(*b*) (gaar) koken; supper is cooking in
the oven; how long does this meat take
to cook? the chicken isn't cooked enough;
a cooked breakfast = eieren met spek
etc.
cooks—cooking—cooked—has
cooked

cooker, *zn*
fornuis; we have a fridge and a gas
cooker in the kitchen.
cookie, *zn*
(*Amerikaans voor* **biscuit**) koekje/bis-
cuitje.

cool [kuːl] **1.** *bn*
koel, fris; the weather has suddenly
become cooler; keep this bottle in a cool
place; what I want is a long, cool drink.
cool—cooler—coolest

2. *ww*
(af)koelen; wait until your soup has
cooled; put the milk in the fridge to cool.
cools—cooling—cooled—has
cooled

cool down, *ww*
afkoelen; has your soup cooled down
enough? we sat in the shade of a tree to
cool down.
cool off, *ww*
afkoelen; we cooled off by going for a
swim.

copy ['kɒpɪ] **1.** *zn*
(*a*) kopie; this isn't a real picture by
Picasso, it's only a copy; to type a letter
and make two copies.
(*b*) exemplaar; have you got a copy of
Shakespeare's plays? I've lost my copy
of 'The Times'.
meervoud **copies**

2. *ww*
kopiëren; nadoen; she copied the letter;
he copies his father's way of walking.
copies—copying—copied—has
copied

cork [kɔːk] *zn*
(*a*) kurk; the floor was covered with
cork.
(*b*) kurk; he pulled the cork out of the
bottle; the cork won't go back into the
bottle.
corkscrew, *zn*
kurketrekker.

corn [kɔːn] *zn*
(*a*) koren, graan; the farmer grows corn.
(*b*) sweet corn = maïs.
geen meervoud

cornflakes, *zn meervoud*
cornflakes.

corner ['kɔːnə] *zn*
hoek; the shop is on the corner of the
street; put the chair in the far corner of
the room; the police car went round the
corner at top speed; she was waiting at
the street corner; he turned the corner =
hij sloeg de hoek om.

correct [kə'rekt] **1.** *bn*
juist; what is the correct time? you have

to give correct answers to all the questions if you want to win a prize; your answer isn't correct—try again.
2. *ww*
corrigeren; **the teacher is correcting our homework** = de onderwijzer(es) kijkt ons huiswerk na; **you must try to correct your spelling; the car keeps turning to the left—can you correct this fault?**
corrects—correcting— corrected—has corrected

correction [kə'rekʃn] *zn*
correctie, verbetering.

correctly, *bw*
juist; **he answered all the questions correctly and won the prize.**

corridor ['kɒridɔː] *zn*
gang; **his room is at the end of the corridor; she ran down the corridor.**

cost [kɒst] **1.** *zn*
prijs; kosten; **what is the cost of a cinema ticket? the cost of living** = de kosten van het levensonderhoud.
2. *ww*
kosten; **apples cost 50p a kilo; petrol seems to cost more all the time; this table cost me £50; what does it cost?**
costs—costing—cost—has cost

cotton ['kɒtn] *zn*
katoen; garen; **a cotton shirt; I'm trying to thread the cotton through this needle.**
cotton wool, *zn*
watten.

cough [kɒf] **1.** *zn*
hoest; kuch; **he gave a little cough to attract the waiter's attention; I have got a bad cough** = ik heb een akelige hoest.
2. *ww*
hoesten; kuchen; **the smoke made me cough; he has a cold and keeps on coughing and sneezing.**
coughs—coughing—coughed— has coughed

could [kʊd] *hulpww*
(*a*) kon(den); zou(den) kunnen; **he fell down and couldn't get up; you could still catch the train if you ran fast.**
(*b*) mocht(en); **the policeman said we could cross the road.**

(*c*) (*in beleefde vragen*) zou(den) ... kunnen; **could you pass me the sugar, please? could you shut the door?**
Ontkennend: **could not,** *meestal* **couldn't**
Let op: **could** *is de verleden tijd van* **can; could** *wordt zonder* **to** *gebruikt en alleen samen met andere werkwoorden*

council ['kaʊnsl] *zn*
raad; **town council** = gemeenteraad; **he lives in a council house** = gemeentewoning.

count [kaʊnt] *ww*
(*a*) tellen; **the little girl can count up to ten; count to three, and then start running.**
(*b*) (op)tellen; **can you count how many books we have? he counted up the figures on the bill.**
(*c*) (mee)tellen; **there were thirty people, if you count the children; we have four television sets, not counting the one which doesn't work.**
counts—counting—counted—has counted

count on, *ww*
rekenen op; **can I count on you to help? don't count on having fine weather for your wedding.**

country ['kʌntrɪ] *zn*
(*a*) land; **the countries of Western Europe; the countries in the United Nations.**
(*b*) (platte)land; buiten; **he has a house in the country/a country house.**
meervoud **countries,** *maar geen meervoud voor* (*b*)

countryside, *zn*
platteland; **the English countryside.**
geen meervoud

couple [kʌpl] *zn*
paar; een paar; **it will only take a couple of minutes; there are a couple of questions I want to ask; he ate a couple of sandwiches; the book only costs a couple of pounds** = ongeveer 2 pond; **a married couple** = echtpaar.

Countryside *Platteland*

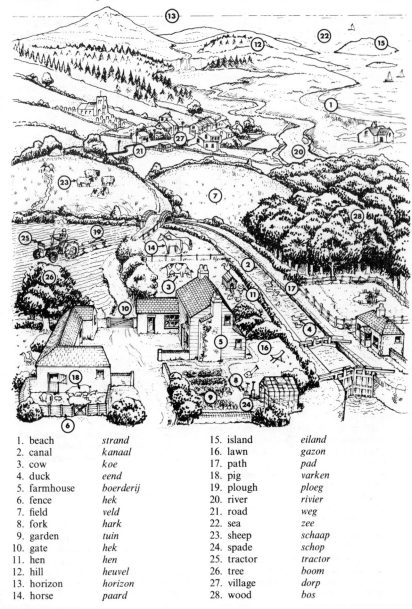

1. beach	*strand*	15. island	*eiland*
2. canal	*kanaal*	16. lawn	*gazon*
3. cow	*koe*	17. path	*pad*
4. duck	*eend*	18. pig	*varken*
5. farmhouse	*boerderij*	19. plough	*ploeg*
6. fence	*hek*	20. river	*rivier*
7. field	*veld*	21. road	*weg*
8. fork	*hark*	22. sea	*zee*
9. garden	*tuin*	23. sheep	*schaap*
10. gate	*hek*	24. spade	*schop*
11. hen	*hen*	25. tractor	*tractor*
12. hill	*heuvel*	26. tree	*boom*
13. horizon	*horizon*	27. village	*dorp*
14. horse	*paard*	28. wood	*bos*

course [kɔːs] *zn*
(*a*) loop; **in the course of the last few years** = gedurende.
(*b*) cursus; **I'm taking a course in mathematics; she's taking a painting course.**
(*c*) gang (*van maaltijd*); **the first course is soup, and then you can have roast chicken.**
of course = natuurlijk; **he is rich, so of course he has a big car; are you coming with us?—of course! do you want to lose all your money?—of course not!**

cousin [ˈkʌzn] *zn*
neef/nicht; **he went to stay with his cousin; I've had a letter from Cousin Charles.**

cover [ˈkʌvə] **1.** *zn*
(*a*) hoes, omslag; **keep a cover over your typewriter when you are not using it; book with a hard cover** = (harde) kaft.
(*b*) **to take cover** = dekking zoeken; **when people began to shoot, the policeman took cover behind a wall.**
2. *ww*
bedekken; **you should cover the floor with newspapers before you start painting the ceiling; she covered her face with her hands.**
covers—covering—covered—has covered

cover up, *ww*
bedekken, verbergen; **he covered up the mark on the wall with white paint.**

cow [kaʊ] *zn*
(*a*) koe; **a field of cows; the farmer was milking a cow.**
(*b*) wijfje (*van olifant etc.*); **a cow elephant.**
Let op: het vlees van een **cow** *is* **beef**
cowboy, *zn*
cowboy.

crack [kræk] **1.** *zn*
barst; spleet; **there's a crack in this glass; we looked through a crack in the fence.**
2. *ww*
(*a*) breken; (doen) barsten; **the stone cracked the window; she cracked a bone in her leg; he dropped the cup and it cracked.**

(*b*) **to crack a joke** = een mop vertellen.
cracks—cracking—cracked—has cracked

crane [kreɪn] *zn*
hijskraan; **they lifted the parts of the factory roof with a crane.**

crash [kræʃ] **1.** *zn*
(*a*) verkeersongeluk; **he was killed in a car crash; none of the passengers was hurt in the crash; crash helmet** = valhelm.
(*b*) klap; **the chair fell over with a crash; there was a crash, and the plates lay on the floor in pieces.**
meervoud **crashes**
2. *ww*
(*a*) botsen (tegen); verongelukken; **the car crashed into the wall; the plane crashed.**
(*b*) met luid geraas vallen; **the tree came crashing down; the pile of plates crashed on to the floor.**
crashes—crashing—crashed—has crashed
3. *bn*
spoed; **he took a crash course in German** = spoedcursus.

cream [kriːm] *zn*
(*a*) room; **I like fruit and cream; single cream** = dunne room; **double cream** = slagroom.
(*b*) crème; **face cream.**

creep [kriːp] *ww*
sluipen; kruipen; **he crept into the bank; she crept downstairs in the dark; he crept up behind the policeman and hit him with a stick.**
creeps—creeping—crept [krept]—has crept

crew [kruː] *zn*
bemanning; **the plane had twenty passengers and a crew of six; when the ship began to sink, the crew jumped into the water.**

cricket [ˈkrɪkɪt] *zn*
cricket; **I haven't played cricket this year; our school has a cricket match this**

afternoon; we beat the Australians at cricket last year.

cried [kraɪd], **cries** [kraɪz] *zie* **cry**

crime [kraɪm] *zn*
misdaad; it is a crime to steal someone's money; the police are trying to reduce crime in London = criminaliteit.
criminal [ˈkrɪmɪnl] *zn*
misdadiger; the policeman arrested a group of criminals.

crisp [krɪsp] **1.** *bn*
fris; knerpend; bros; the snow is crisp; the biscuits aren't crisp—they must have got wet.
crisp—crisper—crispest
2. *zn*
(aardappel)chip; a bag of crisps; do you like crisps which taste of bacon, or just with salt?

crop [krɒp] *zn*
oogst; we have a good crop of tomatoes this year; the apple crop will be small; root crops = knolgewassen.

cross [krɒs] **1.** *bn*
boos; mother's cross with you for drawing on the dining room wall; don't be cross—he didn't do it on purpose.
2. *zn*
kruis; there is a cross on the top of the church; the Red Cross = het Rode Kruis.
***meervoud* crosses**
3. *ww*
oversteken; kruisen; don't cross the road without looking to see if there is any traffic coming; he crossed the river in a small boat; the road crosses the railway line about 2 km from here; she sat down and crossed her legs = ze zat met ge-kruiste benen.
crosses—crossing—crossed—has crossed

crossing, *zn*
(*a*) oversteek, overtocht; how long is the crossing from England to France? we had a rough crossing = een woelige over-tocht.
(*b*) oversteekplaats; you must cross the

street at the zebra crossing = zebra-(pad); cars have to take care at the rail-way crossing = spoorwegovergang.
cross off, cross out, *ww*
doorhalen; he was ill, so we crossed his name off the list; I can't read her letter—she's crossed out so many words.
crossroads, *zn*
(weg)kruising.
crossword, *zn*
kruiswoord(raadsel); I can't do today's crossword in the paper; he's mad about crosswords; I finished the crossword in 25 minutes.

crowd [kraʊd] **1.** *zn*
(mensen)massa, menigte; there were crowds of people trying to do their Christmas shopping; a crowd of tourists rushed into the museum.
2. *ww*
zich verdringen; people crowded into the shops to do their Christmas shopping; the train was crowded = vol, druk.
crowds—crowding—crowded—has crowded

cruel [kruːl] *bn*
wreed; it is cruel to hit your dog with a stick.

crush [krʌʃ] *ww*
platdrukken; he sat on my hat and crushed it flat.
crushes—crushing—crushed—has crushed

cry [kraɪ] **1.** *zn*
kreet; roep; no one heard his cries for help.
***meervoud* cries**
2. *ww*
huilen; she cried when her mother took away her toys; onions make me cry; why is the baby crying? she cries every time she sees this film.
cries—crying—cried—has cried

cup [kʌp] *zn*
(*a*) kop(je); tea cup = theekop(je); coffee cup = koffiekop(je); he was drinking milk out of a cup.
(*b*) kop(je); would you like a cup of tea? she drank two cups of coffee.

(c) beker; **he has won three cups at sailing; cup final** = bekerfinale.
cupful [ˈkʌpfʊl] zn
een kop(je) vol/met.

cupboard [ˈkʌbəd] zn
kast; **put the flour in the cupboard; the plates are on the top shelf in the kitchen cupboard; the cupboard doors are painted white.**

cure [ˈkjʊə] 1. zn
(genees)middel; **there is no cure for an ordinary cold.**
2. ww
genezen; **he was completely cured; can you cure bad eyesight? this disease can't be cured.**
cures—curing—cured—has cured

curious [ˈkjʊərɪəs] bn
(a) nieuwsgierig, benieuwd; **I am curious to know if they are married; she is curious to find out who sent the flowers.**
(b) eigenaardig; **what a curious house! he has the curious habit of pulling the end of his nose.**

curl [kɜːl] 1. zn
krul.
2. ww
krullen; **her hair curls; the smoke curled up from the fire.**
curls—curling—curled—has curled

curl up, ww
(zich) oprollen; **the cat was curled up in front of the fire; the little girl was curled up in the armchair.**
curly, bn
krul-; gekruld; **she has long, curly hair.**
curly—curlier—curliest

current [ˈkʌrənt] 1. zn
stroom; stroming; **the current in the river is strong; the boat was carried away by the current; the electric current is too weak to make the machine work.**
2. bn
actueel; **current affairs** = actualiteiten; **current account** = lopende rekening.
currently, bw
momenteel; thans.

curtain [ˈkɜːtən] zn
(a) gordijn; **can you open the curtains? draw the curtains—it is getting cold.**
(b) (theater) doek; **the curtain goes up at 8.30** = het doek gaat om half negen op.

curve [kɜːv] 1. zn
bocht; **be careful when you drive round this curve; the car takes the curves very well; the cloth has a pattern of curves and straight lines** = kromme lijnen.
2. ww
(zich) buigen, krommen; **the road curves round the hill.**
curves—curving—curved—has curved

curved, bn
gebogen, krom; **a curved line; a curved front window in a car.**

cushion [ˈkʊʃn] zn
kussen; **the sofa has three cushions; the chair with a red cushion.**

customer [ˈkʌstəmə] zn
klant; **will you serve this customer, please? we had no customers, so we shut the shop early.**

customs [ˈkʌstəmz] zn meervoud
douane; **when you come into the country, you have to pass through customs; the customs officer asked me to open my suitcase; customs duty** = invoerrechten.

cut [kʌt] 1. zn
snee; **I had a bad cut on my leg; put a bandage on your cut.**
2. ww
(a) snijden; knippen; **he cut the meat with his knife; she cut her finger on the broken glass; when are you going to get your hair cut? cut the cake into six pieces; he cut himself shaving.**
(b) verminderen; **accidents have been cut by 10%.**
cuts—cutting—cut—has cut

cut down, ww
(a) omhakken; **he cut the tree down/he cut down the tree.**

(*b*) beperken; **he's trying to cut down the number of cigarettes he smokes; the police hope that speed limits will cut down the number of accidents.**

cut off, *ww*

(*a*) afsnijden/knippen; **he cut off a piece of cake; she cut off a little piece of string.**

(*b*) afsnijden; afsluiten; **she was cut off from her friends by a crowd of school-children; the tide came in and cut off the children on some rocks.**

cut out, *ww*

(*a*) uitknippen; **she cut out the photograph from the newspaper; he cut the photograph out with a pair of scissors.**

(*b*) opgeven; **he's trying to cut out smoking; she's decided to cut out sweets.**

cut up, *ww*

fijnsnijden; **cut the meat up into little pieces.**

Let op: **he cut the tree down** *of* **he cut down the tree; she cut out the picture** *of* **she cut the picture out,** *etc., maar alleen* **he cut it down, she cut it out,** *etc.*

cycle [saɪkl] **1.** *zn*
fiets; **he fell off his cycle; let's go for a cycle ride.**
2. *ww*
fietsen; **he cycles to school every day; he was cycling down the hill.**

cycles—cycling—cycled—has cycled

cyclist, *zn*
fietser; **hundreds of cyclists crossed the bridge.**

Dd

dad [dæd], **daddy** [ˈdædɪ] *zn*
pa(ppa); **come over here, Dad, and look at my book; my dad has bought a new car.**
Let op: wordt **Dad** *of* **Daddy** *gespeld wanneer het als aanspreekvorm gebruikt wordt, maar* **dad** *en* **daddy** *als ermee over een vader gesproken wordt.*

daily [ˈdeɪlɪ] **1.** *bn*
dagelijks; **a daily newspaper** = dagblad; **you should do daily exercises to keep fit.**
2. *bw*
dagelijks; **take the medicine twice daily** = twee maal daags.

damage [ˈdæmɪdʒ] **1.** *zn*
schade; **the storm caused a lot of damage; flood damage.**

geen meervoud

2. *ww*
beschadigen; **the car was badly damaged in the accident; if it rains hard it'll damage the crops.**

damages—damaging—damaged—has damaged

dance [dɑːns] **1.** *zn*
dans; **dance band** = dansorkest(je).
2. *ww*
dansen; **he was dancing with my sister; the crowds were dancing in the streets; I'm having dancing lessons.**

dances—dancing—danced—has danced

danger [ˈdeɪndʒə] *zn*
gevaar; **in dry weather there's a danger of forest fires; he's in danger of losing his job** = hij loopt het gevaar zijn baan te verliezen; **she's out of danger** = buiten (levens)gevaar.

dangerous, *bn*
gevaarlijk; **don't touch the electric wires—they're dangerous; it's dangerous to walk on railway lines.**

dare [ˈdeə] *ww*
(*a*) durven; **I would never dare (to) jump**

from that wall; he doesn't dare/he dare not go out of the house; how dare you tell me what to do! I dare say he's ill = zal wel ziek zijn.

(b) uitdagen; **I dared him to steal some sweets from the shop.**

dares—daring—dared—has dared
Let op: he doesn't dare = he dare not

dark [dɑːk] **1.** *bn*
(a) donker; **during the storm the sky turned quite dark; switch the lights on—it's getting too dark to read; in the winter it gets dark early; the sky got darker and darker as night came on.**
(b) donker-; **his shirt is dark green.**
(c) donker(harig); **he's dark, but his sister is fair; he has dark hair.**

dark—darker—darkest

2. *zn*
donker; **she is afraid of the dark; cats can see in the dark; we're completely in the dark** = we tasten volledig in het duister.

darkness, *zn*
duister(nis); **the house was in complete darkness** = in volledige duisternis gehuld.

date [deɪt] *zn*
(a) datum; jaartal; **what's the date today? what are the dates of the Second World War? do you remember the date of your last letter?**
(b) afspraak; **I asked her out for a date; let's make it a date, shall we?** = is dat afgesproken?

up to date = modern; **the new telephone book is completely up to date** = bijgewerkt tot op heden; **keep me up to date on what has been happening** = op de hoogte.

out of date = verouderd; verlopen; **this old book is quite out of date.**

daughter [ˈdɔːtə] *zn*
dochter; **they have two sons and one daughter; have you met my daughter, Mary?**

day [deɪ] *zn*
(a) dag, etmaal; **there are 365 days in**

the year; July has 31 days; Christmas Day is December 25th; what day is it today?** = dag van de week; **I saw him the day before yesterday** = eergisteren; **we will meet the day after tomorrow** = overmorgen; **he phones me every other day** = om de andere dag; **I saw him only the other day** = nog pas.
(b) dag; **he works all day in the office, and then goes to German classes in the evening; it will take me two days to finish this work.**

a day = per dag; **he eats a loaf of bread a day.**
all day = de hele dag; **he's been working hard all day.**

daylight, *zn*
daglicht; **the robbers attacked the bank in full daylight** = op klaarlichte dag.

daytime, *zn*
dag; overdag; **he works at night, and sleeps during the daytime.**

dead [ded] *bn*
(a) dood; overleden; **my grandparents are both dead; dead fish were floating in the lake; the wind blew piles of dead leaves into the road.**
(b) volstrekt; **dead silence; the car came to a dead stop** = de auto stopte plotseling.

deadly, *bn*
dodelijk; **these plants are deadly poisonous.**

deadly—deadlier—deadliest

deaf [def] *bn*
doof; **you have to shout when you speak to Mr Jones because he's deaf.**

deaf—deafer—deafest

deal [diːl] **1.** *zn*
(a) (zaken)overeenkomst; **we did a deal with a German company to buy steel.**
(b) **a good deal of/a great deal of** = heel wat; veel; **he made a great deal of money; we wasted a good deal of time.**

2. *ww*
(a) geven (kaarten); **he dealt me three cards.**
(b) **to deal with** = behandelen; aanpakken; te doen hebben met; **don't worry about the passports—I will deal with**

them; the government is trying to deal
with the problem of crime; I don't like
dealing with difficult people.
(c) to deal in = handelen (in); he deals
in old cars.

deals—dealing—dealt [delt]**—has
dealt**

dear [dɪə] bn
(a) dierbaar; lief; **a very dear friend; I
met dear old Mrs Jones.**
(b) (briefaanhef) geachte; beste; **Dear
Mr Smith; Dear John; Dear Sir.**
(c) duur; **oranges are dearer than apples;
he always orders the dearest food in the
restaurant.**
(d) **oh dear!** = lieve hemel!

dear—dearer—dearest

death [deθ] zn
dood; **his sudden death shocked his
friends; he met his death in a car crash**
= hij is omgekomen bij een auto-on-
geluk.

debt [det] zn
schuld; **he got into debt** = hij heeft
schulden gemaakt; **he is in debt** = hij
zit in de schuld(en); **he is out of debt** =
hij heeft geen schulden meer.

December [dɪ'sembə] zn
december; **her birthday is in December;
she was born on December 20th; we went
on holiday last December; today is December 6th.**
Let op: **December 6th:** zeg 'the sixth
of December' of 'December the sixth'
Let op: **December** wordt altijd met
een hoofdletter geschreven.

decide [dɪ'saɪd] ww
besluiten; **have you decided where to go
for your holiday? they decided to stay at
home; he decided not to go away.**

**decides—deciding—decided—
has decided**

decision [dɪ'sɪʒn] zn
besluit, beslissing; **they have been talking
for hours, but still haven't reached a decision.**

deck [dek] zn
dek; **the restaurant is on the third deck;**

there are seats on the top deck =
bovenste verdieping van dubbeldeks-
bus.

declare [dɪ'kleə] ww
aangeven (bij douane); **anything to declare? I want to declare three bottles of
wine.**

**declares—declaring—declared—
has declared**

deep [diːp] bn
(a) diep; **be careful—the water is very
deep here; this is the deepest mine in
Europe; the water is only two metres
deep.**
(b) (van kleur) diep-; **the carpet is a
deep chocolate colour.**

deep—deeper—deepest

defeat [dɪ'fiːt] 1. zn
nederlaag; **the government had to resign
after its defeat in the election** = na een
nederlaag geleden te hebben bij de verkiezingen moest; **the defeat of the French
army at Agincourt.**
2. ww
verslaan; **the government was
defeated; Napoleon defeated the German
army.**

**defeats—defeating—defeated—
has defeated**

defend [dɪ'fend] ww
verdedigen; **the town was defended by a
large army.**

**defends—defending—
defended—has defended**

defence, zn (Amer. **defense**)
verdediging; **defence of a country against
an enemy.**

degree [dɪ'griː] zn
(a) graad; **a circle has 360°** (zeg 'three
hundred and sixty degrees'); **the temperature is only 20°** (zeg 'twenty degrees').
(b) **he has a degree in English** =
(universitaire) graad.
Let op: in getallen wordt **degree**
geschreven als °

delay [dɪ'leɪ] 1. zn
oponthoud, vertraging; uitstel; **the
meeting started after twenty minutes'**

delay/after a delay of twenty minutes; I am sorry for the delay in answering your letter.
2. *ww*
vertragen, ophouden; uitstellen; **the train was delayed by snow; the fog has delayed all planes.**
delays—delaying—delayed— has delayed

delight [dɪ'laɪt] 1. *zn*
plezier; genot; **he takes delight in being rude to people** =hij heeft er plezier in etc.; **our cat's greatest delight is sleeping in front of the fire.**
2. *ww*
to delight in = genieten; **he delights in being rude to his friends.**
delights—delighting— delighted—has delighted

delighted, *bn*
erg blij; **she was delighted with her present; I'd be delighted to come to your party** = ik kom heel graag etc.
delightful, *bn*
heerlijk; enig; **what delightful weather! they gave a delightful party.**

deliver [dɪ'lɪvə] *ww*
bezorgen; afleveren; bestellen; **the postman delivers the mail to our house; can you deliver this parcel for me? the shop will deliver the new table tomorrow.**
delivers—delivering—delivered— has delivered

demand [dɪ'mɑːnd] 1. *zn*
(aan)vraag; **this book is in great demand** = er is veel vraag naar dit boek.
2. *ww*
eisen; **she demanded to see the manager; he is demanding his money back.**
demands—demanding— demanded—has demanded

dentist ['dentɪst] *zn*
tandarts; **I must go to the dentist—I've got toothache; she had to wait for an hour at the dentist's; I hate going to see the dentist.**

department [dɪ'pɑːtmənt] *zn*
afdeling; **if you want cheese, you must go to the food department; he is manager**

of the sales department; Department of Education = Ministerie van Onderwijs en Wetenschappen.

departure [dɪ'pɑːtʃə] *zn*
vertrek; (*vliegveld*) **departures** = vertrekhal.

depend on [dɪ'pend ɒn] *ww*
(*a*) rekenen op; **he depends on his wife to look after the house; we're depending on you to pay for the food.**
(*b*) (ervan) afhangen; **whether or not we go on a picnic depends on the weather; depending on her exam results she will go to university or start work in an office.**
depends—depending— depended—has depended

depth [depθ] *zn*
diepte; **what is the depth of the pool? the river is at least 6 metres in depth.**
geen meervoud

describe [dɪ'skraɪb] *ww*
beschrijven; **can you describe the man who stole the money? she described how her car suddenly hit a tree; the police asked her to describe what happened.**
describes—describing— described—has described

description [dɪ'skrɪpʃn] *zn*
beschrijving; **her description of the accident.**

desert ['dezət] *zn*
woestijn; **the Sahara desert; he lived for three years on a desert island.**

deserted [dɪ'zɜːtɪd] *bn*
verlaten; **the town is quite deserted on Sunday afternoons; they camped in a deserted spot in the mountains.**

deserve [dɪ'zɜːv] *ww*
verdienen; **he ﹐ deserves a prize; she deserves to be punished.**
deserves—deserving—deserved —has deserved

desk [desk] *zn*
bureau; **put the papers away in your desk; he was sitting at his desk when the telephone rang.**

dessert [dɪˈzɜːt] *zn*
dessert, toetje; **what's for dessert? we'll have ice cream for dessert.**

destroy [dɪˈstrɔɪ] *ww*
vernietigen; **the house was destroyed by fire; she destroyed all his letters.**
destroys—destroying—destroyed—has destroyed

detail [ˈdiːteɪl] *zn*
detail, bijzonderheid; **he went into a lot of detail when describing the accident; she told us how to get to her house, but left out the most important detail—the name of the street.**

develop [dɪˈveləp] *ww*
(a) (zich) ontwikkelen; ontginnen; **the town is going to develop the land near the railway station; tourism is a rapidly developing industry.**
(b) ontwikkelen, krijgen; **she developed a cold; he developed a liking for chocolate.**
(c) (film) ontwikkelen.
develops—developing—developed—has developed

development, *zn*
ontwikkeling.

diamond [ˈdaɪəmənd] *zn*
(a) diamant.
(b) (*van kaartspel*) ruiten; **the ten of diamonds.**

dictionary [ˈdɪkʃənrɪ] *zn*
woordenboek; **a French dictionary; if you don't understand the word, look it up in a dictionary.**
meervoud **dictionaries**

did [dɪd], **didn't** [dɪdnt] *zie* **do**

die [daɪ] *ww*
(a) doodgaan, overlijden; **his father died last year; if you take a fish out of water it will die; she died in a car crash** = zij kwam om.
(b) **dying for** = smachten naar; **I'm dying for a cup of tea.**
dies—dying—died—has died

die away, *ww*
wegsterven; **the sound of the car died away.**

die down, *ww*
bedaren, luwen, uitgaan; **the fire began to die down.**

difference [ˈdɪfrəns] *zn*
verschil; **can you tell the difference between butter and margarine?** = kun jij boter en margarine uit elkaar houden? **you can use water or oil—it doesn't make any difference** = het maakt niets uit.

different, *bn*
anders (dan); verschillend; **living in the country is different from living in the town; I went to six different shops, but couldn't find what I wanted; he looks different—I think he has had his hair cut.**

difficult [ˈdɪfɪkəlt] *bn*
moeilijk; **the examination was very difficult—half the students failed; it is difficult to find somewhere to park on Saturday mornings.**

difficulty, *zn*
moeilijkheid; **the difficulty is how to start the car; she has difficulty in getting up in the morning** = ze vindt het moeilijk om etc.
meervoud **difficulties**

dig [dɪg] *ww*
graven; **he was digging in his garden; the prisoner dug a hole under the prison wall; we dug up an old coin** = we hebben een oude munt opgegraven.
digs—digging—dug—has dug

dining room [ˈdaɪnɪŋ rʊm] *zn*
eetkamer; **we were sitting in the dining room having supper; come into the dining room—dinner is ready; he was doing his homework on the dining room table.**

dinner [ˈdɪnə] *zn*
middageten/avondeten; diner; **we were having dinner in the dining room when the telephone rang; we always have dinner at 7.30; would you like to come to dinner next week?** = wil je komen eten? **eat up your dinner; hurry up, it's almost time for dinner** = etenstijd; **what's for dinner?** = wat eten we vanavond/vanmiddag?
Let op: als je het middageten dinner *noemt, heet het avondeten* supper; *als je het avondeten* dinner *noemt, heet het middageten* lunch

fifty-three 53

dinnertime *zn*
etenstijd; **it's almost dinnertime; 7
o'clock is my dinnertime.**

direct [daɪ'rekt *of* dɪ'rekt] **1.** *bn & bw*
(regel)recht; **the plane flies direct to Paris;
a direct flight to Paris** = rechtstreeks.
2. *ww*
regelen; **the policeman was directing the
traffic; can you direct me to the Post
Office?** = de weg wijzen.
**directs—directing—directed—
has directed**

direction [daɪ'rekʃn *of* dɪ'rekʃn] *zn*
(*a*) richting; **turn round—you are going
in the wrong direction; the station is in
the other direction; leaves were blowing
in all directions.**
(*b*) **directions** = aanwijzingen; **the
policeman gave us directions for getting
to the station; I can't use this, as there
are no directions how to switch it on.**

dirt [dɜːt] *zn*
vuil(igheid); **don't sit in the dirt—
you'll get your clothes dirty.**
dirty, *bn*
vies, vuil; **if you lie on the ground you
will get your clothes dirty; we must wash
all these dirty plates; you can't have any
dinner if your hands are dirty.**
dirty—dirtier—dirtiest

disappear [dɪsə'pɪə] *ww*
verdwijnen; **the thieves disappeared when
they heard the police coming; the sun
disappeared behind the clouds.**
**disappears—disappearing—
disappeared—has disappeared**

disappointed [dɪsə'pɔɪntɪd] *bn*
teleurgesteld; **she is very disappointed
because she did not get the job; they were
disappointed with the hotel.**
disappointment, *zn*
teleurstelling; **to her great disappointment she didn't get the job.**

discover [dɪ'skʌvə] *ww*
ontdekken; **who discovered America?
scientists are trying to discover a cure
for this disease; he discovered a hole in
the floor under his bed.**
**discovers—discovering—
discovered—has discovered**

discuss [dɪ'skʌs] *ww*
bespreken; **they started discussing politics; we were discussing how to get to
Scotland; they discussed the best way of
getting to Scotland.**
**discusses—discussing—
discussed—has discussed**

discussion [dɪ'skʌʃn] *zn*
discussie; bespreking; **the discussion
went on for hours, but no decision was
taken.**

disease [dɪ'ziːz] *zn*
ziekte; **he caught a disease in the tropics;
she is suffering from a very serious
disease.**

dish [dɪʃ] *zn*
(*a*) schotel; **a vegetable dish.**
(*b*) **dishes** = serviesgoed; **can I wash all
these dirty dishes?**
(*c*) gerecht; **you ought to have a meat
dish to start with.**
meervoud **dishes**

dishcloth, *zn*
vaatdoek.
dishwasher, *zn*
afwasmachine; **put all the dirty plates in
the dishwasher.**

distance ['dɪstəns] *zn*
afstand; **what is the distance between the
police station and the post office? can you
see that white house in the distance?** = in
de verte; **long distance race** = marathon.

district ['dɪstrɪkt] *zn*
buurt, streek; **he lives in a country district; district nurse** = wijkverpleegster.

disturb [di'stɜːb] *ww*
storen; **don't disturb him when he's
working; sorry to disturb you, but could
you lend me your pen?**
**disturbs—disturbing—
disturbed—has disturbed**

dive [daɪv] *ww*
duiken; **he dived into the water; she dived
off the rocks into the sea.**
dives—diving—dived—has dived

divide [dɪ'vaɪd] *ww*
(*a*) verdelen; **he divided the cake up between the children.**

(b) delen door; **can you divide 27 by 9?
27 divided by 9 gives 3.**
**divides—dividing—divided—has
divided**

division [dɪ'vɪʒn] *zn*
(ver)deling; **I am good at multiplication
but not at division.**

do [du:] *ww*
(a) (*hulpww van vragende vorm*) **does it
matter? did he laugh? do your parents live
in England? do you smoke? did she go
with them?**
(b) (*hulpww van de ontkennende vorm*) **it
doesn't matter; he didn't laugh; my
parents don't live in England; I don't
smoke; she didn't go with them.**
(c) (*voor extra nadruk*) **please do sit
down; he does like ice cream!**
(d) (*met* so *en* neither *vervangt* do *een
ander werkwoord*) **I don't smoke—
neither do I; he likes chocolate—so does
she** = en zij ook.
(e) (*in korte antwoorden in plaats van
een ander werkwoord*) **does it matter?—
yes, it does; do you live here?—yes, I do;
did he laugh?—no, he didn't; do your
parents live in England?—yes, they do.**
(f) (*in aanhangszinnen in plaats van een
ander werkwoord*) **you live here, don't
you? it doesn't look very nice, does it? it
rains a lot, doesn't it!**
(g) (*ter vervanging van een ander werkwoord*) **I don't eat as much as she does;
she arrived before we did; he speaks
English better than I do.**
(h) (*in een negatief bevel*) **don't play in
the road! don't put that chair there! don't
go away!**
(i) (*met zelfstandige naamwoorden op
-ing*) **she's doing the washing up; he
always does the cooking.**
(j) (*in vaste uitdrukkingen*) **how do you
do? he's doing very well in his new job;
he's a difficult person to do business with;
that will do** = zo is het goed; **that won't
do at all** = dat gaat niet; **the car was
doing 100 miles an hour** = de auto reed
met een snelheid van 160 km per uur;
what do you do for a living? = wat voor
werk.
(k) (*overgankelijk werkwoord*) **go and do**

your teeth = ga je tanden poetsen; **I
must do my hair** = ik moet m'n haar
(nog) doen; **he's doing the dishes** = hij
doet de afwas; **have you done your
homework? what have you been doing?**
zie ook **make do with.**
I do/you do/he, she, it does [dʌz]/
they do
doing—did [dɪd]—**has done** [dʌn]
Ontkennend: **do not,** *meestal* **don't**
[dəʊnt]; **does not,** *meestal* **doesn't**
[dʌznt]; **did not,** *meestal* **didn't**
[dɪdnt]

do away with, *ww*
afschaffen; **the government did away
with tax on food.**
do up, *ww*
vastmaken/dichtmaken; **do up your buttons; can you do up the zip at the back
of my dress?**
Let op: **do your buttons up** *of* **do
up your buttons** *maar alleen* **do
them up**
do with, *ww*
(a) betreffen, te maken hebben; **it is
nothing to do with me; it is something to
do with my new book.**
(b) **what have you done with my hat?** =
waar heb je m'n hoed gelaten?
do without, *ww*
het stellen zonder; **can you do without a
car? we had to do without tea; plants
can't do without water.**

dock [dɒk] **1.** *zn*
dok; **dry dock** = droogdok; **the ship is
in dock.**
2. *ww*
dokken; **we will be docking in twenty
minutes.**
**docks—docking—docked—has
docked**

doctor ['dɒktə] *zn*
arts, dokter; **I have an appointment with
Dr Jones; if you have a pain in your
chest, you ought to see a doctor; he has
gone to the doctor's.**
doctor *wordt tot* **Dr** *afgekort voor
een naam*

does [dʌz], **doesn't** [dʌznt] *zie* **do**

dog [dɒg] *zn*
hond; **our dog bit the postman; I must take the dog out for a walk.**

dollar [ˈdɒlə] *zn*
dollar; **this book costs four dollars ($4)** *in bedragen wordt* **dollar** *als $ geschreven:* **$20, $525,** *etc.*
Let op: voor **bill,** *komt* **dollar** *in het enkelvoud:* **five dollars,** *maar* **a five dollar bill**

donkey [ˈdɒŋkɪ] *zn*
ezel; **I haven't seen him for donkey's years** = in geen jaren.

don't [dəʊnt] *zie* **do**

door [dɔː] *zn*
deur; **our house has a blue door; shut the oven door; he opened the door with his key; the back door leads out into the garden, and the front door on to the street; someone is knocking at the door; they live two doors away** = twee huizen verder; *zie ook* **next door.**

dot [dɒt] *zn*
stippel(tje), nop; **her dress is blue with white dots.**

double [dʌbl] **1.** *bn*
(*a*) dubbel; **double figures** = getallen tussen 10 en 99.
(*b*) dubbel; **I am double your age** = twee keer zo oud; **double bed** = tweepersoonsbed.
2. *ww*
verdubbelen; **think of a number, and then double it.**
doubles—doubling—doubled—has doubled

doubt [daʊt] *ww*
(be)twijfelen; **I doubt if he will come** = hij komt waarschijnlijk niet.
doubts—doubting—doubted—has doubted

doubtful, *bn*
twijfelachtig; onzeker; **I am doubtful if he will ever come.**

down [daʊn] **1.** *vz*
(*a*) af; **he went down the stairs; she fell down the ladder; they ran down the hill.**

(*b*) beneden; **he is not down here; it was cool down below.**
(*c*) verderop; **I'm just going down the road to buy something.**
2. *bw*
(*a*) neer; **put your case down on the floor; he sat down on the sofa** = hij ging zitten; **she lay down on the carpet** = ze ging liggen.
(*b*) opschrijven/neerschrijven; **did you write down the phone number? I'll just take down your address.**
(*c*) naar het zuiden; **I'm going down to London tomorrow (from Edinburgh).**
3. *bn*
onder; **the sun is down.**
Let op: **down** *wordt vaak met werkwoorden gebruikt:* **to go down; to break down; to fall down,** *etc.*

downhill, *bw*
omlaag; bergafwaarts; **the road went downhill for three kilometres.**

downstairs, *bw & zn*
(naar) beneden; **he lives downstairs; the downstairs of the house is larger than the upstairs; the dining room is downstairs; come downstairs at once! did you leave your watch downstairs?**

downwards, *bw*
naar beneden; **he put the card face downwards on the table** = omgekeerd.

dozen [dʌzn] *zn*
(*a*) dozijn; twaalftal; **two dozen eggs** = 24 eieren; **a dozen bottles of beer.**
(*b*) **dozens** = massa's; **I've been there dozens of times** = ontelbare keren.
Let op: na getallen heeft **dozen** *geen* **-s: two dozen, ten dozen,** *etc.*

drag [dræg] *ww*
slepen; zeulen; **he dragged the sack into the corner; he was dragging a table behind him.**
drags—dragging—dragged—has dragged

drain [dreɪn] **1.** *zn*
afvoerbuis; riool; **there is an awful smell—the drains must be blocked.**
2. *ww*
afvoeren; draineren; weglopen; **the**

water will slowly drain away; the land
needs draining.
**drains—draining—drained—has
drained**

drainpipe, *zn*
afvoerbuis; regenpijp; **he got into the
house by climbing up a drainpipe.**

drank [dræŋk] *zie* **drink**

draw [drɔ:] **1.** *zn*
remise, gelijk spel; **the game ended in
a draw, 2–2.**
2. *ww*
(*a*) tekenen; **he drew a picture of the
church; what is he doing?—he is drawing
the church.**
(*b*) trekken; **can you draw the curtains—
it is getting dark** = sluiten/dichttrek-
ken.
(*c*) gelijk spelen; **the teams drew 1–1.**
**draws—drawing—drew—has
drawn**

drawer, *zn*
la(de); **my desk has three drawers; chest
of drawers** = ladenkast.

drawing, *zn*
tekening; **here is a drawing of the church;
drawing pin** = punaise; **drawing room**
= zitkamer.

draw up, *ww*
(*a*) stilhouden; **the car drew up to the
side of the road.**
(*b*) opstellen; **he drew up a plan to build
three new schools; we've drawn up a list
of people to invite to the party.**

dream [dri:m] **1.** *zn*
droom; **I had a bad dream about spiders.**
2. *ww*
dromen; **I dreamt I was swimming; I
wouldn't dream of wearing green shoes**
= ik zou er niet aan denken.
**dreams—dreaming—dreamed/
dreamt** [dremt]**—has dreamed/
dreamt**

dress [dres] **1.** *zn*
(*a*) jurk; **she was wearing a green dress.**
(*b*) tenue, toilet; **he was wearing evening
dress** = in rok.
meervoud **dresses** *voor* (*a*); *geen
meervoud voor* (*b*)

2. *ww*
(zich) aankleden; **he (got) dressed, and
then had breakfast; she was dressed in
white.**
**dresses—dressing—dressed—has
dressed**

drew [dru:] *zie* **draw**

dried [draɪd], **drier** ['draɪə], **dries**
[draɪz], **driest** ['draɪəst] *zie* **dry**

drink [drɪŋk] **1.** *zn*
(*a*) drank; dronk; **have a drink of water;**
= een glas water; **I always have a hot
drink before I go to bed; would you like
a drink?** = iets te drinken; **soft drinks**
= frisdranken.
(*b*) alcoholische drank; **would you like a
drink? I'll order drinks.**
2. *ww*
(*a*) drinken; **he drank two cups of coffee;
someone has drunk my beer! what would
you like to drink?**
(*b*) (alcohol) drinken; **he never drinks/
he doesn't drink.**
**drinks—drinking—drank—has
drunk**

drink up, *ww*
opdrinken; **drink up your milk.**
Let op: **drink your milk up** *of* **drink
up your milk** *maar alleen* **drink it
up**

drip [drɪp] *ww*
druppelen; druipen; **the water dripped
off the table on to the floor; your coat is
dripping wet** = druipnat; **the tap is
dripping.**
**drips—dripping—dripped—has
dripped**

drive [draɪv] **1.** *zn*
(auto)rit; **let's go for a drive; I don't like
long drives.**
2. *ww*
(*a*) (auto)rijden; besturen; **I can swim,
but I can't drive; he's taking driving lessons; he was driving a tractor; can I drive
you to the station?; in Great Britain, cars
drive on the left hand side of the road.**
(*b*) drijven; **the noise is driving her mad**
= maakt.
drives—driving—drove [drəʊv]**—
has driven**

driver, *zn*
bestuurder; chauffeur; **he's a bus driver;
the driver of the car was injured in the
accident.**
driving test, *zn*
rijexamen; **he's just passed his driving
test; she is taking her driving test tomorrow.**

drop [drɒp] **1.** *zn*
(*a*) druppel; **a drop of water fell on my
head; drops of rain splashed into the
river; would you like a drop of wine?** =
een slokje.
(*b*) val; **there is a drop of four metres
from the window to the ground.**
2. *ww*
(laten) vallen; **he dropped the cup and
broke it; prices are dropping.**
**drops—dropping—dropped—has
dropped**
drop in, *ww*
aanlopen; langskomen; **he dropped in to
have a cup of tea; drop in for coffee if
you're passing.**
drop off, *ww*
in slaap vallen; insluimeren; **she dropped
off in front of the TV.**

drove [drəʊv] *zie* **drive**

drown [draʊn] *ww*
verdrinken; **he fell into the sea and (was)
drowned; the drowning man shouted for
help; six people drowned when the boat
sank.**
**drowns—drowning—drowned—
has drowned**

drug [drʌg] *zn*
(*a*) medicijn; geneesmiddel; **the doctors
are trying to cure him with a new drug.**
(*b*) verdovend/verslavend middel; **he
takes drugs.**

drum [drʌm] *zn*
trommel; **he plays the drums in a band**
= de drums/het slagwerk.

drunk [drʌŋk] *bn*
dronken; *zie ook* **drink.**

dry [draɪ] **1.** *bn*
droog; **don't sit on that chair—the paint**
isn't dry yet; it hasn't rained for weeks
so the earth is very dry.
dry—drier—driest
2. *ww*
drogen; afdrogen; **the washing is drying
in the sun; can you dry the dishes for
me?**
dries—drying—dried—has dried
dry out, *ww*
(door en door) drogen; **hang up your
coat until it dries out; I must dry out my
wet shoes.**
Let op: **dry your coat out** *of* **dry out
your coat** *maar alleen* **dry it out**

duck [dʌk] **1.** *zn*
eend; **we're going to feed the ducks; we're
having roast duck for dinner.**
Let op: bij het voedsel **duck** *wordt
geen meervoud gebruikt:* **some
duck; a slice of duck**
2. *ww*
(zich) bukken; (onder)duiken; **he ducked
as the stone went past his head; tall
people have to duck as they go through
that door.**
**ducks—ducking—ducked—has
ducked**

due [djuː] **1.** *bn*
(*a*) verwacht; **the train is due to arrive at
10.00** = moet ... aankomen.
(*b*) (ver)schuldig(d); **the rent is due
next week.**
(*c*) **due to** = vanwege; **the cracks in the
wall are due to the traffic; the plane is
late due to fog.**
2. *bw*
pal; **the boat sailed due west.**

dug [dʌg] *zie* **dig**

dull [dʌl] *bn*
(*a*) saai; **he went to sleep watching a
rather dull film on TV; life here is very
dull—nothing ever happens.**
(*b*) dof; **the car is painted dull grey; dull
weather** = somber.
dull—duller—dullest

dumb [dʌm] *bn*
stom/sprakeloos.

during ['djʊərɪŋ] *vz*
gedurende, tijdens; **he went to sleep during the TV film; during the war we never had any butter.**

dust [dʌst] **1.** *zn*
stof; **the table is covered with dust; wipe the dust off your shoes.**
2. *ww*
stoffen; **have you dusted the dining room table?**
dusts—dusting—dusted—has dusted

dustbin, *zn*
vuilnisbak.
dustman, *zn*
vuilnisman.
meervoud **dustmen**

dusty, *bn*
stoffig; **the top of the car is dusty; we walked for miles along a dusty road.**
dusty—dustier—dustiest

Dutch 1. *bn*
Nederlands; **a Dutch family has come to live next door to us; my sister is married**
to a Dutch doctor; we went to the States on a Dutch ship; we all like Dutch cheese. Dutch people are fond of the sea = Nederlanders/Hollanders; **she's Dutch, but her husband isn't** = zij is Nederlandse, maar haar man is geen Nederlander.
2. *zn*
(*a*) Nederlands; **I can read Dutch, but I can't speak it; what's the Dutch for 'chips'? 'Kool' is the Dutch for 'cabbage'.**
(*b*) **the Dutch** = (de) Nederlanders; **the Dutch like drinking beer.**
Let op: **Dutch** wordt altijd met een hoofdletter geschreven

duty ['dju:tɪ] *zn*
(*a*) invoerrechten/uitvoerrechten; **you have to pay duty if you want to bring cigarettes into the country.**
(*b*) plicht; functie; **what are your duties as manager of the sales department?**
meervoud **duties**

dying ['daɪɪŋ] *zie* **die**

Ee

each [i:tʃ] **1.** *bn*
elk, ieder (apart); **each house has a number; he was holding a knife in each hand; each one of us has a bicycle.**
2. *vnw*
(*a*) ieder, elk; **they have two cars each/ each of them has two cars; she gave them each a cake/she gave them a cake each.**
(*b*) ieder, elk; **each of the houses has three bedrooms/the houses have three bedrooms each.**
each other = elkaar; **they were talking to each other; we always send each other Christmas cards; the cups fit into each other.**

eager ['i:gə] *bn*
felgebrand op; **he is eager to get into the**
top team; she was eager to start work as soon as possible = ze wilde erg graag etc.

ear ['ɪə] *zn*
(*a*) oor; **donkeys have long ears; have you washed your neck and ears? he's up to his ears in work** = tot over z'n oren.
(*b*) oor/gehoor (voor muziek); **he has a good ear for music; she can play the piano by ear** = op het gehoor.
earache ['ɪəreɪk] *zn*
oorpijn.

early ['ɜ:lɪ] **1.** *bw*
(*a*) (te) vroeg; **the train arrived five minutes early; we must get up early tomorrow as we have a lot of work to do; can you come earlier next time?**

earn   educate

(*b*) aan het begin, vroeg; **we went out early in the afternoon; early in the year. 2.** *bn*
vroeg; **early vegetables;** = eerste groenten; **I caught an early train; these flowers open in early summer; we hope to meet you at an early date** = binnenkort; **early closing day** = dag dat winkels 's middags dicht zijn.
early—earlier—earliest

earn [ɜːn] *ww*
verdienen; **he earns £50 a week; how much does a taxi driver earn?**
earns—earning—earned—has earned

earnings, *zn meervoud*
loon, inkomen; **he gave all his earnings to his wife.**

earth [ɜːθ] *zn*
(*a*) aarde, aardbol; **the earth goes round the sun; the space station came back to earth.**
(*b*) aarde, grond; **sow your seeds in fine earth.**
on earth (*voor extra nadruk in vragen*)
in ('s) hemelsnaam; **why on earth did you do that? who on earth is going to read this book? how on earth did he find all that money?**

easier [ˈiːzɪə], **easiest** [ˈiːzɪəst], **easily** [ˈiːzɪlɪ] *zie* **easy**

east [iːst] **1.** *zn*
oosten; **the sun rises in the east and sets in the west; the town is to the east of the mountains; the Far East/the Middle East/the Near East** = het Verre/Midden/Nabije Oosten. **2.** *bn*
oost-; **the East End of London; the east coast. 3.** *bw*
naar het oosten; in oostelijke richting; **the ship is sailing east; go due east for ten kilometres.**
eastern, *bn*
oostelijk, oost-; **Poland is in eastern Europe** = Oost Europa; **the capital is in the eastern part of the country.**

Easter [ˈiːstə] *zn*
Pasen; **Easter egg** = paasei; **we have two days off at Easter; are you going away for the Easter holidays?** = paasvakantie; **we often have a picnic on Easter Monday;** = Paasmaandag, tweede Paasdag; **we went to Germany last Easter.**

easy [ˈiːzɪ] *bn*
(ge)makkelijk; **the exam is too easy—everyone passed; it's easy to understand why he passed the exam; the house is within easy reach of the station** = makkelijk te bereiken.
easy—easier—easiest

easily, *bw*
(ge)makkelijk; zonder moeite; **I could do the exam easily; she is easily the tallest in the class** = verreweg.

eat [iːt] *ww*
eten; **can I have something to eat? I haven't eaten anything since breakfast; he ate all the cakes; who has eaten my chocolates?** = opeten.
eats—eating—ate [et]—has eaten [ˈiːtn]

eat away, *ww*
wegeten; afvreten; **the rocks have been eaten away by the sea.**
eat up, *ww*
opeten; **eat up your meat!**
Let op: **eat up your meat** *of* **eat your meat up,** *maar alleen* **eat it up**

edge [edʒ] *zn*
(*a*) rand, kant; **don't put your cup so close to the edge of the table; he lay down on the flat roof of the building and looked over the edge; she stood the coin on its edge; the knife has a very sharp edge** = snee/snede.
(*b*) rand, zoom; **he stood at the edge of the water; the house is built on the edge of the town.**

educate [ˈedjuːkeɪt] *ww*
opleiden; **he was educated in Scotland** = hij is in Schotland op school geweest.
educates—educating—educated—has educated

education [edjuːˈkeɪʃn] *zn*
onderwijs/opleiding; **adult education** =

60   *sixty*

voor volwassenen; **further education** =
voortgezet; **higher education** = hoger.

effect [ɪ'fekt] *zn*
effect, resultaat; **he poured water on the
fire but it had no effect; this rule comes
into effect on January 1st** = deze regel
wordt van kracht op 1 januari.
effective, *bn*
effectief, doelmatig; **his way of making
the children keep quiet is very effective.**

effort ['efət] *zn*
inspanning; **he made an effort and
painted the whole house;** = hij heeft zich
ingespannen; **it took a lot of effort to
carry the food to the top of the mountain; if
he made an effort he would pass his exams.**

e.g. ['iː'dʒiː]
b.v., bijvoorbeeld; **some fruit, e.g.
lemons, are very sour.**

egg [eg] *zn*
(a) ei; **the birds have laid three eggs in
their nest.**
(b) kippeëi, ei; **I had a boiled egg for
breakfast; can I have bacon and eggs?
this cake is made with three eggs.**

eight [eɪt] acht
**she ate eight sandwiches; he's eight
(years old); come to see us at eight
(o'clock).**
eighteen, achttien
**there are eighteen children in the class;
she's eighteen (years old); the train leaves
at eighteen fifteen (18.15).**
eighteenth, 18th, *bn & zn*
achttiende; **the eighteenth of May/May
the eighteenth (May 18th); the eighteenth
name on the list; it's her eighteenth
birthday tomorrow.**
eighth, 8th, *bn & zn*
achtste; **the eighth of May/May the
eighth (May 8th); an eighth of the time;
Henry the Eighth (Henry VIII); her
eighth birthday is next Tuesday.**
Let op: in een datum wordt **eighth**
meestal als **8th** *geschreven:* **May
8th, 1979; October 8th, 1880;** *Bij
de namen van Koningen en Koninginnen schrijft men* **eighth** *meestal
als* **VIII: King Henry VIII**

eightieth, 80th, *bn & zn*
tachtigste; **an eightieth of the money;
tomorrow is grandfather's eightieth
birthday.**
eighty, tachtig
**you need more than eighty bricks to build
a wall; he's eighty (years old); she's in
her eighties** = in de tachtig.
Let op: **eighty-one** (81), **eighty-
two** (82) *maar* **eighty-first** (81st),
eighty-second (82nd), *etc.*

either ['aɪðə] **1.** *bn & vnw*
(a) de een of de ander; **you can use either
car—it doesn't matter which; I don't believe either of them** = geen van beiden.
(b) een/elk van beiden; **they sat on either
side of him** = ieder aan een kant.
2. *vw*
of (wel) ... of (wel); **either you come to
see us or we'll go to see you; he's either
ill or he doesn't want to come.**
3. *bw*
ook niet; **he isn't French, and he isn't
English either; you don't want to go, and
I don't want to either; it wasn't on the
TV news, and it wasn't on the radio
either.**

elbow ['elbəʊ] *zn*
elleboog; **don't put your elbows on the
table; he pushed me with his elbow.**

elect [ɪ'lekt] *ww*
(ver)kiezen; **he was elected Prime
Minister.**
**elects—electing—elected—has
elected**
election [ɪ'lekʃn] *zn*
verkiezing; **general election** = algemene
verkiezingen; **he was elected a member
of parliament in the last general election.**

electricity [ɪlek'trɪsəti] *zn*
elektriciteit; **the motor is run by electricity; the house is in the country and
doesn't have any electricity.**
geen meervoud

electric [ɪ'lektrɪk] *bn*
elektrisch; **electric light; an electric saw;
don't touch that electric wire.**
electrical, *bn*
elektro-; **he is studying electrical en-**

gineering; they are mending an electrical **fault** = stroomstoring.
electrician [elek′trɪʃn] *zn*
elektriciën.

elephant [′elɪfənt] *zn*
olifant; **you can go for a ride on an elephant.**

elevator [′elɪveɪtə] *zn*
(*Amerikaans voor* **lift**) lift.

eleven [ɪ′levn] elf
you can't eat eleven ice creams all by yourself! he's eleven (years old); come and see me at eleven (o'clock).
eleventh, 11th, *bn & zn*
elfde; **the eleventh of May/May the eleventh (May 11th); he came eleventh in the race; it's his eleventh birthday tomorrow.**

else [els] **1.** *bn*
(*na voornaamwoorden*) ander(s); **anyone else** = ieder ander; **anything else** = iets anders; **somebody else** = iemand anders; **is there anyone else who hasn't got a ticket? did you see anyone else? is there anything else you would like to eat? I couldn't go to the concert, so someone else took my ticket; who else was there?** = wie was er nog meer? **there was nowhere else to put it** = nergens anders; **can we go somewhere else?** = ergens anders.
2. *bw*
or else = of (... anders); anders; **come in or else stay outside; you must have a ticket, or else you won't be able to get in.**
elsewhere, *bw*
ergens anders, elders; **if you can't find it here, I should look elsewhere.**

employ [ɪm′plɔɪ] *ww*
(*a*) in dienst hebben; **the factory employs a staff of two hundred; she is employed as a secretary** = zij heeft een baan als sekretaresse.
(*b*) gebruiken, aanwenden; **don't employ too much force.**
employs—employing—
employed—has employed

employee [emplɔɪ′i:] *zn*
werknemer; employé; **the firm has two hundred employees.**
employer [ɪm′plɔɪə] *zn*
werkgever.
employment, *zn*
baan, betrekking; werk.

empty [′emtɪ] **1.** *bn*
leeg; **the bottle is empty; find an empty bottle and fill it with water; the fridge is empty—we must buy some more food.**
empty—emptier—emptiest
2. *ww*
legen, leegmaken; **he emptied the water out of the bottle; she emptied the box on to the table.**
empties—emptying—emptied—
has emptied

end [end] **1.** *zn*
(uit)eind(e); **tie the ends of the piece of string together; go to the end of the road and turn left; we missed the end of the TV film, because we had to go to dinner; wait until the end of the month.**
in the end = tenslotte; uiteindelijk; **in the end the police let him go home.**
on end = onafgebroken, aan een stuk; **he worked for hours on end.**
2. *ww*
eindigen; **the film ends with the wedding of the boy and girl; the game ended in a draw; the game should end about 4 o'clock** = afgelopen zijn.
ends—ending—ended—has
ended

end up, *ww*
terecht komen; ergens op uitlopen; **we all ended up at my girl friend's house; he ended up getting arrested by the police.**

enemy [′enəmɪ] *zn*
vijand; **the enemy aircraft dropped bombs on our town** = het vijandelijke vliegtuig etc.
meervoud **enemies**

engine [′endʒɪn] *zn*
motor; **my car has a small engine and can't go very fast; the train is driven by an electric engine.**

engineer [endʒɪ'nɪə] *zn*
mecaniciën; ingenieur; technikus; **he works as a telephone engineer.**
engineering, *zn*
machinebouwkunde.
geen meervoud

England ['ɪŋglənd] *zn*
Engeland; **they have come to live in England; why do you want to go to England for your holiday? England is north of France.**
English ['ɪŋglɪʃ] **1.** *bn*
Engels; **do you like English cheese? English weather can be very good; is she English or American?**
2. *zn*
(*a*) **the English** = de Engelsen; **the English like playing cricket.**
(*b*) Engels; **he speaks English very well; what is the English for 'pommes frites'?**
Englishman, Englishwoman, *zn*
Engelsman, Engelse.
meervoud **Englishmen, English-women**

enjoy [ɪn'dʒɔɪ] *ww*
genieten(van); leuk vinden; **I enjoy going to the cinema; did you enjoy the film on TV last night? we didn't enjoy the game at all; to enjoy yourself** = zich amuseren/vermaken; **the children are making a lot of noise—they must be enjoying themselves; did she enjoy herself at the party?**
enjoys—enjoying—enjoyed—has enjoyed

enjoyable, *bn*
prettig, leuk, fijn; **we had an enjoyable day by the sea.**
enjoyment, *zn*
genot, plezier.

enough [ɪ'nʌf] **1.** *bn*
genoeg; voldoende; **have you got enough money to pay the bill? there isn't enough light to take a photograph.**
2. *vnw*
genoeg; **have you had enough to eat?**
3. *bw*
genoeg; **you are not walking quickly enough; your hands aren't clean enough; this knife isn't sharp enough; he doesn't work hard enough.**

enquire [ɪŋ'kwaɪə], **enquiry** [ɪŋ'kwaɪərɪ] *zie* **inquire, inquiry**

enter ['entə] *ww*
binnengaan/binnenkomen; **he entered the room; the burglars entered the house through a bedroom window.**
enters—entering—entered—has entered

entrance, *zn*
ingang; binnenkomst; **this is the main entrance** = hoofdingang; **entrance—10p** = .10p entrée.

envelope ['envələʊp] *zn*
envelop(pe); **don't forget to lick the envelope and put a stamp on it.**

equal ['i:kwəl] **1.** *bn*
gelijk, hetzelfde; **weigh three equal amounts of sugar; the two bits of string are not equal in length** = niet even lang.
2. *ww*
(*a*) gelijk zijn aan; geven; **two and four equals six** $(2 + 4 = 6)$; **ten take away two equals eight** $(10 - 2 = 8)$.
(*b*) evenaren; **he equalled the world record; there's no one to equal him at tennis.**
equals—equalling—equalled—has equalled
Let op: in rekensommen wordt **equals** *als* = *geschreven:* $6 + 4 = 10$

equipment [ɪ'kwɪpmənt] *zn*
uitrusting/toerusting; benodigdheden; **office equipment; he brought his camping equipment with him; the soldiers carried their equipment on their backs.**
geen meervoud: **some equipment; a piece of equipment**

escape [ɪ'skeɪp] **1.** *ww*
ontsnappen; **he escaped from prison by climbing over a wall.**
escapes—escaped—escaping—has escaped
2. *zn*
ontsnapping; **we had a narrow escape when the train hit our car** = wij zijn ternauwernood aan de dood ontsnapt etc.

especially [ɪ'speʃlɪ] *bw*
vooral, bijzonder; **he's especially fond of**

chocolates; you mustn't go out without a coat, especially when it's raining.

etc. [et′setərə]
etcetera, enzovoort; **vegetables, such as carrots, potatoes, etc.**

Europe [′jʊərəp] *zn*
Europa; **Germany and Holland are countries in Europe; many tourists come to Europe for their holidays.**
European [jʊərə′piːən] *bn*
Europees; **the European countries; he collects European stamps.**

even [′iːvn] **1.** *bn*
(*a*) **even numbers** = even getallen; **on the left side of the street, all the houses have even numbers.**
(*b*) gelijk; **at the end of the competition, the two teams were even.**
2. *bw*
zelfs (nog); **even the cleverest students can make silly mistakes; even the biggest apples were rotten; he even tried to swim across the lake; that film was bad, but this one is even worse.**
even if = ook al, zelfs al; **he never wears a coat, even if it's snowing.**
even so = toch, niettemin; **it poured with rain, but even so we had our picnic.**
even though = hoewel; **he didn't wear a coat, even though it was snowing.**

evening [′iːvnɪŋ] *zn*
avond; **this evening** = vanavond; **I'll meet you this evening after work; I saw him yesterday evening** = gisteravond; **the accident took place at 9 o'clock in the evening** = 's avonds; **we arrived in New York in the morning, having left London the evening before** = de avond tevoren; **on Sunday evening we stayed in to watch television; we always watch television on Sunday evenings** = 's zondagsavonds.

event [ɪ′vent] *zn*
(*a*) gebeurtenis, voorval; **strange events took place in the church at night.**
(*b*) (sport) evenement; **field events** = lichte atletiek; **track events** = baansporten/nummers.

ever [′evə] *bw*
(*a*) ooit; **nothing ever happens; did you ever meet Mr Smith? have you ever been to the USA? I hardly ever see her** = bijna nooit; **he sang better than ever.**
(*b*) altijd; **ever since** = vanaf die tijd, sindsdien; **for ever** = voorgoed; **it has gone for ever;** *zie ook* **however, whatever, whenever, wherever, whoever.**

every [′evrɪ] *bn*
elk(e), ieder(e); **every day; every evening; we have a party every Christmas; every time we go on a picnic it rains; I bought six apples and every one of them was rotten; every other day** = om de andere dag; **every two hours** = om de 2 uur; **have your car checked every 5,000 miles** = na iedere 5000 mijl.
everybody, everyone, *vnw*
iedereen; **everybody/everyone is going to the party; I sent Christmas cards to everybody/everyone at work; everybody/everyone has to show their tickets; everybody is here, aren't they?**
Let op: **everybody** *en* **everyone** *worden gevolgd door* **they/their/ themselves,** *etc. maar het werkwoord wordt in het enkelvoud gebruikt tenzij er een vraag volgt:* **is everyone enjoying themselves?** *maar* **not everyone works here do they?**
everything, *vnw*
alles; **have you brought everything with you? everything was dark in the house; the burglars stole everything that was valuable** = alles wat.
everywhere, *bw*
overal; **there were papers everywhere; I have looked everywhere for the key and I can't find it; everywhere was white after the snow had fallen.**

exact [ɪg′zækt] *bn*
nauwkeurig, precies; **this is an exact copy; what is the exact time?** = hoe laat is het precies?
exactly, *bw*
precies; **the time is exactly 16.24; he looks exactly like his brother.**

exam [ɪg'zæm] *zie* **examination**

examine [ɪg'zæmɪn] *ww*
examineren; onderzoeken; **the doctor examined the sick man's heart; the boxes were examined by the customs men.**
examines—examining—examined—has examined

examination [ɪgzæmɪ'neɪʃn], **exam** [ɪg'zæm] *zn*
examen; onderzoek; **there is a written examination in French; he passed his English exam; she was sad when she failed her music exams.**
Let op: **exam** *wordt voornamelijk in de spreektaal gebruikt*

example [ɪg'zɑ:mpl] *zn*
voorbeeld; **this is a good example of German poetry; for example** = bijvoorbeeld; **he is keen on keeping fit—for example, he goes running every morning; to set an example** = een voorbeeld stellen; **he sets everyone a good example by getting up early; she sets a bad example to everyone else in the office.**

excellent ['ekələnt] *bn*
uitstekend, voortreffelijk; **we had an excellent meal.**

except [ɪk'sept] *vz & vw*
behalve; **you can eat anything except fish; the party was very good, except that there wasn't enough to eat; he doesn't do anything except sit and watch television** = niets anders dan.

excited [ɪk'saɪtɪd] *bn*
opgewonden; **the children were excited at the thought of going on holiday; don't get too excited—you may not win the prize.**
excitement, *zn*
opwinding, drukte; **what's all the excitement about? the children are in a state of excitement before Christmas.**
exciting, *bn*
opwindend, spannend; **an exciting film; the news is really exciting.**

excuse 1. *zn* [ɪk'skju:s]
excuus; **his excuse for not coming was that he had a cold.**

2. *ww* [ɪk'skju:z]
vergeven; **excuse me** = neemt u mij niet kwalijk; **excuse me, can you tell me how to get to the post office?** = pardon; **excuse me for being so late/for interrupting** = vergeef me dat ik stoor/zo laat ben.
excuses—excusing—excused—has excused

exercise ['eksəsaɪz] *zn*
(*a*) oefening; (lichaams)beweging; **regular exercise is good for your heart; you ought to do five minutes' exercises every morning; he doesn't get/take enough exercise—that's why he's too fat.**
(*b*) oefening, opgave] **have you done all your maths exercises?**
exercise book, *zn*
schrift.

exhibition [eksɪ'bɪʃn] *zn*
tentoonstelling, expositie; **an exhibition of modern art; we went to a furniture exhibition.**

exist [ɪg'zɪst] *ww*
bestaan; **can fish exist out of water? don't be silly—such a thing doesn't exist.**
exists—existing—existed—has existed

exit ['egzɪt] *zn*
uitgang; **use the exit at the back of the room; passengers must go in by the front door—the back door is the exit; turn off the motorway at exit 12** = afslag.

expect [ɪk'spekt] *ww*
verwachten; aannemen; **I expect it will rain; I expect she is tired after a day at the office; he expects his wife to do all the work for him; do you think it's going to snow?—yes, I expect so** = ik verwacht van wel.
expects—expecting—expected—has expected

expensive [ɪk'spensɪv] *bn*
duur, kostbaar; **he was wearing an expensive watch; I'll buy two watches—they're not very expensive; this hotel is more expensive than I expected.**

experiment [ɪk'sperɪmənt] *zn*
experiment, proef; **he did some experiments to show that water boils at a temperature of 100°.**

explain [ɪk'spleɪn] *ww*
uitleggen; verklaren; **can you explain why it is colder in winter than in summer? she tried to explain what had happened, but the policeman didn't listen; he explained that the car hadn't stopped at the red light.**

explains—explaining—explained—has explained

explanation [eksplə'neɪʃn] *zn*
uitleg, verklaring; **the police asked him for an explanation of his strange behaviour; there is no explanation for this sudden cold weather.**

expression [ɪk'spreʃn] *zn*
(*a*) uitdrukking; **'for donkey's years'** is an expression meaning 'for a long time'.
(*b*) (gezichts)uitdrukking; **she had a sad expression; his expression showed that he was annoyed** = aan z'n gezicht was te zien etc.

extra ['ekstrə] *bn & bw*
extra; **the first class ticket will cost you an extra £10/will cost you £10 extra; you should find some extra strong string/ some extra thick paper.**

extremely [ɪk'striːmlɪ] *bw*
uiterst; buitengewoon; **he is extremely small; this watch is extremely expensive.**

eye [aɪ] *zn*
oog; **she has blue eyes; shut your eyes while we all hide; I've got something in my eye; to keep an eye on something** = een oogje op houden; **can you keep an eye on the house while we are on holiday?**
eyebrow, *zn*
wenkbrauw; **he raised his eyebrows** = hij fronste zijn wenkbrauwen.
eyelid, *zn*
ooglid.
eyesight, *zn*
gezichtsvermogen; **he has got very good eyesight** = goede ogen.
geen meervoud

Ff

face [feɪs] **1.** *zn*
(*a*) gezicht; **don't forget to wash your face and hands; he tried to keep a straight face** = hij probeerde zijn gezicht in de plooi te houden; **he was making funny faces and the children laughed** = hij trok gekke gezichten etc.
(*b*) voorkant; **a clock face** = wijzerplaat; **he put the picture face downwards on the table** = omgekeerd.
2. *ww*
het gezicht toekeren; liggen/staan tegenover; **please face the camera** = kijk alstublieft in de lens; **the house faces east** = het huis ziet uit op het oosten.
faces—facing—faced—has faced

facecloth, *zn*
washandje.
face up to, *ww*
onder (de) ogen zien; **he faced up to the fact that he wasn't fit enough for the race; you must try to face up to the problem.**

fact [fækt] *zn*
feit; **it is a fact that he did well in his exams; tell me all the facts so that I can decide what to do.**
in fact = in feite; in werkelijkheid; **he said he was going to the office when in fact he went to the cinema.**

factory ['fæktrɪ] *zn*
fabriek; **a shoe factory; he works in a**

car factory; **he runs a factory which makes furniture** = hij exploiteert een meubelfabriek.
meervoud **factories**

fail [feɪl] *ww*
falen; mislukken; (*van examen*) zakken; **the car failed to stop at the red light; she has failed her exams again; he failed his driving test three times.**
fails—failing—failed—has failed

failure [ˈfeɪljə] *zn*
mislukking; falen; **he tried to make a machine to change gas into oil, but it was a failure.**

faint [feɪnt] **1.** *ww*
flauw vallen; **she fainted when she saw the blood; it was so hot standing in the sun that he fainted.**
faints—fainting—fainted—has fainted
2. *bn*
vaag; flauw; zwak; **we could hear a faint noise behind the door; there's a faint smell of paint.**
faint—fainter—faintest

fair [feə] *bn*
(*a*) blond; **she's got fair hair; he's dark, but his sister is fair.**
(*b*) middelmatig; **her work was only fair.**
(*c*) juist, eerlijk; **it isn't fair to eat all the cake yourself; that's not fair—you must let everyone play with the ball; the teacher was very fair when she marked our exams.**
(*d*) (*van weer*) goed; **the TV says it will be fair tomorrow.**
fair—fairer—fairest

fairly, *bw*
nogal, vrij; **I'm fairly certain I have met him before; he has been working here a fairly short time.**
Let op de woordvolgorde: **he's a fairly good student** *maar* **he's quite a good student**

fall [fɔ:l] **1.** *zn*
(*a*) val, vallen; **there has been a heavy fall of snow; falls** = waterval.
(*b*) val; **she had a fall and hurt her back** = zij viel etc.

(*c*) (*Amerikaans voor* **autumn**) herfst.
2. *ww*
(om)vallen; **he fell down the stairs; she fell off the wall; did he fall into the water or did someone push him? don't put the bottle on the cushion—it will fall over.**
falls—falling—fell—has fallen

fall asleep, *ww*
in slaap vallen, inslapen; **he fell asleep in front of the TV.**

fall off, *ww*
verminderen, afnemen, teruglopen; **the number of tourists has fallen off this summer.**

fall through, *ww*
niet doorgaan, in duigen vallen; **the trip to London fell through.**

family [ˈfæmlɪ] *zn*
familie; gezin; **John is the youngest in our family; the Jones family have gone on holiday to Spain; they have a very big family—two sons and three daughters.**
meervoud **families, maar family** *kan als meervoud gebruikt worden*

famous [ˈfeɪməs] *bn*
beroemd; **he's a famous singer; that restaurant is famous for its cakes.**

far [fɑ:] *bw & bn*
(*a*) ver; **the post office is not far from here; how far is it from London to Edinburgh?**
(*b*) veel; **it is far cheaper to go by bus than to take a taxi; the food in this restaurant is far nicer than at home.**
by far = verreweg; **it is by far the cheapest way to travel; this car uses by far the least amount of petrol.**
so far = tot nu toe; **so far the weather has been beautiful; have you enjoyed the holiday so far?**
far—farther/further—farthest/furthest

fare [feə] *zn*
reisgeld, reiskosten; **bus fares have increased again** = bustarieven; **what is the fare from London to Edinburgh? the return fare is twice the ordinary fare** = retourprijs.

farm [fɑːm] zn
boerderij; **he's going to work on the farm during the holidays; we spent six weeks on a farm; you can buy eggs and vegetables at the farm.**
farmer, zn
boer.
farmhouse, zn
boerderij.
farmyard, zn
(boeren)erf.

fast [fɑːst] bn & bw
(a) vlug, snel; **this is a fast train to London—it doesn't stop anywhere** = sneltrein; **if you walk fast you can catch up with the children in front; my watch is five minutes fast** = mijn horloge loopt vijf minuten vóór.
(b) **fast asleep** = diep in slaap.
fast—faster—fastest

fasten ['fɑːsn] ww
vastmaken, sluiten; **fasten your seat belt when you drive a car; the dress is fastened with a zip down the back.**
fastens—fastening—fastened—has fastened
fasten up, ww
dichtmaken; **you should fasten up your coat.**
Let op: **you fasten your coat up** *of* **you fasten up your coat,** *maar* *alleen* **you fasten it up**

fat [fæt] **1.** bn
dik; **you ought to eat less—you're getting too fat; that fat man has a very thin wife; he's the fattest boy in the class.**
fat—fatter—fattest
2. zn
vet; **if you don't like the fat, cut it off; fry the eggs in some fat.**

father ['fɑːðə] zn
vader; **ask your father if you can borrow his car; Jane is coming to tea with her father and mother.**

faucet ['fɔːsət] zn
(*Amerikaans voor* **tap**) kraan.

fault [fɒlt] zn
fout, defect; schuld; **whose fault is it that**

we haven't any food? it's all your fault— if you hadn't stayed in bed all morning we would be at the seaside by now; the engineer is trying to mend an electrical fault.

favourite ['feɪvrɪt] bn & zn (*Amer.* favorite)
favoriet; lievelings-; **what is your favourite ice cream? which film star is your favourite? this is my favourite TV programme.**

feather ['feðə] zn
veer; **a duck with green feathers on its head.**

February ['februərɪ] zn
februari; **his birthday is in February; she died on February 6th; we are moving to a new house next February; today is February 7th.**
Let op: **February 7th:** *zeg* 'the seventh of February' *of* 'February the seventh'
Let op: **February** *wordt altijd met een hoofdletter geschreven*

fed [fed] *zie* **feed**
fed up ['fed'ʌp] bn
het beu zijn; ergens genoeg van hebben; **I'm fed up with listening to all this talk; she's fed up with school.**

feed [fiːd] ww
voeden, voederen, te eten geven; zich voeden (met); **it's time to feed the cows; how can you feed the family when you haven't any money? cows feed on grass.**
feeds—feeding—fed [fed]—**has fed**

feel [fiːl] ww
(a) (be)voelen, (be)tasten; **feel how soft the cushion is; when the lights went out we had to feel our way to the door** = toen de lichten uitgingen, moesten we op de tast de deur vinden.
(b) aanvoelen; **the knife felt cold; the floor feels hard.**
(c) (zich) voelen; **I felt the table move; did you feel the lift go down suddenly? I feel cold/warm/happy/hungry, etc.** = ik heb het koud/warm/ik voel me gelukkig/

ik heb honger etc.; **when she saw the film she felt sad; are you feeling better?**

(*d*) het gevoel hebben, vinden; **he feels it would be wrong to leave the children alone in the house; the police felt that the accident was the fault of the driver of the car.**

feels—feeling—felt [felt]**—has felt**

feeling, *zn*
gevoel sensatie; **I had a feeling that someone was watching me.**

feel like, *ww*
I felt like going for a swim = zin hebben/krijgen in; **do you feel like a cup of tea?**

feet [fi:t] *zie* **foot**

fell [fel] *zie* **fall**

felt [felt] *zie* **feel**

female ['fi:meıl] *bn & zn*
vrouw; wijfje; vrouwelijk; **a female cat.**

fence [fens] *zn*
hek, omheining; **you need a strong wire fence round the chickens; the sheep pushed through the hole in the fence; he was leaning on the garden fence.**

ferry ['ferı] *zn*
veerboot, (veer)pont; **we will take the ferry to France; a car ferry** = autoveer.
meervoud **ferries**

fetch [fetʃ] *ww*
(af)halen/(op)halen; **it's time to fetch the children from school; I'll come and fetch you from the office** = ik kom je met de auto van kantoor halen; **can you fetch another bag of sugar from the grocer's?**
fetches—fetching—fetched—has fetched

fever ['fi:və] *zn*
koorts; **you must stay in bed until the fever has gone.**

few [fju:] *bn & zn*
(*a*) weinig(e); **he has few friends; we go to fewer parties than last year.**
(*b*) **a few** = een paar, enkele; **take a few photographs and we will choose which one is best; I'll be ready in a few minutes.**
few—fewer—fewest

field [fi:ld] *zn*
(*a*) veld, wei; grasveld; **the cows are all in the field; a field of grass.**
(*b*) (sport)veld/(sport)terrein; **the crowd is going to the football field.**

fifteen [fɪf'ti:n] vijftien
there are fifteen players in a rugby football team; he's fifteen (years old); come and see me in fifteen minutes time; the train leaves at eighteen fifteen (18.15).

fifteenth, 15th, *bn & zn*
vijftiende; **the fifteenth of May/May the fifteenth (May 15th); that's the fifteenth phone call I've had this morning; it's his fifteenth birthday next week.**

fifth [fɪfθ] **5th,** *bn & zn*
vijfde; **the fifth of June/June the fifth (June 5th); Henry the Fifth (Henry V); a fifth** = 20%; **he spends a fifth of his time writing letters; it's her fifth birthday tomorrow.**

Let op: in een datum wordt **fifth** *meestal als* **5th** *geschreven:* **June 5th, 1935; December 5th, 1981;** *bij de namen van koningen en koninginnen schrijft men* **fifth** *meestal als* **V: King Henry V**

fifty [fɪftı] vijftig
I've made fifty pots of marmalade; he's fifty (years old); she's in her fifties = in de vijftig.
Let op: **fifty-one** (51), **fifty-two** (52), *maar* **fifty-first** (51st), **fifty-second** (52nd), *etc.*

fiftieth, 50th, *bn & zn*
vijftigste; **a fiftieth** = 2%; **she came fiftieth in the race; it's his fiftieth birthday on Monday** = maandag wordt hij vijftig.

fight [faıt] *ww*
vechten; (be)strijden; **the boys are fighting in the street; the police are fighting to reduce traffic accidents; doctors are fighting against disease; the two dogs were fighting over a bone.**
fights—fighting—fought [fɔ:t]**—has fought**

figure ['fıgə] *zn*
cijfer; **write two hundred and twenty three in figures; double figures** = getallen

tussen 10 en 99; **his salary is in five figures** = tussen 10,000 en 100,000.

fill [fɪl] *ww*
(*a*) vullen; **he filled the box with books; she was filling the bottle with water.**
(*b*) **to fill a tooth** = vullen, plomberen;
fills—filling—filled—has filled

fill in, *ww*
invullen; **fill in your name and address; fill in the missing words.**

filling, *zn*
vulling; **I had to have two fillings when I went to the dentist's.**

filling station, *zn*
tankstation/benzine station; **stop at the next filling station to ask the way.**

fill up, *ww*
(*a*) (op)vullen; **fill her up** = wilt u de tank volgooien alstublieft; **he filled up the bottle and screwed on the top.**
(*b*) invullen; **fill up the form as soon as possible.**
Let op: **fill the glass up** *of* **fill up the glass** *maar alleen* **fill it up**

film [fɪlm] *zn*
(*a*) film; **have you seen this Charlie Chaplin film? we watched the film on TV.**
(*b*) film; **I must buy a film before I go on holiday; do you want a colour film or a black and white one?**

finally ['faɪnəlɪ] *bw*
tenslotte, uiteindelijk; **the car wouldn't start, there were no buses, so finally we had to walk; we waited for half an hour, and he finally arrived at 8.30.**

find [faɪnd] *ww*
(*a*) vinden, ontdekken; **I found a 50p coin in the street; did she find the book she was looking for? scientists have found that cold water helps a headache; doctors are still trying to find a cure for colds** =doktoren zijn nog steeds op zoek naar etc.
(*b*) (leuk/interessant etc.) vinden; **I found this film very interesting; he finds his work too easy.**
finds—finding—found [faʊnd]—has found

find out, *ww*
uitzoeken; **the police are trying to find out why she went to Edinburgh; I'm going to the library to find out about how to look after tropical fish.**

find time, *ww*
kans zien om; **in spite of all his work, he found time to phone his wife.**

fine [faɪn] **1.** *bn*
(*a*) goed, mooi (*van weer*); **we'll go for a picnic if it is fine tomorrow; let's hope it stays fine for the cricket match.**
(*b*) goed, uitstekend; **I was ill yesterday, but I'm feeling fine today; how are things?—fine!**
(*c*) fijn; **sharpen your pencil to a very fine point; I can't read this book—the print is too fine.**
fine—finer—finest
2. *zn*
boete; **I had to pay a £10 fine for parking on the yellow lines.**
3. *ww*
beboeten; een boete krijgen/opleggen; **he was fined £10 for parking on yellow lines.**
fines—fining—fined—has fined

finger ['fɪŋgə] *zn*
vinger; **she wears a ring on her little finger; he touched the switch with his finger; to keep your fingers crossed** = duimen voor.

fingernail, *zn*
(vinger)nagel; **she painted her fingernails red.**

fingerprint, *zn*
vingerafdruk; **the police found fingerprints near the broken window.**

finish ['fɪnɪʃ] *ww*
afmaken; eindigen; **I've finished my homework; tell me when you've finished reading the book; we can't watch TV until we've finished the washing up; the film finished at 10.30.**
finishes—finishing—finished—has finished

finish off, *ww*
voltooien, afmaken; **have you finished off your work?**

finish up, *ww*
(*a*) terecht komen; **we got lost and finished up in south London.**

(*b*) opmaken, opeten; **you must finish up your potatoes.**

Let op: **he finished his work off** *of* **he finished off his work, finish up your meat** *of* **finish your meat up,** *etc., maar alleen* **finish it off, finish it up,** *etc.*

finish with, *ww*
klaar zijn; **can I borrow the tin opener when you've finished with it?; have you finished with the newspaper?** = hebt u de krant uit?

fire ['faɪə] **1.** *zn*
vuur; brand; kachel; **we sat in front of a gas fire; we made a big fire in the garden to burn the dead leaves.**
to catch fire = vlam vatten, in brand vliegen; **the house caught fire; take that carpet away—it might catch fire.**
to set fire to = in brand steken; **his cigarette set fire to the chair.**
on fire = in brand (staan); **phone the fire station—the house is on fire.**
2. *ww*
(af)vuren; **the police fired at the car; we could hear the guns firing in the distance.**
fires—firing—fired—has fired

fireman, *zn*
brandweerman; **the firemen were fighting the fire in the town centre.**
meervoud **firemen**

fireplace, *zn*
open haard.

firm [fɜ:m] **1.** *zn*
firma, zaak; **he works for a firm of engineers; it is the biggest engineering firm in the country.**
2. *bn*
stevig, vast, solide; flink, ferm; **make sure that chair is firm before you sit on it.**
firm—firmer—firmest

firmly, *bw*
ferm, flink, beslist; stevig, vast; **she told them firmly to keep quiet.**

first [fɜ:st] **1. 1st** *bn & zn*
eerst(e); **my birthday is on the first of**

August/August the first (August 1st); King Charles the First (Charles I); it's the baby's first birthday on Tuesday; the post office is the first building on the left.

Let op: in een datum wordt **first** *meestal als* **1st** *geschreven:* **August 1st, 1980; December 1st, 1669;** *bij de namen van vorsten en vorstinnen schrijft men* **first** *meestal als* **I: King Charles I**

2. *bw*
(*a*) (het) eerst(e); **he came first in the race; do your homework first, and then we can go out.**
(*b*) voor het eerst; **when did you first go to Germany?**
at first = in het begin, eerst; **he didn't like his job at first but later got used to it; at first I didn't want to go to the party, but then I changed my mind.**
first class, *zn & bw*
(de)eerste klas(se); **a first class ticket to Edinburgh; he always travels first class; send that letter first class—I want it to arrive quickly; first class is always very comfortable.**

fish [fɪʃ] *zn*
vis; **look at all those fish in the lake; I caught six little fish; we're having fish and chips for dinner.**
meervoud meestal **fish: some fish; three fish**

fishing, *zn*
vissen; **he goes fishing every weekend.**

fit [fɪt] **1.** *bn*
fit, in goede conditie; geschikt; **he isn't fit enough to work; you'll have to get fit before the football match.**
fit—fitter—fittest

2. *ww*
(*a*) passen; **he's grown so tall that his trousers don't fit him any more; these shoes don't fit me—they're too tight.**
(*b*) zetten, monteren; **I want to fit a new bath in the bathroom; the sitting room has a fitted carpet** = vaste vloerbedekking.
fits—fitting—fitted—has fitted

fit in, *ww*
inpassen; **I don't think I can fit in any**

holidays this year as I have too much
work; how can you fit everything into
that little box? = hoe krijgen we alles
in dat doosje?

five [faɪv] vijf
she drank five cups of coffee; he's five
(years old); come for tea at five
(o'clock).

fix [fɪks] ww
(a) bevestigen; vastmaken; he fixed the
cupboard to the wall; she fixed a notice
to the post with string.
(b) repareren; herstellen; can you fix the
car engine for me?
(c) vaststellen; organiseren; the meeting
has been fixed for next week.
fixes—fixing—fixed—has fixed

fix up, ww
organiseren; voorzien van; we've fixed
up for a car to meet us at the airport;
can you fix me up with a room for two
nights?

flag [flæg] zn
(a) vlag; each ship carries the flag of its
country; a ship flying the British flag; for
the party, we hung flags across the
street.
(b) vlaggetje, speldje; he was selling
flags for the Red Cross.

flame [fleɪm] zn
vlam; the flame of a candle; the house
was in flames = in lichterlaaie staan;
the car burst into flames = de auto
vloog in brand.

flash [flæʃ] 1. zn
straal, flits; vlam; a flash of lightning; if
you want to take a photograph in the
dark, you should use a flash; a news flash
= extra (nieuws)bericht.
meervoud flashes
2. ww
(a) (kort) schijnen op; flitsen; the light
flashed twice; he flashed his torch in my
eyes; a police car has a blue flashing light
= zwaailicht.
(b) (langs)flitsen; the car flashed past the
traffic lights.
**flashes—flashing—flashed—has
flashed**

flat [flæt] 1. bn & bw
plat, vlak; a flat road; spread the paper
out flat on the table; the soldiers lay flat
on the ground; a flat tyre = een lekke
band.
flat out = keihard, uit alle macht; he
worked flat out to finish his work on
time.
2. zn (Amer. apartment)
flat; they live in a block of flats =
flat(gebouw); their flat is on the top
floor = zij wonen op de bovenste verdieping; he has a flat in London and a house
in the country = hij heeft een apparte-
ment in Londen en een huis buiten.

Flemish 1. bn
Vlaams; Antwerp is in the Flemish part
of Belgium.
2. zn
(a) Vlaams; Flemish is spoken in the
Northern part of Belgium; what is the
Flemish for 'chips'? she lives in the Flem-
ish-speaking part of Belgium.
(b) the Flemish = de Vlamingen.
Let op: Flemish wordt altijd met een
hoofdletter geschreven.

flew [fluː] zie **fly**

flies [flaɪz] zie **fly**

flight [flaɪt] zn
(a) vlucht; the flight to New York leaves
in 15 minutes; there are six flights a day
to Glasgow; when does the New York
flight leave? how long is the flight from
London to Madrid? the flight lasts about
3 hours.
(b) flight of stairs = trap; turn left at
the top of the first flight of stairs = ga
bovenaan de eerste trap naar links.

float [fləʊt] ww
drijven; zweven; leaves were floating on
the lake; he put his model boat into the
water and it floated.
**floats—floating—floated—has
floated**

flood [flʌd] 1. zn
overstroming; after the rainstorm there
were floods in the valley.
2. ww
overstromen; onder water staan/zetten;

blank staan; **the fields were flooded; the washing machine flooded the kitchen floor.**

floods—flooding—flooded—has flooded

floor [flɔ:] *zn*
(*a*) vloer; **put that box down on the floor; she lay on the floor and looked up at the ceiling.**
(*b*) verdieping; **the shop is on the ground floor** = begane grond; **his office is on the second floor; he walked up the stairs to the top floor.**

flour ['flaʊə] *zn*
(tarwe)bloem; **brown flour** = volkoren bloem; **white flour** = witte bloem.
geen meervoud

flow [fləʊ] *ww*
vloeien, stromen; **the water flowed down the pipe; the traffic was flowing around the square; the river flows into the sea.**

flows—flowing—flowed—has flowed

flower ['flaʊə] **1.** *zn*
bloem; **she picked a bunch of flowers; the apple trees are in flower** = staan in bloei.
2. *ww*
bloeien; **the apple trees flowered early this year; this plant only flowers once every ten years.**

flowers—flowering—flowered—has flowered

flown [fləʊn] *zie* **fly**

flu [flu:] *zn*
griep, influenza; **he's in bed with flu; she caught flu and had to stay at home; there is a lot of flu about in the winter.**

fly [flaɪ] **1.** *zn*
vlieg; **try to kill that fly; flies can walk on the ceiling.**
meervoud **flies**
2. *ww*
(*a*) vliegen; **he is flying his own plane; the birds flew away; I'm flying to Hong Kong next week; to go from London to Italy you have to fly over France; he has flown across the Atlantic twice.**

(*b*) (*van vlag*) voeren; **the ship was flying a British flag.**

flies—flying—flew—has flown

fog [fɒg] *zn*
mist; **the planes couldn't take off because of fog; the fog is so thick that you must drive slowly.**
foggy, *bn*
mistig, nevelig; **foggy weather; he walked around the foggy streets; don't drive fast when it's foggy.**

foggy—foggier—foggiest

fold [fəʊld] *ww*
(op)vouwen; **he folded the letter and put it in an envelope; he folded up the newspaper; to fold your arms** = je armen over elkaar slaan.

folds—folding—folded—has folded

follow ['fɒləʊ] *ww*
(*a*) volgen; **follow me and I will show you the way; C follows B in the alphabet; the police followed the man across the town; look at the following pages.**
(*b*) volgen (uit iets); **if he wrote the letter, it follows that he must have known the news.**

follows—following—followed— has followed

fond of ['fɒnd 'ɒv] *bn*
lekker vinden; houden van; **I'm fond of food; she's fond of dancing** = dol/verzot zijn op; **he's very fond of cheese; I'm not very fond of loud music.**

fond—fonder—fondest

food [fu:d] *zn*
eten, voedsel; **this restaurant is famous for its food; do you like Chinese food? we went on a picnic but forgot to bring the food; this food tastes funny.**
food *wordt meestal in het enkelvoud gebruikt*

foot [fʊt] *zn*
(*a*) voet; **he has got big feet; you trod on my foot; on foot** = te voet; **we went to the shops on foot; don't wait for the bus—it's quicker to go on foot; he put his foot in it** = hij heeft een blunder begaan.

(*b*) voet; **he sat at the foot of the stairs; the house is at the foot of the hill; the page number is at the foot of the page** = onderaan.

(*c*) voet (= 30 centimeter); **the table is three feet/three foot wide; he is almost six foot tall; she is five foot six inches tall** (**5′ 6″**; *zeg* 'she's five foot six').

meervoud **feet**
Let op: samen met getallen is het niet **feet** *maar* **foot: six foot tall; three foot wide**
Let op: bij cijfers wordt **foot** *aangegeven met':* **a 6′ ladder; he is 5′ 6″ (five foot six);** *zie ook* **inch**

football, *zn*
(*a*) voetbal; **he was kicking a football about in the garden; throw me that football.**
(*b*) voetbalspel/voetbalsport; **rugby football** = rugby; **a football match; they were playing football in the field; come and have a game of football; do you always watch the football matches/games on TV?**
football field, football ground, *zn*
voetbalveld/voetbalterrein.
footpath, *zn*
voetpad.
footstep, *zn*
voetstap; **we heard quiet footsteps outside the room.**

for [fɔ:] *vz*
(*a*) voor; **this box is for old papers; what's that key for? what did she say that for?** = waarom zei ze dat?
(*b*) voor, met; **what did your parents give you for Christmas? what shall we buy John for his birthday?**
(*c*) (bestemd) voor; **the postman has brought a parcel for you; this present is for your mother.**
(*d*) voor; **he has gone to the United States for a week; I have been waiting for hours** = ik sta/zit al uren te wachten.
(*e*) voor, naar; **is this the train for London?**
as for = wat betreft; **as for me, I'm going to bed.**
for ever = altijd; **I will love you for ever.**

for example/for instance = bijvoorbeeld; **large animals, for example elephants, are expensive to feed.**
Let op: **for example** *wordt vaak als* **e.g.** *geschreven.*

for good = voorgoed; **he left the house for good.**

forbid [fə'bɪd] *ww*
verbieden; **smoking is forbidden in the cinema; the committee has forbidden any discussion of the plan; the rules of football forbid you to touch the ball.**
forbids—forbidding—forbade [fə'bæd]—**has forbidden**

force [fɔ:s] **1.** *zn*
(*a*) kracht; geweld; **the tree was blown down by the force of the wind.**
(*b*) macht; **the police force** = de politiemacht; **the armed forces** = de strijdkrachten.
2. *ww*
dwingen; **they forced him to lie on the floor; she was forced to do whatever they wanted.**
forces—forcing—forced—has forced

forehead ['fɒrɪd] *zn*
voorhoofd.

foreign ['fɒrɪn] *bn*
vreemd, buitenlands; **he speaks several foreign languages.**
foreigner, *zn*
buitenlander.

forest ['fɒrɪst] *zn*
woud, bos; **many wild animals live in the forests of South America.**

forgave [fə'geɪv] *zie* **forgive**

forget [fə'get] *ww*
vergeten; **he forgot to put on his trousers; he's forgotten how to play cricket; I forgot all about my appointment with the dentist; don't forget to lock the door.**
forgets—forgetting—forgot [fə'gɒt]—**forgotten** [fə'gɒtn]

forgive [fə'gɪv] *ww*
vergeven; **she forgave him when he said he was sorry; please forgive me for**

being so late = neemt u mij alstublieft
niet kwalijk dat ik zo laat ben.

forgives—forgiving—forgave
[fə'geɪv]—has forgiven

forgot [fə'gɒt], **forgotten** [fə'gɒtn],
zie **forget**

fork [fɔːk] *zn*
vork; **you can't eat soup with a knife and
fork; use your fork to eat your meat—
don't use your fingers; each person had a
knife, fork and spoon; garden fork** =
hark.

form [fɔːm] *zn*
(*a*) vorm; **she has a ring in the form of a
letter A.**
(*b*) formulier; **you have to fill in a form
when you want to pay your tax.**
(*c*) vorm, conditie; **our team was in good
form and won easily; he's in good form
today** = goed op dreef; **off form** = niet
in vorm.
(*d*) (*van school*) klas; **he's in the top
form; the little children are in the first
form; sixth form** = hoogste klas van de
middelbare school.

former ['fɔːmə] *bn*
vroeger; **he's a former army officer** =
voormalig.
formerly, *bw*
vroeger, eertijds; **this house was formerly
a railway station; she was formerly the
headmistress of the local school.**

fortnight ['fɔːtnaɪt] *zn*
veertien dagen/twee weken; **we are going
away for a fortnight to France; I'll see
you in a fortnight's time; we met a fortnight ago.**

fortunate ['fɔːtʃənət] *bn*
gelukkig; **how fortunate that you
happened to be there!** = wat een geluk!
fortunately, *bw*
gelukkig.

forty ['fɔːtɪ] veertig
**he's forty (years old); she has forty pairs of
shoes; he's in his forties** = in de veertig.
Let op: **forty-one** (41), **forty-two**
(42), *maar* **forty-first** (41st), **forty-**
second (42nd), *etc.*

fortieth, 40th, *bn & zn*
veertigste; **she came fortieth in the race;
it's my fortieth birthday tomorrow.**

forward ['fɔːwəd] **1.** *bw* (*ook* **for-**
wards)
naar voren, voorwaarts; **he ran forward
to shake my hand; the police asked the
crowd to move forward;** *zie ook* **back-**
wards.
2. *zn*
(van sport) voorspelen.

fought [fɔːt] *zie* **fight**

found [faʊnd] *zie* **find**

four [fɔː] vier
**she's four (years old); come and see me at
four (o'clock); a square has four corners.**
fourteen, veertien
**I have fourteen books to read for my
exam; she's fourteen (years old).**
fourteenth, 14th, *bn & zn*
veertiende; **she came fourteenth in her
race; the fourteenth of July/July the
fourteenth (July 14th); it was his fourteenth birthday yesterday.**
fourth, 4th, *bn & zn*
vierde; **they live in the fourth house from
the corner; the fourth of August/August
the fourth (August 4th); Charles the
Fourth (Charles IV); it's her fourth
birthday tomorrow; a fourth** = 25%.
Let op: in plaats van **'a fourth'** *of* **'a**
fourth part' *zegt men meestal* **'a**
quarter'.
Let op: in een datum wordt **fourth**
meestal als **4th** *geschreven:* **June**
4th, 1979; August 4th, 1981; *bij de*
namen van koningen en koninginnen
schrijft men **fourth** *meestal als* **IV:**
King Charles IV

frame [freɪm] *zn*
(*van fiets*) frame; (*van schilderij*) lijst;
(*van gebouw*) geraamte; (*van schip*)
spanten; (*van bril*) montuur; **the bicycle
has a very light frame; I've broken the
frame of my glasses; picture frame.**

free [friː] *bn*
(*a*) vrij, onbezet; **are you free tonight?
there is a table free in the corner of the
restaurant.**

freeze

(b) gratis; **if you cut off the top of the cereals box you can get a free book; I didn't pay anything for my ticket—I got it free! children are admitted free, but adults have to pay £1.**
(c) vrij; **he's free to do what he wants; it's a free country.**
free—freer—freest

freeze [fri:z] *ww*
(a) vriezen; **it is freezing outside; they say it will freeze tomorrow; I'm freezing** = ik sterf van de kou.
(b) (be)vriezen, invriezen; **I'll cook some frozen peas to eat with the fish** = diepvries; **we freeze a lot of vegetables from our garden; the river has frozen over** = is dichtgevroren.
freezes—freezing—froze [frəʊz]—**has frozen** ['frəʊzn]

freezer, *zn*
diepvries(kast/kist)
freeze up, *ww*
bevriezen; **all the pipes in the house froze up.**

frequent ['fri:kwənt] *bn*
frequent, veelvuldig; **there are frequent trains to London; she is a frequent visitor.**
frequently, *bw*
vaak; **it frequently rains in the west of the country.**

fresh [freʃ] *bn*
(a) fris, schoon; **I'll get some fresh towels; fresh air** = frisse lucht; buitenlucht; **they came out of the mine into the fresh air.**
(b) vers; **fresh bread.**
(c) vers; **fresh fish; fresh fruit salad; fresh vegetables are expensive in winter.**
fresh—fresher—freshest

Friday ['fraɪdɪ] *zn*
vrijdag; **he came to see me last Friday; we always go to the cinema on Fridays; I'll see you next Friday; today is Friday, June 20th.**
Let op: **Friday** *wordt altijd met een hoofdletter geschreven*

fridge [frɪdʒ] *zn*
koelkast; **put the butter in the fridge;**

there's no milk left in the fridge; shut the fridge door.

fried [fraɪd] *zie* **fry**

friend [frend] *zn*
vriend(in); **Henry is my best friend; she's going on holiday with some friends from college; to make friends with someone** = bevriend raken met iemand; **these are the people we made friends with on holiday.**
friendly, *bn*
vriendelijk, behulpzaam; **don't be afraid of the dog—he's very friendly; we're on friendly terms with the people who live next door** = we gaan vriendschappelijk om met de mensen van hiernaast.
friendly—friendlier—friendliest

fries [fraɪz] *zie* **fry**

frighten ['fraɪtn] *ww*
bang maken, angst aanjagen; **the noise frightened me; a frightening film about insects which eat people.**
frightens—frightening—frightened—has frightened
frightened, *bn*
bang; **I'm frightened of spiders; don't leave me alone—I'm frightened of the dark.**

frog [frɒg] *zn*
kikker; **a little green frog jumped into the river.**

from [frɒm] *vz*
(a) van; uit; **take two from three, and you have one left; he comes from America.**
(b) van; vanaf; **the bee moved from flower to flower; I'll be at home from 9 o'clock in the morning; she works from Monday to Friday; it is 2 km from here to the post office; here's a letter from Peter.**
(c) van; **I can't tell butter from margarine** = ik kan boter niet van margarine onderscheiden; **your job is very different from mine** = anders dan.
(d) (*geeft oorzaak aan*) **he died from his disease** = hij overleed aan zijn ziekte; **she suffers from colds.**

front [frʌnt] *zn*
voorkant; **the front of the house faces south; there is a picture of the Tower of London on the front of the book; he spilt soup down the front of his shirt; there was a photograph of him on the front page** (= voorpagina) **of the newspaper.**
in front of = voor; **he was standing in front of the bus when it suddenly started; there are two people in front of me in the queue; park your car in front of the house.**

frost [frɒst] *zn*
vorst; **there was a frost last night.**

froze [frəʊz], **frozen** ['frəʊzn] *zie* **freeze**

fruit [fru:t] *zn*
vrucht; fruit; **can you buy me some fruit at the market? his garden is full of fruit trees; we ought to eat all the fruit quickly or it will go bad; fruit salad** = fruitsalade.
geen meervoud: **some fruit/a lot of fruit**

fry [fraɪ] *ww*
bakken; braden; **fried eggs; do you want your eggs fried or boiled? he was frying onions in the kitchen.**
fries [fraɪz]—**frying**—**fried** [fraɪd]—**has fried**

frying pan, *zn*
koekepan, braadpan.

full [fʊl] *bn*
(a) vol; **is the bottle full? the bag is full of apples; the bus was so full we couldn't get on; I'm full up** = ik kan geen hap meer op.
(b) volledig; **you must write down the full details of your job; he got full marks** = het hoogste cijfer; **children over 12 must pay full fare** = vol tarief; **full moon** = volle maan.
full stop = punt (.).
full—fuller—fullest

fun [fʌn] *zn*
plezier; pret; **we had some fun on the beach; to make fun of someone** = de gek steken; **for fun** = voor de grap; **she poured water down his neck for fun.**

funny, *bn*
(a) leuk, grappig; gek; **we saw a funny programme on TV; she wore a funny hat; let me tell you a funny story about my brother.**
(b) vreemd, raar, gek; **he was behaving in a funny way; there's a funny smell in the kitchen.**
funny—funnier—funniest

fur [fɜ:] *zn*
bont; **our cat has soft white fur; the lady was wearing a fur coat.**
furry, *bn*
wollig, zacht, bont-; **a little furry animal.**

furnish ['fɜ:nɪʃ] *ww*
inrichten; **they have a small furnished flat** = gemeubileerd.
furnishes—furnishing—furnished—has furnished

furniture ['fɜ:nɪtʃə] *zn*
meubilair, meubelen; **someone has stolen all our furniture; you should move the furniture out of the room before you paint the ceiling.**
geen meervoud: **some furniture; a lot of furniture; a piece of furniture**

further ['fɜ:ðə] *bw & bn*
(a) verder; **can you move further back? they went further away; the post office is further away than the police station; Edinburgh is further from London than Paris.**
(b) nader; **we want further information; can you give me further details of when the accident took place?**
furthest, *bw & bn*
(het) verst(e); **he lives furthest from the office; the furthest distance I have travelled by train is 800 km.**

future ['fju:tʃə] *zn*
(a) toekomst; **in the future, I will try to eat less; I'll be more careful in future** = voortaan.
(b) (*ook* **future tense**) toekomende tijd van werkwoorden; **'he will go' and 'he is going to go' are forms of the future of 'to go'.**

Gg

gallon [ˈgælən] *zn*
gallon (= 4.5 liter); **the car does thirty miles to the gallon** = de auto rijdt één op tien; **the bucket can hold two gallons.**

game [geɪm] *zn*
(*a*) spel, party; sportwedstrijd; **would you like a game of tennis? he's not very good at games; our side have won all their games this year.**
(*b*) (tennis) game; **he's winning by six games to three.**

garage [ˈgærɪdʒ] *zn*
(*a*) garage; **put the car into the garage; he drove the car out of the garage; don't forget to lock the garage door.**
(*b*) garage(bedrijf); **where's the nearest garage?—my car has broken down; I can't drive you to the station—my car is in the garage.**

garden [ˈgɑːdn] *zn*
(*a*) (*Amer.* **yard**) tuin; **he grows tomatoes in his back garden; your mother's sitting in the garden.**
(*b*) **public gardens** = park.
garden centre, *zn*
tuincentrum.
gardener, *zn*
tuinman.
gardening, *zn*
tuinieren; **he likes gardening; she does some gardening every Saturday.**

gas [gæs] *zn*
(*a*) gas; **a gas cooker; we heat our house by gas; there is a gas fire in the dining room.**
(*b*) (*Amerikaans voor* **petrol**) benzine.
het meervoud **gases** *wordt alleen gebruikt om verschillende soorten gas aan te duiden.*

gate [geɪt] *zn*
(*a*) hek; poort; **if you leave the gate open,** the sheep will get out of the field; shut the gate; there is a white gate in the garden wall.
(*b*) (*vliegveld*) uitgang, poort; 'gate'; **go to gate 25 for flight AB193.**

gather [ˈgæðə] *ww*
(*a*) oogsten; verzamelen; zich scharen/verzamelen; **she was gathering peas; the speaker gathered up his papers; the children gathered round the Christmas tree.**
(*b*) afleiden, opmaken (uit); **I gather you're leaving for Africa tomorrow; did you gather who will be speaking at the ceremony?**
gathers—gathering—gathered—has gathered

gave [geɪv] *zie* **give**

general [ˈdʒenrəl] **1.** *bn*
algemeen; **there was a general feeling of excitement; a general election** = algemene verkiezingen; **in general** = in het algemeen; **in general, the winters are wet and cold.**
2. *zn*
generaal; **General Robinson.**
generally, *bw*
over het algemeen, gewoonlijk; **we generally spend our holidays in Holland.**

generous [ˈdʒenrəs] *bn*
mild, gul; edelmoedig; **she is very generous with her money; that's very generous of you; the firm will give a very generous sum** = royaal.

gentle [ˈdʒentl] *bn*
zacht, vriendelijk; **the doctor has gentle hands; you must be gentle when you are holding a little baby.**
gentle—gentler—gentlest
gentleman, *zn*
(*a*) heer; **well, gentlemen, you may sit down.**

(b) heer, 'gentleman'; **he's a real gentleman.**

geography [ˈdʒɒɡrəfɪ] *zn*
geografie, aardrijkskunde; **geography is my best subject; he got top marks in geography; I've lost my geography book.**
geen meervoud

get [get] *ww*
(a) krijgen; **I got a letter this morning; she will get £10 for cutting the grass; he gets more money than I do.**
(b) komen, arriveren; **we got home late; when will you get to London?**
(c) worden; **he's getting old; she got fat from eating too much; the light got brighter and brighter; this towel's getting dirty.**
(d) (iets) laten (doen); **can you get the garage to fill up my car?; I'll try and get him to bring his car; I must get my shoes mended** = ik moet mijn schoenen laten maken.
(e) **to have got to** = moeten; **you have got to come** = je moet komen; **he left early because he had got to drive a long way; has she got to work all night?**
(f) oplopen, vatten; **I think I'm getting a cold; she's got flu.**
(g) (*bij bijvoeglijke naamwoorden of de verleden tijd van werkwoorden betekent het* doen/maken) **she's getting the dinner ready; I got my work finished in time** = ik heb mijn werk op tijd afgekregen.
gets—getting—got [gɔt]—*has got*

get across, *ww*
(a) oversteken; **they got across the river by boat.**
(b) zijn mening duidelijk maken/iemand iets duidelijk maken; **we managed to get the message across, although no one understood English; I'm trying to get across to him that he has to work harder.**

get along, *ww*
afkunnen, het kunnen stellen; **we seem to get along quite well without any electricity.**

get around, *ww*

zich verplaatsen; de ronde doen; **since she had the accident she gets around on two sticks; the news soon got around that he was married.**

get away, *ww*
ontsnappen, wegkomen; **the burglars got away in a stolen car.**

get back, *ww*
(a) terugkomen; **we got back home very late; when did you get back from holiday?**
(b) terugkrijgen; **he got his book back; I want to get my coat back.**

get down, *ww*
(a) naar beneden/omlaag komen; **she got down off the ladder.**
(b) omlaag/naar beneden halen/brengen; **can you get that box down for me?**

get down to, *ww*
aanpakken; aan de slag gaan; **he will have to get down to work if he wants to pass his exams.**

get dressed, *ww*
zich aankleden; **he got dressed quickly because he didn't want to be late for work; she was getting dressed when the phone rang.**

get in, *ww*
instappen, binnenkomen; **hurry up and get in—the train is waiting to leave; she got in and sat down; the burglars got in through the kitchen window.**

get into, *ww*
gaan/komen/instappen in; **he got into the car and sat down; I was getting into bed when the phone rang; the burglars got into the house through the kitchen window.**
Let op: **get into** *wordt door een zelfstandig naamwoord gevolgd*

get off, *ww*
afstappen/uitstappen; **he got off his bicycle; you must get off the bus at the next stop.**

get on, *ww*
(a) instappen/opstappen; **we got on the bus at the post office; she got on her bike and rode away.**
(b) op leeftijd komen, ouder worden; **he's getting on and is quite deaf.**

get on with, *ww*
(a) kunnen opschieten met; **he gets on**

very well with everyone; I didn't get on with the boss.

(b) doorgaan; **I must get on with my homework.**

get out, *ww*

(a) voor de dag halen; **get your books out of the box; he was getting his car out of the garage.**

(b) wegkomen; uitstappen; **she was getting out of her car; the lorry stopped and the driver got out; the burglars got out through the front door.**

get over, *ww*

ergens overheen komen/raken; **he got over his cold; she never got over her mother's death.**

get through, *ww*

(a) komen door; **the sheep got through the hole in the hedge.**

(b) (*van examen*) halen; **she got through all her exams.**

get up, *ww*

opstaan; **he got up from his chair and walked out of the room; what time did you get up? I was getting up when the phone rang.**

girl [gɜːl] *zn*

meisje; **she's only a little girl; they have three children—two boys and a girl; he met a girl at the bus stop; my sister goes to the girls' school.**

give [gɪv] *ww*

geven; **I gave him a watch for his birthday; give me another apple; she gave him a kiss; you ought to give that book to the teacher.**

gives giving gave [geɪv] has given

give back, *ww*

teruggeven; **give me back my watch/ give me my watch back; he gave back everything he had stolen.**

give in, *ww*

(het) opgeven; toegeven; **we asked him every day if we could go to the cinema, and in the end he gave in.**

give out, *ww*

opraken; uitgaan; **the battery has given out so I can't use my radio.**

give up, *ww*

opgeven; **he's given up smoking; I give up!** = ik geef het op!

glad [glæd] *bn*

blij; **I'm glad to see you; we're glad you came; she was glad to sit down.**

glass [glɑːs] *zn*

(a) glas; van glas; **the doors are made of glass; a glass roof** = glazen dak; **the car has black glass windows.**

geen meervoud: **some glass; a piece of glass**

(b) (drink)glas; **put the glasses on the table; he broke a glass as he was washing up; give him some more milk, his glass is empty.**

(c) glas(vol); **he drinks a glass of milk every evening; two glasses of wine.**

meervoud **glasses** *voor* (b) *en* (c)

glasses, *zn meervoud*

bril; **he has glasses with gold frames; can you see my glasses anywhere?; she was wearing dark glasses** = zonnebril.

glove [glʌv] *zn*

handschoen; **the doctor was wearing rubber gloves; I've bought a new pair of gloves; put your gloves on if you are going to play in the snow.**

glue [gluː] **1.** *zn*

lijm; **you can mend the broken cup with glue; he put some glue on the teacher's chair.**

geen meervoud: **some glue; a tube of glue**

2. *ww*

lijmen; **he glued the handle on to the cup; she's glued the pieces together.**

glues glueing glued has glued

go [gəʊ] *ww*

(a) gaan; lopen; **he has gone to New York; she went from London to Berlin; they all went across the street; he went down the stairs; the car went up the hill; do you go to school by bus? she has gone shopping; we all went for a walk.**

(b) werken, lopen; **my watch won't go; the car is going smoothly; I'm trying to get my motorbike to go** = ik probeer mijn motorfiets aan de gang te krijgen.

(*c*) weggaan; **it's time for us to go.**

(*d*) passen; horen; **this box won't go into the back of the car; this book goes on the top shelf.**

(*e*) worden; **she went pale; he went bright red; the old lady is going deaf.**

goes—going—went [went]—has gone [gɔn]

to be going to, *ww*
op het punt staan; van plan zijn; **that tree is going to fall down; are you going to sing? I am going to read my newspaper; it's going to be fine tomorrow** = het wordt morgen mooi weer.

go away, *ww*
weggaan; **they went away and we never saw them again.**

go back, *ww*
teruggaan/-keren; **he went back home; let's all go back to the bus stop.**

go on, *ww*
(*a*) doorgaan; **go on, don't stop; he went on singing; go on with your work.**
(*b*) gebeuren; **what has been going on here?**

go without, *ww*
het stellen/doen zonder; **he got up late and had to go without breakfast; we haven't enough money so we'll have to go without a holiday this year.**

goal [gəʊl] *zn*
(*a*) (*van sport*) doel.
(*b*) doelpunt, goal; **he scored a goal; our team scored six goals.**
goalkeeper, *zn*
doelverdediger/keeper.

God [gɒd] *zn*
God.

gold [gəʊld] *zn*
goud; van goud; gouden; **a gold chain; she has a gold ring on her left hand; that ring isn't made of gold; gold is worth more than silver.**
geen meervoud: some gold; a piece of gold

golden, *bn*
gouden; gulden; **her golden hair; golden wedding** = gouden bruiloft.
goldfish, *zn*
goudvis; **he has two goldfish in a glass bowl.**
geen meervoud: one goldfish; three goldfish

good [gʊd] *bn*
(*a*) goed; **we had a good meal; did you have a good time at the party?** = heb je je geamuseerd op het feest?
(*b*) handig; **he's good at making things out of wood; she's good with her hands.**
(*c*) zoet, braaf; **be a good girl and I'll give you a sweet.**
(*d*) **a good deal of/a good many** = heel wat; **he made a good deal of money; a good many people know her.**
for good = voorgoed; **he left the town for good.**
no good = waardeloos; **this radio's no good.**
good—better ['betə]—best [best]

goodbye, *zn & interj*
da-ag; tot ziens; **Goodbye! we'll see you again next week; say goodbye to Aunt Anne** = zeg tante Anne eens gedag.
good-looking, *bn*
aantrekkelijk; knap; **she's a good-looking girl; he's very good-looking.**
good morning/good afternoon/ good evening, *interj*
goedemorgen; goedemiddag; goedenavond; **good morning, Mrs Smith; I must say good afternoon to Aunt Jane.**
goodnight, *interj*
goedenacht, welterusten; **goodnight! sleep well!**
goods, *zn meervoud*
goederen; artikelen; koopwaar; **the goods will be on sale tomorrow; the shop sells goods from various countries.**

got [gɒt] *zie* get

govern ['gʌvn] *ww*
regeren; **the country is governed by a group of army officers.**
governs—governing— governed—has governed

government ['gʌvnmənt] *zn*
regering; **the Prime Minister is head of the government; a military government; government employees are asking for more money.**

gradually ['grædʒʊəlɪ] *bw*
geleidelijk, langzamerhand; **he gradually got better after his operation; the snow gradually melted.**

gram [græm] *zn*
gram; **a thousand grams make one kilogram; I want 500 g.** (*zeg* five hundred grams) **of butter.**
Let op: met cijfers wordt **gram** *meestal als* **g** *geschreven*

grand [grænd] *bn*
(*a*) groots; **a grand entrance; grand piano** = vleugel.
(*b*) uitstekend, voortreffelijk; **that's a grand idea; it's a grand day for a picnic.**
grand—grander—grandest

grandchild, *zn*
kleinkind; **old Mr and Mrs Smith have one son and three grandchildren.**
meervoud **grandchildren**

granddaughter, *zn*
kleindochter; **old Mr and Mrs Smith have only girls in their family—they have a daughter and three granddaughters.**

grandfather, *zn*
grootvader, opa; **both my father's father and my mother's father are still alive, so I have two grandfathers; grandfather clock** = staande klok.
Let op: wordt vaak **grandad** *of* **grandpa** *genoemd*

grandmother, *zn*
grootmoeder, oma; **both my grandmothers are still alive.**
Let op: wordt vaak **granny** *of* **grandma** *genoemd*

grandparents, *zn meervoud*
grootouders; **my wife's grandparents are staying with us.**

grandson, *zn*
kleinzoon; **old Mr and Mrs Smith have three grandsons.**

grape [greɪp] *zn*
druif; **have another grape; what a beautiful bunch of grapes!**

grapefruit ['greɪpfruːt] *zn*
grapefruit; **we had grapefruit for breakfast; a jar of grapefruit marmalade.**
geen meervoud: **one grapefruit, two grapefruit**

grass [grɑːs] *zn*
gras; **the grass is getting too long; keep off the grass! we'll sit on the grass and have our picnic.**
geen meervoud

grateful ['greɪtfʊl] *bn*
dankbaar; **she was grateful for all the help she received.**

grave [greɪv] *zn*
graf; **his grave is covered with flowers.**

gray [greɪ] *bn*
(*Amerikaans voor* **grey**) grijs.

grease [griːs] **1.** *zn*
vet, smeer; **have you put any grease on your back wheel?**
2. *ww*
(be)smeren, invetten, oliën; **he was greasing the engine.**
greases—greasing—greased—has greased

greasy, *bn*
vet(tig); vuil; **don't wipe your greasy hands on your shirt.**
greasy—greasier—greasiest

great [greɪt] *bn*
(*a*) groot; **he was carrying a great pile of books; she's eating a great big sandwich; a great deal of** = een heleboel; **there's a great deal of work to do.**
(*b*) belangrijk, voornaam; groot; **London is a great city; Picasso was a great artist.**
great—greater—greatest

Great Britain, *zn*
Groot-Brittannië; **he came to live in Great Britain ten years ago.**
greatly, *bw*
enorm, zeer; **we greatly enjoyed the party.**

greedy ['griːdɪ] *bn*
gulzig; hebzuchtig; **don't be greedy—leave some for the others.**
greedy—greedier—greediest

green [griːn] *bn & zn*
groen; **her coat is bright green; I have painted the door dark green; he was dressed all in green; have you any paint**

greet   **guard**

of a lighter green than this? you can go
ahead—the traffic lights are green.

greengrocer, *zn*
groentehandelaar/-man/-boer; the greengrocer's = de groenteboer/-man; **can
you go to the greengrocer's and buy some
potatoes? I buy all my fruit at the greengrocer's in the High Street.**

greet [gri:t] *ww*
(be)groeten; **he greeted his mother as she
got off the bus.**

greets—greeting—greeted—has
greeted

greetings, *zn meervoud*
groeten; beste wensen; **to send someone
birthday greetings.**

grew [gru:] *zie* **grow**

grey [greɪ] *bn & zn* (*Amer.* **gray**)
grijs; **his hair is quite grey; a grey-
haired man; she was dressed all in grey;
the clouds are grey—I think it is going
to rain; he was wearing dark grey
trousers**

grey—greyer—greyest

grocer [ˈgrəʊsə] *zn*
kruidenier; **the grocer's** = de kruidenier; **can you go to the grocer's and get
me a tin of beans? we buy our tea at the
grocer's in the High Street.**

groceries, *zn meervoud*
kruidenierswaren; **my bag is full of groceries.**

ground [graʊnd] *zn*
(*a*) grond, aarde; **you must dig the
ground in the winter.**
(*b*) grond; **the house was burnt to the
ground; it has been so dry that the ground
is hard; let's sit on the ground to have
our picnic; he lay down on the ground
and went to sleep.**
(*c*) terrein; **football ground/cricket
ground.**

ground floor, *zn*
begane grond, parterre; **the clothes
department is on the ground floor; he
lives in a ground floor flat.**

Let op: Amerikanen noemen de
ground floor *de* first floor

grounds, *zn meervoud*
(*a*) terrein, gronden; **they had a party in
the grounds of the castle.**
(*b*) gronden, redenen; **what grounds have
you got for saying that he should have
more money?**

group [gru:p] *zn*
(*a*) groep; **a group of policemen waited
at the corner of the street; let's meet at
that group of trees over there.**
(*b*) groep(ering); **blood group** = bloed-
groep; **age group** = leeftijdsgroep.
(*c*) (muziek)groep.

grow [grəʊ] *ww*
(*a*) groeien; **these trees grow very tall;
cabbages grow well in our garden.**
(*b*) verbouwen, kweken; **we are growing
cabbages; farmers grow grass to feed
their cows.**
(*c*) groeien; **your son has grown since I
last saw him; the population is growing
very fast.**
(*d*) worden; **it's growing colder at nights
now; he grew richer all the time.**

grows—growing—grew [gru:]—
has grown

grown-up, *zn & bn*
volwassen(e); **there are three grown-ups
and ten children.**

grow up, *ww*
opgroeien; **what do you want to do when
you grow up/when you've grown up?** =
wat word je als je groot bent?

growth, *zn*
groei; **the growth of the population since
1960** = bevolkingsgroei/bevolkings-
aanwas.

guard [gɑ:d] **1.** *zn*
(*a*) wacht, bewaker; **armed guards were
at the door of the bank.**
(*b*) bewaking, wacht; **he is on guard** =
op z'n hoede; hij staat op wacht; **to be
caught off guard** = overrompeld
worden.
(*c*) conducteur.
2. *ww*
bewaken, beschermen; **the soldiers were
guarding the castle.**

guards—guarding—guarded—has
guarded

guess [ges] 1. *ww*
(*a*) raden, gissen; **guess who is coming to see us; can you guess what we are having for dinner? he guessed right** = hij heeft juist/goed geraden.
(*b*) veronderstellen; **I guess it's my turn to do the washing up.**
guesses—guessing—guessed—has guessed

2. *zn*
gissing; **do you know who is coming to see us?—I'll give you three guesses** = je mag drie keer raden; **I don't know if the answer is right—I only made a guess.**
meervoud **guesses**

guest [gest] *zn*
gast(e); **all the guests in the hotel had to leave because of the fire.**

guide [gaɪd] 1. *zn*
gids; **I'll act as your guide to London; read this guide to doing repairs in the house.**
2. *ww*
gidsen, rondleiden; **he guided his visitors** round the town; **guided tour** = rondleiding.
guides—guiding—guided—has guided

guide book, *zn*
reisgids; **a guide book to London.**
guide dog, *zn*
blindegeleidehond.

guilty [ˈgɪltɪ] *bn*
schuldig; **the judge decided he was guilty of murder.**
guilty—guiltier—guiltiest

guitar [gɪˈtɑː] *zn*
gitaar; **he likes to play the guitar; Spanish guitar music.**

gum [gʌm] *zn*
(*a*) kauwgom.
(*b*) gom.

gun [gʌn] *zn*
geweer; revolver; **the policeman pulled out his gun; she took his gun and shot him dead.**

gym [dʒɪm] *zn*
gymnastiekzaal; **we are going to watch a tennis game in the school gym.**

Hh

habit [ˈhæbɪt] *zn*
gewoonte; **he got into the habit of swimming every day before breakfast; she's got out of the habit of taking any exercise** = ze is niet meer gewend om; **from force of habit** = (uit) macht der gewoonte; **I wake up at 6 o'clock from force of habit.**

had [hæd] *zie* **have**

hair [heə] *zn*
(*a*) haar; **the dog has left hairs all over the armchair; there's a hair in my soup; you're beginning to get some grey hairs.**
meervoud **hairs**

(*b*) haar, haren; **she's got long black hair; you ought to wash your hair; his hair is too long; he is going to have his hair cut.**
geen meervoud

haircut, *zn*
(haar)knippen; **you need a haircut** = je moet nodig naar de kapper.
hairdresser, *zn*
kapper; **you must go to the hairdresser's before the party; I met her at the hairdresser's.**

hairy, *bn*
harig, behaard; **a hairy dog; he's got hairy arms.**
hairy—hairier—hairiest

half [hɑːf] **1.** *zn*
helft; **he cut the apple in half** = in tweeën, doormidden; **half the apple fell on the floor** de halve appel; **our team scored a goal in the first half; half of six is three.**

meervoud **halves** [hɑːvz]

2. *bn*
half; **half an apple; two and a half hours; I only want half a cup of coffee.**

3. *bw*
half; **the work is only half finished; this book is half as big/half as thick as that one** = maar half zo groot/dik; **but this book is half as big again** = anderhalf keer zo groot.

half past = 30 minuten over het hele uur; **come and see me at half past six (6.30).**

half term, *zn*
crocusvakantie/herfstvakantie; **we went away for a few days at half term.**

hall [hɔːl] *zn*
(*a*) vestibule; hal; gang; **don't stand in the hall, come into the dining room; I've left my umbrella in the hall.**
(*b*) zaal; **we all eat in the school hall; concert hall** = concertgebouw; **town hall** = stadhuis.

hallo [həˈləʊ] *interj* (*Amer.* **hi**)
hallo, da-ag; **hallo, John, I'm glad to see you; he called hallo from the other side of the street**

ook gespeld **hello, hullo**

ham [hæm] *zn*
ham; **he had a ham salad; can I have two ham sandwiches, please? would you like another slice of ham?**

geen meervoud: some ham; a slice of ham

hammer [ˈhæmə] *zn*
hamer; **he hit his thumb with the hammer.**

hand [hænd] **1.** *zn*
(*a*) hand; **he had a cup in each hand; to shake hands** = de hand schudden; **he shook hands with me; can you lend a hand?** = kun je me een handje helpen? **give me a hand with the washing up** =

help eens mee etc; **the car has changed hands** = de auto heeft een nieuwe eigenaar; **they walked along hand in hand.**
(*b*) wijzer; **the hour hand/the minute hand.**
by hand = met de hand; **he made the table by hand.**

2. *ww*
aanreiken, overhandigen; **can you hand me that book? he handed me all his money.**

hands—handing—handed—has handed

handbag, *zn*
(hand)tas

handful, *zn*
handvol; **he gave me a handful of pound notes; only a handful of people came** = handjevol.

handkerchief [ˈhæŋkətʃiːf] *zn*
zakdoek; **he blew his nose into his handkerchief; have you got a handkerchief, my glasses are dirty?**

handmade, *bn*
handwerk, met de hand gemaakt; **a handmade table; a box of handmade chocolates.**

handle [ˈhændl] **1.** *zn*
handvat, knop, kruk, oor; **he turned the door handle; she broke the handle off the cup; the handle of my suitcase is broken.**

2. *ww*
(*a*) hanteren; aanraken; **don't handle the fruit, please.**
(*b*) ofhandelen/behandelen; **do you think she can handle all the work in the department?**

handles—handling—handled—has handled

handlebars, *zn meervoud*
(fiets)stuur; **hold on to the handlebars.**

handsome [ˈhænsəm] *bn*
aantrekkelijk, knap; **a handsome young man.**

Let op: wordt meestal alleen voor mannen gebruikt, niet voor vrouwen of kinderen

handwriting [ˈhændraɪtɪŋ] *zn*
handschrift; **his handwriting is very difficult to read;** *zie ook* **writing.**

handy ['hændɪ] *bn*
nuttig, handig; **a handy hammer; keep
the salt handy when you are cooking; the
shops are handy; these scissors will come
in handy** = deze schaar zal van pas
komen.
handy—handier—handiest

hang [hæŋ] *ww*
(op)hangen; **hang your coat on the hook;
I like that picture hanging over the fireplace; she hung the photograph over her
bed; he's hanging the lights on the
Christmas tree.**
hangs—hanging—hung ['hʌŋ]—
has hung

hang on, *ww*
wachten; **hang on a moment please.**

happen ['hæpn] *ww*
(*a*) gebeuren; **the accident happened
at the corner of the street; how did it
happen? something has happened to
make the train late; she's late—something must have happened; what's
happened to his brother?** = wat is er van
z'n broer geworden?
(*b*) toevallig (zijn/hebben etc.); **I
happened to be there when the fire
started; the house happened to be empty;
we happened to meet him at the pub** =
we troffen hem toevallig in het café; **do
you happen to have a map of London?** =
heb je soms een kaart van Londen?
happens—happening—
happened—has happened

happy ['hæpɪ] *bn*
blij, gelukkig; **I'm happy to say we're
going to have a holiday; we're so happy
to hear that you are better; she's not
very happy in her job; are you happy
with the plans for the new school?
Happy Birthday/Happy Christmas/
Happy New Year** = Welgefeliciteerd/
gelukkig Kerstfeest/Nieuwjaar; **many
Happy Returns of the Day** = en nog
vele jaren!
happy—happier—happiest

happily, *bw*
vrolijk, blij; gelukkig; **the children played
happily for hours.**

harbour ['hɑːbə] *zn* (*Amer.* **harbor**)
haven; **the sailing boats are all in the
harbour; the ships tried to reach the
harbour in the storm.**

hard [hɑːd] **1.** *bn*
(*a*) hard; **this bed is too hard; the cake is
so hard I can't bite it.**
(*b*) moeilijk, zwaar; **today's crossword is
too hard—I can't finish it; if the exam is
too hard, nobody will pass; he's hard of
hearing** = hardhorend.
(*c*) **a hard winter** = streng.
hard—harder—hardest
2. *bw*
hard, hevig; **hit the nail hard with the
hammer; it's snowing hard; if we all work
hard, we'll earn a lot of money.**

hardly, *bw*
nauwelijks; **I hardly know her; it hardly
ever rains in the desert** = bijna nooit;
hardly anyone came to the meeting =
bijna niemand.

hard up, *bn*
platzak, blut; **I'm rather hard up at the
moment so I can't lend you any money.**

harm [hɑːm] **1.** *zn*
schade, kwaad; **walking to work every
day won't do you any harm; I hope my
guitar won't come to any harm if I leave
it on the chair** = ik hoop dat er niets
met mijn gitaar gebeurt etc; **there's no
harm in phoning him** = hem bellen kan
geen kwaad.
2. *ww*
kwaad doen, schaden; **the dog won't
harm you; walking to work every day
won't harm you.**
harms—harming—harmed—has
harmed

harmful, *bn*
schadelijk; **bright light can be harmful to
your eyes.**

harmless, *bn*
onschadelijk; **the dog is old—he's quite
harmless.**

hat [hæt] *zn*
hoed; **take your hat off when you go into
a church; she put on her new hat; keep it
under your hat!** = houd het geheim!

hate [heɪt] *ww*

haten; **I hate cold eggs; she hates getting up in the morning.**

hates—hating—hated—has hated

have [hæv] *ww*

(a) (*ook* **to have got**) bezitten, hebben; **he has (got) a lot of money; she has (got) a new green car; have you got enough to eat? do you have enough to eat? he has (got) very big muscles.**

(b) hebben/nemen; **have you had any breakfast? I have sugar in my coffee; I'm going to have a bath; we had a long walk** = we hebben een lange wandeling gemaakt.

(c) laten (doen); **he is having his house painted; you ought to have your hair cut.**

(d) (*hulpww van de voltooid tegenwoordige en voltooid verleden tijd*) **he has eaten his breakfast; have you finished your work? she hadn't seen him for two days; if they had asked me I would have said yes.**

Tegenwoordige tijd: **I/you have; he/she/it has; we/you/they have having—had—has had**

Ontkennend: **I haven't**, *etc.;* **he hasn't**, *etc.*

Let op: de afgekorte vormen worden alleen gebruikt samen met **got** *en om de voltooid tegenwoordige en voltooid verleden tijd van werkwoorden te vormen:* **I've; you've; he's; she's; it's; we've; they've**

have got, *ww*

(a) bezitten, hebben; **he's got a lot of money; she has got a new green car; have you got enough to eat? he's got very big muscles.**

(b) moeten; **you've got to do what the doctor says; have they got to get up early tomorrow? have you got to go so soon?**

have (got) to do with, *ww*

aangaan; te maken hebben met; betreffen; **that's got nothing to do with you.**

have to, *hulpww*

moeten; **you have to do what the policeman says; in England you have to drive on the left; I had to walk to work because I missed the bus; do you have to go so soon?**

he [hiː] *vnw*

hij; **he's my father; he and I went there together; I'm angry with John—he's eaten all the chocolates; don't be frightened of the dog—he won't hurt you.**

Let op: als lijdend voorwerp gebruikt, wordt **he him: he hit the ball/the ball hit him;** *na het werkwoord* **be,** *wordt meestal* **him** *in plaats van* **he** *gebruikt:* **who's that?—it's him, the man who stole my bike!**

head [hed] **1.** *zn*

(a) hoofd; kop; **can you stand on your head? he hit his head on the low branch; she rolled head over heels down the hill** = hals over kop; **he shook his head** = hij schudde zijn hoofd; **she tried to do the sum in her head** = uit haar hoofd.

(b) hoofd; **he stood at the head of the queue; whose name is at the head of the list?** = bovenaan.

(c) hoofd, chef; **he's the head of the sales department; head waiter** = ober, kelner; **head teacher** = schoolhoofd.

(d) (*van geldstuk*) kruis; **let's play heads or tails** = kruis of munt; **heads you win** = als het kruis is winje.

2. *ww*

(a) aanvoeren; bovenaan staan; **his name heads the list.**

(b) koers zetten naar; **they are heading north; he headed for the manager's office.**

heads—heading—headed—has headed

headache [ˈhedeɪk] *zn*

hoofdpijn; **I must lie down—I have a headache; she can't come with us because she's got a headache.**

headlights, *zn meervoud*

koplichten/lampen.

headline, *zn*

(krante)kop; **did you see the headlines about the Prime Minister? the newspaper headline says TAXES TO BE RAISED.**

headmaster, *zn*

schoolhoofd, direkteur.

headmistress, *zn*

schoolhoofd, direktrice

meervoud **headmistresses**

health [helθ] *zn*
gezondheid; **he's in good health; your health/good health!** = proost/op je gezondheid! **health service** = (nationale) gezondheidszorg.
healthy, *bn*
gezond; **being a farmer is a healthy job; this town is the healthiest place in England.**
healthy—healthier—healthiest

heap [hi:p] **1.** *zn*
hoop, stapel; **he brushed the dead leaves into heaps; he threw the papers on to the heap in the middle of the table.**
2. *ww*
(op)stapelen, ophopen; overladen; **he heaped his plate with potatoes; the snow is heaped up by the wall of the house.**
heaps—heaping—heaped—has heaped

hear ['hɪə] *ww*
(*a*) horen; **can you hear footsteps? I can't hear what you're saying because of the noise of the aircraft; I heard her shut the front door; we heard him singing in the bath.**
(*b*) horen, vernemen; **I hear you're going to Denmark on holiday; have you heard that the Prime Minister has died? where did you hear that?—I heard it on the news.**
hears—hearing—heard [hɜːd]—has heard

heart [hɑːt] *zn*
(*a*) hart; **the doctor listened to his heart; he has heart trouble.**
(*b*) hart; centrum; **he lives in the heart of the forest; she has a house in the heart of the city.**
(*c*) **he learnt the whole book by heart** = uit het hoofd, van buiten; **don't take it to heart** = trek het je niet aan; **his heart isn't in it** = het interesseert hem niet; **my heart sank when I heard the news** = het hart zonk mij in de schoenen.
(*d*) (*van kaartspel*) harten; **the six of hearts.**
heart attack, *zn*
hartaanval.

hearty, *bn*
hartig, stevig; **she ate a hearty breakfast.**

heat [hi:t] **1.** *zn*
(*a*) hitte; **the heat of the sun made the road melt.**
(*b*) (*van sport*) serie; **there are three heats before the main competition; dead heat** = gelijk eindigende ronde, 'kamp' ronde.
2. *ww*
opwarmen; **heat up the soup while I'm getting the table ready; a heated swimming pool** = verwarmd.
heats—heating—heated—has heated

heater, *zn*
kachel; **water heater** = geiser, boiler; **electric heater** = elektrisch kacheltje.
heating, *zn*
verwarming; **the heating has been switched off; central heating** = centrale verwarming.

heavy ['hevɪ] *bn*
(*a*) zwaar; **this box is so heavy I can hardly lift it.**
(*b*) hevig, zwaar; **heavy rain fell; don't go to bed after you've had a heavy meal; there has been a heavy fall of snow during the night; there was heavy traffic in the centre of town** = druk; **he's making heavy weather of it** = hij neemt het zwaar op.
heavy—heavier—heaviest

heel [hi:l] *zn*
(*a*) hiel; **you've got a hole in the heel of your stocking.**
(*b*) hak; **she wore shoes with very high heels.**

height [haɪt] *zn*
hoogte; **the height of the ceiling is 3 m; what is the height of that mountain?**

held [held] *zie* **hold**

helicopter ['helɪkɒptə] *zn*
helikopter.

hello [hə'ləʊ] *interj.*
hallo, da-ag; **Hello, James, where have**

you been? **say hello to her from me** =
doe haar de groeten van me; **he called
out hello from the other side of the
street.**
ook gespeld **hallo, hullo**

helmet [ˈhelmɪt] *zn*
helm; **if you ride a motorbike you have
to wear a helmet.**

help [help] **1.** *zn*
(*a*) hulp; **he cleaned the car with the help
of a big brush** = met behulp van; **do
you need any help?**
(*b*) (te) hulp; **they went to his help** = zij
gingen hem te hulp; **she was calling for
help.**
2. *ww*
(*a*) helpen; **can you help me with my
homework? I got a friend to help put the
piano into the bedroom; he helped the old
lady across the street.**
(*b*) (*met* **cannot**) iets niet kunnen
helpen; **he couldn't help laughing; he
can't help it if he's deaf.**
(*c*) **help yourself** = zichzelf helpen/
bedienen; **he helped himself to some
pudding; if you want anything to eat just
help yourself.**
3. help! *interj.* = help! **help, help, call a
doctor quickly! help, the brakes aren't
working.**
**helps—helping—helped—has
helped**

helper, *zn*
helper.
helpful, *bn*
behulpzaam; hulpvaardig; nuttig; **he
made a helpful suggestion.**
helpless, *bn*
hulpeloos; machteloos.

hen [hen] *zn*
kip, hen; **the hen has laid an egg.**

her [hɜː] **1.** *vnw*
haar; **have you seen her? tell her to go
away; that's her in the white dress;
there's a letter for her.**
2. *bn*
haar, d'r; **she had lost all her money; have
you seen her brother? the cat won't eat**

her food; **Germany is helping her industry
to sell more goods abroad.**
hers, *vnw*
het hare, van haar; haar; **this book is
hers, not mine; she introduced me to a
friend of hers** = één van haar vrienden.
herself, *vnw*
zichzelf/haarzelf; zelf; **the cat was
washing herself; she is all by herself** =
ze is helemaal alleen; **she did it all by
herself** = helemaal zelf; **she wrote to me
herself; the nurse is ill herself; did your
mother enjoy herself?**

here [ˈhɪə] *bw*
hier; **I put the book down here next to
my cup; we have been living here in
London for twenty years; can you come
here, please? they brought the money
here; here's the newspaper; here comes
Frank; here you are** = alstublieft (*bij
het overhandigen van iets*).
Let op: in een met **here** *beginnende
zin komt het onderwerp ná het werkwoord als het een zelfstandig naamwoord is; en ervóór in het geval van
een voornaam woord:* **here comes
the bus/here it comes**

hesitate [ˈhezɪteɪt] *ww*
aarzelen; **I'm hesitating about what to do
next; he hesitated for a few seconds, then
went into the shop.**
**hesitates—hesitating—
hesitated—has hesitated**

hesitation, *zn*
aarzeling; **after a few minutes' hesitation
he went into the shop.**

hi [haɪ] *Amer. interj.*
hallo; **hi John, did you have a good day?**

hide [haɪd] *ww*
(*a*) verbergen, verstoppen; **he hid the
gold coins under the bed; someone has
hidden the key to the school.**
(*b*) zich verstoppen/verbergen/ver-
schuilen; **he's hiding from the police; they
hid behind the door.**
hides—hiding—hid [hɪd]—**has
hidden** [ˈhɪdn]

high [haɪ] **1.** *bn*
(*a*) hoog; **the office building is 60 m high;**

which is the highest mountain in the world? the living room has a high ceiling.
(b) (van getallen) hoog, groot; the car goes well at high speeds; prices seem to be higher every year; glass will melt at very high temperatures.
Let op: high wordt ook met cijfers gebruikt: the mountain is 700 metres high
2. bw
hoog, in de lucht; the balloon flew high up into the sky; aircraft fly high to avoid storms; the bird went up higher and higher.
high—higher—highest
highly, bw
he thinks highly of her = hij heeft een hoge dunk van haar.
High School, zn
Amerikaanse middelbare school.
High Street, zn
Hoofdstraat; he has a shop in the High Street; go down the High Street until you come to the traffic lights.
Let op: wordt vaak als High St *geschreven.*

hill [hɪl] zn
heuvel; his house is on top of a hill; if you climb up the hill, you will get a good view.

him [hɪm] vnw
hem; have you seen him lately? tell him to come in; there is a letter for him; that's him over there.
himself, vnw
zichzelf/hemzelf; zelf; he's all by himself = hij is helemaal alleen; he did it all by himself = hij deed het helemaal zelf; he wrote to me himself; the doctor is ill himself; did your father enjoy himself? = heeft je vader zich geamuseerd?

hire ['haɪə] ww
(a) huren; he hired a car for his holiday
(b) (ook to hire out) verhuren; a car hire firm = autoverhuurbedrijf.
hires—hiring—hired—has hired

his [hɪz] **1.** bn
zijn, z'n; he's lost all his money; have

you met his mother? our dog wants his food.
2. vnw
van hem, het zijne; this book is his, not mine; he introduced me to a friend of his called Anne.

history ['hɪstrɪ] zn
geschiedenis; he is writing a history of the First World War; she's reading a history book; I got best marks in History.
geen meervoud

hit [hɪt] ww
raken; slaan, stoten; the car hit the lamppost and knocked it down; she was hitting her husband with a bottle; he hit the ball so hard, that we can't find it; I hit my head on the door.
hits—hitting—hit—has hit

hobby ['hɒbɪ] zn
hobby, liefhebberij; his hobby is collecting stamps; do you have any hobbies?
meervoud hobbies

hold [həʊld] ww
(a) (vast)houden; zich vasthouden; he was holding a gun in his right hand; she held the knife between her teeth; hold tight—the ship is moving fast.
(b) (kunnen) bevatten; this bottle holds two litres; will the car hold six people? = is er in de auto plaats voor zes mensen? the box isn't big enough to hold all the potatoes.
(c) houden; we held the meeting in the Town Hall; we are holding the flower show next week.
(d) aanhouden; will the fine weather hold until next week?
holds—holding—held [held]—has held

holder, zn
houder; etui; he put the pen back into its holder.
hold on, ww
(a) (zich) stevig vasthouden; hold on to the handle; hold on, we're turning.
(b) wachten; hold on a moment; you want to speak to Mr Smith—hold on, I'll find him for you.

hold up, *ww*
(a) ophouden, rechtop houden; in de lucht steken; **he held up his hand; the tent is held up by four posts.**
(b) ophouden, vertragen; **we were held up in a traffic jam; the train was held up by the snow.**
(c) overvallen; **three men held up the bank.**
Let op: the accident held the traffic up *of* held up the traffic *maar alleen* the accident held us up

hold-up, *zn*
(a) oponthoud; **the accident caused a hold-up on the motorway.**
(b) (roof)overval; **two people were injured in the bank hold-up.**

hole [həʊl] *zn*
gat; hol; **the boys looked through the hole in the fence; I've got a hole in my sock; the rabbit ran down its hole; you must try to pull the piece of wool through the hole in the needle** = oog.

holiday ['hɒlɪdeɪ] *zn* (*Amer.* **vacation**)
vakantie; **we always spend our holidays by the sea; how many days' holiday do you have each year? teachers can rest during the school holidays; Mr Brown isn't in the office—he's on holiday; when do you go on holiday?**
Let op: wordt meestal zonder **the** *gebruikt.*

Holland ['hɒlənd] *zn*
Holland; **we went to Holland on holiday; my sister lives in Holland; many people from Holland come to spend their holidays in England.**

home [həʊm] **1.** *zn*
(a) huis; thuis; woning; **are you going to be at home tomorrow? our home is the house at the corner of the street; she's staying at home instead of going to work; when do you leave home in the morning?** = van huis gaan; **make yourself at home!** = doe, alsof je thuis bent!
(b) tehuis; **an old people's home** = bejaardentehuis; **a children's home** = kindertehuis.
(c) (*van sport*) **at home** = thuiswed-

strijd; **our team is playing at home next Saturday.**
2. *bw*
naar huis; thuis; **I'm going home; I usually get home at 7 o'clock; I'll take it home with me; she can take the bus home.**
Let op: wordt zonder voorzetsel gebruikt: **he went home; she's coming home,** *etc.*

homemade, *bn*
eigengemaakt; **a pot of homemade jam.**
homesick, *bn*
to be homesick = heimwee hebben.
homework, *zn*
huiswerk; **have you done your maths homework? I haven't got any homework, so I can watch TV.**
geen meervoud

honest ['ɒnɪst] *bn*
eerlijk.

honey ['hʌnɪ] *zn*
honing; **put some honey on your bread.**
geen meervoud

hook [hʊk] **1.** *zn*
haak(je); (vis)haak; **hang your coat on the hook behind the door; he caught a fish on his hook.**
2. *ww*
haken over/aan etc.; aan de haak slaan; **he hooked his umbrella over the back of the chair; she hooked a huge fish.**
hooks—hooking—hooked—has hooked

hop [hɒp] **1.** *zn*
sprongetje op één voet; hink.
2. *ww*
wippen, springen; hinkelen; **he hopped up and down; the birds were hopping about on the grass.**
hops—hopping—hopped—has hopped

hope [həʊp] *ww*
hopen; **we hope to be back home at 6 o'clock; I had hoped to be there, but in the end I couldn't go; I hope our team wins; she hoped she would soon be able to drive a car; I hope so** = ik hoop van wel; **I hope not** = ik hoop van niet; **will**

you come to the party?—yes, I hope so;
is it going to rain tomorrow?—I hope not!
hopes—hoping—hoped—has
hoped

hopped [hɒpt], **hopping** [ˈhɒpɪŋ] *zie*
hop

horizon [həˈraɪzn] *zn*
horizon; can you see that ship on the
horizon?

horizontal [hɒrɪˈzɒntl] *bn*
horizontaal; a horizontal line.

horn [hɔːn] *zn*
(*a*) hoorn, horen; the cow tried to push
him with its horns.
(*b*) hoorn, claxon; he plays the horn in
an orchestra; sound your horn when you
come to the corner.

horrible [ˈhɒrəbl] *bn*
verschrikkelijk, vreselijk, afschuwelijk; I
had a horrible dream last night; the meal
in the restaurant was horrible; what
horrible weather!

horrid [ˈhɒrɪd] *bn*
afschuwelijk, vreselijk; she's a horrid old
woman; what horrid weather!

horse [hɔːs] *zn*
paard; she goes out on her horse every
morning; some farmers still use horses to
plough the fields.
on horseback = te paard; there
were six policemen on horseback =
bereden politie.

hose [həʊz] *zn*
slang; he was watering his garden with a
hose; the firemen used their hoses to put
out the fire.

hospital [ˈhɒspɪtl] *zn*
ziekenhuis; she's so ill, she has been sent
to hospital; he's been in hospital for
several days; the children's hospital is at
the end of our street.

hot [hɒt] *bn*
heet; the water in my bath is too hot;
what hot weather we're having! it's
usually hot in August; if you're hot, take
your coat off = als je het warm hebt etc.
hot—hotter—hottest

hot dog, *zn*
hotdog; broodje warme worst.

hotel [həʊˈtel] *zn*
hotel; all the rooms in the hotel are
booked; which is the best hotel in the
town? we're staying at the Grand Hotel;
aren't there any hotels near the sea? ask
the hotel manager if he has found your
keys.

hour [ˈaʊə] *zn*
uur; there are 24 hours in the day; he is
paid by the hour = per uur; the hours of
work are from 9 to 5; when is your lunch
hour? = lunchpauze/middagpauze; I'll
be ready in a quarter of an hour/in half
an hour = een kwartier, een half uur; the
car was travelling at over 100 miles an
hour = per uur.
hourly, *bn*
uur-; ieder uur; there's an hourly news
programme.

house [haʊs] *zn*
huis; he has a flat in town and house in
the country; all the houses in our street
look the same; his house has six bedrooms.
Let op: **houses** [ˈhaʊzɪz]

household, *zn & bn*
huishouden; household goods department = afdeling huishoudelijke artikelen.

housework, *zn*
huishoudelijk werk; I have a lot of
housework to do.

how [haʊ] *bw*
(*a*) hoe; how do you make chocolate
biscuits? how can you get to the post
office from here? tell me how fish
breathe.
(*b*) hoe; how big is your car? how long is
the flight to Copenhagen? how often do
you have a holiday? he showed how
strong he was.
(*c*) wat; how hot it is today!
how blue the sky is! how she cried when
she hit her thumb with the hammer!
how are you?/how do you do?
hoe gaat het met u?/ hoe maakt u het?
how do you do, Mrs Jones; hello,

Charles, how are you? the headmaster asked me how I was.

however, *bw*
(*a*) hoe ... ook, toch; **however hard he tried, he couldn't swim; I must buy that old clock, however expensive it is.**
(*b*) echter, evenwel; toch; **I never go out on Saturdays, however this Saturday I'm going to a wedding.**

hullo [həˈləʊ] *interj.*
hallo, da-ag; **Hullo John, I'm glad to see you; say hullo to your mother from me; he called hullo from the other side of the street**
ook gespeld hallo, hello

human [ˈhjuːmən] **1.** *bn*
menselijk; **a human being** = mens.
2. *zn*
mens; **most animals are afraid of humans.**

humour [ˈhjuːmə] *zn* (*Amer.* **humor**)
humor; **he's got no sense of humour** = hij heeft geen gevoel voor humor.

hundred [ˈhʌndrəd] honderd
he's over a hundred (years old); the house was built several hundred years ago; hundreds of people caught the disease = honderden mensen.
Let op: in getallen verandert **hundred** *niet en wordt gevolgd door* **and** *bij het uitspreken:* **491** = four hundred and ninety one; **102** = a hundred and two
Let op: **a hundred and one** (101), **three hundred and six** (306), *etc.,* *maar* **hundred and first** (101st), **three hundred and sixth** (306th), *etc.*

hundredth, 100th *bn & zn*
honderdste; **the clock is correct to one hundredth of a second (100th of a second); tomorrow is grandfather's hundredth birthday.**

hung [hʌŋ] *zie* **hang**

hungry [ˈhʌŋgrɪ] *bn*
hongerig; **I'm hungry** = ik heb honger; **are you hungry? you must be hungry after that long walk** = je zult wel honger

hebben; **I'm not very hungry—I had a big breakfast; hurry up with the dinner—we're getting hungry.**
hungry—hungrier—hungriest

hunt [hʌnt] *ww*
(*a*) jacht maken op; zoeken; **the police are hunting for the people who held up the bank; I've been hunting in all the shops, but I can't find any shoes that fit me.**
(*b*) jagen; **the cat went out hunting mice** = op muizenjacht; **the farmer's sons are hunting rats.**
hunts—hunting—hunted—has hunted

hunter, *zn*
jager.

hurry [ˈhʌrɪ] **1.** *zn*
haast; **he's always in a hurry** = hij heeft altijd haast; **out of the way—we're in a hurry! what's the hurry?** = waarom zo'n haast?
geen meervoud
2. *ww*
(zich) haasten, voortmaken, opschieten; **she hurried along the passage; you'll have to hurry if you want to catch the train; don't hurry—we've got plenty of time; don't hurry me, I'm going as fast as I can.**
hurries—hurrying—hurried—has hurried

hurry up, *ww*
opschieten; laten opschieten; **hurry up—we'll be late; can't you make the waiter hurry up? we'll have to hurry them up if we want them to be there in time.**

hurt [hɜːt] *ww*
(zich) pijn doen; geblesseerd/gewond raken; **he's hurt his hand; she fell down and hurt herself; are you hurt? is he badly hurt? my foot hurts; he was slightly hurt in the crash; two players got hurt in the football game.**
hurts—hurting—hurt—has hurt

husband [ˈhʌzbənd] *zn*
echtgenoot, man; **he's my secretary's husband; I know Mrs Jones, but I have never met her husband.**

hut [hʌt] *zn*
hut(je).

Ii

I [aɪ] *vnw*

ik; he said: 'I can do it', and he did it; he and I are great friends; the manager said I could have a holiday; I told you I was going to be late.

Let op: I wordt me als lijdend voorwerp: I gave it to him/he gave it to me; I hit him/he hit me; als I het werkwoord be volgt, wordt het meestal me: who is it?—it's me!

ice [aɪs] *zn*

(*a*) ijs; when the lake freezes, ice covers the surface; don't try to walk on the ice, it isn't thick enough yet; do you want some more ice in your drink? my hands are like ice = ijskoud.

(*b*) (room)ijs; I'll have an ice for my pudding; two chocolate ices, please.

geen meervoud voor (a): some ice; a lump of ice; ices betekent ice creams

ice cream, *zn*

ijs(je); roomijs; a chocolate ice cream; what sort of ice cream do you want—lemon or coffee? come and help me—I can't carry six ice creams.

icicle, *zn*

ijspegel.

icy, *bn*

ijzig; glad; be careful, the pavements are icy.

icy—icier—iciest

idea [aɪ'dɪə] *zn*

idee; I've had an idea—let's all go swimming; what a good idea! I have an idea that the buses don't run on Sundays = ik heb het idee dat etc.; where's your brother?—I've no idea = ik heb geen (flauw) idee; I had no idea it was so late = ik had geen idee etc.

ideal [aɪ'dɪəl] *bn*

ideaal, perfect; this is an ideal place for a picnic; a small car is ideal for shopping in town.

i.e. ['aɪ'i:]

dat wil zeggen, d.w.z.; you must obey the rules, i.e. don't walk on the grass.

if [ɪf] *vw*

(*a*) als; if it rains, you'll get wet; if I'm free, I'll come for a walk; if you'd told me you were ill, I'd have come to see you; if I won £1000, I'd take a long holiday.

(*b*) of; do you know if the train is going to be late? I wonder if you've ever been to Russia?

(*c*) wanneer, als; if she goes out, she always wears a coat; if he was late, he always used to telephone.

ill [ɪl] *bn*

ziek; eating green apples will make you ill; if you feel ill, you ought to see a doctor; he's not as ill as he was last week.

ill—worse—worst

illness, *zn*

ziekte; his illness makes him very tired; a lot of children stay away from school because of illness.

meervoud illnesses

imagine [ɪ'mædʒɪn] *ww*

zich verbeelden/voorstellen; imagine yourself sitting on the beach in the sun; you can't imagine how difficult it is to get a new telephone; I thought I heard someone shout, but I must have imagined it because there is no one there.

imagines—imagining—imagined—has imagined

imagination [ɪmædʒɪ'neɪʃn] *zn*

verbeelding;   voorstellingsvermogen; fantasie; in his imagination he saw himself sitting on a beach in the sun.

imitate ['ımıteıt] *ww*
imiteren, nadoen; **when he walks he imitates his father; she is very good at imitating the English teacher.**
imitates—imitating—imitated—has imitated

immediate [ı'mi:djət] *bn*
onmiddellijk; dringend; **this letter needs an immediate reply.**
immediately, *bw*
meteen, direct, onmiddellijk; **he became ill immediately after he came back from holiday; she will telephone you immediately (after) she comes home; if the house catches fire, you must call the firemen immediately.**

important [ım'pɔ:tnt] *bn*
belangrijk; **is it important for you to get to London tomorrow? I must go · to London, because I have an important meeting; he has an important job in the government.**

impossible [im'pɒsıbl] *bn*
onmogelijk; **it's impossible to get tickets for the concert; it was impossible to get the car out of the garage because of the snow; driving to London is impossible because of the traffic.**

impress [ım'pres] *ww*
imponeren, indruk maken; **I'm very impressed by your work** = ik ben zeer onder de indruk van je werk; **she isn't very impressed by the new maths teacher.**
impresses—impressing—impressed—has impressed

improve [ım'pru:v] *ww*
verbeteren; vooruitgaan; **he has improved the look of his house by painting it white; he was very ill, but he is improving now; I scored two—can you improve on that?** = kun jij dat beter doen?
improves—improving—improved—has improved

improvement, *zn*
verbetering, vooruitgang; **there is no improvement in his work.**

in [ın] *vz & bw*
(*a*) (*van plaats*) in; **they live in Japan; in**

Russia it can be very cold during the winter; he's in the bathroom; she's in bed; why are you sitting outside in the snow? is your mother in? = thuis; **the train isn't in yet** = de trein is nog niet.
(*b*) (*van tijd*) in; **in autumn the leaves fall off the trees; in the evening we sit and watch TV** = 's avonds; **he was born in 1963; I will be back home in January; she should be here in half an hour; he finished the crossword in 20 minutes.**
(*c*) (*van staat*) in; **she was dressed in white; he ran outside in his pyjamas; she's in a hurry** = ze heeft haast; **the dictionary is in alphabetical order.**
in for, *bw*
I think we're in for some rain = ik denk dat we regen kunnen verwachten; **he's in for a nasty shock** = hem staat een flinke schok te wachten.
in on, *bw*
op de hoogte; van de partij; **is he in on the secret?**

inch [ıntʃ] *zn*
inch (= 2.54 cm); **the table is 18 inches (18″) across; she is 5 foot 6 inches tall (5′6″)** (*zeg* 'she's five foot six').
meervoud **inches**
Let op: met cijfers wordt **inch** *vaak als* ″ *geschreven:* $7\frac{1}{2}″$ = seven and a half inches

include [ın'klu:d] *ww*
meerekenen; **did you include your mother in the people you have asked to the party? there were ten of us, if you include the children; I will be on holiday up to and including next Tuesday; every one had a good time, including the grown-ups** = inbegrepen.
includes—including—included—has included

income ['ıŋkʌm] *zn*
inkomen; **his income isn't enough to pay the rent.**

increase 1. *zn* ['ınkri:s]
toename, stijging; **an increase in the price of petrol; he asked for an increase** = (salaris) verhoging
2. *ww* [ın'kri:s]
toenemen, vermeerderen, stijgen,

omhoog gaan; **the price of petrol has
increased twice this year; his salary was
increased by 10 per cent.**
**increases—increasing—
increased—has increased**

indeed [ɪnˈdiːd] *bw*
(*a*) werkelijk; **thank you very much
indeed for your letter** = heel hartelijk;
**she is very kind indeed to have given you
so much money.**
(*b*) inderdaad, in feite; **he is poor—
indeed he has no money at all.**

independent [ɪndɪˈpendənt] *bn*
onafhankelijk; **she's a very independent
girl; the country became independent on
January 1st; an independent member of
parliament.**

indoors [ɪnˈdɔːz] *bw*
(naar) binnen; **you ought to stay
indoors until your cold is better; they
were playing tennis, but when it started
to rain they went indoors.**
indoor [ˈɪndɔː] *bn*
binnen; **the room's full of indoor plants**
= kamerplanten; **there's an indoor
swimming pool in the town, so we can
swim even in winter** = overdekt zwembad.

industry [ˈɪndəstrɪ] *zn*
industrie; **the car industry; heavy industry** = zware industrie; **light industry** =
lichte industrie.
meervoud **industries**

industrial [ɪnˈdʌstrɪəl] *bn*
industrie-, industrieel; **an industrial
town** = industriestad.

infectious [ɪnˈfekʃəs] *bn*
besmettelijk; **mumps and measles are
common infectious diseases; he is covered
with red spots—is it infectious?**

influence [ˈɪnflʊəns] **1.** *zn*
invloed; **the moon has an influence on
the tide; the headmaster has no influence
over the teachers in the school.**
2. *ww*
beïnvloeden; invloed hebben op; **the
crops have been influenced by the bad
weather; the government has tried to influence the voters; I liked the film—I**
wasn't influenced by what the papers said
about it.**
**influences—influencing—
influenced—has influenced**

inform [ɪnˈfɔːm] *ww*
berichten, mededelen; inlichten; **have
you informed the police that your car has
been stolen? I must inform you that you
will be arrested.**
**informs—informing—informed
—has informed**

information [ɪnfəˈmeɪʃn] *zn*
informatie, inlichting(en); **have you any
information about holidays in Greece?
the police won't give me any information
about how the accident happened; could
you send me some more information
about the job; you haven't given me
enough information about your stolen
car; that's a very useful piece/ bit of information**
geen meervoud: **some information;
a piece of information**

injure [ˈɪndʒə] *ww*
verwonden; gewond raken; **six people
were injured in the accident.**
**injures—injuring—injured—has
injured**

ink [ɪŋk] *zn*
inkt; **he wrote his name in red ink; my
pen's dry—have you any blue ink? she
dropped a bottle of ink on the floor.**

inquire [ɪŋˈkwaɪə] *ww*
informeren; **have you inquired at the
police station about your lost cat? she
inquired about the weather in Spain.**
**inquires—inquiring—inquired—
has inquired**
Let op: wordt ook gespeld **enquire**

inquiry, *zn*
navraag, onderzoek; **she is making inquiries about her cat which is missing** =
ze is inlichtingen aan het inwinnen etc.;
**he wrote in answer to my inquiry about
holidays in Greece.**
meervoud **inquiries**
Let op: wordt ook gespeld **enquiry**

insect [ˈɪnsekt] *zn*
insekt; **flies and butterflies are insects but**

spiders aren't; lots of insects were flying round the lamp.

inside [ɪnˈsaɪd] **1.** *bw*
(naar) binnen; **come inside**—it's starting to rain; **the weather was so bad that we just sat inside and watched TV; the house is dark inside.**
2. *vz*
in; binnen; **there is nothing inside the box; he was sitting inside his car listening to the radio; I know his house from the outside, but I've never been inside it.**
3. *zn*
binnenkant, binnenste; **I know his house from the outside, but what is the inside like? the inside of this cake is quite hard; he put his pyjamas on inside out** = binnenste buiten; **he knows London inside out** = door en door.

instant [ˈɪnstənt] **1.** *zn*
moment, ogenblik; **come here this instant!** = ogenblikkelijk; **he stopped running for an instant, and then started again.**
2. *bn*
instant coffee = oploskoffie.
instantly, *bw*
onmiddellijk; **all the passengers were killed instantly in the crash** = op slag.

instead (of) [ɪnˈstedəv] *bw*
in plaats van; **he'll go instead of me; instead of talking to the police, he just ran away; instead of playing football, why don't you help me clean the car? would you like an orange instead of that apple? if she can't go, can I go instead?** = in haar plaats; **we haven't any coffee—would you like some tea instead?** = wil je in plaats daarvan thee?

instructions [ɪnˈstrʌkʃnz] *zn meervoud*
(gebruiks)aanwijzing; instructies; **the instructions are written on the bottle of medicine; I can't use this machine because I have lost the book of instructions; she gave the taxi driver instructions how to get to her house.**

instrument [ˈɪnstrəmənt] *zn*
(*a*) instrument; (stuk) gereedschap; **the doctor had a box of instruments; I can't**

test your car—I haven't brought the right instruments.
(*b*) (muziek)instrument; **wind instruments** = blaasinstrumenten; **string instruments** = snaarinstrumenten.

insure [ɪnˈʃʊə] *ww*
verzekeren; **is your car insured? I insured my luggage for £200.**
insures—insuring—insured—has insured

insurance, *zn*
verzekering; **she has an insurance against fire; life insurance** = levensverzekering; **accident insurance** = ongevallenverzekering.

intelligent [ɪnˈtelidʒənt] *bn*
intelligent; knap; **he's the most intelligent boy in the class.**

intend [ɪnˈtend] *ww*
van plan zijn; **they intend to go to Spain for their holidays; she's intending to study English at university.**
intends—intending—intended—has intended

interest [ˈɪntrəst] **1.** *zn*
(*a*) belangstelling, interesse; **he takes a lot of interest in his students; she has no interest in plants; why doesn't he take more interest in what his sister is doing?**
(*b*) interesse; **her main interest is the cinema; do you have any special interests apart from your work?**
(*c*) rente; **if you put your money in the bank you'll get 10% interest on it; this type of bank account pays 10% interest; what's the interest I'll have to pay if I borrow £1000?**
2. *ww*
interesseren; **he's specially interested in the cinema; nothing seems to interest her very much; the film didn't interest me at all.**
interests—interesting—interested—has interested

interesting, *bn*
interessant; **there's an interesting article on fishing in the newspaper; I didn't find the TV programme at all interesting; what's so interesting about old churches?—I find them dull.**

interjection [ɪntə'dʒekʃn] *zn*
uitroep, tussenwerpsel; **'oh!' and 'help!' are interjections.**

international [ɪntə'næʃnl] *bn*
internationaal; **an international agreement; I have to make an international phone call.**

interrupt [ɪntə'rʌpt] *ww*
onderbreken; **I was just starting to tell my story, when I was interrupted by the telephone; he couldn't finish his speech because he was being interrupted all the time; I'm sorry to interrupt, but your wife wants to speak to you on the phone.**
interrupts—interrupting— interrupted—has interrupted
interruption, *zn*
onderbreking; **he couldn't finish his work because of all the interruptions.**

into ['ɪntʊ] *vz*
(*a*) ... binnen, ... in; in, binnen; **he went into the house; she fell into the swimming pool; put the knives back into their box; you can't get 150 people into that bus; when he came into the room we were all talking about him; are you driving into the centre of the town?** = het centrum in.
(*b*) tegen; **the car ran into a tree.**
(*c*) in; **it turned into a butterfly; when does water turn into steam? you ought to change into some clean clothes for the party; she burst into tears** = ze barstte in tranen uit.
(*d*) in; **cut the cake into six pieces; four into three won't go** = op.

introduce [ɪntrə'djuːs] *ww*
voorstellen; **I will introduce you to my sister; can I introduce my new assistant?**
introduces—introducing— introduced—has introduced

invent [ɪn'vent] *ww*
(*a*) uitvinden; bedenken; **he invented a new type of engine; who invented the telephone? he invents new machines.**
(*b*) verzinnen, bedenken; **he invented the whole story.**
invents—inventing—invented— has invented
invention, *zn*

uitvinding; **we have seen his latest invention—a machine for putting fruit into jars.**

invite [ɪn'vaɪt] *ww*
uitnodigen, inviteren; **how many people have you invited to your party? we invited them to come in; don't invite him—he's too rude; he's been invited to speak at the meeting.**
invites—inviting—invited—has invited
invitation [ɪnvɪ'teɪʃn] *zn*
uitnodiging, invitatie; **I've had an invitation to their party; he's had an invitation to speak at the meeting.**

Ireland ['aɪələnd] *zn*
Ierland; **we're going to Ireland for our holidays; they live in Ireland.**
Northern Ireland *zn*
Noord-Ierland, Ulster.
Irish ['aɪrɪʃ] **1.** *bn*
Iers; **he speaks English with an Irish accent; the Prime Minister of the Irish Republic.**
2. *zn*
the Irish = (de) Ieren; **the Irish are good at rugby.**

iron [aɪən] **1.** *zn*
(*a*) ijzer; **the house has an iron roof; this hammer is made of iron.**
geen meervoud: some iron; lumps of iron/pieces of iron
(*b*) strijkijzer/strijkbout; **she has two irons—but only one of them works; if the iron is too hot it will make a brown mark on my shirt.**
2. *ww*
strijken; **he was ironing his shirt when the telephone rang; that shirt doesn't look as though it has been ironed.**
irons—ironing—ironed—has ironed
ironing, *zn*
strijk; **she was doing the ironing** = ze was aan't strijken.

is [ɪz] *zie* **be**

island ['aɪlənd] *zn*
eiland; **he lives on a little island in the**

middle of the river Thames; Australia is really a very large island.

isn't [ɪznt] *zie* **be**

it [ɪt] *vnw*
(a) (*verwijst naar dier of zaak*) hij, zij, hem, haar, het; **he picked up an apple and then dropped it on the ground; I put my hat down somewhere, and now I can't find it; where's my book?—it's on the chair; the dog's hungry—give it something to eat.**
(b) (*algemeen*) het; **it's raining; it's a long way from here to the post office; is it Tuesday today? it's very difficult to get a ticket at this time of year; what time is it?—it's 6 o'clock; it's silly to walk when we've got a car.**
Let op: **it's** = **it is** *of* **it has**

its [ɪts] *bn*
zijn, haar, ervan; **I can't use my bicycle—one of its tyres is flat; that firm pays its staff very badly.**
Let op: je schrijft **its**, *niet* **it's**

itself [ɪt'self] *vnw*
(zich)zelf; zelf; **the house stands all by itself** = helemaal alleen; **the horse seems to have hurt itself; the car started to move all by itself** = vanzelf; **the cat is washing itself; the wires are all right, so there must be something wrong with the TV itself.**

Jj

jacket ['dʒækɪt] *zn*
jasje, colbert; **he took his jacket off because it was hot; he was wearing grey trousers and a blue jacket.**

jam [dʒæm] *zn*
(a) jam; **have some jam on your bread; she made jam out of all the fruit in the garden; open another jar of jam—this one is empty.**
(b) traffic jam = (verkeers)opstopping; file; **the accident caused a big traffic jam; there are jams every Friday evening.**
geen meervoud voor (a): **some jam; a pot of jam**

January ['dʒænjʊərɪ] *zn*
januari; **her birthday is in January; he was born on January 26th; we never go on holiday in January; he went to Canada last January; today is January 6th.**
Let op: **January 6th** *zeg* 'the sixth of January' *of* 'January the sixth'
Let op: **January** *wordt altijd met een hoofdletter geschreven*

jar [dʒɑː] *zn*
pot(je), (stop)fles; **a jar of fruit; put those nuts into that glass jar.**

jaw [dʒɔː] *zn*
kaak; **your teeth are fixed in your jaw; he fell down and broke his jaw.**

jealous ['dʒeləs] *bn*
jaloers; **I'm jealous of him because he gets more money than I do; don't be jealous—he works harder than you do; we're all jealous of his long holidays.**

jeans [dʒiːnz] *zn meervoud*
jeans; **she was wearing jeans and a red pullover; I've bought a new pair of jeans/some new jeans.**
Let op: zeg **a pair of jeans** *om aan te geven dat het om één broek gaat.*

jewel ['dʒuːəl] *zn*
juweel; **she had jewels in her hair.**
jewellery, *zn*
juwelen, sieraden; **a burglar stole all her jewellery.**
geen meervoud

job [dʒɒb] *zn*
(*a*) karwei(tje) werkje; **you've made a good job of mending that table** = je hebt die tafel mooi opgeknapt; **I have a couple of jobs for you to do; have you any little jobs you want doing in the house?**
(*b*) werk, baan; **he's got a job in a car factory; he's finding it difficult to get a job because he can't drive; she's applied for a job as a teacher; he lost his job when the factory closed.**
(*c*) probleem; **I had a job to find your house; what a job!** = dat valt niet mee!
(*d*) **good job** = uitkomst; **it's a good job he can drive** = het komt goed uit dat hij kan rijden.
(*e*) **it's just the job** = dat komt prachtig van pas!

join [dʒɔɪn] *ww*
(*a*) samenvoegen, verbinden; samenkomen. **the two roads join about three kilometres further on; you must join the two wires together.**
(*b*) meegaan/meedoen; lid worden van; **we are going to the theatre tomorrow—why don't you join us? will you join me for a cup of coffee? his daughter is going to join the police** = gaat bij de politie; **he's joined the army** = hij heeft dienst genomen.
joins—joining—joined—has joined

joint [dʒɔɪnt] *zn*
(*a*) gewricht, scharnier; **your elbow is a joint in your arm.**
(*b*) groot stuk vlees, bout; **we have a joint of beef for dinner.**

joke [dʒəʊk] *zn*
grap, mop; **he was cracking jokes all the time; she made jokes about his hat.**

journey ['dʒɜːnɪ] *zn*
reis; **he went on a journey across Russia; he has a difficult journey to work every day.**

judge [dʒʌdʒ] **1.** *zn*
rechter; jurylid; **the judge ordered him to pay a £50 fine; she's the judge in the flower competition; he's one of the judges in the Olympics.**
2. *ww*
(*a*) (be)oordelen; achten; **she's judging the flowers in the flower show.**
(*b*) schatten; **I'm no good at judging distances.**
judges—judging—judged—has judged

jug [dʒʌg] *zn*
kan(netje); **milk jug; a jug of milk.**

juice [dʒuːs] *zn*
(vruchten)sap; **a glass of orange juice; a tin of tomato juice.**
juicy, *bn*
sappig; **a juicy orange.**
juicy—juicier—juiciest

July [dʒuːˈlaɪ] *zn*
juli; **he was born in July; she died last July; we are going to Spain next July; today is July 25th.**
Let op: **July 25th:** *zeg* 'the twenty-fifth of July' *of* 'July the twenty-fifth'
Let op: **July** *wordt altijd met een hoofdletter geschreven.*

jump [dʒʌmp] **1.** *zn*
sprong; **long jump** = verspringen; **high jump** = hoogspringen.
2. *ww*
springen; **he jumped over the wall; can you jump across this stream? jump on to that bus—it's going to leave; she jumped down from the chair** = ze sprong van de stoel af; **when they fired the gun, it made me jump** = het maakte me aan het schrikken, toen ze etc.
to jump the gun = te vroeg starten/handelen.
to jump the queue = voordringen, voor je beurt gaan.
jumps—jumping—jumped—has jumped

June [dʒuːn] *zn*
juni; **he was born in June; her birthday is on June 15th; last June we went to the USA; today is June 7th.**
Let op: **June 7th:** *zeg* 'the seventh of June' *of* 'June the seventh'
Let op: **June** *wordt altijd met een hoofdletter geschreven.*

just [dʒʌst] *bw*
(*a*) precies, juist; net; **it's just by the door; don't come in just yet—we're not ready; just how many of the children can read? she's just sixteen—her birthday was yesterday; what time is it?—it's just six o'clock.**
(*b*) net; **I had just got into my bath when the phone rang; I'm just going to the shops; I was just going to phone her, when she phoned me; they've just arrived from New York; he's just leaving for the office.**
(*c*) enkel; **I've been there just once; wait**

just a minute! = een ogenblikje!
just about = ongeveer, min of meer; **I've just about finished my homework.**
just about to = op het punt; **he's just about to leave; we were just about to go to bed when the phone rang.**
just as (*a*) net . . . toen; **just as I got into the bath the phone rang.**
(*b*) net/precies zo; **this book is just as good as the film; it is just as cold inside the house as it is outside.**
just now = (*a*) momenteel, nu net; **we're very busy just now.**
(*b*) net; **I saw him just now in the bank.**

Kk

keen [ki:n] *bn*
(*a*) fel/gebrand op; iets dolgraag willen; **he's keen to do well at school; I'm not very keen to go to see that film; she's keen on dancing** = zij danst erg graag; **he's keen on football.**
(*b*) scherp; **he has a keen sense of smell.**
keen—keener—keenest

keep [ki:p] *ww*
(*a*) houden; **can I keep the book I borrowed from you? I don't want that paper any more—you can keep it; he's kept my watch and won't give it back.**
(*b*) doorgaan; blijven + *ander werkwoord of bijvoeglijk naamwoord;* **this watch will keep going even under water; he had to keep running so that the police wouldn't catch him; keep quiet or they'll hear you; the weather has kept fine.**
(*c*) (op)houden; **what kept you?** = waar ben je zo lang gebleven? **he kept us waiting for twenty minutes** = laten wachten; **this coat will keep you warm.**
(*d*) **to keep an eye on** = ergens een oogje op houden; **he's keeping an eye on the shop while I'm away.**
keeps—keeping—kept [kept]—has kept

keep off, *ww*
(af)blijven (van); **keep off the grass!**

keep on, *ww*
doorgaan, blijven + *ander werkwoord;* my watch keeps on stopping; the traffic kept on moving although the snow was very deep.

keep up, *ww*
volhouden; in stand houden; onderhouden; **you're doing very well—keep it up! he finds it difficult to keep up his French** = bijblijven met.

keep up with, *ww*
bijhouden; gelijke tred houden met; **he couldn't keep up with a car on his bicycle; wages can't keep up with the cost of food; she walked so fast that I had difficulty in keeping up with her.**

kettle ['ketl] *zn*
ketel; **the kettle's boiling—let's make the tea** = het water kookt etc.

key [ki:] **1.** *zn*
(*a*) sleutel; **I can't get into the house—I've lost the key to the front door; where did you put your car keys?**
(*b*) toets; klep.
(*c*) uitleg, sleutel; **is there a key to explain what these signs mean?**
2. *bn*
sleutel-, essentieel; **he has the key position in the firm; oil is a key industry.**

kick [kɪk] **1.** *zn*
trap, schop; **he gave the ball a kick.**
2. *ww*
schoppen, trappen; **he kicked the ball into the goal.**
kicks—kicking—kicked—has kicked

kill [kɪl] *ww*
doden, laten doodgaan; **the dry weather has killed all my plants; the car hit the dog and killed it; he was killed in a plane crash** = hij kwam om bij een vliegtuigongeluk.
kills—killing—killed—has killed

kilogram ['kɪləgræm], **kilo** ['kiːləʊ] *zn*
kilo(gram); **two kilos of sugar; he weighs 62 kilos (62 kg).**
*Let op: met cijfers wordt **kilos** meestal geschreven **kg***

kilometre [kɪ'lɒmɪtə] *zn* (*Amer.* kilometer)
kilometer; **it is about twenty kilometres (20 km) from here to the railway station; the speed limit is 80 kilometres per hour (80 kmh).**
*Let op: met cijfers wordt **kilometres** meestal geschreven **km**: 26 km; Let ook op: **kilometres per hour** wordt meestal geschreven **kmh**: eighty kilometres per hour = 80 kmh*

kind [kaɪnd] **1.** *zn*
soort/type; **a butterfly is a kind of insect; how many kinds of apples do you have in your garden? we were talking about all kinds of things** = allerlei dingen.
2. *bn*
aardig, vriendelijk; **it's very kind of you to lend me your car; how kind of him to ask you to the party; you always should be kind to animals; she's the kindest old lady I know.**
kind—kinder—kindest

king [kɪŋ] *zn*
koning; **King John; the King and Queen came to visit the town.**
*Let op: **king** wordt met een hoofdletter gespeld als het met een naam gebruikt wordt of naar een bepaalde persoon verwijst.*

kiss [kɪs] **1.** *zn*
kus, zoen; **she gave her mother a kiss.**
meervoud **kisses**
2. *ww*
kussen, zoenen; **they kissed each other goodbye; he kissed his daughter and went away.**
kiss—kissing—kissed—has kissed

kitchen ['kɪtʃn] *zn*
keuken; **don't come into the kitchen with your dirty shoes on; he put the bread down on the kitchen table; the ice cream is in the fridge in the kitchen.**

knee [niː] *zn*
knie; **he was on his knees looking for something under the bed; the baby can go quite fast on his hands and knees** = de baby kan tamelijk snel kruipen; **the little girl sat on her grandfather's knee.**

kneel [niːl] *ww*
knielen; **he kneeled/knelt down to look under the car; she was kneeling by the bed.**
kneels—kneeling—kneeled/ knelt [nelt]**—has kneeled/knelt**

knew [njuː] *zie* **know**

knife [naɪf] *zn*
mes; **to lay the table, you put a knife, fork and spoon for each person; cut your meat up with your knife; bread knife** = broodmes.
meervoud **knives** [naɪvz]

knit [nɪt] *ww*
breien; **she's knitting a pair of socks; he was wearing a red knitted hat; my mother knitted this scarf for me.**
knits—knitting—knitted—has knitted

knock [nɒk] **1.** *zn*
(*a*) klop; **there was a knock at the door.**
(*b*) klap, slag, stoot; **he had a knock on the head.**
2. *ww*
kloppen; slaan, stoten; **he knocked on the door before going in; you need a hammer to knock that nail in.**
knocks—knocking—knocked— has knocked

Kitchen *Keuken*

1.	cooker	*fornuis*	14.	matchbox	*lucifersdoosje*
2.	cup	*kopje*	15.	oven	*oven*
3.	cupboard	*kast(je)*	16.	pan (saucepan)	*(steel)pan*
4.	electric light	*licht, lamp(je)*	17.	plate	*bord*
5.	electric plug	*stekker*	18.	saucer	*schoteltje*
6.	fridge	*koel-/ijskast*	19.	shelf	*plank*
7.	frying pan	*koekepan*	20.	sink	*gootsteen*
8.	glasses	*glazen*	21.	steam	*stoom*
9.	handle	*(deur)knop*	22.	tap	*kraan*
10.	jug	*kan(netje)*	23.	teacloth	*theedoek*
11.	kettle	*ketel*	24.	teapot	*theepot*
12.	kitchen scales	*weegschaal*	25.	tin opener	*blikopener*
13.	lid	*deksel*			

knot

knock down, *ww*
omstoten; afbreken; aanrijden; **they are going to knock down the old church to build a new one; he was knocked down by a car.**
Let op: **they knocked the church down** *of* **they knocked down the church** *maar alleen* **they knocked it down**

knock off, *ww*
(*a*) omstoten, afslaan; **the cat knocked the milk jug off the table.**
(*b*) ophouden met werken; **the workmen all knocked off at 4.30.**

knock out, *ww*
bewusteloos slaan; **he was knocked out by a blow on the head.**

knot [nɒt] *zn*
knoop; **he tied a knot at the end of the piece of string; tie the two ropes together with a knot.**

land

know [nəʊ] *ww*
(*a*) weten; **do you know how to get to London from here? I didn't know she was married; he knew he would have to spend a lot of money; do you know the German for 'one—two—three'? he doesn't know where she has gone; I didn't know when he was going to come.**
(*b*) kennen; **I know your brother—we were at school together; I used to know a man called Johnson; I know Scotland very well.**
knows—knowing—knew [njuː]—**has known**

knowledge [ˈnɒlɪdʒ] *zn*
kennis; **he has no knowledge of what is happening** = hij is niet op de hoogte etc.; **he has a good knowledge of French.**

LI

lack [læk] **1.** *zn*
gebrek, gemis; **the plants are dying through lack of rain; they could not go** on holiday for lack of money = wegens gebrek aan.
2. *ww*
gebrek hebben aan; ontbreken, missen; **the plants lack water; he lacks strength** = hij mist de kracht.
lacks—lacking—lacked—has lacked

ladder [ˈlædə] *zn*
ladder; **he climbed up a ladder to look at the roof; you have to go down a ladder to get into the hole in the ground.**

lady [ˈleɪdɪ] *zn*
dame; **there's a lady waiting to see you; a lady doctor** = een vrouwelijke dokter.
meervoud **ladies**

laid [leɪd] *zie* **lay**

lain [leɪn] *zie* **lie**

lake [leɪk] *zn*
meer; **they went out in a boat on the lake; he swam across the lake.**

lamb [læm] *zn*
(*a*) lam(metje); **we saw hundreds of lambs in the fields.**
(*b*) lamsvlees; **we had roast lamb for dinner.**
Let op: geen meervoud als het vlees betekent: **some lamb; a slice of lamb**

lamp [læmp] *zn*
lamp; **an electric lamp; street lamp** = straatlantaarn
lamppost, *zn*
lantaarnpaal; **the car hit a lamppost and stopped.**

land [lænd] **1.** *zn*
(*a*) land; **I am glad to be on land again after ten days at sea.**
(*b*) land, natie; **people of many lands.**
c) land, grond; **he owns land in Scot-**

land; **I have bought a piece of land to build a house on.**
2. *ww*
landen; **the plane landed at the airport; we will be landing at London Airport in 15 minutes.**

lands—landing—landed—has landed

landing, *zn*
(*a*) landing; **the plane made a good landing.**
(*b*) overloop, trapportaal; **go up the stairs and wait for me on the landing.**

land up, *ww*
terechtkomen; **we set off for London and landed up in Oxford; he tried to steal a car and landed up in prison.**

language ['læŋgwɪdʒ] *zn*
taal; **Swedish is a very difficult language; English is a language which is used everywhere; I don't enjoy holidays in a country where I don't speak or understand the language; Chinese is the language spoken by most people in the world.**

large [lɑːdʒ] *bn*
groot; **he was carrying one large suitcase and two small ones; I want a large cup of coffee, please; how large is your office?**

large—larger—largest

largely, *bw*
grotendeels, hoofdzakelijk; **the country is largely forest.**

last [lɑːst] **1.** *bn*
(*a*) (het)laatste; **they live in the last house on the right; you must pay me by the last day of the month; December 31st is the last day of the year; last but one** = op één na laatste; **they live in the last house but one.**
(*b*) laatst, vorig; **last Monday** = afgelopen maandag; **last week** = afgelopen week; **I saw her last Thursday; where did you go on holiday last year? last month it rained almost every day; she's been ill for the last ten days.**
(*c*) **before last** = voorlaatste; **the Monday before last** = maandag twee weken geleden; **the week before last** = twee weken geleden.
2. *zn*
de/het laatste; **she was the last to arrive;**

that's the last of the apples = nu zijn de appels op.
3. *bw*
(*a*) het laatst; **he came last in the race.**
(*b*) voor het laatst; **when did you see her last? she was looking ill when I saw her last.**
4. *ww*
duren; aanhouden; **the fine weather won't last; our holidays never seem to last very long; the storm lasted all night.**

lasts—lasting—lasted—has lasted

at last/at long last = tenslotte, (uit)eindelijk; **I walked for hours, and got home at last at 6 o'clock; at long last the train arrived.**

lastly, *bw*
tot slot, tenslotte; **lastly I want to thank my friends for their help.**

late [leɪt] **1.** *bn*
(*a*) te laat; **the train is ten minutes late; it's too late to change your ticket; if you don't hurry you'll be late.**
(*b*) laat; **we had tea in the late afternoon; there are always films on the late evening programmes on TV.**
(*c*) laat; **it's late—I'm going to bed.**
(*d*) **latest** = laatste, nieuwste; **the radio gives the latest news at 10.00; have you read his latest book?**

late—later—last/latest

2. *bw*
(*a*) (te)laat; **the train arrived late; we went to bed late last night; she got up late this morning.**
(*b*) later; **he came a month later; can I see you later this afternoon? see you later!** = tot straks!/tot ziens!

late—later—last

lately, *bw*
onlangs, de laatste tijd; **have you seen her lately? he's been quite busy lately.**

laugh [lɑːf] **1.** *zn*
lach; **she's got a lovely laugh; he said it with a laugh; he did it for a laugh** = voor de grap.
2. *ww*
lachen; **they all laughed at his jokes;**

when he fell off his bicycle everyone laughed; don't laugh at him because he's so fat = lach hem niet uit etc.; **you mustn't laugh at her hat.**
laughs—laughing—laughed—has laughed

laundry ['lɔːndrɪ] *zn*
(*a*) wasserij; **you had better send your shirts to the laundry.**
(*b*) was(goed); **have you any laundry to be washed?**
meervoud **laundries**, *maar geen meervoud voor* (*b*)

lavatory ['lævətrɪ] *zn*
W.C., toilet; **the ladies' lavatory is to the right.**
meervoud **lavatories**

law [lɔː] *zn*
wet, recht(en); **you must always obey the law; driving at night without lights is against the law; Parliament has passed a law forbidding the use of dangerous drugs.**
lawyer ['lɔːjə] *zn*
jurist, advocaat; **if you are arrested, you must try to speak to your lawyer.**

lawn [lɔːn] *zn*
gazon; **let's have tea outside on the lawn; the lawn needs cutting; the town hall has a large lawn in front of it.**

lay [leɪ] *ww*
(*a*) leggen; **he laid the book down on the table; they are laying a new carpet in the dining room; the hen has laid an egg.**
(*b*) **to lay the table** = (de) tafel dekken; **the table is laid for four people.**
(*c*) *zie ook* **lie.**
lays—laying—laid—has laid

lay out, *ww*
uitspreiden; **the map was laid out on the table; the presents are laid out under the Christmas tree.**

lazy ['leɪzɪ] *bn*
lui; **he's too lazy to earn a lot of money; she's the laziest girl in the school.**
lazy—lazier—laziest

lb, *zie* **pound**

lead¹ [led] *zn*
(*a*) lood; **you should tie a piece of lead to your fishing line to make it sink.**

(*b*) (potlood)stift; **the lead's broken—I must sharpen the pencil.**
geen meervoud voor (*a*)

lead² [liːd] **1.** *zn*
(*a*) lijn, riem; **dogs must be kept on a lead.**
(*b*) voorsprong, eerste plaats; **he went into the lead; who's in the lead?**
2. *ww*
(*a*) de leiding/een voorsprong hebben, voor liggen; **our team was leading at half time; he is leading by two metres.**
(*b*) leiden; **she led us to the post office; the path leads to the top of the hill.**
(*c*) de leiding hebben, aanvoeren; **he is leading a group of businessmen on a tour of Italian factories.**
(*d*) **to lead to** = leiden tot; **the discussion led to a violent argument.**
leads—leading—led [led]**—has led**

leader, *zn*
leider; **he is the leader of the group.**

lead up to, *ww*
voorafgaan aan; leiden tot; **the events leading up to the war; the discussion led up to an agreement.**

leaf [liːf] *zn*
blad; **in the winter the leaves fall off the trees and grow again in the spring; insects have eaten the leaves of the cabbages.**
meervoud **leaves** [liːvz]; *zie ook* **leave**

lean [liːn] *ww*
leunen; zetten tegen; **lean the ladder against the wall; he leant his elbows on the table; the ladder is leaning up against the wall; don't lean over the edge of the roof; he was leaning out of the window.**
leans—leaning—leaned/leant [lent]**—has leaned/leant**

learn [lɜːn] *ww*
(*a*) leren; **she's learning to swim; we learn English at school; have you learnt how to drive yet?**
(*b*) horen, vernemen; **I learnt that they were leaving; when did you learn that she was getting married?**
learns—learning—learnt/learned—has learnt/learned

learner, *zn*
pupil, leerling; **a learner driver** = aspirant automobilist.

least [li:st] *bw, bn & zn*
(het) minst(e); **that's the least of my problems; it's the thing I worry about least of all; it doesn't matter in the least** = niet in het minst.
at least = tenminste; **even if the job is dull, at least you have enough money to live on.**

leather ['leðə] *zn*
leer; **a leather belt; her jacket is made of leather.**
geen meervoud

leave [li:v] *ww*
(a) weggaan; vertrekken; verlaten; **he left the house; the train leaves at 10.00; when does the train leave for Edinburgh?**
(b) (achter-/aan-/etc.) laten; laten liggen; **she left her toothbrush at home; someone has left the light on; did you leave the door locked?**
(c) overlaten; **leave a piece of cake for your brother.**
(d) left *of* left over = overhebben; **after paying for the meal and the theatre tickets, I've still got £3 left over; if you eat three apples there will be only two left; there is nobody left in the office** = niemand meer.
leaves—leaving—left [left]—has left

leave behind, *ww*
achterlaten, laten liggen; **he left his keys behind in the shop; we had to leave the dog behind at home.**
leave off, *ww*
(a) ophouden met; **he suddenly left off smoking; leave off!** = hou op!
(b) weglaten; **she left the address off the envelope; the waiter left the drinks off the bill.**
leave out, *ww*
nalaten; laten ... uit; **he left out the most important detail when he reported the accident to the police; we left him out of the team because he's got a cold.**
Let op: **don't leave your sister out of** don't leave out your sister *maar alleen* don't leave her out

led [led] *zie* **lead²**

left [left] *bw, bn & zn*
links; linker-; **he can't catch with his left hand; in England, cars drive on the left; his house is on the left side of the street** = aan de linkerkant; **go down the street and turn left at the traffic lights** = en ga linksom/sla linksaf etc; **keep going left if you want to get to the beach** = links aanhouden; *zie ook* **leave.**
left-hand, *bn*
aan de linkerkant; links; **look in the left-hand drawer; they live on the left-hand side of the street.**
left-handed, *bn*
linkshandig, links; **he's left-handed.**

leg [leg] *zn*
(a) been; poot; **he's standing on one leg; the table has got four legs; some dogs can stand on their back legs; she fell off the wall and broke her leg; he's pulling your leg** = hij houdt je voor de gek.
(b) poot; **a leg of lamb; would you like a chicken leg?**

lemon ['lemən] *zn*
citroen; **put some lemon juice on your fish; do you want a piece of lemon in your drink?**
lemonade [lemə'neid] *zn*
limonade; **can I have a glass of lemonade?**

lend [lend] *ww*
(uit)lenen; **can you lend me your dictionary? can you lend me £5 till Monday? I lent her my bike and now she won't give it back; to lend a hand** = een handje helpen; **can you lend a hand with the cooking?**
lends—lending—lent [lent]—has lent
Let op: vergelijk **borrow**

length [leŋkθ] *zn*
lengte; afstand; **the garden is 25 metres in length; he swam a length of the pool** = een baan.

lent [lent] *zie* **lend**

less [les] **1.** *bn & zn*
minder; **you ought to eat less bread; the**

lesson

bill comes to less than £10; he finished his work in less than an hour.
2. *bw*
minder; **she's trying to eat less; the second book is less well known than the first; I want a suitcase which is less heavy than this one.**

lesson ['lesn] *zn*
les, lesuur; **he went to sleep during the maths lesson; we have six lessons of English a week; he's taking/having driving lessons; she gives English lessons at home in the evenings.**

let [let] *ww*
(*a*) laten, toestaan; **let me wash the car; will he let us go home early today? can you let me have two kilos of sugar?** = kan ik twee kilo suiker van je krijgen? **they let her borrow their car; let them come in—it's raining hard; can you let me know as soon as possible?** = kun je het me zo gauw mogelijk laten weten?
(*b*) verhuren; **I'm letting my house to an American family for the summer; this flat is to let at £100 a month.**
(*c*) laten; **let's all go to the cinema; don't let's start yet/let's not start yet.**

lets—letting—let—has let

let down, *ww*
(*a*) laten zakken; **they let down the bucket on a rope.**
(*b*) leeg laten lopen; **he let down my back tyre.**
(*c*) teleurstellen, duperen; **I asked him to speak at the meeting but he let me down.**
let go, *ww*
loslaten; **don't let go of the handle; he held on to the branch, and then had to let go of it.**
let in, *ww*
binnenlaten; **don't let the dog in if he's wet; these shoes are no good—they let in water/they let the water in.**
let yourself in for, *ww*
zich op de hals halen/(zich) aanhalen; **he didn't realise what he was letting himself in for when he said he would paint the house.**
let off, *ww*
(*a*) af laten gaan, afvuren; **the gun made a loud noise when they let it off.**

level

(*b*) kwijtschelden; vrijstellen; ergens vanaf laten komen; **he was arrested for stealing, but the judge let him off with a fine; the teacher has let us off our homework.**
let on, *ww*
laten blijken; verklappen; **don't let on that I was there.**
let out, *ww*
laten gaan/ontsnappen; **they let the sheep out of the field; don't let the dog out when the postman is coming; he let the air out of my back tyre** = hij heeft mijn achterband leeg laten lopen.
let up, *ww*
ophouden, uitscheiden; langzamer aan doen; **the rain didn't let up all day; he's working too hard—he ought to let up a bit.**

Let op: **don't let the dog in** *of* **don't let it in the dog; he let the bucket down** *of* **he let down the bucket, etc., maar alleen don't let it in, he let it down, etc.**

letter ['letə] *zn*
(*a*) brief; **the postman has brought two letters for you; I must write a letter to my mother to tell her how we all are; I've had a letter from the bank manager; can you post this letter for me?**
(*b*) letter; **A is the first letter of the alphabet; can you think of a word with eight letters beginning with A and ending with T?**
letterbox, *zn*
(*a*) (*op straat*) brievenbus; **can you post these letters for me?—there's a letterbox at the corner of the street**
(*b*) (*in deur*) brievenbus; **the newspaper is too thick to go into the letterbox.**

level ['levl] **1.** *bn*
(*a*) gelijk; vlak, horizontaal; **this table isn't level, put a piece of wood under the leg.**
(*b*) op één lijn, gelijk; **can you hang this picture level with the other one? the water is level with the top of the glass.**
2. *zn*
niveau, hoogte, stand; **the room is on a level with the garden; the town is 900 metres above sea level** = zeespiegel; the

government wants to reduce the level of
public spending.
3. *ww*
gelijk maken, effenen; vlak lopen; **they
are levelling the ground before they start
building; the road goes up and down, and
then levels out for a few miles.**
levels—levelling—levelled—has
levelled

library ['laɪbrərɪ] *zn*
bibliotheek; **he has a big library of records; don't forget to take your books
back to the library; this book isn't
mine—it's a library book.**
meervoud libraries

librarian [laɪ'breərɪən] *zn*
bibliothecaris, bibliothecaresse.

lick [lɪk] *ww*
likken; **she was licking an ice cream; the
cat licked up the spilt milk; he forgot to
lick the envelope.**
licks—licking—licked—has licked

lid [lɪd] *zn*
deksel; **put the lid back on the jam jar;
I've lost the lid of the kettle.**

lie [laɪ] **1.** *zn*
leugen; **he's been telling lies about his
brother.**
2. *ww*
liegen; **he was lying when he said he
hadn't touched the money; he lied to the
police about the accident.**
lies—lying—lied—has lied
3. *ww*
liggen; **the dog was lying in front of the
fire; snow lay 6 inches deep on the
ground; there were leaves lying all over the
pavement; we lay in the sun all afternoon.**
lies—lying—lay [leɪ]—has lain

lie down, *ww*
gaan liggen; **she lay down on the floor;
just as I was lying down the telephone
rang.**
lie in, *ww*
uitslapen.

life [laɪf] *zn*
leven; **he spent his whole life working on
the farm; a miner has a hard life; life
insurance** = levensverzekering; **she**

saved my life = ze heeft mijn leven gered;
there's no sign of life in the house = geen
teken van leven.
lifebelt, *zn*
reddingsgordel.
lifeboat, *zn*
reddingsboot; **the lifeboat rescued the
crew of the sinking ship.**

lift [lɪft] **1.** *zn*
(*a*) (*Amer.* elevator) lift; **take the lift to
the sixth floor; push the button to call
the lift.**
(*b*) lift; **can I give you a lift to the station
in my car?**
2. *ww*
(op)heffen, (op)tillen; **this case is so
heavy, I can't lift it off the floor; he hurt
his back lifting a box down from the
shelf.**
lifts—lifting—lifted—has lifted

light [laɪt] **1.** *bn*
(*a*) licht, luchtig; **I can carry this case
easily—it's quite light; she was only
wearing a light coat; he's not fit, and so
can only do light work.**
(*b*) licht-; blond; **a light blue shirt; our
house has a light green door; she has light
hair.**
(*c*) licht, helder; **the kitchen is lighter
than our dining room; at six o'clock in
the morning it was just getting light.**
(*d*) **light music** = lichte muziek.
light—lighter—lightest
2. *zn*
(*a*) licht; **you can't read by the light of
the moon; the light of the sun makes
plants green; there's not enough light in
here to take a photo.**
(*b*) licht; lamp(je); **switch on the lights—
it's getting dark; the car was travelling
with no lights; I could see the red lights of
the car in front of me; I'm going to put a
light on the wall so that I can read in bed.**
(*c*) **can you give me a light?** = hebt u
een vuurtje voor me?
3. *ww*
aansteken; **can you light the gas under
the kettle? I can't get the fire to light;
light a match—we can't see in the dark.**
lights—lighting—lit—has lit

lighter, *zn*
aansteker; **can I borrow your lighter—mine has run out of gas?**
lighthouse, *zn*
vuurtoren.
lighting, *zn*
verlichting; **the lighting is very bad in the dining room—we can't see what we are eating.**
lights, *zn meervoud*
stoplichten/verkeerslichten; **turn right at the lights; he went across the crossroads when the lights were red.**

lightning ['laɪtnɪŋ] *zn*
bliksem; **during the storm, lightning struck the town hall clock; a flash of lightning lit the sky** = een bliksem-straal/bliksemschicht/bliksemflits.
geen meervoud: **some lightning; a flash of lightning**

like [laɪk] **1.** *vz*
(zo)als, lijkend op; **he's very like his father** = hij lijkt erg op etc; **the photo doesn't look like her at all** = lijkt niet; **what was the weather like on holiday?** = wat voor weer; **he swims like a fish; it tastes like jam; it sounds like Beethoven; it feels like rain** = het ziet ernaar uit dat het gaat regenen; **I feel like a cup of tea** = ik heb zin in een kopje thee.
2. *ww*
(*a*) houden van; lusten; aardig/leuk etc. vinden; **do you like butter? he doesn't like fish; I like my new teacher; do you like driving? I like to sit and read quietly in the evening.**
(*b*) graag willen; **I'd like you to meet my father; we'd like to go to Sweden; take as much sugar as you like.**
likes—liking—liked—has liked
likely, *bn*
waarschijnlijk; **it's likely to rain** = het gaat waarschijnlijk regenen; **he's not likely to win** = hij heeft niet veel kans om te winnen.
likely—likelier—likeliest
liking, *zn*
dol zijn op; **he has a liking for sweets; I've taken a liking to her** = ik ben haar aardig gaan vinden.

limit ['lɪmɪt] **1.** *zn*
limiet, beperking; grens; **there is a speed limit of 30 miles per hour in towns; there is no age limit for joining the club** = leeftijdsgrens.
2. *ww*
beperken; **the club is limited to 200 members; parking is limited to 30 minutes; limited company** = naamloze vennootschap; **John Smith, Limited** = John Smith N.V.
limits—limiting—limited—has limited
Let op: in namen van firma's wordt **limited** *vaak geschreven* **Ltd.**

line [laɪn] **1.** *zn*
(*a*) lijn; rimpel; **he drew a straight line with his pencil; she has lines on her forehead; you must not park on the yellow lines; I want some notepaper without any lines; the football went over the line.**
(*b*) lijn, snoer; **fishing line; telephone line; speak more clearly—the line's bad; we had a crossed line** = er kwam een gesprek tussendoor; **he's on the line now** = aan de lijn.
(*c*) rij; file; regel; **we stood in line for half an hour waiting to get into the exhibition; no buses came for a long time, then three of them came in a line** = achter elkaar; **the line of cars stretched for three miles from the accident; she only typed two lines and made six mistakes; start at the top line on page 6; can you read that line again?**
(*d*) **railway line** = spoorbaan; **don't cross the lines when a train is coming.**
2. *ww*
(*a*) opstellen; **the soldiers lined the streets** = stonden opgesteld langs; **lined paper** = gelinieërd.
(*b*) voeren; **she was wearing a dress lined with silk** = zij droeg een met zijde gevoerde jurk; **have you any fur-lined boots?**
lines—lining—lined—has lined

line up, *ww*
in de rij gaan staan; zich opstellen; **if you want tickets, line up over here.**
lining, *zn*
voering; **a dress with a silk lining.**

lip [lɪp] *zn*
lip; **he licked his lips when he thought of dinner; she fell over and cut her top lip** = bovenlip.
lipstick, *zn*
lippenstift, lipstick; **she put her lipstick on.**

liquid ['lɪkwɪd] *bn & zn*
vloeibaar; vloeistof; **heat the butter until it is quite liquid; he's ill and needs a lot of liquids.**

list [lɪst] **1.** *zn*
lijst; **there is a list of names in alphabetical order; we couldn't remember what to buy because we forgot the shopping list** = boodschappenlijst; **he's on the danger list** = hij is levensgevaarlijk ziek.
2. *ww*
noteren; een lijst maken; catalogiseren. **the streets are listed at the back of the book; all the restaurants are listed in the yellow pages.**
lists—listing—listed—has listed

listen ['lɪsn] *ww*
luisteren; **be quiet—I'm listening to the news; if you listened to what I tell you, you wouldn't make so many mistakes; will you listen for the telephone while I'm in the garden?** = wil jij luisteren of je de telefoon hoort etc.?
listens—listening—listened—has listened
listener, *zn*
luisteraar.

lit [lɪt] *zie* **light**

litre ['liːtə] *zn* (*Amer.* liter)
liter; **can you buy a litre of milk? this bucket contains two litres.**

little ['lɪtl] **1.** *bn*
(*a*) klein; **they have two children—a boy and a little girl; he has a ring on his little finger** = pink; **she stood on my little toe.**
(*b*) weinig; **she eats very little bread; the car uses very little petrol.**
little—less—least
2. *zn*
a little = een beetje; **give me a little of that soup; would you like some more coffee?—just a little, please.**

3. *bw*
weinig; **it was little more than fifteen minutes ago** = nog geen kwartier geleden; **I see her very little these days.**
little by little = langzamerhand, stukje bij beetje; **little by little, he got better.**

live 1. *bn* [laɪv]
(*a*) levend, in leven; **a real live film star** = heus, echt.
(*b*) direct, regelrecht; 'live'; **a live TV programme.**
(*c*) onder spanning/stroom; **don't walk on the live rail; watch out—that's a live wire.**
2. *ww* [lɪv]
(*a*) wonen; **we live in London; they used to live in Germany; do you like living in the town better than in the country? they live in a house by the river; where do your parents live? they live at 15, London Road.**
(*b*) leven; **Queen Elizabeth lived in the 16th century; he is very ill, and the doctor doesn't expect him to live much longer.**
lives—living—lived—has lived

lively [laɪvlɪ] *bn*
levendig, actief; **my grandfather is very lively; we had a very lively party with dozens of guests.**
live on, *ww*
leven op/van; **he lives on eggs and bread; you can't live on £10 a week; he doesn't earn enough to live on** = om van te bestaan.
living room, *zn*
woonkamer; **we sat in the living room and watched TV; the living room door is shut; they were having tea in the living room.**

load [ləʊd] **1.** *zn*
lading/vracht; **a lorry with a load of potatoes; the aircraft had a load of supplies; loads of** = massa's; **he's got loads of money.**
2. *ww*
(in)laden; **we're loading the lorry with bags of coal; the ship's loading in the harbour; the aircraft was loaded with supplies for the soldiers.**
loads—loading—loaded—has loaded

Living Room *Woonkamer*

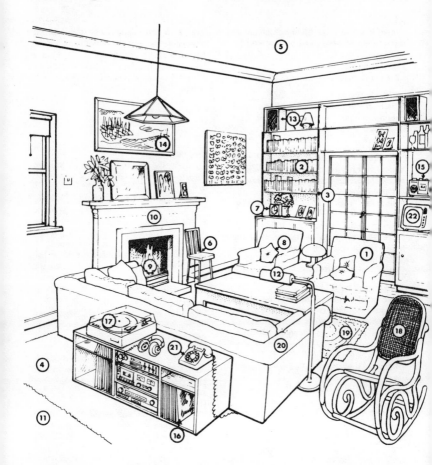

1. armchair	*leunstoel*	12. lamp	*lamp*
2. bookcase	*boekenkast*	13. loudspeaker	*luidspreker*
3. bookshelf	*boekenplank*	14. picture	*plaat, schilderij*
4. carpet	*kleed, tapijt*	15. radio	*radio*
5. ceiling	*plafond*	16. record	*grammofoonplaat*
6. chair	*stoel*	17. record player	*platenspeler*
7. clock	*klok*	18. rocking chair	*schommelstoel*
8. cushion	*kussen*	19. rug	*kleedl(je)*
9. fire	*vuur*	20. sofa	*bank*
10. fireplace	*open haard*	21. telephone	*telefoon*
11. floor	*vloer*	22. television	*televisie*

one hundred and twelve

loaf [ləʊf] *zn*
brood; can you buy me one white loaf and a brown one? have you eaten all that loaf of bread? the baker took the loaves out of the oven.
meervoud **loaves** [ləʊvz]

local ['ləʊkl] *bn*
plaatselijk, lokaal; buurt; we do all our shopping in the local shops; local government = plaatselijk bestuur.

lock [lɒk] 1. *zn*
slot; you left the key in the lock, so anyone could have opened the door; the lock is very stiff—I can't turn the key.
2. *ww*
op slot doen; afsluiten; the door's locked—can you climb in through a window? did you remember to lock the car? my father locks all the doors each night before he goes to bed.
locks—locking—locked—has locked

lock in/lock out, *ww*
binnensluiten/buitensluiten; my mother went shopping and locked my father out; he came back late and found he was locked out; I've left the keys inside and locked myself out; I think we've been locked in.

lock up, *ww*
(*a*) (voor de nacht) sluiten; don't forget to lock up before you go home; he was locking up the shop when a customer called.
(*b*) opsluiten; I'll lock up these jewels in the safe/I'll lock these jewels up in the safe; the police locked him up in prison for the night.
Let op: he locked the jewels up *of* he locked up the jewels *maar alleen* he locked them up

lonely ['ləʊnlɪ] *bn*
eenzaam; come and stay with me—it's lonely being in this big house all by myself; she was so lonely on holiday that she came back early.
lonely—lonelier—loneliest

long [lɒŋ] 1. *bn*
lang; a long piece of string; what a long film—it lasted for more than three hours;

we've been waiting for a long time; do you have long holidays in your job? how long is it before the holidays begin? the table is three feet long; is the Amazon the longest river in the world? your hair is getting long—it needs cutting.
long—longer—longest
Let op: wordt ook met cijfers gebruikt: the road is six miles long; a piece of string a metre long
2. *bw*
lang; have you been waiting long? I couldn't wait any longer; she died long ago.
long—longer—longest
as long as/so long as = zolang (als); it's nice to go on a picnic as long as it doesn't rain.
3. *ww*
verlangen naar; I'm longing for a cup of tea; they long to be back home.
longs—longing—longed—has longed

look [lʊk] 1. *zn*
(*a*) blik; kijkje; take a look at this picture = kijk eens naar etc.; they had a quick look round the town.
(*b*) uiterlijk, aanzien; he has a foreign look about him.
(*c*) good looks = knap uiterlijk.
2. *ww*
(*a*) kijken; look at this picture; we spent all evening looking at TV; can you look in the oven and see if the meat is cooked? she looked out of the window and saw the postman; he was looking under the bed.
(*b*) (er)uitzien, lijken; he looks ill; she looks at least eighty = ze ziet eruit als minstens tachtig; that cake looks good; what does she look like? he looks like his father; it looks as if it may rain/it looks like rain = het ziet ernaar uit etc.
looks—looking—looked—has looked

look after, *ww*
verzorgen, zorgen voor, the nurses looked after their patients; who's looking after your cat when you're away?
look for, *ww*
zoeken; he looked everywhere for his missing watch; the police are looking for the prisoner who has escaped.

look forward to, *ww*
zich verheugen op; **I'm looking forward
to my holidays; he isn't looking forward
to his exams; I'm looking forward to
seeing her again.**

look in, *ww*
aanlopen/binnenwippen; **I'll look in on
my way home.**

look out, *ww*
uitkijken; **look out! the pavement is
covered with ice.**

look out for, *ww*
(*a*) uitkijken naar; **he's looking out for
new staff to work in the office; I'll look
out for you at the party.**
(*b*) oppassen/uitkijken voor; **look out for
ice on the road.**

look round, *ww*
(*a*) omkijken; **when he heard footsteps in
the road he quickly looked round.**
(*b*) rondkijken; **did you look round the
museum? do you want to buy something?—no, I'm just looking round.**

look up, *ww*
(*a*) opkijken; **he looked up and saw a bird
on the roof; if you look up the chimney
you can see the sky.**
(*b*) opzoeken; **I'll look him up in the
telephone book to try to find his address;
look up the word in the dictionary if you
don't know what it means.**
Let op: **look the words up** *of* **look
up the words** *maar alleen* **look
them up**

loose [luːs] *bn*
los, slap; **part of the engine is loose; tie
the rope with a loose knot; the knot came
loose and the boat floated away.**
loose—looser—loosest

loosely, *bw*
losjes; **the boat was only loosely tied to
the tree.**

loosen, *ww*
losmaken; **loosen the rope; she loosened
the knot.**
**loosens—loosening—loosened—
has loosened**

lorry ['lɒrɪ] *zn*
vrachtwagen; **he was putting the
potatoes on to his lorry; the big lorries**

make a lot of noise as they go past the
house; *zie iij* **truck.**
meervoud **lorries**

lose [luːz] *ww*
(*a*) verliezen; **I can't find my watch—I
think I lost it on the bus; don't lose your
ticket or you'll have to buy another one.**
(*b*) kwijt raken; **she has lost weight since
last summer** = ze is afgevallen sinds
verleden zomer; **my watch loses 10
minutes every day** = mijn horloge loopt
per dag 10 minuten achter; **don't lose
any time in posting the letter** = verlies
geen tijd etc.; **has he lost his way?** = is
hij de weg kwijt? **he lost his temper** =
hij verloor zijn kalmte.
(*c*) een nederlaag lijden, verliezen (van);
**we lost the match 10–0; did you win?—
no, we lost!**
loses—losing—lost [lɒst]**—has lost**

get lost, *ww*
verdwalen; **we went for a walk in the
woods and got lost; they're very late—do
you think they've got lost?**

loss [lɒs] *zn*
(*a*) verlies; **loss of weight; with no loss of
time** = zonder tijd te verspillen.
(*b*) verlies (lijden); **he made a loss of
£10; we sold the car at a loss** = we
hebben de auto met verlies verkocht.
(*c*) verlies, nederlaag; **the loss of a battle;
our team had a series of losses this summer.**
meervoud **losses**

lot [lɒt] *zn*
(*a*) **a lot of/lots of** = massa's, een heleboel; **we've lots of time; what a lot of
apples! I've seen him quite a lot recently;
I'm feeling a lot better now** = een stuk
beter; **lots of people go to Spain for their
holidays; a lot of people were waiting for
the bus.**
(*b*) **the lot** = alles; de hele partij; **that's
the lot; we sold the lot for £10; we bought
pounds of potatoes and ate the lot for
dinner.**

loud [laʊd] *bn & bw*
luid, hard; **don't talk too loud—your father
is asleep; a loud noise made him jump.**
loud—louder—loudest

loudspeaker, *zn*
luidspreker.

love [lʌv] **1.** *zn*
liefde; groeten; **give my love to your parents; her great love is music; to fall in love with someone** = verliefd worden op iemand.
2. *ww*
houden van; dol zijn op; **he loves his children; the children love their teacher; we love going to the sea; he loves cream cakes; I'd love to come with you** = ik wil dolgraag mee; **but I've got too much work to do.**
loves—loving—loved—has loved

lovely, *bn*
heerlijk, enig; **a lovely warm day; she was wearing a lovely blue hat.**
lovely—lovelier—loveliest

low [ləʊ] *bn & bw*
laag; **he hit his head on the low ceiling; this shop has the lowest prices in town; the town is surrounded by low hills; the engine works best at low speeds; that aircraft is flying too low—it'll hit the trees; the temperature is too low for oranges to grow here.**
low—lower—lowest

lower [ləʊə] *ww*
laten zakken, verlagen; **we lowered a bucket into the water; the shops are lowering their prices to attract customers.**
lowers—lowering—lowered—has lowered

Ltd *zie* **limit**

luck [lʌk] *zn*
toeval; geluk; bof; **good luck with your exams!** = veel succes! **bad luck! hard**

luck! = pech gehad! **I wear this ring for luck** = dit is mijn geluksring; **just my (bad) luck to have homework to do when everyone else is swimming.**

lucky, *bn*
gelukkig, geluks-; **13 is my lucky number; he is lucky not to have been sent to prison** = hij boft dat hij etc.
lucky—luckier—luckiest

luckily, *bw*
gelukkig; **it started to rain, but luckily I had taken my umbrella.**

luggage ['lʌgɪdʒ] *zn*
bagage; **put all the luggage into the back of the car; we have too much luggage—we will have to pay extra; I can't carry all that luggage—can someone help me?**
geen meervoud: **some luggage; a piece of luggage**

lump [lʌmp] *zn*
brok, stuk; **he made a bowl out of a lump of wood; how many lumps of sugar do you take in your tea?** = (sui-ker)klontje.

lunch [lʌntʃ] *zn*
lunch; **hurry up—lunch is ready; will it soon be time for lunch? we always have lunch at one o'clock; we are having fish and chips for lunch; I'm not hungry so I don't want a big lunch.**
meervoud **lunches;** *zie ook* **dinner**

lunchtime, *zn*
lunchpauze; **it's half past twelve—almost lunchtime.**

lung [lʌŋ] *zn*
long; **the doctor listened to his chest to see if his lungs were all right.**

lying [laɪŋ] *zie* **lie**

Mm

machine [mə'ʃiːn] *zn*
machine; **washing machine; sewing machine; the factory has put in a new machine for making electric light bulbs.**
machinery, *zn*
machines; machinerie; **the factory has put in a lot of machinery.**
geen meervoud: **some machinery; a piece of machinery**

.. **mad** [mæd] *bn*
(*a*) gek, krankzinnig; **you're mad to go out in the snow without a coat; he had a mad idea to walk across America.**
(*b*) dol, razend; **this noise is driving me mad; I'll go mad if you don't stop that singing.**
(*c*) dol op; **she's mad about film stars; he's mad on old cars.**
mad—madder—maddest

madam ['mædəm] *zn*
mevrouw; **after you, madam;** (*als brief-aanhef boven 'n brief aan een onbekende dame*) **Dear Madam.**

made [meid] *zie* **make**

magazine [mægə'ziːn]·*zn*
tijdschrift; **the gardening magazine comes out on Tuesdays; have you got this week's TV magazine?**

mail [meil] *zn*
(*a*) post; **you should send the letter by air mail; if the present is valuable, send it by registered mail.**
(*b*) post; brieven; **has the mail come yet? he opened his mail before he had his breakfast.**

main [mein] **1.** *bn*
hoofd-, voornaamste; **the main thing is to work well; our main office is in London; there is always a lot of traffic on main roads; August is the main month for holidays.**
2. *zn*
(*a*) hoofdkabel, hoofdleiding; **a water main burst in the High Street.**
(*b*) **the mains** = elektriciteitsnet, hoofdleiding; **that machine is connected to the mains; does it use a battery or the mains?**
mainly, *bw*
hoofdzakelijk, voornamelijk; **we have mainly women working in our office; people mainly go on holiday in August.**

make [meik] **1.** *zn*
merk; **an Italian make of car; what make is your new record-player?**
2. *ww*
(*a*) maken; **he made a table out of pieces of wood; this cup is made of plastic** = dit kopje is van plastic; **he is making a cake.**
(*b*) (klaar)maken; **do you want me to make the breakfast? have you made your bed?** = heb je je bed opgemaakt?
(*c*) opleveren; **two and three make five.**
(*d*) verdienen; **he made £10 from selling old newspapers.**
(*e*) maken; **the smell of cooking makes me hungry; the movement of the boat made him sick; will the present make him happier? he made himself comfortable in the armchair.**
(*f*) laten; **I made him clean his shoes; the teacher made him stay in after school; the rain will make the grass grow; can't you make the car go any faster?**
makes—making—made [meid]—**has made**

make do with, *ww*
genoegen nemen (met); **I lost my toothpaste, so I had to make do with soap; the**

baker had run out of brown bread, so we had to make do with white; all the plates were dirty, so we made do with paper ones.

make for, *ww*
zich begeven naar; **he is making for London; when he saw her he made straight for the door.**

make of, *ww*
denken van; **what do you make of the news? I don't know what to make of it.**

make off with, *ww*
ervandoor gaan met; **the burglar made off with the jewellery.**

make out, *ww*
(*a*) onderscheiden; begrijpen; **I can't make out the details in the photo because the light is bad; she couldn't make out why he didn't want to come.**
(*b*) beweren; voorgeven; **is English weather really as bad as it is made out to be? stop trying to make out that you're the best singer in the world.**
(*c*) (*van cheque*) uitschrijven; **he made out the cheque to Mr Smith.**
Let op: can you make the writing out? *of* can you make out the writing? *maar alleen* can you make it out?

make up, *ww*
(*a*) verzinnen; **he told the police he had seen a man steal a car but in fact he made the whole story up.**
(*b*) **to make up your mind** = besluiten; **I can't make up my mind what to do; his mind is made up** = zijn besluit staat vast.
Let op: he made the story up *of* he made up the story *maar alleen* he made it up

make-up, *zn*
make-up.

male [meɪl] *bn & zn*
mannelijk, mannetjes-; man; **a male spider; the male is stronger than the female.**

man [mæn] *zn*
(*a*) man; **my father is a very tall man; ask that old man if he wants some tea.**
(*b*) mens; **men have only existed on earth for a short time compared to fish.**

(*c*) persoon; **the man in the street** = de gewone man, het grote publiek; **the man in the street isn't interested in politics.**
meervoud **men** [men]

manage [ˈmænɪdʒ] *ww*
(*a*) beheren; leiden; **she manages our London office; we want to appoint someone to manage our sales department.**
(*b*) slagen; (het) redden; lukken; **did you manage to phone your mother? he managed to get the lid off; can she manage all by herself? how are we going to manage without her?**
manages—managing— managed—has managed

manager, *zn*
manager, chef, leider; **the sales manager; the manager of the sports department.**

manner [ˈmænə] *zn*
(*a*) manier/wijze (van doen); **he was behaving in a strange manner.**
(*b*) **manners** = (goede) manieren; **he has very good table manners; it's bad manners to put your knife in your mouth.**

many [ˈmenɪ] *bn & vnw*
vele/veel; **many old people live by the seaside; many of us knew him when he was at school; so many people wanted tickets that they sold out quickly; how many apples have you got? he ate twice as many slices of bread as you did; a good many** = heel wat; **a good many people thought the film was no good.**
many—more [mɔː]**—most** [məʊst]
Let op: **many** *wordt met telbare zelfstandige naamwoorden gebruikt:* **not many apples** *maar* **not much bread**

map [mæp] *zn*
kaart, plattegrond; **here's a big map of Germany; have you got a street map of London? can you show me the mountains on the map? we soon got lost because we'd forgotten to take a map.**

March [mɑːtʃ] *zn*
maart; **his birthday is in March; today is**

March 6th; last March we went to Germany.

Let op: **March 6th:** *zeg* 'the sixth of March' *of* 'March the sixth'

Let op: **March** *wordt altijd met een hoofdletter geschreven*

march [mɑːtʃ] *ww*
marcheren; **the soldiers marched up the street; quick march!** = voorwaarts mars!

marches—marching—marched—has marched

margarine [mɑːgəˈriːn] *zn*
margarine; **spread some margarine on your bread; she fried the fish in margarine.**

mark [mɑːk] **1.** *zn*
(*a*) plek; vlek; **he has ink marks on his shirt; your cup has made a mark on the table; there's a red mark where you hit your head; on your marks!** = klaar voor de start!
(*b*) cijfer, punt; **he got top marks in French** = hij kreeg het beste cijfer van de klas voor Frans; **did you get a good mark for your maths homework? the teacher took marks off for spelling mistakes; is 8 out of 10 a good mark? 2.** *ww*
(*a*) merken; **the table is marked by coffee cups** = de tafel heeft kringen etc.; **the tin is marked 'dangerous'** = op het blik staat 'gevaarlijk'
(*b*) corrigeren, nakijken; **the teacher is marking our homework; has the maths exam been marked yet?**

marks—marking—marked—has marked

market [ˈmɑːkɪt] *zn*
markt; **we bought some vegetables and fish at the market; market day is Saturday.**

marmalade [ˈmɑːməleɪd] *zn*
marmelade; **do you want toast and marmalade for your breakfast? open another pot of marmalade—this one is empty.**

geen meervoud

marry [ˈmærɪ] *ww*
trouwen; **he married the girl next door;**

they were married in church; how long have you been married? she's married to a soldier; they got married last Saturday.

marries—marrying—married—has married

mass [mæs] *zn*
massa; **there's a mass of dead leaves on the lawn; masses of people went to the exhibition; have some more meat—there's masses left; a mass meeting.**

meervoud **masses**

master [ˈmɑːstə] *zn*
leraar; meester, onderwijzer; **Mr Jones is the English master.**

mat [mæt] *zn*
(*a*) mat; **wipe your shoes on the mat; bath mat**
(*b*) onderzetter; **put table mats out for everyone.**

match [mætʃ] *zn*
(*a*) wedstrijd; **are you going to watch the football match? I won the last two tennis matches I played.**
(*b*) lucifer; **a box of matches; he struck a match and lit the fire; the matches are wet—they won't light.**

meervoud **matches**

matchbox, *zn*
lucifersdoosje.

meervoud **matchboxes**

material [məˈtɪərɪəl] *zn*
(*a*) materiaal; **building materials** = bouwmaterialen; **raw materials** = grondstoffen.
(*b*) materiaal, stof; **I bought some cotton material to make a skirt.**

mathematics [mæθəˈmætɪks], **maths** [mæθs] *zn*
wiskunde; **the maths teacher; I found the maths exam very difficult; my sister is no good at maths; maths is my best subject.**

Let op: het werkwoord wordt hierbij in het enkelvoud gebruikt: **maths is an important subject**

matter [ˈmætə] **1.** *zn*
probleem, zaak; **what's the matter?**

there's something the matter with the
engine = er is iets aan de hand etc.; **it's
a matter for the police** = het is een zaak
voor de politie; **as a matter of fact** = in
feite; **as a matter of course** = vanzelf
sprekend.
2. *ww*
van belang zijn, ertoe doen; **it matters a
lot to him; does it matter where we sit?
it doesn't matter if you're late** = het
hindert niet als je te laat bent.
matters—mattering—mattered—
has mattered

mattress [ˈmætrəs] *zn*
matras; **this mattress has lumps in it.**
meervoud **mattresses**

May [meɪ] *zn*
mei; **she was born in May; today is May
15th; last May we moved to London; are
you going away next May?**
Let op: **May 15th:** *zeg* 'the fifteenth
of May' *of* 'May the fifteenth'
Let op: **May** *wordt altijd met een
hoofdletter geschreven*

may [meɪ] *hulpww*
(*a*) misschien kunnen; **if he doesn't hurry
he may miss the train; take your umbrella, it may rain; he may be waiting
outside; you may have left your gloves
on the train; it may not rain after all; she
may not have heard.**
(*b*) mogen; **mother says we may come in;
you may sit down if you want to; may I
ask you a question? may we have tea
early today?**
I may, you may, he may, we may,
they may
Verleden tijd: [*alleen* (*a*)] **might,
might not,** *meestal* **mightn't**
Let op: **may** *en* **might** *worden zonder*
to *en altijd met andere werkwoorden
gebruikt*
maybe, *bw*
misschien; **maybe it will be fine tomorrow.**

me [miː] *vnw*
mij, me; **give it to me; can you hear me? he
is taller than me** = hij is langer dan ik;
who is it?—it's me! = ik ben het!

meal [miːl] *zn*
maal(tijd); **we have three meals a day—
breakfast, lunch and dinner; you should
only have a light meal in the evening;
when they had eaten their evening meal
they went for a walk.**

mean [miːn] **1.** *bn*
(*a*) gemeen, laag; **he played a mean trick
on his sister; that was a mean thing to say.**
(*b*) krenterig; onaardig; **don't be mean—
lend me your football; he's very mean
with his money.**
mean—meaner—meanest
2. *ww*
(*a*) bedoelen; **did he mean Uncle Richard
when he was talking about fat men? what
do you mean?**
(*b*) betekenen; **a red light means that you
have to stop; 'Tisch' in German means
'table'; what does that sign mean?—I
know what it means, it means that you
can't park here on Saturdays.**
(*c*) **to be meant to** = het is de bedoeling,
dat; **we're meant to be there by nine
o'clock; this medicine is meant to be used
only for coughs; a train is meant to leave
every half hour.**
means—meaning—meant [ment]—
has meant

meaning, *zn*
betekenis; **if you want to find the meaning of this word, look it up in the dictionary.**

means, *zn*
(*a*) manier; middel(en); **is there any
means of getting to London tonight? a
motorbike is a cheap means of travelling.**
by all means = vooral, in elk geval;
natuurlijk; **by all means telephone the
office if you want to.**
by no means = geenszins, in geen
geval; **he's by no means rich.**
(*b*) inkomen; **it is beyond my means** =
dat kan ik me niet permitteren.

meanwhile, *bw*
ondertussen; **he hid in an empty house—
meanwhile, the police were coming
nearer.**

measles [ˈmiːzlz] *zn meervoud*
mazelen; **she's in bed with measles; have**

you had measles? he's got measles; they caught measles from their friends at school.

measure ['meʒə] 1. *zn*
maat(staf); maatregel; a metre is a measure of length; tape measure = centimeter.
2. *ww*
(op)meten; the room measures 3 metres by 2 metres; a thermometer measures temperature; how much do you measure round the waist? she measured the room before buying the carpet.
measures—measuring—measured—has measured

measurement, *zn*
maat; afmeting; what are the measurements of the tent? do you know your waist measurement? he had to take the measurements of the room to calculate how much paint he needed.

meat [mi:t] *zn*
vlees; can I have some more meat? would you like another slice of meat? this meat is very well cooked.
geen meervoud: some meat; a piece of meat/a slice of meat

medicine ['medsɪn] *zn*
(a) medicijn, geneesmiddel; take some cough medicine if your cough is bad; you should take the medicine three times a day.
(b) medicijnen; he is studying medicine because he wants to be a doctor.
geen meervoud voor (b)

medical ['medikl] *bn*
medisch; a medical student; medical help was provided by the Red Cross.

meet [mi:t] *ww*
(a) ontmoeten, treffen; I'll meet you at the bus stop; they met at the railway station; let's arrange to meet somewhere before we go to the theatre; I'm meeting her at the post office at six o'clock.
(b) ontmoeten, leren kennen; I think I have met him before; I have never met your mother—come and meet her, then.
meets—meeting—met—has met

meeting, *zn*
ontmoeting; vergadering; bijeenkomst; there will be a meeting of the stamp club next Thursday; there were only six people at the meeting.

melt [melt] *ww*
smelten; the butter has melted in the sun; you must melt the chocolate in a pan and pour it over the ice cream.
melts—melting—melted—has melted

member ['membə] *zn*
lid; he is a member of the golf club; the club is limited to 250 members; Member of Parliament = kamerlid, parlementslid.

memory ['memərɪ] *zn*
(a) geheugen; he has a very good memory for dates; I have no memory for names; he said the whole poem from memory = hij zei het hele gedicht uit zijn hoofd op.
(b) herinnering; I have wonderful memories of our last holiday.
meervoud memories

men [men] *zie* **man**

mend [mend] *ww*
maken, repareren; herstellen; can you mend my watch? he's trying to mend his car; my trousers are torn—can they be mended?
mends—mending—mended—has mended

mention ['menʃn] *ww*
vermelden, noemen; opmerken; he mentioned that he was going away for a few days; did she mention the results of the exam? they don't know about the party—shall I mention it to them?
mentions—mentioning—mentioned—has mentioned

menu ['menju:] *zn*
menu; (menu)kaart; have you any fish on the menu? the waiter brought us the menu; she always chooses the most expensive dish on the menu.

merry ['merɪ] *bn*
vrolijk; Merry Christmas; he wished us a Merry Christmas.
merry—merrier—merriest

✥ MENU ✥

<u>LUNCH</u>

vegetable soup 40p
tomato soup 40p
fruit juices, tomato juice 25p

chicken, rice 1.50
roast lamb 1.50
meat pie .... 1·00
ham & salad 1.25

vegetables: boiled potatoes, chips, peas,
beans, carrots, cabbage .... 30p extra

cheese & biscuits 60p
fresh fruit salad 50p
apple pie & cream 75p
ice cream 30p
pancakes (two) 60p
pastries .... 45p each

coffee, tea .... per cup 25p
milk shakes 50p
beer .... per glass 45p
wine .... per glass 60p

<u>SNACKS</u>

sandwiches ....35p each
hot dogs ....45p each
sausage rolls ....30p each

Service not included.

mess [mes] *zn*
viezigheid; rommel; **the builders made a
mess all over the floor; the room is in a
mess—you'll have to tidy it up; he made
a mess of mending his car** = van het
repareren van zijn auto heeft hij niets
terechtgebracht.
meervoud **messes**

message ['mesɪdʒ] *zn*
boodschap; **he got a message telling him
to go to the police station; your boss has
left a message for you; here's a phone
message for you.**

messenger ['mesɪndʒə] *zn*
boodschapper, koerier, (voor)bode.

met [met] *zie* **meet**

metal ['metl] *zn*
metaal; **a metal teapot; the spoons are
plastic but the knives are metal; this table
is made of metal.**

method ['meθəd] *zn*
methode; **he showed me a new method of
making bread.**

metre ['miːtə] *zn* (*Amer.* **meter**)
meter; **the room is four metres by three;
one square metre** = vierkante meter; **the
area of the stage is ten square metres.**
Let op: met cijfers wordt **metre**
meestal geschreven **m** *en* **square
metre** *meestal als* **m²** **(four metres
= 4m; six square metres = 6m²)**

mice [maɪs] *zie* **mouse**

mid- [mɪd] *prefix*
midden; **the two aircraft hit each other
in mid-air** = in de lucht; **we will be going
on holiday in mid-August.**

midday [mɪd'deɪ] *zn*
twaalf uur 's middags; tussen de
middag; **he caught the midday train to
Scotland; she won't be back to her office
before midday.**

middle ['mɪdl] *zn*
(*a*) midden; **he was standing in the middle
of the room; Zaire is a country in the
middle of Africa; I woke up in the middle
of the night; she was in the middle of**
making the dinner when we called; the
telephone rang in the middle of the meeting.
(*b*) middel, taille; **the water came up to
my middle; how much do you measure
round the middle?**
middle-aged, *bn*
van middelbare leeftijd; **he's middle-
aged; three middle-aged women got on to
the bus.**

midnight ['mɪdnaɪt] *zn*
middernacht; **you must go to bed before
midnight; I heard the clock strike midnight and then went to sleep.**

might [maɪt] *hulpww*
(*a*) zou(den) kunnen; **it might rain; he
might be waiting outside; you might have
left your gloves on the train.**
(*b*) had(den) wel eens kunnen; **he might
have done something to help** = hij zou
hulp hebben kunnen bieden; **you might
have told me** = dat had je me wel eens
kunnen/mogen vertellen.
**I might, you might, he might, we
might, they might**
Ontkennende wijs: **might not,** *meestal* **mightn't**
Let op: **might** *wordt zonder* **to** *en
altijd met andere werkwoorden gebruikt.* **Might** *is de verleden tijd van*
may, *maar kan als beleefdere vorm van
de tegenwoordige tijd gebruikt
worden in verzoeken om iets te mogen
doen.*

mild [maɪld] *bn*
mild, zacht; licht; **we had a very mild
winter; she's had a mild attack of
measles; I like strong mustard—this sort
is too mild** = deze soort is niet scherp
genoeg.
mild—milder—mildest

mile [maɪl] *zn*
(*a*) mijl (= 1625 meter); **we walked for
miles before we found the post office; the
car was travelling at 60 miles per hour;
it's 24 miles from here to the sea; it's a
three mile walk from here.**
(*b*) **miles** = heel veel; **it's miles too big**

= veel te groot; **the string is miles too long** = veel te lang.

met cijfers wordt **miles per hour** *meestal geschreven* **mph: 60 miles per hour** = 60 mph

military ['mɪlɪtrɪ] *bn*
militair; **he was wearing military uniform; a military hospital** = legerhospitaal.

milk [mɪlk] **1.** *zn*
melk; **have you drunk your milk? can I have a glass of milk, please? I must buy some milk; have you enough milk? we've got no milk left.**
geen meervoud: **some milk; a glass of milk/a bottle of milk**
2. *ww*
melken; **the farmer was milking the cow; the cows haven't been milked yet.**
milks—milking—milked—has milked

milkman, *zn*
melkboer/melkman; **tell the milkman to leave six bottles of milk today.**
meervoud **milkmen**

milk shake, *zn*
milkshake; **he drank two chocolate milk shakes.**

millimetre ['mɪlɪmiːtə] *zn* (*Amer.* **millimeter**)
millimeter; **the wood is only 10 millimetres thick; there are ten millimetres in a centimetre, and a thousand in a metre.**
met cijfers wordt **millimetre** *meestal geschreven* **mm: 26 mm** = 26 millimetres

million ['mɪljən] miljoen, 1.000.000
the population of the country is 60 million; millions of trees were burnt in the forest fire; the country spends millions of dollars on oil; millions of people spend their holidays in Spain.
Let op: geen meervoud met cijfers: **sixty million;** *met cijfers kan* **million** *ook geschreven worden* **m: £2m** = two million pounds

millionth, *bn & zn*
miljoenste; **a millionth of a second; con-**

gratulations—you're our **millionth customer!**

mind [maɪnd] **1.** *zn*
geest; gedachte(n); **what do you have in mind?** = wat hebt u in gedachten? **he's got something on his mind** = er zit hem iets dwars; **let's try to take her mind off her exams** = laten we haar gedachten afleiden van haar examens.
state of mind = gemoedstoestand; **he's in a very miserable state of mind.**
to make up your mind = besluiten; **I can't make up my mind whether to go on holiday or stay here and work; she couldn't make up her mind what hat to wear.**
to change your mind = van gedachten/mening veranderen; **I have decided to go on holiday, and nothing will make me change my mind; he took out his bike, but then changed his mind and went by bus.**
2. *ww*
(*a*) opletten, oppassen; zorgen voor; **mind the step! mind you ride carefully on your bike; mind you get back in time for tea; mind the oven—it's hot!**
(*b*) zich aantrekken; **never mind** = het hindert niet; **you must learn to mind your own business** = je moet je met je eigen zaken leren bemoeien.
(*c*) bezwaar tegen iets hebben; **do you mind if I close the window? they won't mind if you're late; I wouldn't mind a cup of tea** = ik heb best zin in een kopje thee; **do you mind if we sit down? I don't mind standing up.**
minds—minding—minded—has minded

mine [maɪn] **1.** *vnw*
van mij, de/het mijne; **that bike is mine; can I borrow your pen, I've lost mine? Paul is a friend of mine.**
2. *zn*
(*a*) mijn; **a coal mine; a gold mine.**
(*b*) (land)mijn; **the lorry went over a mine and was blown up.**
3. *ww*
exploiteren; winnen; in de mijnen werken; **they are mining gold here.**
mines—mining—mined—has mined

miner, *zn*
mijnwerker.

mineral ['mınrəl] *zn*
mineraal, delfstof; **they mine coal and other minerals in the north of the country; mineral water** = (*a*) mineraalwater; (*b*) frisdrank.

minister ['mınıstə] *zn*
minister; **the Foreign Minister** = de minister van Buitenlandse Zaken; *zie ook* **Prime Minister.**

minute¹ ['mınıt] *zn*
(*a*) minuut; **there are sixty minutes in an hour; 12 minutes to four** = 3.48; **12 minutes past three** = 3.12; **I'll meet you in fifteen minutes; the house is about five minutes' walk from the station/is a five minute walk from the station; minute hand** = grote wijzer.
(*b*) minuutje, ogenblik(je); **why don't you sit down for a minute? I won't be a minute** = ik ben zo terug; **can you wait a minute?**

minute² [maı'nju:t] *bn*
minuskuul; **a minute piece of dust got in my eye.**

mirror ['mırə] *zn*
spiegel; **he looked at his face in the bathroom mirror; driving mirror** = achteruitkijkspiegel.

miserable ['mızrəbl] *bn*
ongelukkig; ellendig; **she was miserable when he didn't write to her; the weather on holiday was really miserable** = miserabel.

Miss [mıs] *zn*
(me)juffrouw; **Miss Jones; Miss Anne Jones; please, Miss, can I have the bill?**
Let op: met een naam kan **Miss** *zowel voor de voor- als achternaam staan; zonder naam wordt* **Miss** *gebruikt om een serveerster of onderwijzeres aan te spreken.*

miss [mıs] **1.** *zn*
misslag; 'misser'; **he scored a goal and then had two misses; let's give it a miss** = laten we er wegblijven.
meervoud **misses**

2. *ww*
(*a*) missen; **he missed the goal; they tried to shoot the rabbit but missed.**
(*b*) missen, mislopen; **we missed the house in the dark; they missed the bus and had to walk home; I missed the article about farming in yesterday's paper; you didn't miss much** = je hebt niet veel gemist; **he just missed being knocked down** = hij was bijna aangereden.
(*c*) missen; **do you miss your dog? I miss those long walks we used to take; they'll miss you if you go to work in another office.**
misses—missing—missed—has missed

missing, *bn*
kwijt, zoek(geraakt); **we're looking for my missing keys; there is a lot of money missing; the police searched for the missing children.**

miss out, *ww*
weglaten; **you missed out the most important part of the letter.**
Let op: **he missed the best part out of** **he missed out the best part** *maar alleen* **he missed it out**

mistake [mı'steık] **1.** *zn*
vergissing; fout; **I made a mistake; I got on the wrong bus by mistake; by mistake he tried to eat his soup with his fork; there are several mistakes in her work.**
2. *ww*
zich vergissen; **I mistook him for his brother** = ik zag hem bij vergissing aan voor zijn broer; **he is mistaken in thinking I am your brother; if I'm not mistaken, Dr Smith is your brother.**
mistakes—mistaking—mistook [mı'stʊk]—has mistaken

mix [mıks] *ww*
(ver)mengen; **mix the flour and milk in a bowl; if you mix blue and yellow you will get green.**
mixes—mixing—mixed—has mixed

mixture ['mıkstʃə] *zn*
mengsel; drankje; **the walls are painted in a mixture of red and blue; the doctor**

gave me an unpleasant mixture to drink;
cough mixture = hoestdrank(je).

mix up, *ww*
verwarren; door elkaar halen/raken; **I'm
always mixing him up with his brother;
all the books got mixed up in the box.**

model ['mɒdl] *zn*
(*a*) model; **he is making a model plane;
have you seen his model trains?**
(*b*) model; mannequin.
(*c*) model, type; **this is the latest model;
he has a 1979 model Ford.**

modern ['mɒdn] *bn*
modern; **their house is very modern;
modern languages; he's studying French
and Spanish in the modern languages
department.**

moment ['məʊmənt] *zn*
moment, ogenblik; **please wait a
moment; I only saw him for a moment;
we expect him to arrive at any moment**
= we verwachten hem elk ogenblik; **we
only heard of it a moment ago** = we
hebben het net pas gehoord.
at the moment = op het ogenblik;
I'm rather busy at the moment.
for the moment = voorlopig; **we
won't disturb you for the moment.**

Monday ['mʌndɪ] *zn*
maandag; **the shops are shut on Mondays; I saw her last Monday; we're going
on holiday next Monday; will you be in
the office on Monday afternoon? we go
to the cinema every Monday.**
Let op: **Monday** *wordt altijd met een
hoofdletter geschreven*

money ['mʌnɪ] *zn*
geld; **how much money have you got? I
haven't any money with me; we ran out
of money** = ons geld raakte op; **you
spent too much money last week; I want to
change my pounds into Spanish money.**
geen meervoud

month [mʌnθ] *zn*
maand; **January is the first month of the
year; February is the shortest month;
what day of the month is it today? I'm
going on holiday next month; it rained a
lot last month, in fact it rained all month;**

a month from today I'll be sitting on the
beach =over een maand etc.; **we haven't
had any homework for months** = we
hebben in geen maanden huiswerk
gehad; **he's taken a month's holiday.**

moon [muːn] *zn*
maan; **it is difficult to think that men
have walked on the moon; the moon is
very bright tonight; there was no moon
because there were too many clouds; it
only happens once in a blue moon** = het
gebeurt slechts een doodenkele keer.

more [mɔː] **1.** *bn*
meer; nog; **do you want some more
coffee? we need two more men to make a
football team; there are many more
trains on weekdays than on Sundays;
£10—that's more than I can pay.**
2. *zn*
(nog) meer; **is there any more of this
jam?**
3. *bw van de vergrotende trap*
**he was more surprised than I was; she is
more intelligent than her brother; it was
even more unpleasant than I had thought
it would be.**
more or less = min of meer, ongeveer; **I've more or less finished my
homework.**
not ... any more = niet meer/
langer; **he doesn't write to me any more;
we don't go abroad on holiday any more.**
Let op: **more** *wordt gebruikt om de
vergrotende trap te vormen van bijvoeglijke naamwoorden die niet de uitgang -er krijgen*

morning ['mɔːnɪŋ] *zn*
morgen, ochtend; **I go to the office every
morning; tomorrow morning he's going to
talk on the radio; we'll meet on Tuesday
morning; I woke up at four in the morning** = ik werd om vier uur 's nachts
wakker; **have you read the morning
paper? we must get the morning plane to
Stockholm.**

most [məʊst] **1.** *bn*
(het/de) meeste; **most people have
breakfast at about 8 o'clock; most children like watching TV; most apples are
sweet.**

2. *zn*
het/de meest(e); **most of the work has been done; he sits and writes most of the time; it rained for most of the day; most of the children are over 11.**
3. *bw*
(*a*) (*van de overtreffende trap*) meest; **he's the most intelligent child in his class; the most important thing is to be able to speak Russian.**
(*b*) hoogst, zeer; **I find it most annoying that the post doesn't come until 10 o'clock; most probably he will be held up by the fog; you are most kind.**
Let op: **most** *wordt gebruikt om de overtreffende trap te vormen van bij-voeglijke naamwoorden die niet de uitgang* **-est** *krijgen*

mostly, *bw*
meestal; **sometimes we go abroad for our holidays, but mostly we stay in Britain.**

mother ['mʌðə] *zn*
moeder; **he lives with his mother; my mother's a doctor; Mother! there's someone asking for you on the telephone**
Let op: **Mother** *wordt soms als aan-spreekvorm voor een moeder gebruikt, maar* **Mum** *en* **Mummy** *komen vaker voor*

motor ['məʊtə] *zn*
motor; **switch on the motor; the model boat has an electric motor.**
motorbike, motorcycle, *zn*
motor(fiets); **he fell off his motorbike; I'm learning to ride a motorcycle.**
motorboat, *zn*
motorboot.
motorcyclist, *zn*
motorrijder.
motorist, *zn*
automobilist.
motorway, *zn*
snelweg; **we drove north along the new motorway; if we take the motorway we will get there more quickly; there is a lot of traffic on the motorway.**

mountain ['maʊntn] *zn*
berg; **Everest is the highest mountain in the world; we go climbing in the moun-**

tains every weekend; are we nearly at the top of the mountain yet? mountain railway = bergspoorlijn.**

mouse [maʊs] *zn*
muis; **a mouse ran under the bed; my sister is afraid of mice; John brought a white mouse to school.**
meervoud **mice** [maɪs]

moustache [məˈstɑːʃ] *zn*
snor; **the policeman had a big black moustache.**

mouth [maʊθ] *zn*
mond; **don't talk with your mouth full; she was sleeping with her mouth open; the cat was carrying a bird in her mouth.**
meervoud **mouths** [maʊðz]
mouthful, *zn*
mondvol; **he had a mouthful of bread.**

move [muːv] **1.** *zn*
beweging; zet (*bij spel*); **we must make a move** = we moeten ervandoor; **get a move on!** = schiet op! **what's the next move?** = wat is de volgende stap?
2. *ww*
(*a*) (zich) bewegen, (zich) verplaatsen; **move the chairs away from the table; an animal was moving in the bushes; only the end of the cat's tail was moving; who's moved my book?—I left it on the table; he moved his head; don't move!** = verroer je niet!
(*b*) verhuizen; **they moved from Edinburgh to London; my husband has got a job in Oxford, but I don't want to move; we are moving back to London.**
moves—moving—moved—has moved
move about, *ww*
(zich) heen en weer bewegen; **he moved the boxes about; crowds of people were moving about in the street.**
move away, *ww*
(zich) verwijderen; **the ship moved away from the harbour; we're moving away from London** = we gaan naar buiten verhuizen (uit Londen).
move in, *ww*
een woning betrekken.

movement, *zn*
beweging; **there was a movement in the
trees; all you could see was a slight
movement of the cat's tail.**
move off, *ww*
zich verwijderen; zich in beweging
zetten; **the car moved off; he tried to get on
to the train as it was moving off.**

Mr ['mɪstə] *zn*
meneer; de heer; **Mr Jones; Mr John
Jones; Dear Mr Smith** (*als briefaanhef*);
Mr and Mrs Smith.
Mr *wordt met een achternaam gebruikt en soms met zowel voor- als
achternaam*

Mrs ['mɪsɪz] *zn*
mevrouw; **Mrs Jones; Mrs Anne Jones;
Dear Mrs Jones** (*als briefaanhef*); **Mr
and Mrs Smith.**
Mrs *wordt met een achternaam gebruikt en soms met zowel voor- als
achternaam*

Ms [mɪz] *zn*
mw.; **Ms Jones; Dear Ms Jones** (*als
briefaanhef*).
Ms *wordt met een achternaam gebruikt*

much [mʌtʃ] **1.** *bn*
veel; **with much love; how much bread do
you want? I never carry much money with
me; he eats too much meat; how much
does it cost?** = hoeveel kost dat? **how
much is that book?**
as much as = zoveel als, evenveel
als; **you haven't eaten as much as she has;
he spends as much money as me.**
Let op: **much** *wordt met niet telbare
zelfstandige naamwoorden gebruikt:*
not much money *maar* **not many
boys**
2. *bw*
veel; **she's feeling much better today; it's
much less cold in the south of the
country; does it matter very much? that
book is much too expensive.**
much—more [mɔː]**—most** [məʊst]
3. *zn*
veel; **much of the work has been done;
you didn't write much in your exam; do**

you see much of him? = zie je hem
vaak?

mud [mʌd] *zn*
modder; **we were up to our ankles in
mud; the tractor got stuck in the mud.**
geen meervoud
muddy, *bn*
modderig; **don't walk across the kitchen
in your muddy boots; he dropped his hat
into a pool of muddy water.**
muddy—muddier—muddiest
mudguard, *zn*
spatbord.

multiply ['mʌltɪplaɪ] *ww*
vermenigvuldigen; **if you multiply 240 by
2 the answer is 480.**
**multiplies—multiplying—
multiplied—has multiplied**
multiplication [mʌltɪplɪ'keɪʃn] *zn*
vermenigvuldiging; **I can do division but
I'm no good at multiplication.**

mum [mʌm], **mummy** ['mʌmɪ] *zn*
mam(ma); **go and tell your mum I want
to see her; is your mummy at home? my
mummy's gone shopping; Mummy! can I
have a biscuit?**
Wordt **Mum** *of* **Mummy** *gespeld als
aanspreekvorm, maar* **mum** *of
mummy* *als over een moeder wordt
gesproken*

mumps [mʌmps] *zn meervoud*
de bof; **he caught mumps from the children next door; she's in bed with mumps;
he can't go to school—he's got mumps.**

murder ['mɜːdə] **1.** *zn*
moord; **he was arrested for murder; the
police are looking for the knife used in
the murder.**
2. *ww*
vermoorden; **he was charged with murdering the old man; she was murdered
while she was sleeping.**
**murders—murdering—
murdered—has murdered**
murderer, *zn*
moordenaar.

muscle ['mʌsl] *zn*
spier; **if you do a lot of exercises you
develop strong muscles.**

museum [mju:'zɪəm] *zn*
    museum; **a railway museum** = spoor-
wegmuseum; **war museum** = oorlogs-
museum; **a museum of country life; a
museum of modern art; the British
Museum.**

music ['mju:zɪk] *zn*
    (*a*) muziek; **do you like modern music?
he's taking music lessons; her music
teacher says she plays the piano very well.**
    (*b*) muziek; **here's some piano music—
try and play it; he can play the piano
without any music.**
    geen meervoud: **some music; a
piece of music**

musical, *bn*
    muzikaal, muziek-; **he doesn't play any
musical instrument.**

must [mʌst] *hulpww*
    (*a*) moeten; **you must do your homework
or the teacher will be angry; we mustn't
be late or we'll miss the TV programme;
you must hurry up if you want to catch
the bus; must you go so soon?**
    Ontkennend: **mustn't, needn't**
    Let op: **mustn't** = niet mogen,
needn't = niet hoeven; **we mustn't
be late/you needn't hurry**
    (*b*) moeten, zullen (wel); **I must have left
my umbrella on the train; there's a knock
at the door—it must be the doctor; they
must be wet after walking in the rain.**
    Ontkennend: **can't: it can't be the
doctor.**
    **I must, you must, he must, we
must, they must**
    Verleden tijd: **had to: I must go to
the dentist's/I had to go to the
dentist's yesterday**

    Ontkennend: **didn't have to**
    Voltooid tegenwoordige tijd: **must
have: I must have left it on the
train**
    Ontkennend: **can't have: I can't
have left it on the train**
    Let op: **must** *wordt zonder* **to** *en
altijd met andere werkwoorden ge-
bruikt*

mustard ['mʌstəd] *zn*
    mosterd; **do you want some mustard with
your beef? have you put any mustard on
the ham sandwiches?**
    geen meervoud

mutton ['mʌtn] *zn*
    schapevlees; **we're having a leg of mutton
for lunch on Sunday.**
    Let op: **mutton** *wordt minder vaak
gebruikt dan* **lamb**

my [maɪ] *bn*
    mijn, van mij; **that's my pen you're
using! have you seen my new car? I broke
my leg when I was playing football.**

myself, *vnw*
    (me-/mij)zelf; **I've hurt myself; I saw it
myself; I enjoyed myself very much** = ik
heb me erg vermaakt; **I did it all by
myself** = ik heb het helemaal zelf
gedaan; **I don't like being all by myself
in the big house** = ik ben niet graag
helemaal alleen in dat grote huis.

mystery ['mɪstrɪ] *zn*
    raadsel, mysterie; **it is a mystery how the
burglar got into the house; the police are
trying to clear up the mystery of the
missing jewels.**
    meervoud **mysteries**

Nn

nail [neɪl] **1.** *zn*
    (*a*) nagel; **she painted her nails red; nail
scissors** = nagelschaartje; *zie ook*
fingernail, toenail

    (*b*) spijker; **hang that picture on the nail;
put in another nail—the piece of wood is
loose.**
    2. *ww*

(vast)spijkeren; **she nailed the pieces of wood together; they were nailing the carpet to the floor; they nailed down the lid of the box.**

nails—nailing—nailed—has nailed

name [neɪm] **1.** *zn*
naam; **his name's John; I've forgotten the name of the shoe shop; Christian name/ first name** = voornaam; **her Christian name/her first name is Anne, but I don't know her surname; I know him by name** = ik ken hem van naam; **don't call the teacher names** = niet je onderwijzer(es) uitschelden! *zie ook* **surname**
2. *ww*
noemen; **he's named John after his grandfather** = hij heet John naar zijn grootvader; **can you name the largest town in the USA?**

names—naming—named—has named

narrow [ˈnærəʊ] *bn*
nauw; **the road is too narrow for two cars to pass; we had a narrow escape** = we zijn door het oog van een naald gekropen.

narrow—narrower—narrowest

narrowly, *bw*
ternauwernood, net; **we narrowly missed hitting the lamppost.**

nasty [ˈnɑːstɪ] *bn*
vervelend, naar, akelig; vies; **this medicine has a nasty taste; he's a nasty man— I don't like him; there's a nasty smell coming from the kitchen.**

nasty—nastier—nastiest

nation [ˈneɪʃn] *zn*
natie; **all the nations of the world.**
national [ˈnæʃnl] *bn*
nationaal; **she's wearing national costume; they're singing a national song.**
nationality [næʃəˈnælɪtɪ] *zn*
nationaliteit; **he's of French nationality; what nationality is she?**

nature [ˈneɪtʃə] *zn*
natuur; **nature study** = biologieles op lagere school.

natural [ˈnætʃrəl] *bn*
(*a*) natuurlijk, normaal; **his behaviour was quite natural; it's quite natural for old people to go deaf.**
(*b*) natuurlijk, aangeboren; **do you think the colour of her hair is natural?** = denk je dat dat haar eigen haarkleur is? **natural gas** = aardgas; **natural history** = natuurlijke historie.
naturally, *bw*
(*a*) natuurlijk, vanzelfsprekend; **naturally the little boy was beaten by the big one; do you want to watch the game?—naturally!**
(*b*) van nature; vanzelf; **she has naturally curly hair.**

naughty [ˈnɔːtɪ] *bn*
stout; **if you're naughty you won't have any ice cream; you naughty boy, stop pulling the cat's tail.**

naughty—naughtier—naughtiest
Let op: **naughty** *wordt meestal voor kinderen of dieren gebruikt.*

navy [ˈneɪvɪ] *zn*
marine, vloot; **he's in the navy; we want to join the navy; navy blue** = marineblauw.

meervoud **navies**

near [ˈnɪə] *bw, vz & bn*
(*a*) dichtbij(zijnd); **the shops are near the post office; bring your chair nearer to the fire; the bus stop is nearer to our house than the pub; which is the nearest police station? we had a near miss** = het scheelde niet veel of we hadden een aanrijding gehad; **the near side** = trottoirkant.
(*b*) vlak voor, tegen; **my birthday is on December 21st—it's quite near to Christmas; phone me again nearer the day when you want to see me.**

near—nearer—nearest

nearby [nɪəˈbaɪ] *bw & bn*
dichtbij/nabij(gelegen); **they live just nearby; we met in a nearby pub.**
nearly, *bw*
bijna, haast; **he's nearly 20 years old; the war lasted nearly ten years; hurry up, it's nearly time for the bus to come; this film isn't nearly as good as the one we saw**

last week = deze film is lang niet zo
goed als etc.

neat [ni:t] *bn*
net(jes); **her room is always neat and
tidy; why is his homework never neat?**
neat—neater—neatest

necessary ['nesəsərı] *bn*
noodzakelijk, nodig; **it's necessary to
pay your tax at the correct date; if you
are going abroad it's necessary to have a
passport; is all this equipment really
necessary?**

neck [nek] *zn*
(*a*) nek; **I've got a stiff neck; she wears a
gold chain round her neck; he's breathing
down my neck all the time** = hij kijkt
steeds over mijn schouder; **they're neck
and neck** = ze liggen nek aan nek.
(*b*) hals(opening); **a pullover with a V
neck; what size neck shirts do you wear?**
(*c*) hals; **the neck of a bottle; a neck of
land** = landtong.
necklace ['nekləs] *zn*
ketting, halssnoer.

need [ni:d] **1.** *zn*
behoefte; noodzaak; **there's no need for
us to wait** = we hoeven niet te wachten;
to be in need of = nodig hebben, behoefte hebben aan; **they're in need of
food; are you in need of help?**
2. *ww*
nodig hebben; vereisen; moeten/(niet)
hoeven; **we shall need foreign money for
our holiday; painting needs a lot of skill;
do you need help? the house needs painting; I'm afraid the TV needs mending
again; do you really need all this equipment? the police need to know who saw
the accident; you don't need to come
if you have a cold; will you be needing
me any more or can I go home? I need
you to help me with the cleaning; you
can take the book—I don't need it any
more.**
**needs—needing—needed—has
needed**

needn't *hulpww*
niet hoeven; **you needn't come if you
have a cold; he needn't have phoned; he**

**needn't make so much noise in the
bath.**
Let op: **needn't** *wordt zonder* **to** *en
alleen met andere werkwoorden gebruikt*

needle ['ni:dl] *zn*
naald; **she's lost her knitting needles;
don't sit down, I've left a needle on that
chair.**

negative ['negətıv] *bn & zn*
ontkennend(e vorm);   ontkenning;
**'didn't' is the negative of 'did'; the
answer's in the negative** = het antwoord
luidt ontkennend.

neighbour ['neıbə] *zn* (*Amer.* **neigh-
bor**)
buur(man)/buur(vrouw); **our next door
neighbours** = de buren van hiernaast;
the Swedes and Danes are neighbours.
neighbourhood, *zn* (*Amer.* **neigh-
borhood**)
buurt, omgeving; **this is a quiet neighbourhood; the postman knows everyone
in the neighbourhood.**
neighbouring, *bn* (*Amer.* **neigh-
boring**)
naburig, aangrenzend; **we go to the
neighbouring town to see the doctor as
there isn't one in our town; Sweden and
Denmark are neighbouring countries.**

neither ['naıðə] **1.** *bn & vnw*
geen van beide(n); **neither of them
guessed the right answer; neither brother
is fair/neither of the brothers is fair.**
2. *bw & vw*
noch; en ... ook niet; **he doesn't like
fish and neither do I** = en ik ook niet;
**it's neither too hot nor too cold—it's just
right; he isn't tall—but neither is he
really very short** = maar erg lang is hij
ook niet.
*Let op: het werkwoord komt voor het
onderwerp na* **neither**

nephew ['nefju:] *zn*
neef(je); **my sister has two sons, so I have
two nephews; an uncle and his nephews.**

nerve [nɜ:v] *zn*
zenuw; **she's in a state of nerves** = ze is

nest   nice

op van de zenuwen; **he gets on my nerves**
= hij werkt op mijn zenuwen; **he had
the nerve to tell me to be quick when he's
so slow himself** = hij had de brutaliteit
om me te vertellen etc.
nervous, *bn*
nerveus, zenuwachtig; **she's nervous
about her exams; don't be nervous—the
driving test is quite easy.**

nest [nest] *zn*
nest; **the birds have built a nest in the
apple tree.**

net [net] **1.** *zn*
net; **a fishing net; a tennis net; he hit the
ball into the net.**
2. *bn*
netto; **net weight** = netto gewicht; **net
profit** = netto winst.

the Netherlands [ðə'neðələndz] *zn*
meervoud
Nederland; **we went to the Netherlands
on holiday; my sister lives in the Netherlands; many people from the Netherlands
come to spend their holidays in England.**
*Let op: wordt altijd met the ge-
schreven*

never ['nevə] *bw*
nooit; **I'll never forget our holiday in
Sweden: I've never been into that shop
although I've often walked past it; she
never eats meat; never mind!** = het hindert niet!

new [nju:] *bn*
(*a*) nieuw, ongebruikt; **take a new piece
of paper; this is a new model of car; this
bike is new—I didn't buy it secondhand.**
(*b*) nieuw, recent; **here are the new boys
in the school; we bought some new
potatoes.**
(*c*) nieuw; **have you seen his new car? she
introduced me to her new teacher.**
new—newer—newest
New Year, *zn*
Nieuwjaar; **I start my new job in the
New Year; Happy New Year** = vrolijk/
gelukkig Nieuwjaar; **New Year's Day** =
Nieuwjaarsdag.
news, *zn*
nieuws; **he was watching the 9 o'clock**

**news on TV; did you hear the news on
the radio? he told me the news about the
fire; have you heard the news?** = heb je
het nieuws gehoord? **have you had any
news about your new job? we always like
to hear good news.**
*Let op: news is enkelvoud, geen
meervoud*

newsagent, *zn*
sigarenwinkel, tijdschriftenhandel; **go to
the newsagent's and get me today's
newspaper and the TV magazine.**
newspaper, *zn*
krant; **a daily newspaper/a weekly
newspaper** = dag-/weekblad; **has
today's newspaper been delivered? have
you finished the crossword in today's
newspaper? yesterday's newspaper was
full of news of the election.**
*Let op: a newspaper wordt vaak a
paper genoemd*

next [nekst] *bn & bw*
(*a*) volgende; aanstaande; nu, nou; vervolgens; **on Wednesday we arrived in
London and the next day we left for
Scotland; what shall we do next? first the
teacher came into the classroom, and
next came a policeman; come to see me
when you're next in London** = de volgende keer dat je in Londen bent etc.;
**next Monday I start my holidays; the
next time you go to the post office, can
you buy me some of the new stamps?
come to see me the week after next; next
please!** = wie volgt/wie is er aan de
beurt?
(*b*) aangrenzend; naast; **the walls are
thin—we can hear everything that is said
in the next room; he sat down next to
me; it costs next to nothing** = vrijwel
niets.
next door, *bn & bw*
(hier)naast; **she lives next door to my
aunt; our next door neighbours are Germans** = de buren van hiernaast; **they
have a lot of flowers next door.**

nice [nais] *bn*
fijn, leuk, prettig; **what a nice time we
had at the party! come and see us if the
weather's nice; it wasn't fine today, so**

we hope it'll be nicer tomorrow; he had a
nice sleep after lunch; we went for a nice
ride in his new car; that wasn't a very
nice thing to say = het was niet erg
aardig van je om dat te zeggen.
nice—nicer—nicest

niece [ni:s] *zn*
nicht(je); I've got three nieces—they're
my brother's children; the niece looks
like her aunt.

night [naɪt] *zn*
nacht; avond; I don't like going out
alone late at night; it rained a lot during
the night; we stayed at home last night,
but tomorrow night we're going to a
party; if you travel by night you pay less
= als je 's nachts reist, betaal je
minder.

nine [naɪn] negen
he's nine (years old); come to see me
tomorrow morning at nine o'clock;
you've eaten nine cakes! nine times out
of ten = negen van de tien keer.
nineteen, negentien
she's nineteen (years old); the nineteen
fifteen train = de trein van 19.15; in the
1950s = in de vijftiger jaren.
Let op: **1950s:** *zeg* 'the nineteen
fifties'

nineteenth, 19th, *bn & zn*
negentiende; he came nineteenth in the
race; it's her nineteenth birthday tomorrow; the nineteenth century; the nineteenth of June/June the nineteenth (June
19th).
ninety, negentig
she is ninety (years old); her husband is
ninety-two; they are both in their
nineties.
Let op: **ninety-one** (91), **ninety-two**
(92), *etc., maar* **ninety-first** (91st),
ninety-second (92nd), *etc.*

ninetieth, 90th, *bn & zn*
negentigste; a ninetieth of a second; she
was ninetieth in the competition; it will
be grandmother's ninetieth birthday next
month.
ninth, 9th, *bn & zn*
negende; at least a ninth of the children
are ill; she was ninth in her exam; today

is the ninth of September /September the
ninth (September 9th); tomorrow is his
ninth birthday.

no [nəʊ] *bn & bw*
(a) nee; we asked him if he wanted to
come, and he said 'no'; do you want some
more coffee?—no, thank you.
(b) geen; there's no butter left; there are
no shops for miles around; I've had no
reply to my letter; no parking/no smok-
ing/no exit = niet parkeren/roken; geen
uitgang.
(c) niet; this book is no better than the
last one I read; he's no longer here; he's
no good at his job.

nobody ['nəʊbədɪ] *vnw*
niemand; there's nobody in the bathroom; I saw nobody I knew; nobody likes
sour milk; nobody else wears long socks
like you.

nod [nɒd] **1.** *zn*
knik(je); he gave me a nod; when we
asked if he wanted an ice cream, he gave
a nod.
2. *ww*
knikken; he nodded to me in the street;
when she asked if anyone wanted an ice
cream all the children nodded.
**nods—nodding—nodded—has
nodded**

nod off, *ww*
indommelen; he nodded off in his chair;
give me a pinch if I nod off; she's nodding
off over her book.

noise [nɔɪz] *zn*
geluid; lawaai; don't make so much
noise—I'm trying to work; the car's
making strange noises—perhaps something's wrong with the engine; I thought
I heard a noise in the kitchen; he's
making such a lot of noise that he can't
hear the telephone; we were woken up by
noises in the night.
noisy, *bn*
lawaai(e)rig; luidruchtig; a noisy car; a
crowd of noisy children.
noisy—noisier—noisiest

none [nʌn] *vnw*
(a) geen; a little money is better than

none at all; none of the houses has a red door; he was none the worse for his accident = hij is er bij dat ongeluk heelhuids vanaf gekomen; her health is none too good = haar gezondheid is bepaald niet zo best.

(b) geen (enkele); none of the teachers has a beard; none of the guests left the party early.

nonsense ['nɒnsəns] zn
onzin, nonsens; you're talking nonsense; it's nonsense to say that money doesn't matter; take an umbrella!—nonsense, it won't rain; stop that nonsense at once!

no one ['nəʊwʌn] vnw
niemand; there's no one in the room; I saw no one I knew; no one here likes sour milk; no one else wears long socks like you.

nor [nɔː] vw
neither ... nor = (noch ...) noch; she's neither English nor German; neither you nor she looks very well.

normal ['nɔːml] bn
gewoon, normaal; wet weather is quite normal at this time of year; after the Christmas holidays the trains went back to their normal service.
normally, bw
gewoonlijk, normaal; I normally have a cup of chocolate before going to bed; we normally go on holiday in August.

north [nɔːθ] **1.** zn
(het) noorden; snow fell in the north of the country; the wind is blowing from the north.
2. bn
noord-, noorden-; the north coast of Scotland; the north side of the house never gets any sun.
3. bw
noordwaarts; naar/op het noorden; we were travelling north; the house faces north.
North America, zn
Noord-Amerika.
northern, ['nɔːðn] bn
noordelijk; they live in the northern part of the country.

North Pole, zn
noordpool.
North Sea, zn
Noordzee.

nose [nəʊz] zn
neus; he has a red nose; dogs have wet noses; she must have a cold—her nose is running = ze heeft een druipneus; don't wipe your nose on your sleeve—use a handkerchief; he blew his nose several times =hij snoot verschillende keren zijn neus; to speak through your nose; to look down your nose at something = op iets neerkijken, minachten; to turn up your nose at something = je neus voor iets ophalen.

not [nɒt] bw
(a) (afgekort **n't**) niet; he won't come; she isn't there; he didn't eat his meat; they couldn't go home because of the snow; the service charge is not included.
(b) niet; it is not at all funny; is he coming?—I hope not = ik hoop van niet; I don't want to go—why not? all the family was there—not forgetting old Aunt Jane = niet te vergeten onze oude tante Jane; not a few = heel wat; not very well = niet zo goed/gezond; I'm not sorry to leave = ik ben blij weg te kunnen.
not ... either = niet ... en ook niet; I don't like meat and I don't like fish either; it wasn't fine but it wasn't raining either.
not only ... but also = niet alleen ... maar ook; he isn't only blind, but he's also deaf; the book is not only very long but it's also very bad.

note [nəʊt] **1.** zn
(a) kort briefje; lijstje; notitie; I sent him a note to say I was ill; he made some notes before giving his speech; we must make a note of what we need before we go on holiday.
(b) (Amer. **bill**) bankbiljet; he only had a five pound note to pay for the newspaper.
(c) toon; noot; toets; he can't sing the high notes; he only played the black notes on the piano.

2. *ww*
(*a*) noteren; **the policeman noted down down the details of the accident.**
(*b*) opmerken, notitie nemen van iets; **please note that the film starts at 7 o'clock.**
notes—noting—noted—has noted

notebook, *zn*
aantekenboekje
notepaper, *zn*
schrijfpapier.
geen meervoud: **some notepaper; a piece of notepaper**

nothing [ˈnʌθɪŋ] *zn*
niets; **there's nothing in the box; when asked about the accident he said nothing; he said nothing about the accident; he thinks nothing of cycling ten miles to work** = hij draait zijn hand niet om voor etc.; **it's nothing to do with you** = dat gaat jou niets aan; **nothing much happened** = er gebeurde niets bijzonders; **there was nothing interesting on the news; there's nothing more to be done; he has nothing left in the bank** = hij heeft geen geld meer op de bank.

notice [ˈnəʊtɪs] **1.** *zn*
(*a*) bericht, aankondiging; **he pinned up a notice about the meeting.**
(*b*) waarschuwing; **they had to leave with ten minutes' notice; it had to be done at short notice** = op korte termijn; **if you want to leave your job, you have to give a month's notice** = je moet een maand van tevoren je ontslag indienen als etc.
(*c*) aandacht; **take no notice of what he says** = besteed (er) geen aandacht aan/trek het je niet aan wat hij zegt.
2. *ww*
opmerken; **nobody noticed that I was wearing one blue and one white sock; did you notice what the time was when I started boiling the egg?**
notices—noticing—noticed—has noticed

noticeboard, *zn*
mededelingenbord.

nought [nɔːt] nul
a million is written as a one and six noughts.

noun [naʊn] *zn*
zelfstandig naamwoord; **'man', 'stone' and 'colour' are all nouns.**

November [nəˈvembə] *zn*
november; **today is November 5th; he was born in November; we didn't go away last November.**
Let op: **November 5th:** *zeg* 'the fifth of November' *of* 'November the fifth'
Let op: **November** *wordt altijd met een hoofdletter geschreven*

now [naʊ] **1.** *bw*
nu, nou; **I can hear the car coming now; can we go to the beach now? he ought to be in Germany by now; now's the best time for picking apples; a week from now we'll be on holiday** = over een week; **until now she has never had to see a doctor** = tot nu toe.
2. *vw*
nu; **now (that) I know how to drive I can go on holiday by myself; now that you've reminded me, I do remember seeing him last week.**
3. *tw*
(*a*) nou, nu; **now then, let's get ready; come on now, pull hard!**
(*b*) vooruit, nou; **now, let's begin.**
nowadays, *bw*
tegenwoordig, nu; **everything is very different nowadays from what it was fifty years ago; nowadays most people have cars and fridges.**

nowhere [ˈnəʊweə] *bw*
(*a*) nergens; **the cat was nowhere to be found; where are you going?—nowhere! there is nowhere else to put the typewriter.**
(*b*) **nowhere near** = op geen stukken na; **the house is nowhere near finished; he has nowhere near done his homework.**

nuisance [ˈnjuːsns] *zn*
last(post); **that little boy is a real nuisance; what a nuisance—I've lost my**

front door key! = wat lastig/vervelend etc.

number ['nʌmbə] *zn*
(*a*) nummer; getal; **13 is my lucky number; they live in flat number 48b; what is your telephone number? I can't remember the number of our car.**
(*b*) aantal; **a large number/large numbers of people are waiting to take their driving tests; a large number of houses were damaged in the fire; only a small number of people were there; I've seen that film a number of times** = verscheidene keren; **I've been to London any number of times** = ik ben talloze keren in Londen geweest; **you could take your driving test any number of times but you still wouldn't pass it.**

Let op: als **number** *bij een meervoudig zelfstandig naamwoord hoort, volgt er een werkwoord in het meervoud:* **a number of houses were damaged**

nurse [nɜːs] **1.** *zn*
verpleegster; **she works as a nurse in the local hospital; she's training to be a nurse; male nurse** = verpleger.
2. *ww*
verplegen; **when he was ill, his sister nursed him until he was better.**
nurses—nursing—nursed—has nursed

nursery school, *zn*
kleuterschool; **now she is three, we may send her to nursery school in the mornings.**

nut [nʌt] *zn*
noot; **he was eating a bar of milk chocolate with nuts.**

Oo

oar [ɔː] *zn*
roeiriem.

obedient [ə'biːdiənt] *bn*
gehoorzaam; **our dog isn't very obedient—he won't sit down when we tell him to.**

obey [ə'beɪ] *ww*
gehoorzamen; **you ought to obey your father; you must obey the rules.**
obeys—obeying—obeyed—has obeyed

object 1. *zn* ['ɒbdʒɪkt]
(*a*) voorwerp; **a big black object fell into the middle of the field.**
(*b*) doel; **what's the object of your plan?**
(*c*) lijdend voorwerp, object; **in the sentence 'the dog chased the cat', the word 'cat' is the object of the verb 'chased'.**
2. *ww* [əb'dʒekt]
bezwaar maken (tegen); **I object to**

having to attend long meetings; he objected to my going on holiday; does anyone object if I smoke my pipe?
objects—objecting—objected—has objected

observe [əb'zɜːv] *ww*
gadeslaan, observeren; opmerken; **a policeman observed them putting the boxes into a van.**
observes—observing—observed—has observed

obvious ['ɒbviəs] *bn*
duidelijk; **it's obvious that the car is no good; he made a very obvious mistake.**
obviously, *bw*
duidelijk; **obviously he was very pleased when he passed his exam.**

occupy ['ɒkjʊpaɪ] *ww*
bezetten, in beslag nemen; bezig houden; **the table occupies the whole corner of the room; how do you occupy**

your time when you are on holiday? the
soldiers occupied the town; is this seat
occupied? I'm afraid the manager is
occupied at the moment = het spijt
me, maar de manager is nu niet te
spreken.
**occupies—occupying—
occupied—has occupied**
occupation [ɒkjʊˈpeɪʃn] *zn*
beroep; what is his occupation?

ocean [ˈəʊʃn] *zn*
oceaan; the Pacific Ocean; the Atlantic
Ocean.

o'clock [əˈklɒk] *bw bijzin*
uur; it's 6 o'clock; I never get up before
8 o'clock; by 10 o'clock everyone was
asleep.
*Let op: o'clock wordt alleen voor het
hele uur gebruikt, niet voor tijden
waarin minuten voorkomen. Het kan
ook weggelaten worden: we got
home at eleven = we got home
at eleven o'clock*

October [ɒkˈtəʊbə] *zn*
oktober; were you born in October?
today is October 21st; last October we
went to Germany.
*Let op: October 21st: zeg 'the
twenty-first of October' of 'October
the twenty-first'*
*Let op: October wordt altijd met een
hoofdletter geschreven*

odd [ɒd] *bn*
(a) vreemd, raar; I find it odd that he
hasn't written to us; how odd that the
door wasn't locked; isn't it odd that he is
afraid of the telephone?
(b) oneven (getal); 3, 5, 7 are all odd
numbers; the houses with odd numbers
are on this side of the street.
(c) enkel, één enkel(e); I have two odd
socks = twee verschillende sokken;
there was an odd glove left on the table.
(d) ongeregeld; he does odd jobs in the
house = hij knapt klusjes op etc.; she
writes the odd article for the newspaper
= ze schrijft nu en dan een artikel voor
de krant.
odd—odder—oddest

of [ɒv] *vz*
(a) van; he's the son of the man who
mended my car; she's a friend of mine;
where's the lid of the black saucepan?
what are the dates of Henry VIII?
(b) (er)van; how much of it do you want?
today is the first of June; there are six of
them = er zijn er zes; half of the team
were ill with flu; a pint of milk; two kilos
of potatoes.
(c) van; a child of ten = een kind van
tien (jaar); the town of Bath is an important town in the west.
(d) van, aan; he lives south of the town;
the pullover is made of wool; he died of
his wounds.
*Let op: of wordt vaak na werkwoor-
den of bijvoeglijke naamwoorden
gebruikt: to think of; to be fond of;
to be tired of; to smell of; to be
afraid of, etc.*

off [ɒf] *bw & vz*
(a) weg; (er)af; van hier/daar; uit; van-
(af); I'm off to France tomorrow; the post
office is just off the High Street = ligt
vlak achter de hoofdstraat; she got off
the bus; take your shoes off if they are
wet; take the cloth off the table; he fell
off his horse; he's taking a day off = hij
neemt een dag vrij(af); the off side = de
kant van de rijweg.
(b) uit; af; switch all the lights off; is the
TV off?
*Let op: off wordt vaak na werkwoor-
den gebruikt: to keep off; to take
off; to fall off; to break off, etc.*

offer [ˈɒfə] 1. *zn*
aanbieding, aanbod; £10 is the best offer
I can make = meer dan £10 kan ik niet
bieden; we had offers of help from
everyone in the village; special offer =
speciale aanbieding.
2. *ww*
aanbieden; did he offer to help? they
didn't even offer me a cup of tea; I
offered to go with her to the bus stop.
**offers—offering—offered—has
offered**

office [ˈɒfɪs] *zn*
kantoor; he works in an office in

Office *Kantoor*

1.	book	*boek*	12.	notice	*berichtje*
2.	calculator	*rekenmachine*	13.	noticeboard	*mededelingenbord*
3.	card	*kaart*	14.	page	*bladzij*
4.	cassette	*cassette*	15.	parcel	*pakje*
5.	cheque	*cheque*	16.	pen	*pen*
6.	drawing pin	*punaise*	17.	pencil	*potlood*
7.	envelope	*envelop*	18.	ruler	*lineaal*
8.	ink	*inkt*	19.	safe	*kluis*
9.	letter	*brief*	20.	telephone	*telefoon*
10.	magazine	*tijdschrift*	21.	telephone book	*telefoonboek*
11.	notebook	*aantekenboekje*	22.	typewriter	*schrijfmachine*

London; **I'll be staying late at the office this evening; she's the manager of our London office; Miss Jones's office is next door to mine;** zie ook **post office**

officer [ˈɒfɪsə] zn
officier; **he's an army officer; a police officer came to look at the damage** = een politieagent.

official [əˈfɪʃl] 1. bn
officieel; **an official report; his official title is Manager of the Sales Department.**
2. zn
ambtenaar, functionaris; **an official from the Tax Office came to look at our accounts; she's an official in the Department of Education.**

often [ˈɒfn] bw
vaak, dikwijls; **I often go to Paris on business; do you often have chicken for dinner? how often do the trains go to London? I go to the cinema every so often** = ik ga nu en dan naar de bioskoop.

oh [əʊ] tw
oh! **Oh look, there's the train! Oh stop it, I can't hear the radio! Oh, Mr Jones, can you come here, please? you must come to the police station—Oh no I won't!**

oil [ɔɪl] 1. zn
olie; **cooking oil; vegetable oil; he's fond of painting in oils** = hij schildert graag met olieverf; **an oil painting; an oil well; an oil field.**
2. ww
oliën, smeren; **you should oil the car door because it makes a noise.**
oils—oiling—oiled—has oiled

OK [əʊˈkeɪ] zn & tw
ok, goed; **shall we start now?—OK, let's go; I was ill yesterday, but I'm OK now; he gave our plan the OK** = hij keurde ons plan goed.

old [əʊld] bn
(a) oud; **my grandfather is an old man —he's eighty; my mother's getting old; an old church; I don't like this old music—play something modern.**

(b) oud; **I'll have to wear my old clothes to paint the house; she sold her old car and bought a new one.**
(c) oud; **she's ten years old today; how old are you?**
(d) (vriendelijke manier om over iemand te praten) oud; **hello, old boy!** = hallo, ouwe jongen! **the old man** = de oude baas; **my old man** = mijn ouwe (man); pa.
old—older—oldest

on [ɒn] 1. vz
(a) op; **put the book on the table; flies can walk on the ceiling.**
(b) aan; **hang the picture on the hook.**
(c) op; aan; **he got on the train** = hij stapte in de trein; **it's on page 4; the house is on the right side of the road.**
(d) in, bij; **she's on the staff of the school; he's on the committee.**
(e) voor, op; **he's gone to Germany on business; they're on holiday.**
(f) op; **on Sundays; on Monday we went to the zoo; on December 25th; on my arrival** = bij (mijn) aankomst.
(g) op, per; te (voet); **he went away on foot; she's going on her bike.**
(h) over; **he wrote a book on African animals.**
(i) op, aan (de telefoon); **he played a piece of music on the piano; she was on the telephone for half an hour; the play was on the radio yesterday; I watched the football game on TV.**
2. bw
(a) op, aan; **put the kettle on; have you put your boots on? because it was cold he kept his coat on in the house.**
(b) aan; **the gas is on; you've left the light on; turn the engine on; switch the TV on; what's on at the cinema?** = wat draait er in de bioskoop?
(c) door, verder; **he worked on until the evening; she went on talking; go on— don't stop.**
(d) verder, van ... af (aan); **from that time on; later on** = naderhand;
Let op: on *wordt vaak na werkwoorden gebruikt* to sit on; to jump on; to put on; to lie on, *etc.*

once [wʌns] 1. bw
(a) eens, één keer; **take the medicine once**

a day; the magazine comes out once a
month; how many times did you see the
dentist?—only once.
(b) eens, ooit; I knew him once; once,
when I was going home, I fell off my
bike.
2. vw
zodra; once you start you can't stop;
once I'm on holiday, I'll swim every day.
at once, bw
(a) meteen, onmiddellijk; do it at once!
the doctor came at once.
(b) tegelijk; don't all speak at once.

one [wʌn] 1.
(a) één; our little boy is one year old; his
grandfather is a hundred and one.
(b) één; there's only one left; this is the
last page but one = de op één na laatste
bladzij.
2. bn & vnw
(a) één; there's only one cake left; which
one do you want—the green one or the
black one? one of the boys will help you;
I've lost my pen—have you got one?
(b) men, je; one just can't do that sort of
thing, can one? one can't afford to drive
a large car these days.
(c) one another = elkaar; you should
write to one another more often.
Let op: **one** (1) maar **first** (1st)

one-way street, zn
straat met eenrichtingsverkeer; you
can't turn left—it's a one-way street.

onion ['ʌnjən] zn
ui; we had onion soup for dinner.

only ['əʊnlɪ] 1. bn
enige; it's the only watch I've got; she's
an only child = een enig(st) kind.
2. bw
(a) alleen, enkel; I've only got three
pounds; only you can help us; staff only
can use this lift; only children are allowed
in free.
(b) nog pas; only yesterday I got a postcard from her.
if only als ... maar = if only I had
known; if only she had phoned the police.
only just = maar net; he only just
caught the bus = hij haalde de bus maar
net.

only too = maar al te; I'm only too
happy to help.

open ['əʊpn] 1. bn
(a) open; that box is open; leave the door
open—it's hot in here; why is the oven
door open?
(b) open/geopend; are the shops open on
Sundays? the exhibition is open from 10
a.m. to 5 p.m.
(c) open, toegankelijk; the field is open
on three sides; I like being out in the open
air; the competition is open to everyone
= iedereen kan meedoen aan de wedstrijd.
2. ww
(a) openen, open maken; open the
door—the cat wants to go out; can you
open that box?
(b) openen, open gaan; a new shop is
going to open next door to us; the shops
open early in the morning.
opens—opening—opened—has
opened

opener, zn
opener; a tin opener; a bottle opener.
opening, zn
(a) opening; opening time for the exhibition is 10.00 a.m.
(b) opening; gat; the sheep got out
through an opening in the hedge.
open on to, ww
uitkomen op; the door opens directly on
to the garden; the windows open on to
the street.

operation [ɒpə'reɪʃn] zn
operatie; she's had an operation on her
foot; the operation was successful.

opinion [ə'pɪnjən] zn
opinie, mening; what's your opinion of
the situation? ask the bank manager for
his opinion about what we should do; he
has a very high/a very low opinion of his
assistant = hij heeft een erg hoge/lage
dunk van zijn assistent.

opportunity [ɒpə'tjuːnɪtɪ] zn
gelegenheid, kans; if you start work
early, that will give you the opportunity
to finish before dinner; I'd like to learn

to fly a plane, but I've never had the opportunity to do so.
meervoud **opportunities**

oppose [ə'pouz] *ww*
zich verzetten (tegen); **he opposed his boss at the meeting; she is opposed to taking a long holiday this year.**
opposes—opposing—opposed—has opposed

opposite ['ɒpəzɪt] **1.** *bn & vz*
tegenover(gelegen),   tegenovergesteld; **their house is just opposite the post office; it's not on this side of the street—it's on the opposite side; his car hit a lorry going in the opposite direction; will you sit opposite my mother?**
2. *zn*
tegendeel; tegenovergestelde; **'big' is the opposite of 'small'; what's the opposite of 'black'? he's just the opposite of his brother; he said one thing, and then did the opposite.**

or [ɔː] *vw*
(*a*) of; **you can come with us or you can stay at home; I don't mind if I have tea or coffee; did she die in an accident or was she murdered?**
(*b*) (een stuk) of; **six or seven people came; it costs £4 or so** = het kost ongeveer £4.
or èlse = anders; **you must wear a coat or else you'll catch cold; he has to get up early or else he'll miss his train.**

orange ['ɒrɪnʒ] **1.** *zn*
sinaasappel; **I have an orange for breakfast; I like orange ice cream; can I have a glass of orange juice?**
2. *bn & zn*
oranje; **does he always wear an orange tie? they painted the kitchen ceiling orange; I'd like to paint the front door a dark orange.**

orchestra ['ɔːkɪstrə] *zn*
orkest; **the school orchestra played music by Beethoven.**

order ['ɔːdə] **1.** *zn*
(*a*) bevel, order; **he gave an order to the soldiers; if you can't obey orders, you shouldn't be a policeman.**

(*b*) bestelling; opdracht; **we've had a large order for machinery from Japan; he gave the waiter his order; the waiter brought him the wrong order.**
(*c*) (volg)orde; **the names on the list are in alphabetical order; the books in the library are all in the wrong order/all out of order** = staan door elkaar.
(*d*) orde; **the lift is out of order** = defect; **are your papers in order?** = zijn uw papieren in orde?
in order that = zodat; teneinde; **people on bikes should wear orange coats in order that drivers can see them in the dark.**
in order to = om; **he ran fast in order to catch the bus; she bent down in order to pick up her book.**
2. *ww*
(*a*) bevelen, voorschrijven; **he ordered the gate of the castle to be shut; the doctor ordered three weeks' rest; I don't like being ordered about** = ik hou er niet van gecommandeerd te worden.
(*b*) bestellen; **he ordered chicken and chips and a glass of beer; we've ordered a new electric typewriter.**
orders—ordering—ordered—has ordered

ordinary ['ɔːdnrɪ] *bn*
gewoon; normaal; **I'll wear my ordinary suit to the office; he leads a very ordinary life; the film is quite out of the ordinary** = buitengewoon.

organize ['ɔːgənaɪz] *ww*
organiseren/regelen; **you must organize your work properly; she organized a meeting to complain about the noise.**
organizes—organizing—organized—has organized

organization, *zn*
(*a*) organisatie; **you have to have good organization if you want the factory to work well.**
(*b*) organisatie/instelling; **a youth organization; an organization which sends food to poor people; she belongs to an organization which looks after old people.**

other ['ʌðə] *bn & vnw*
(*a*) ander(e); **the two boys went swim-**

ming while the other members of the family sat on the beach; I don't like these cakes —can I have one of the other ones/ one of the others? which others do you want? any other sort would do; can't we go to some other place on holiday next year?
(b) (het/de) ander(e); one pencil is red, and the other (one) is blue; one girl is tall, but the other (one) is short.
(c) een of ander; he went to stay in some village or other by the sea; she met some boy or other at the party; the other day/ the other week = een dag/week of wat geleden.
one after the other = de een na de ander; they fell down one after the other; they all got colds one after the other.
every other = om de andere; the police stopped every other car = elke tweede; he wrote a letter every other day = hij schreef om de andere dag een brief.

ought [ɔ:t] *hulpww*
(a) (be)horen, eigenlijk moeten; you ought to go to the cinema; he ought to see a doctor if his cough is no better; you oughtn't to eat so many cakes; she ought to have told you before she went away.
(b) zou(den) moeten; he ought to pass his exams easily; she ought to get home by 6 o'clock; they ought to have arrived by now.

I ought, you ought, he ought, we ought, they ought
Verleden tijd: ought to have
Ontkennend: ought not, ought not to have, *meestal* oughtn't, oughtn't to have
Let op: ought *wordt gevolgd door* to. ought *en* ought to have *worden met andere werkwoorden gebruikt en bezitten geen onbepaalde wijs*

our [ˈaʊə] *bn*
ons/onze; our house is near the post office; we have lost our dog; one of our children has got measles.
ours, *vnw*
van ons; de/het onze; that house is ours; is that their son?—no, he's ours; some

friends of ours told us to go; can we borrow your car, ours won't start?
ourselves, *vnw*
ons(zelf); we organized ourselves into two groups; we were enjoying ourselves; we did it all by ourselves = we hebben het helemaal zelf gedaan; we don't like being all by ourselves = we zijn niet graag helemaal alleen.

out [aʊt] *bw*
(a) uit; weg; tevoorschijn; no one answered the phone—they must all be out; the rabbit got out of its cage; he pulled out a gun; take the camera out of its box; the water came out of the hole in the pipe.
(b) weg; the tide is out = het is eb; the ship is out at sea = het schip is op zee.
(c) ernaast; mis; I am £10 out = ik heb me £10 verrekend; she was out in her answer to the sum.
(d) van, uit; he got 10 out of 12 for his exam; nine times out of ten she's wrong = negen van de tien keer.
Let op: out *wordt vaak na werkwoorden gebruikt:* to jump out; to get out; to come out, *etc.*
Let op: out *wordt vaak gevolgd door of*

outdoor, *bn*
buiten; an outdoor swimming pool = openluchtzwembad.
outdoors, *bw*
buiten; you should sit outdoors instead of sitting in the house.
outing, *zn*
uitje; uitstapje; dagje uit; we're going on an outing to the seaside.
output, *zn*
produktie; output is falling; the factory has an output of 200 tons per day.
outside 1. *zn*
buitenkant; the outside of the house is painted white; the apple looked nice on the outside, but the inside was rotten.
2. *bn*
buiten; the outside walls of the house.
3. *bw & vz*
buiten; I left my bike outside the front door; come and sit outside in the garden;

his coat's all wet—it must be raining outside.

oven ['ʌvn] *zn*
oven; **I've put a cake in the oven; your dinner's in the oven.**

over ['əʊvə] **1.** *vz*
(*a*) over; boven; over ... heen; **she spread a cloth over the table; the plane flew over our house; the water was soon over her ankles.**
(*b*) over, aan de overkant; **he lives over the road from the post office; she threw the bottle over the wall; they jumped over the railway lines.**
(*c*) over; **he fell over the edge; she looked over the edge.**
(*d*) gedurende; tijdens; **over the last few months he's grown quite tall; we talked about it over dinner.**
(*e*) boven; meer dan; **children over 5 years old; it costs over £50; we've been waiting for over two hours.**
2. *bw*
(*a*) overal; helemaal; **he's dirty all over.**
(*b*) (telkens) weer; **he played the record over and over again; they did it ten times over** = zij herhaalden het tien keer.
(*c*) om, voorover; **the bottle fell over; he knocked the bottle over; she leaned over and picked up the cushion.**
(*d*) over, voorbij, afgelopen; **is the game over yet? when the war was over we had more food to eat.**
(*e*) boven; meer dan; **children of 14 and over pay full price; there are reduced prices for groups of 30 and over.**
(*f*) over; **you can keep what's left over; I have two cards over.**
Let op: **over** *wordt na veel werkwoorden gebruikt:* **to run over; to fall over; to come over; to look over,** *etc.*

overalls, *zn meervoud*
overal; **he was wearing a pair of blue overalls.**

overcoat, *zn*
overjas; **put on your overcoat—it's snowing.**

overcrowded, *bn*
overvol/overladen; **the building is overcrowded; the overcrowded boat sank.**

overnight, *bw & bn*
's nachts; **we stayed overnight in France** = we overnachtten etc.; **will the food stay fresh overnight?** = zou het eten tot morgen goed blijven? **they took the overnight train to Scotland** = de nachttrein.

overtake, *ww*
inhalen; **he overtook three lorries on the motorway; we were overtaken by a bus.**
overtakes—overtaking—overtook—has overtaken

owe [əʊ] *ww*
(*a*) schuldig zijn; **he owes me £5; how much do I owe you for the petrol?**
(*b*) verschuldigd zijn, te danken hebben; **I owe him my life** = ik heb mijn leven aan hem te danken; **he owes a lot to his father** = hij heeft veel aan zijn vader te danken.
owing to = vanwege; **the train is late owing to fog.**
owes—owing—owed—has owed

own [əʊn] **1.** *bn*
eigen; **I have my own car; he has his own shop.**
2. *zn*
(*a*) **my own/his own, etc.** = mijn/zijn etc. eigen; **he has a car of his own;** = hij heeft z'n eigen auto; **she has a house of her own** = ze heeft een eigen huis; **they have a garden of their own.**
(*b*) **on my own/on his own, etc.** = alleen; **I'm on my own today; he did it on his own.** = hij deed het zelf.
3. *ww*
bezitten/hebben; **I don't own a car; who owns this land?** = van wie is dit land?
owns—owning—owned—has owned

owner, *zn*
eigenaar; **the police are looking for the owner of the car; who's the owner of this house?**

own up (to), *ww*
bekennen; toegeven; **she owned up to having stolen the jewels; he owned up to his mistake; the teacher asked who had written rude words on the board, but no one would own up.**

Pp

p [pi:] *letter*
wordt gebruikt om een bedrag in pence
aan te geven; this book costs 60p; you
should get a ticket from the 20p machine
= de automaat voor kaartjes van
twintig pence; *zie ook* **penny**

pack [pæk] 1. *zn*
pak(je); **a pack of cards.**
2. *ww*
(*a*) (in)pakken/(ver)pakken; **she's
packed her suitcase; have you finished
packing yet, it's time to start? I packed
my toothbrush at the bottom of the bag;
the glasses are packed in boxes to stop
them being broken.**
(*b*) (vol)proppen; **how can you pack ten
people into that little car? the trains
are packed with people going on holiday; the shelves were packed with
books.**
packs—packing—packed—has
packed

package ['pækɪdʒ] *zn*
pakje, pakket; **the postman brought this
package for you; tie the package carefully before taking it to the post
office; package tour** = geheel verzorgde
reis.

packet, *zn*
pakje; **a packet of cigarettes; how many
packets do you smoke a day?** = hoeveel
pakjes rook je per dag?

pack up, *ww*
(*a*) (in)pakken; **they packed up the picnic
things when the rain started.**
(*b*) met iets uitscheiden; **the engine
packed up when we were on the motorway** = de motor begaf het.

page [peɪdʒ] *zn*
bladzij/pagina; **the paper has 32 pages;
turn over the page; look at the next page;**

the answer to the crossword is on page
23; open the book at page 24.
Let op: bij getallen wordt het woordje
the weggelaten: on the next page;
on page 50

paid [peɪd] *zie* **pay**

pain [peɪn] *zn*
(*a*) pijn; **I have pains in my legs after
playing tennis; she says she has a pain in
her back.**
(*b*) **to take pains** = moeite doen op/om;
**he took a lot of pains with his homework;
they took great pains to be at the meeting
on time.**
painful, *bn*
pijnlijk; **his foot is so painful he can
hardly walk; your eye looks very red—is
it painful?**

paint [peɪnt] 1. *zn*
verf; **we gave the front door two coats of
paint; she got a box of paints for her
birthday; I need a 2½ litre tin of blue
paint; the paint's coming off the ceiling.**
2. *ww*
(*a*) verven, schilderen; **he's painting the
outside of the house; we painted the front
door red.**
(*b*) schilderen; **he painted a picture of his
mother; she's painting the old church; the
sea is very difficult to paint.**
paints—painting—painted—has
painted

painter, *zn*
schilder; **the painter's coming today to
paint the bathroom; Rembrandt was a
famous painter.**
painting, *zn*
schilderij; **do you like this painting of my
mother?**

pair [peə] *zn*
(*a*) paar; **she's bought a new pair of**

shoes; these socks are a pair = deze sokken horen bij elkaar.
(b) I'm looking for a clean pair of pyjamas = ik zoek een schone pyjama; where's my pair of brown trousers? this pair of scissors isn't very sharp.

pajamas [pə'dʒɑ:məz] zn *meervoud* (*Amerikaans voor* **pyjamas**) pyjama.

palace ['pæləs] zn
paleis; the soldiers stood in front of the president's palace; the Queen lives in Buckingham Palace.

pale [peɪl] bn
bleek, licht; she turned pale at the sight of blood = ze verbleekte; he was wearing pale grey trousers; this blue is too dark—have you something paler?

pale—paler—palest

palm [pɑ:m] zn
(a) (hand)palm; he held the egg in the palm of his hand; if you look at the lines on your palm you can see what will happen to you in the future.
(b) palm(boom); he climbed up a palm tree.

pan [pæn] zn
pan; put the potatoes into a pan of boiling water; use a larger pan if you're boiling lots of eggs; the handle of the frying pan is hot; *zie ook* **frying pan, saucepan**

pancake, zn
pannekoek; we eat pancakes with jam; who wants another pancake?
Let op: **pancakes** *worden in Engeland altijd op Vastenavond gegeten* (*Shrove Tuesday of Pancake Day*)

paper ['peɪpə] zn
(a) papier; she uses pink paper when she writes to her friend; the parcel was wrapped up in brown paper; can you give me another piece of paper/another sheet of paper? this paper's too thin to write on; I bought a box of paper handkerchiefs; he floated a paper boat on the lake.
(b) krant; I read the paper in the train on my way to work; did you see the picture of our school in yesterday's paper?;

the local paper comes out on Fridays; has the evening paper been delivered yet? Sunday papers are so big that it takes me all day to read them.
(c) examen; the French paper was very hard; she wrote a good maths paper.
Let op: geen meervoud voor (a); **some paper; a sheet of paper/a piece of paper**

paper boy, zn
krantenjongen.

paragraph ['pærəgrɑ:f] zn
alinea; look at the second paragraph on page 2; start a new paragraph.

parallel ['pærəlel] bn
parallel/evenwijdig; railway lines are parallel; the lines of writing should be parallel to the top of the page.

parcel ['pɑ:sl] zn
pakje, pakket(je); the postman brought this parcel for you; look at all the parcels round the Christmas tree! tie that parcel up well before you take it to the post office.

pardon ['pɑ:dn] 1. zn
gratie; vergiffenis; I beg your pardon = neemt u mij niet kwalijk; pardon? = pardon, wat zegt u?
2. ww
vergeven; gratie verlenen.

pardons—pardoning—pardoned—has pardoned

parents ['peərənts] zn *meervoud*
ouders; my parents live in London; she went to live with her parents; did your parents tell you they had sold their house?
Let op: het enkelvoud **parent** *wordt zelden gebruikt*

park [pɑ:k] 1. zn
(a) park; Hyde Park is in the middle of London; you can ride across the park on a horse, but cars are not allowed in.
(b) car park = parkeerplaats/parkeerterrein; leave your car in the hotel car park; the car park's full.
2. ww
parkeren; you can park your car at the

back of the hotel; don't park on the grass; the bus ran into a parked car = de bus reed tegen een geparkeerde auto op; no parking = verboden te parkeren.
parks—parking—parked—has parked

parliament ['pɑːləmənt] *zn*
parlement; he was elected to Parliament in 1970; Parliament will meet again next week; the Houses of Parliament = het parlementsgebouw; Member of Parliament = parlementslid/kamerlid.
Let op: **Parliament** *wordt meestal zonder* **the** *gebruikt*

part [pɑːt] *zn*
(a) deel, gedeelte, stuk; parts of the book are good; we live in the south part of London; part of the year he works in France; spare parts = reserveonderdelen.
(b) to play a part = een rol spelen/een aandeel hebben (in); he played an important part in putting out the fire; to take part = deelnemen; he took part in the battle; did she take part in the fight?
partly, *bw*
gedeeltelijk; the house is partly finished; I'm only partly happy with the result.

particular [pə'tɪkjʊlə] *bn*
bijzonder, speciaal; bepaald; I don't like that particular restaurant.
in particular = in het bijzonder/speciaal; he's good at languages, in particular Italian and Greek; she likes Shakespeare's plays, 'Hamlet' in particular.
particularly, *bw*
bijzonder; he is particularly fond of cakes.

party ['pɑːtɪ] *zn*
(a) feest/partij; we're having a party on Saturday night; can you come to our party next Saturday? she had fifteen people to her birthday party.
(b) groep; there were parties of tourists visiting all the churches.
(c) partij; he joined a political party; which party does the Prime Minister belong to?
meervoud **parties**

pass [pɑːs] *ww*
(a) passeren; voorbijgaan; on the way to

the bank you pass the church on your left; I passed him on the stairs; when you're passing the post office, can you put this letter in the letter box?
(b) aangeven, aanreiken, doorgeven; can you pass me the sugar? he passed the ball to the goalkeeper; they passed the dirty plates to the person at the end of the table.
(c) slagen, halen; he passed in maths, but failed in English; she passed her driving test.
(d) (*van wet*) aannemen; Parliament has passed a law against drugs.
passes—passing—passed—has passed

pass out, *ww*
flauw vallen; when we told her her father was ill, she passed out.

passage ['pæsɪdʒ] *zn*
gang; I passed her in the passage; he rushed down the passage and into the street; go to the end of this passage and turn left.

passenger ['pæsɪndʒə] *zn*
passagier; the car can take three passengers on the back seat; the plane is carrying 125 passengers and a crew of 6.

passive ['pæsɪv] *zn*
lijdende vorm.

passport ['pɑːspɔːt] *zn*
paspoort.

past [pɑːst] 1. *vz*
(a) na; over; it's past ten o'clock; it was past dinner time; the train leaves at twenty past two; it's already half past three; it's five past nine—we've missed the news on TV.
(b) voorbij, langs; go past the post office and turn left; he walked past me without saying hello; the car drove past at 50 miles an hour.
2. *bn*
afgelopen; voorbij; she has spent the past hour talking about her holidays.
3. *zn*
(a) verleden; in the past we always went to Scotland for our holidays.

(b) (ook **past tense**) verleden tijd; 'he went' is the past of the verb 'to go'.

Let op: **past** *wordt gebruikt voor tijdstippen tussen* **o'clock** *en* **half past:** **4.05 = five past four; 4.15 = a quarter past four; 4.25 = twenty five past four; 4.30 = half past four.** *Voor tijdstippen na* **half past,** *zie* **to**
past *wordt ook bij veel werkwoorden gebruikt:* **to go past; to drive past; to fly past,** *etc.*

paste [peɪst] **1.** *zn*
(a) lijm, plaksel; **put some paste on the back of the picture before you stick it in the book.**
(b) pasta; **he spread fish paste on his bread; do you like meat paste sandwiches?** *zie ook* **toothpaste**
2. *ww*
(aan)plakken/(op)plakken; **he pasted the pictures into his book; they pasted the picture on to the wall.**
pastes—pasting—pasted—has pasted

pastry [ˈpeɪstrɪ] *zn*
deeg; gebak; **she was rolling the pastry on the kitchen table; these pies are made of very hard pastry.**
geen meervoud: **some pastry;** *het meervoud* **pastries** *betekent gebakjes*

path [pɑːθ] *zn*
(a) pad, paadje; **the path goes across the field; follow the path until it comes to the river.**
(b) weg, pad, baan; **the house stood in the path of the motorway** = in de weg.

patience [ˈpeɪʃns] *zn*
(a) geduld; **if you want to catch a fish, you must have patience; he lost patience waiting for the bus.**
(b) patience; **she was playing patience.**
geen meervoud

patient 1. *bn*
geduldig; **you have to be patient if you are at the end of a long queue.**
2. *zn*
patiënt; **the patients are all asleep in their beds; the doctor is taking the patient's temperature.**

patiently, *bw*
geduldig; **they waited patiently for two hours.**

pattern [ˈpætən] *zn*
(a) patroon; **to knit this pullover, you have to follow the pattern.**
(b) patroon; motief; **her dress has a pattern of white and red spots; I don't like the pattern on this carpet.**

pause [pɔːz] **1.** *zn*
pauze; onderbreking; **there was a pause in the conversation.**
2. *ww*
pauzeren, (even) rusten; **he paused for a moment and then went on speaking.**
pauses—pausing—paused—has paused

pavement [ˈpeɪvmənt] *zn* (*Amer.* sidewalk)
stoep; trottoir; **the restaurant has put some tables out on the pavement; you can park your car on the pavement for a few minutes; it's dangerous to cycle on the pavement; the pavements are slippery after yesterday's snow.**

pay [peɪ] *ww*
(a) betalen (voor); **I paid £100 for my watch; did he pay for the coffee? how much do you pay for petrol? I'll pay for both of us.**
(b) betalen (aan); **please pay the waiter for your meal; I paid him 50p for washing the car; I'll pay you 50p to wash the car; they paid him £10 for his old bike.**
(c) **to pay a visit** = een bezoek brengen; **we'll pay my mother a visit when we are in town.**
pays—paying—paid [peɪd] **—has paid**
Let op: **you pay him to wash the car** *drukt een doel uit, maar* **pay him for washing the car** *gebeurt nadat de auto gewassen is*

pay back, *ww*
terugbetalen; **I paid for your meal— when will you pay me back?**
pay up, *ww*
(af)betalen; **he paid up quickly when they started to take out their guns.**

pea [pi:] *zn*
erwt; **with the meat we'll have potatoes and peas; don't eat your peas with your knife!**

peace [pi:s] *zn*
(*a*) vrede; **after the long war, there were thirty years of peace.**
(*b*) rust, vrede, kalmte; **I like the peace of the country better than the noise of the town.**
geen meervoud
peaceful, *bn*
vredig; rustig; **the village is so peaceful.**

peanut ['pi:nʌt] *zn*
pinda; **he bought a bag of peanuts to eat in the cinema; peanut butter = pindakaas.**

pedal ['pedl] *zn*
pedaal; trapper; **bicycle pedal; he took his feet off the pedals as he was riding down the hill; brake pedal = rempedaal.**

pedestrian [pɪ'destrɪən] *zn*
voetganger; **you have to watch out for pedestrians when you're driving in a busy town; always cross the road at a pedestrian crossing** = je moet altijd bij een voetgangersoversteekplaats oversteken.

peel [pi:l] **1.** *zn*
schil; **put the apple peel into the dustbin; you can boil potatoes with their peel on.**
geen meervoud
2. *ww*
schillen; **he was peeling an orange; peel the potatoes before you cook them.**
peels—peeling—peeled—has peeled

pen [pen] *zn*
pen; **I've lost my pen—can I borrow yours? if you haven't got a pen you can write in pencil.**

pence [pens] *zie* **penny**

pencil ['pensl] *zn*
potlood; **can I borrow your knife?—I want to sharpen my pencil; you must not write your examination answers in pencil.**

penknife ['pennaɪf] *zn*
zakmes; **he cut his name on the table with his penknife.**
meervoud **penknives** ['pennaɪvz]

penny ['penɪ] *zn*
penny; **this book only costs 60 pence; the meat came to £3.25, and you gave me £4, so I must give you seventy five pence change.**
Let op: het meervoud **pennies** *wordt voor de munt gebruikt, maar* **pence** *voor de prijs. In prijzen wordt,* **pence** *altijd geschreven* **p** *en vaak uitgesproken* [pi:]; **this book costs 60p** (*zeg* **sixty p** *of* **sixty pence**)

people ['pi:pl] *zn meervoud*
mensen; **how many people are there in the room? there were thirty people waiting to see the doctor; so many people tried to see the film that they had to go on showing it for several months; several people in our office went to Spain on holiday; here's a photograph of the people we met on holiday.**

pepper ['pepə] *zn*
peper; **pepper makes me sneeze; don't put so much pepper in your soup.**
geen meervoud

per [pɜ:] *vz*
(*a*) per; **ten per thousand** = tien op de duizend; **there are about six bad eggs per hundred.**
(*b*) per; **the car can't go faster than sixty miles per hour; we eat about 10 loaves of bread per week. tomatoes cost 10p per kilo; we paid her £3 per hour.**
per cent, *bw & zn*
procent; **fifty per cent of the people (50%) voted in the election; seventy five per cent (75%) of the cars are less than two years old.**
Let op: **per cent** *wordt* % *geschreven als het met cijfers gebruikt wordt*

perfect ['pɜ:fɪkt] *bn*
perfect/volmaakt; **he speaks perfect English; she drew a perfect circle; it's a perfect day for a picnic.**
2. *zn* (*ook* **perfect tense**)
voltooid tegenwoordige tijd; **'he has gone' is the perfect of 'to go'.**

perfectly, *bw*
voortreffelijk, volmaakt; **she can speak English perfectly; it was a perfectly beautiful holiday.**

perform [pə'fɔːm] *ww*
(a) opvoeren/uitvoeren; **the school performed Shakespeare's 'Hamlet'.**
(b) (het) (goed/slecht) doen; **our Rugby team performed very well; the car hasn't been performing very well.**
performs—performing—
performed—has performed

performance, *zn*
voorstelling; opvoering; **did you enjoy the performance of 'Hamlet'?**

perhaps [pə'hæps] *bw*
misschien; **perhaps he'll come; they're late—perhaps the snow's very thick; do you think it's going to rain?—perhaps not, I can see some blue sky.**

period ['pɪərɪəd] *zn*
(a) periode; tijd; **I can swim under the water for short periods; this happened at a period when food was scarce.**
(b) lesuur; **we have three periods of maths a week; I had to miss the English period because I was seeing the headmaster.**

permission [pə'mɪʃn] *zn*
permissie, toestemming; **you have my permission to use the telephone; he left the school without permission.**

permit 1. *zn* ['pɜːmɪt]
pasje; vergunning; **he has a permit to use the library; you must have a permit to park in the college car park; the shop has a permit to sell alcohol.**
2. *ww* [pə'mɪt]
toestaan; **smoking is not permitted in the theatre; this ticket permits you to park at any time** = met dit kaartje heb je altijd het recht om te parkeren.
permits—permitting—
permitted—has permitted

person ['pɜːsn] *zn*
persoon; **this ticket admits three persons; she's a very interesting person; he was there in person** = hij was in eigen persoon /zelf aanwezig.

personal, *bn*
persoonlijk; **he lost all his personal property in the fire.**

persuade [pə'sweɪd] *ww*
overreden, overhalen; **he persuaded me to sing a song; the policeman persuaded her not to shoot.**
persuades—persuading—
persuaded—has persuaded

pet [pet] *zn*
huisdier; **we keep a lot of pets—a cat, two dogs and a white mouse.**

petrol ['petrəl] *zn* (*Amer.* **gas**)
benzine; **my car doesn't use very much petrol; I ran out of petrol on the motorway; petrol prices seem to be going up all the time.**
geen meervoud: **some petrol; a gallon of petrol**

petrol station, *zn*
benzinestation; garage; **stop at the next petrol station—we've got hardly any petrol left.**

phone [fəʊn] **1.** *zn*
telefoon(toestel); **the phone's ringing; can you answer the phone for me—I'm in the bath; he lifted the phone and called the police** = hij nam de hoorn van de haak etc.
on the phone = (a) aan de telefoon; **don't make a noise—Daddy's on the phone; there's someone on the phone who wants to speak to you.**
(b) met telefoon; **are you on the phone? they're not on the phone** = ze hebben geen telefoon.
2. *ww*
telefoneren, (op)bellen; **your sister phoned yesterday; phone the doctor—the baby's ill; can you phone me tomorrow morning? I want to phone New York.**
phones—phoning—phoned—has phoned

phone back, *ww*
terugbellen; **Mr Smith is out—can you phone back in an hour? she phoned back very late at night.**

phone book, *zn*
telefoonboek; **this restaurant isn't in the phone book.**

phone box, *zn*
telefooncel; **you can call from the phone
box at the corner of the street; I wanted
to use the phone box, but I didn't have
any 10p coins.**

phone number, *zn*
telefoonnummer; **what's your phone
number? if I tell you my phone number
you'll keep on phoning me; my phone
number's 405 9935.**

photo ['fəʊtəʊ] *zn*
foto; **here's a photo of our house; let
me show you our holiday photos.**

photograph ['fəʊtəgrɑ:f] **1.** *zn*
foto; **a black and white photograph of
the church; she's taking a photograph of
the dogs; he pinned her photograph on
the wall; have you got a photograph of
your children?**
2. *ww*
fotograferen; **he was photographing the
birds on the lake.**
**photographs—photographing—
photographed—
has photographed**

photographer [fə'tɒgrəfə] *zn*
fotograaf.

phrase [freiz] *zn*
frase; woordgroep; uitdrukking; **'the big
green door' and 'along the road' are
phrases.**

piano ['pjænəʊ] *zn*
piano; **he's learning to play the piano;
she plays the piano all day long; she
played the song on the piano.**

pick [pɪk] **1.** *zn*
keuze; pluk; **take your pick** = zoek kies
maaruit.
2. *ww*
(*a*) (uit)kiezen; **the captain picked his
team; he was picked to play goalkeeper.**
(*b*) plukken; **we've picked all the apples;
she was picking roses in the garden.**
(*c*) plukken; peuteren; **he picked the bits
of grass off his coat; she was picking her
teeth with a pin** = ze peuterde tussen
haar tanden etc.
(*d*) **to pick someone's pocket** = zakken-
rollen; **my pocket's been picked!**
**picks—picking—picked—has
picked**

pick on, *ww*
het gemikt/gemunt hebben op iemand;
afgeven op; **why do you always pick on
children who are smaller than you? stop
picking on me all the time.**

pick out, *ww*
(uit)kiezen; **he picked out all the good
apples in the box.**

pick up, *ww*
(*a*) oppakken; oprapen; **she picked up
the books which had fallen on the floor;
he dropped his money and bent down to
pick it up.**
(*b*) oppikken; aanleren; **I was never
taught to type—I just picked it up; she
picked up some Chinese when she was
living in China.**
(*c*) oppikken; afhalen; **I'll pick you up
at your office; can you come to pick me
up at 6 o'clock?**
(*d*) oppikken; leren kennen; toevallig
ontmoeten; **he picked up a girl in a snack
bar.**
(*e*) oppikken, arresteren; **the police
picked him up at the airport.**
(*f*) opknappen; **he was ill for months,
but he's picking up now; business is
picking up; the car began to pick up
speed** = de auto begon vaart te krijgen.
Let op: **pick your money up** *of* **pick
up your money** *maar alleen* **pick it
up**

picnic ['pɪknɪk] **1.** *zn*
picknick; **let's go on a picnic on Saturday; we went on a picnic last week and it
rained; they stopped the car and had a
picnic in the wood.**
2. *ww*
picknicken; **we were picnicking by the
side of the road.**
**picnics—picnicking—picnicked—
has picnicked**

picture ['pɪktʃə] *zn*
(*a*) afbeelding, plaat, schilderij; tekening; **he's painting a picture of the church;
have you seen the picture she drew of the
house? the book has several pictures of
wild flowers; he cut out the picture of the
Prime Minister from the newspaper; let**

me put you in the picture = laat mij je
op de hoogte brengen.
(*b*) pictures = bioskoop; we go to the
pictures every Friday evening.

pie [paɪ] *zn*
pastei; taart; we had apple pie and ice
cream; let's buy a pork pie to eat on the
picnic; cottage pie = gehakt met aard-
appelpuree.

piece [piːs] *zn*
stuk(je); can I have another piece of
cake? I want two pieces of paper; the
watch came to pieces in my hand = het
horloge viel in mijn handen uit elkaar;
he dropped the plate and it smashed to
pieces; to mend the clock, he had to take
it to pieces = moest hij hem uit elkaar
halen.
Let op: piece *wordt vaak gebruikt voor
een gedeelte van iets wat geen meervoud heeft:* furniture: a piece of
furniture; wood: a piece of wood;
toast: a piece of toast; news: a
piece of news; advice: a piece of
advice

pig [pɪg] *zn*
varken; the pigs were lying in the mud.
Let op: varkensvlees *heet* pork,
bacon *of* ham

pile [paɪl] 1. *zn*
hoop, stapel; there were piles of old
books on the floor; throw those bricks on
to the pile.
piles of = een heleboel/massa's; we've
got piles of work to do.
2. *ww* (*ook* to pile up)
opstapelen/ophopen; he piled (up) the
bricks by the side of the house; the books
were piled (up) on the table; she was
piling boxes on top of each other.
piles—piling—piled—has piled

pillar box [ˈpɪləbɒks] *zn*
brievenbus (op straat); can you post this
letter in the pillar box at the end of the
road?
meervoud pillar boxes

pillow [ˈpɪləʊ] *zn*
kussen.

pilot [ˈpaɪlət] *zn*
(*a*) piloot, gezagvoerder; don't talk to the
pilot when the plane is landing.
(*b*) loods.

pin [pɪn] 1. *zn*
speld; he kept his trousers up with a pin;
fasten the papers together with a pin;
drawing pin = punaise; he pinned the
notice up with a drawing pin.
2. *ww*
opprikken; vastspelden; the papers were
pinned together; the notices are pinned
to the wall of the office.
pins—pinning—pinned—has
pinned

pin up, *ww*
opprikken; the notice is pinned up outside the entrance; he was pinning the sign
up on a tree.
Let op: pin the notice up *of* pin up
the notice *maar alleen* pin it up

pinch [pɪntʃ] 1. *zn*
kneep(je); snufje; he gave me a pinch; put
a pinch of salt into the water; you can
take what he says with a pinch of salt =
je kunt wat hij zegt het beste met een
korreltje zout nemen.
meervoud pinches

2. *ww*
(*a*) knijpen; she pinched my arm.
(*b*) gappen; they pinched some sweets
from the shop; someone has pinched my
bike.
pinches—pinching—pinched—
has pinched

pink [pɪŋk] *zn & bn*
roze; these pink roses smell nice; her hat
was a dark pink.

pint [paɪnt] *zn*
pint (0.56 liter); ask the milkman to leave
two pints of milk; a pint of beer, please;
he drank half a pint of coffee.

pipe [paɪp] *zn*
(*a*) pijp; buis; leiding; the water pipes are
under the street; he made a hole in the
gas pipe and the gas started to come out.
(*b*) pijp; he was smoking a pipe; can I
have another match—my pipe has gone

out; it's difficult to light a pipe when it is windy.

pity ['pɪtɪ] **1.** *zn*
(*a*) medelijden; **I felt pity for the runner who came last in the race.**
(*b*) (wat) jammer; **it's a pity that . . .** = het is jammer; **it's a pity that it rained when we went on the picnic; what a pity that she was ill and couldn't run in the race.**
geen meervoud
2. *ww*
medelijden hebben met; **I pity you having to stay in and look after the baby when we all go to the cinema.**
pities—pitying—pitied—has pitied

place [pleɪs] **1.** *zn*
(*a*) plaats/plek; **this is the place where we had the accident; put the books back in the right place; there were papers lying all over the place** = overal.
(*b*) huis; woning; **why don't we all go back to my place for a cup of coffee?**
(*c*) (zit)plaats; **this is Mr Smith's place; is this anybody's place? yes, I'm afraid this place is taken; I changed places with Jane** = Jane en ik verwisselden van plaats.
(*d*) plaats; **the German runners were in the first three places** = de Duitse atleten eindigden op de eerste, tweede en derde plaats; **he's in first place** = hij heeft een voorsprong.
(*e*) (*van boek*) **I put a piece of paper to mark my place** = ik stopte een stukje papier op de plaats waar ik was gebleven; **I've lost my place and can't remember where I've got to.**
to take place = plaatsvinden; **the argument took place in the restaurant; the action of the film takes place in Russia.**
2. *ww*
plaatsen; neerzetten; **he placed his hat carefully on the table; can you place the books in the right order?**
places—placing—placed—has placed

plain [pleɪn] **1.** *bn*
(*a*) duidelijk; **it's plain that he didn't hear**

the motorcycle; I want to make it plain that we will not pay you any more money.
(*b*) gewoon; eenvoudig; **I like plain country cooking best; plain chocolate** = pure chocola.
plain—plainer—plainest
2. *zn*
vlakte; **the wind whistled across the plain.**
plainly, *bw*
duidelijk; ronduit; **he was plainly worried by his exams.**

plan [plæn] **1.** *zn*
(*a*) plan; **we've prepared a plan for saving money each week; the burglars made a plan to get into the house by the kitchen window.**
(*b*) schets; ontwerp; **here are the plans for the new school; this is the plan of the office; I can't find our street on the town plan** = plattegrond.
2. *ww*
ontwerpen; van plan zijn; **she planned her kitchen herself; they've planned a whole new town; we are planning to go on holiday in August; I wasn't planning to stay up late** = ik was niet van plan lang op te blijven.
plans—planning—planned—has planned

plane [pleɪn] *zn*
(*a*) vliegtuig; **when does this plane leave for Copenhagen? the plane to Glasgow is full—you will have to wait for the next one; there are six planes a day to New York.**
(*b*) schaaf.

plant [plɑːnt] **1.** *zn*
plant; **a tomato plant; these plants are growing very tall; house plants/pot plants** = kamerplanten; **plant pot** = bloempot.
2. *ww*
planten; **I've planted an apple tree in the garden.**
plants—planting—planted—has planted

plaster ['plɑːstə] *zn*
(*a*) gips; **the ceiling is made of plaster;**

after his accident he had his leg in plaster for two months.

(*b*) **sticking plaster** = pleister; **put a piece of sticking plaster on your cut.**

geen meervoud: **some plaster; some sticking plaster; a piece of sticking plaster**

plastic [ˈplæstɪk] *bn & zn*
plastic; **take the plastic plates on the picnic; I want a plastic bag to put my sandwiches in; don't put that plate in the oven—it's made of plastic; these seats in the car are made of plastic and get very hot in the summer.**

geen meervoud: **it's made of plastic**

plate [pleɪt] *zn*
(*a*) bord; **put the sausages on a plate; pass your dirty plates to the person at the end of the table.**

(*b*) bord (vol); **she held out a plate of cakes; he ate two plates of meat.**

(*c*) plaat; **a plate glass window** = een raam van plaatglas; **number plate** = nummerbord.

platform [ˈplætfɔːm] *zn*
(*a*) perron; **there were crowds waiting on the platform; the train to Edinburgh will leave from platform 6; the Birmingham train is leaving from the next platform; I was in such a hurry that I left my suitcase on the platform.**

(*b*) podium; **the speaker went up on to the platform; someone in the crowd threw tomato at the speaker on the platform.**

play [pleɪ] **1.** *zn*
(*a*) (toneel)stuk; **did you watch the play last night? we're going to see a new play at the National Theatre; we have to read two of Shakespeare's plays for our English exam.**

(*b*) spel; **play will start at 3 o'clock** = de wedstrijd begint etc.; **the ball went out of play** = de bal ging buiten spel; **it's child's play** = het is kinderspel.
2. *ww*
(*a*) spelen; **he was playing with his sister; the children were playing in the garden; let's play at doctors and nurses** = zullen we doktertje spelen?

(*b*) spelen; **he plays football for the**

school team; **can you play cricket? I don't play tennis in the winter.**

(*c*) spelen; **don't talk while he's playing the violin; I can't play the piano very well; let me play you my new record.**

(*d*) (toneel)spelen; **the played Harry Lime in 'The Third Man'.**

plays—playing—played—has played

player, *zn*
speler; **you need eleven players for a football team; tennis players have to be fit; three of our players are ill.**

playground, *zn*
speelplaats; **if it's raining you can't go into the playground during break; they were playing quietly in the playground.**

playing cards, *zn*
speelkaarten; *zie ook* **card**.

playing field, *zn*
sportveld; **two football matches are being played on our playing field.**

pleasant [ˈpleznt] *bn*
prettig; fijn; vriendelijk; aangenaam; **what a pleasant picnic; the weather is very pleasant.**

pleasant—pleasanter—pleasantest

pleasantly, *bw*
vriendelijk; prettig; **he answered me pleasantly.**

please [pliːz] *tw*
alstublieft; **shut the door, please; please come in; can I have another cup of coffee, please? do you want some more cake?— yes, please; who wants some more coffee?—me, please!**

pleased, *bn*
blij, tevreden; **I'm pleased with my new car; she isn't pleased with her exam results; he wasn't pleased when we broke his bedroom window; was she pleased to get your letter? I'd be very pleased to help you if I can** = ik zou je met genoegen willen helpen etc.

pleasure [ˈpleʒə] *zn*
plezier; genot; **sitting in the garden is my greatest pleasure; I'll do the job with pleasure** = met het grootste plezier; **it gives me great pleasure to be here today.**

plenty ['plentɪ] *zn*
een heleboel, massa's; **you've got plenty of time; we've plenty of food left after the party; plenty of people were waiting for the bus; have you enough milk?—yes, we've got plenty.**
geen meervoud

plough [plaʊ] **1.** *zn*
ploeg.
2. *ww*
ploegen; **the farmer was ploughing the field.**
ploughs—ploughing—ploughed—has ploughed

plug [plʌg] **1.** *zn*
(*a*) stekker; **the refrigerator has stopped working—I think that a wire has broken in the plug.**
(*b*) (*van bad etc.*) stop.
2. *ww* (*meestal* **to plug in**)
inschakelen, aansluiten (op het stopcontact); **have you plugged the radio in? the light won't work—it isn't plugged in!**
plugs—plugging—plugged—has plugged

plural ['plʊərəl] *bn & zn*
meervoud; **'children' is the plural of 'child'; 'is' is the third person singular of the verb 'to be' and 'are' is the plural; 'they' is a plural pronoun.**

p.m. ['pi:'em] *bw*
na twaalven; 's middags en 's avonds; **I have to meet someone at 2 p.m.; she's catching the 7 p.m. train to Edinburgh.**
Let op: **p.m.** *wordt gebruikt om het hele uur aan te geven en het woord* **o'clock** *wordt dan weggelaten*

pocket ['pɒkɪt] *zn*
zak; **I've looked in my coat pockets but I can't find my keys; there's a hole in my pocket, and all my money fell out; he was walking along with his hands in his pockets; put your hands in your pockets if you want to keep them warm.**
pocket calculator = zakrekenmachientje.
pocket dictionary = zakwoordenboek.
pocket money = zakgeld; **how much pocket money do you get? I can't**
buy any more sweets, **I spent all my pocket money on a new penknife.**

poem ['pəʊɪm] *zn*
gedicht; **do you like this poem about the autumn? he spends all his time writing poems.**

poet, *zn*
dichter; **Byron and Keats are famous English poets.**

poetry, *zn*
poëzie; **we have to study English poetry of the nineteenth century; he was reading a poetry book.**
geen meervoud

point [pɔɪnt] **1.** *zn*
(*a*) punt; **he's broken the point of his pencil; this needle hasn't got a very sharp point.**
(*b*) punt; (=, in getallen in het Nederlands); **3.256** *zeg* 'three point two five six' = 3,256.
(*c*) punt; **we walked for miles and came back to the point where we'd started from; the lights went off at that point** = op dat punt etc.; **I was on the point of phoning you** = ik stond op het punt je te bellen.
(*d*) zin; bedoeling; **there's no point in trying to phone him—he's gone away; the point of the meeting is to discuss how we can save money; I see your point** = ik begrijp wat je bedoelt.
(*e*) punt; **he scored three points; that shot gives you ten points.**
(*f*) punt; **what's the freezing point of water?**
2. *ww*
wijzen/richten/mikken op; wijzen naar; **the policeman is pointing at you; he pointed his gun at the door; don't point at people—it's rude.**
points—pointing—pointed—has pointed

pointed, *bn*
puntig; **a pointed stick.**

point out, *ww*
aanwijzen; wijzen op; **he pointed out all the mistakes in my homework.**
Let op: **he pointed the mistakes out** *of* **he pointed out the mistakes** *maar alleen* **he pointed them out**

poison [ˈpɔɪzn] *zn*
(ver)gif; **I think someone has put poison in my soup; try putting some poison on the floor if you want to kill the mice.**
poisonous, *bn*
(ver)giftig; **don't eat those seeds—they're poisonous; I wish I knew which leaves are good to eat and which are poisonous.**

pole [pəʊl] *zn*
(a) paal; **the flag is attached to a tall pole; the tent is held up by two poles; the car ran into a telephone pole.**
(b) pool; **who was the first man to get to the North Pole?**
polar, *bn*
pool-; **a polar bear** = ijsbeer.

police [pəˈliːs] *zn (meestal meervoud)*
politie; **the police are looking for three armed men; if someone steals your car, you must tell the police; the phone number of the police is 999; call the police—someone's taken all my money! he was knocked down by a police car.**
policeman, policewoman, *zn*
politieagent(e); **three policemen were hiding behind the wall; if you don't know how to find the post office—ask a policeman.**
meervoud **policemen, police-women**
police station, *zn*
politiebureau; **they arrested two men and took them to the police station.**

polish [ˈpɒlɪʃ] **1.** *zn*
(a) was; (schoen)smeer; **put some polish on the table; we haven't any black shoe polish left.**
(b) glans; (het) oppoetsen; **give the car a good polish; I'll give the table a polish.**
2. *ww*
boenen, opwrijven, poetsen; **you should polish your shoes before you go to the party; has he polished the car?**
polishes—polishing—polished—has polished

polite [pəˈlaɪt] *bn*
beleefd; **you should always be polite to your teacher; it wasn't very polite to go away without saying thank you; it is polite to say 'please' when you are asking for something; he's a very polite little boy.**
politely, *bw*
beleefd; **if you ask her politely she will give you some cake.**

political [pəˈlɪtɪkl] *bn*
politiek; **political party.**
politician [pɒlɪˈtɪʃn] *zn*
politikus.
politics, *zn*
politiek; **he is going into politics** = hij gaat in de politiek.

pool [puːl] *zn*
(a) plas; **there was a pool of blood on the floor.**
(b) **(swimming) pool** = zwembad; **the competition will be held in the open air pool** = in het openluchtzwembad; **our school has an indoor pool** = overdekt zwembad; **come out—you've been in the pool long enough; we have a heated swimming pool in our garden.**

poor [pɔː] *bn*
(a) arm; **they are very poor, now that their father has no work; poor people can get extra money from the government; it is one of the poorest countries in the world.**
(b) armoedig; schraal; slecht; **this soil's poor—it's not good for growing fruit trees; their football team is very poor this year—they haven't won a single match; these bananas are very poor quality; he's in poor health.**
(c) arm; **poor John—he's got to stay in bed while we're going for a picnic; my poor feet—I've been walking all day!**
poor—poorer—poorest

popular [ˈpɒpjʊlə] *bn*
populair/geliefd; **Spain is a popular place for summer holidays; this film has been very popular; cold milk is a popular drink with children; the maths teacher isn't very popular with our class—he gives us too much homework.**

population [pɒpjʊˈleɪʃn] *zn*
bevolking; **the population is increasing**

by 2% each year; what is the population of Denmark?

pork [pɔːk] *zn*
varkensvlees; **we're having roast pork for lunch; would you like some more pork? can I have another slice of pork, please? pork sausages.**
geen meervoud: **some pork; a piece of pork/a slice of pork**

porridge [ˈpɒrɪdʒ] *zn*
pap; **you eat porridge with milk and sugar; do you want any more porridge?**
geen meervoud: **some porridge; a bowl of porridge**

port [pɔːt] *zn*
haven(stad); **Dover is an important port for ferries to France; Grimsby is a big fishing port.**

porter [ˈpɔːtə] *zn*
kruier.

position [pəˈzɪʃn] *zn*
positie/plaats; **it was a difficult job putting the piano into position; she found herself in a very difficult position; he was in third position in the race; you need to have the brush in the right position to paint properly.**

possess [pəˈzes] *ww*
bezitten; **he possessed two large houses; how many cars does she possess?**
possesses—possessing—possessed—has possessed
possession, *zn*
bezitting; **he lost all his possessions in the fire.**

possible [ˈpɒsɪbl] *bn*
mogelijk; **that field is a possible place for a house; it's possible that the train will be late because of the fog.**
as possible (*gebruikt voor de overtreffende trap*) (zo . . .) mogelijk; **go as far away as possible; I would like it done as quickly as possible; give me as much time as possible; this is the cheapest possible way of going to France.**
possibility [pɒsɪˈbɪlɪtɪ] *zn*
mogelijkheid; **is there any possibility that the plane will be late?**

possibly, *bw*
(*a*) mogelijk, misschien; **the train will possibly be late; it is possibly the worst weather we have ever had.**
(*b*) (*voor extra nadruk*) (on)mogelijk; **you can't possibly eat all those sausages!** = je kunt onmogelijk al die worstjes opeten!

post [pəʊst] **1.** *zn*
(*a*) paal, post; **the gate is attached to a gate post; he kicked the ball but it bounced off the post.**
(*b*) positie, post, betrekking; **she has applied for a post in the library.**
(*c*) post; **has the post come yet? there was nothing for you in the post this morning; send the parcel by post; can you put this letter in the post for me?**
2. *ww*
posten; **he went to post his Christmas cards; the letter was posted ten days ago; if you're going to the post office, can you post this parcel for me?**
posts—posting—posted—has posted

postage, *zn*
porto; **what is the postage for a letter to Australia?**
geen meervoud

postcard, *zn*
(ansicht)kaart, briefkaart; **send me a postcard when you get to Italy; she sent me a postcard of the hotel where she was staying.**

postman, *zn*
postbode; **has the postman been yet? give this letter back to the postman—it's not for us.**
meervoud **postmen**

post office, *zn*
postkantoor; PTT kantoor; **can you take this parcel to the post office for me? the post office is shut on Saturday afternoons.**

pot [pɒt] *zn*
pot(je); **plant the flowers in a bigger pot; we made ten pots of jam.**

potato [pəˈteɪtəʊ] *zn*
aardappel; **boiled potatoes; do you want**

any more potatoes? potatoes in their jackets = in de schil geroosterde aardappelen.
meervoud **potatoes**

pound [paʊnd] *zn*
(*a*) pond (450 grams); **I want a pound of onions and three pounds of potatoes; the baby only weighed four pounds when he was born; how much is sugar?—it's 20p a pound.**
Let op: met cijfers wordt **pound** *meestal geschreven* **lb; it weighs 26lb; take 6lb of sugar**

(*b*) pond (sterling); **the meal cost several pounds; he gets more than a pound in pocket money; the price is over fifty pounds (£50); he gave me a five pound note.**
Let op: met cijfers wordt **pound** *meestal geschreven* **£: £20; £6,000,** *etc.*
Let op: samen met **note** *wordt* **pound** *in het enkelvoud gebruikt:* **five pounds** *maar* **a five pound note**

pour [pɔː] *ww*
(*a*) gieten, (in)schenken; **she poured the tea into my cup; pour the dirty water down the sink; he poured out two glasses of water; can you pour me another cup of tea?**
(*b*) stromen; **smoke poured out of the window; people poured on to the platform; oil was pouring out of the hole in the pipe; it was pouring with rain** = het stroomde van de regen.
pours—pouring—poured—has poured

pour down, *ww*
stortregenen; **we couldn't go for a walk because it was pouring down; the rain poured down for days.**

powder [ˈpaʊdə] *zn*
poeder; poeier; **face powder** = poeder.

power [ˈpaʊə] *zn*
(*a*) kracht; energie; **the engine runs on electric power; the wheel is turned by water power; power cut** = elektriciteitsstoring/stroomstoring.
(*b*) macht; **the party has a lot of power**

in the town council; the general came to **power in 1962** = de generaal kwam in 1962 aan de macht.
powerful, *bn*
machtig; krachtig; **the motor isn't powerful enough to drive the car up hills.**

practical [ˈpræktɪkl] *bn*
praktisch; **she gave me some practical advice; he's a practical man.**
practically, *bw*
praktisch/vrijwel; **I've practically finished my homework.**

practice [ˈpræktɪs] *zn*
(*a*) praktijk; **it's a good idea, but will it work in practice?**
(*b*) oefening; **he does his piano practice every day; with practice, you should be able to play tennis quite well.**

practise [ˈpræktɪs] *ww*
oefenen; instuderen; **he practises the piano every day; she's practising her Spanish songs; if you don't practise you'll never play tennis well.**
practises—practising—practised—has practised

praise [preɪz] **1.** *zn*
lof; **he wrote a poem in praise of the new church** = hij schreef een gedicht ter ere van etc.; **she was full of praise for your work.**
2. *ww*
prijzen/loven; **he praised the policeman who had saved the little boy from drowning; the judges praised the winners in the competition.**
praises—praising—praised—has praised

pray [preɪ] *ww*
bidden; **they are praying for fine weather; we prayed for his sister.**
prays—praying—prayed—has prayed

prayer [preə] *zn*
gebed; **he said his prayers before he went to bed.**

prefer [prɪˈfɜː] *ww*
de voorkeur geven aan iets, liever willen; **I don't want to sit in the garden—**

I prefer watching TV inside; which do you prefer—chocolate or orange ice cream? I prefer English cars to foreign ones; we prefer to go on holiday in June because the weather is better; I don't want to go to the cinema—I'd prefer to stay at home.
prefers—preferring—preferred—has preferred

prefix ['pri:fiks] zn
voorvoegsel; in the word 'impossible', 'im-' is a prefix which means 'not'.

prepare [prɪ'peə] ww
(zich) voorbereiden, klaarmaken; they are preparing to go on holiday next week; she was preparing the dinner when the milkman called.
prepares—preparing—prepared—has prepared

prepared, bn
(voor)bereid; are you prepared to leave immediately? they weren't prepared for the letter from the bank manager.

preposition [prepə'zɪʃn] zn
voorzetsel; prepositions are words such as 'near', 'next to', 'through', in the sentences 'his house is near the Post Office', 'she sat down next to me', 'he drove through the town'.

present 1. zn ['preznt]
(a) cadeau; he gave me a watch as a present; do you give your children big presents at Christmas? how many birthday presents did you get? all the Christmas presents are piled under the tree.
(b) heden; at present = op het ogenblik.
(c) tegenwoordige tijd; the present of 'to give' is 'he gives' or 'he is giving'.
2. bn ['preznt]
(a) huidig; what is your present address? the present situation; present tense = tegenwoordige tijd; the present tense of 'to sit' is 'he sits' or 'he is sitting'.
(b) aanwezig; were you present when the old man died?
3. ww [prɪ'zent]
(a) aanbieden; when he retired, the firm presented him with a watch.

(b) presenteren; he's presenting a programme on wild animals.
presents—presenting—presented—has presented

president ['prezɪdnt] zn
president; the President of the USA; we've elected him president for the next year.
Let op: kan met namen gebruikt worden: President Kennedy, *etc.*

press [pres] **1.** zn
pers; the British press reported a plane crash in Africa; the press has not mentioned the problem; I read about it in the press.
geen meervoud
2. ww
(a) drukken; zich verdringen; persen; press the button if you want a cup of coffee; they all pressed round him.
(b) persen; your trousers need pressing.
presses—pressing—pressed—has pressed

pressure ['preʃə] zn
druk; there is not enough air pressure in your tyres; to put pressure on someone to do something = pressie/druk op iemand uitoefenen; he did it under/pressure; blood pressure = bloeddruk.

pretend [prɪ'tend] ww
doen alsof; voorwenden; he got into the house by pretending to be a policeman; she pretended she was Australian; the children were pretending to be doctors and nurses; he hasn't got a headache—he's pretending to have one so that he can go home.
pretends—pretending—pretended—has pretended

pretty ['prɪtɪ] bn
lief; aardig; mooi; he has two pretty daughters; she is prettier than her sister; what a pretty little village!
pretty—prettier—prettiest
Let op: wordt voor dingen of meisjes gebruikt, maar nooit voor mannen

prevent [prɪ'vent] ww
voorkomen; verhinderen/beletten; the fog prevented the planes (from) taking

off; something must have prevented her
(from) coming; we must try to prevent
anyone (from) knowing about this; cars
have red lights to try to prevent accidents.
**prevents—preventing—
prevented—has prevented**

price [praɪs] 1. *zn*
prijs; kosten; the price of meat is going
up; we can't pay such a high price; don't
go to that greengrocer's—his prices are
too high; that TV is very cheap—at that
price you could buy two.
2. *ww*
de prijs bepalen; the table is priced at
£25 = de prijs van de tafel is vast-
gesteld op £25; it won't sell—it is too
highly priced.
**prices—pricing—priced—has
priced**

pride [praɪd] *zn*
trots; he takes pride in always being on
time = hij is er trots op altijd op tijd te
zijn; she takes a lot of pride in her
garden.

primary ['praɪmərɪ] *bn*
(*a*) primair/elementair; the primary
colours = grondkleuren.
(*b*) basis/lager; primary education =
basis/lager onderwijs; primary school =
basisschool/lagere school.

Prime Minister [praɪm'mɪnɪstə] *zn*
minister president, premier; the French
Prime Minister; the Prime Minister of
Australia.
*Let op: wordt soms met een naam
gebruikt:* **Prime Minister Wilson,
etc.**

print [prɪnt] 1. *zn*
(*a*) druk; the print in that book is so
small that I can't read it.
(*b*) (foto)afdruk; can you develop this
film and make black and white prints of
it?
2. *ww*
(*a*) drukken; the book is printed in the
USA; this newspaper is printed on pink
paper.
(*b*) met drukletters/blokletters schrijven;

please print your name and address =
blokletters s.v.p.
**prints—printing—printed—has
printed**

prison [prɪzn] *zn*
gevangenis; he was sent to prison for four
years; his mother's in prison; they
escaped from prison.
*Let op: wordt vaak zonder the ge-
bruikt*

prisoner, *zn*
gevangene; the prisoners tried to escape
by climbing over the wall.

private ['praɪvɪt] *bn*
partikulier, privé; this is a private house;
he won't talk about his private life; we
were having a private conversation = we
waren in een vertrouwelijk gesprek
gewikkeld.

prize [praɪz] *zn*
prijs; the person with the highest marks
has a prize of £10; there are several good
prizes in the competition; a prize pig =
bekroond varken.

probable ['prɒbəbl] *bn*
waarschijnlijk; vermoedelijk; it's probable that the ship sank in a storm; this
horse is a probable winner.
probably, *bw*
waarschijnlijk; they're probably going to
be late because of the fog; he's probably
forgotten about the meeting; we'll
probably see you next week.

problem ['prɒbləm] *zn*
probleem; I couldn't do the problems in
the maths exam; the government is trying
to deal with the problem of crime/with
the crime problem.

produce [prə'djuːs] *ww*
produceren/maken; the company is producing a new sort of toothpaste; he hit
the piano hard, but only produced a little
noise; if you bring the two electric wires
together you'll produce a flash; the
country doesn't produce enough oil; we
produce so many vegetables that we sell
them to our neighbours.
**produces—producing—
produced—has produced**

product [ˈprɒdʌkt] *zn*
produkt; **we sell electrical products; coal is an important product in the north of the country.**
production [prəˈdʌkʃn] *zn*
produktie; **production of cars was held up by the strike; we are trying to increase production.**
geen meervoud

profession [prəˈfeʃn] *zn*
beroep/vak; **the teaching profession; he's a doctor by profession.**
professional, *bn & zn*
professioneel/beroeps-; **a professional footballer; she has become a professional.**

profit [ˈprɒfɪt] *zn*
winst; **we sold the car and made a profit of £200** = en we hebben £200 winst gemaakt; **he sold his car at a profit** = hij heeft zijn auto met winst verkocht.

programme [ˈprəʊɡræm] *zn* (*Amer.* **program**)
(*a*) programma; **we watched a programme on wild animals of the desert; did you see that funny programme last night? there's a sports programme after the news.**
(*b*) programma; **can I look at your programme? the programme costs 25p.**

promise [ˈprɒmɪs] **1.** *zn*
belofte; **he gave his promise that he would work harder; she broke her promise that she would pay us the money** = ze is haar belofte ... niet nagekomen.
2. *ww*
beloven; **he promised to send us a postcard when he arrived; promise me you'll go to bed early; she promised she would pay back the money.**
promises—promising—
promised—has promised
promising, *bn*
veelbelovend; **he's a promising student.**

pronoun [ˈprəʊnaʊn] *zn*
voornaamwoord; **'I', 'you', 'they', etc., are pronouns; 'he', 'it' and 'me' are pronouns in the sentence 'he gave it to me'.**

pronounce [prəˈnaʊns] *ww*
uitspreken; **he didn't pronounce the name very clearly; how do you pronounce the word 'laugh'?**
pronounces—pronouncing—
pronounced—has pronounced
pronunciation [prənʌnsɪˈeɪʃn] *zn*
uitspraak; **the pronunciation is given for the words in this dictionary; what's the correct pronunciation of 'through'?**

proof [pruːf] *zn*
bewijs; **the police have proof that he was not at home when the old woman was murdered; you say he stole your bicycle—but do you have any proof of it?**

propellor [prəˈpelə] *zn*
propeller; **a helicopter has a large propeller on its roof.**

proper [ˈprɒpə] *bn*
juist, behoorlijk; **he didn't put the book back into its proper place; what is the proper way to hold a screwdriver? the envelope did not have the proper address.**
properly, *bw*
goed, juist; **they didn't put the wheel on the car properly; the envelope wasn't properly addressed.**

property [ˈprɒpətɪ] *zn*
(*a*) eigendom; bezit; **that piano is my property; lost property office** = bureau gevonden voorwerpen.
(*b*) bezitting(en), bezit; **he has a lot of property in north London; not much private property was destroyed in the war.**

protect [prəˈtekt] *ww*
beschermen; beschutten; **the house is protected from the wind by a row of tall trees; they were protected from the cold by their thick coats; the harbour is protected by a high wall; the white coat will protect your clothes in the factory; the police were protecting the Prime Minister against attack.**
protects—protecting—
protected—has protected
protection, *zn*
bescherming; **that thin coat is no protection against the rain; the President has**

proud   pump

police protection = onder politiebe-
scherming.

proud [praʊd] *bn*
trots; she was proud of her exam results;
hitting an old lady is nothing to be proud
of; he's very proud of his cooking; she's
proud of her children; I'm proud to be
here today.
proud—prouder—proudest
proudly, *bw*
trots; he proudly showed us his new car.

prove [pruːv] *ww*
(a) bewijzen; the police think he's a burglar, but they can't prove it; can you
prove that you were at home on the day
the old woman was murdered?
(b) blijken; the weather proved to be even
worse than they expected; the film proved
to be very bad.
proves—proving—proved—has
proved

provide [prəˈvaɪd] *ww*
voorzien van, zorgen voor; the hotel will
provide us with sandwiches; they'll bring
the food, but we'll have to provide the
drink.
provides—providing—provided—
has provided
provided that, *vw*
mits, onder voorwaarde dat; I will come
provided that the weather is fine; he said
he would make a speech provided that
someone told him what to say.

pub [pʌb] *zn*
(*afkorting van* **public house**) café; let's
stop at the next pub and get some sandwiches; there's a pub in the village where
children can sit in the garden.

public [ˈpʌblɪk] *bn*
openbaar; go to the public library to see
if there is a book on sailing; the last
Monday in August is a public holiday.
public house, *zn*
café, kroeg; there are three public houses
in the village, but no shops; children are
not allowed in public houses.
Let op: **a public house** *wordt meestal* **pub** *genoemd*

pudding [ˈpʊdɪŋ] *zn*
(a) pudding; **Christmas pudding** =
Kerstpudding; **rice pudding** = rijstebrij.
(b) dessert/toetje; what's for pudding? I've
eaten so much, I don't want any pudding;
we're having ice cream for pudding.

pull [pʊl] *ww*
trekken; you have to pull that door to
open it, not push; the plough is pulled by
a tractor; he pulled a piece of paper out
of his pocket; I don't like people who pull
my hair.
to pull someone's leg = iemand
voor de gek houden; don't believe what
he says—he's pulling your leg.
pulls—pulling—pulled—has
pulled
pull down, *ww*
afbreken; they pulled down an old house
to build a row of shops.
pull in(to), *ww*
aan de kant van de weg stilhouden/
inhouden; he pulled into the side of the
road when he saw the ambulance
coming.
pull off, *ww*
iets klaarspelen, voor elkaar krijgen; the
burglars pulled off a big crime.
pull out, *ww*
wegrijden (met auto).
pullover, *zn*
pullover, trui; I like your new pullover;
my mother's knitting me a pullover.
pull together, *ww*
to pull yourself together = zich ver-
mannen; zich beheersen; although he
was very angry he soon pulled himself
together.
pull up, *ww*
(a) bijschuiven, bijtrekken; pull your
chair up to the table.
(b) (*van auto etc.*) stoppen; a car pulled
up and the driver asked us the way; he
didn't pull up in time and hit the back of
the car in front.

pump [pʌmp] **1.** *zn*
pomp; bicycle pump, petrol pump.
2. *ww*
pompen; he was pumping up his tyres; I
can't pump any more air into this

160   *one hundred and sixty*

balloon; they tried to pump the water out of the boat.

pumps—pumping—pumped—has pumped

punish ['pʌnɪʃ] *ww*
straffen; **you will be punished for talking in class; I'll punish him by taking away his chocolate.**

punishes—punishing—punished—has punished

punishment, *zn*
straf; **as a punishment, you mustn't watch TV for three days.**

pupil ['pju:pl] *zn*
leerling; **how many pupils are there in your school?**

pure ['pjʊə] *bn*
zuiver/puur; **this gold is 100% pure; this pullover is made of pure wool; is the water pure?**

pure—purer—purest

purely, *bw*
zuiver/enkel; **he says he likes you purely because you've got money.**

purpose ['pɜ:pəs] *zn*
doel; **what's the purpose of going by plane when it's much cheaper by car? I think he set fire to the house on purpose** = met opzet/expres.

purposely, *bw*
opzettelijk, expres; **she purposely stayed at home instead of coming to work.**

purse [pɜ:s] *zn*
portemonnaie; **she dropped her purse on the floor of the bus; I put my ticket in my purse so that I wouldn't forget it.**

push [pʊʃ] *ww*
(a) duwen; **they had to push their car to get it to start; we can't lift the piano, we'll have to push it into the corner; I had to push my bike home because I had a flat tyre; did he fall into the river, or was he pushed?**
(b) (in)drukken; **push button A to make the machine start;** (*in een lift*) **which floor number do you want me to push?** = voor welke verdieping moet ik drukken?

pushes—pushing—pushed—has pushed

push off, *ww*
opstappen; **it's time for us to push off now; push off!** = verdwijn!

put [pʊt] *ww*
(a) (neer)leggen; (neer-, op)zetten; **put your books down on the table; he put the milk in the fridge; do you want me to put another record on? can you help me put up the curtains?** = de gordijnen ophangen.
(b) uitdrukken, zeggen; stellen; **if you put it like that, it sounds quite pleasant; I want to put a question to the speaker.**

puts—putting—put—has put

put away, *ww*
wegbergen/wegzetten; **put your toys away before you go to bed.**

put back, *ww*
terugzetten; **put that book back on the shelf; shall I put the milk back in the fridge? to put the clocks back** = achter-uitzetten.

put off, *ww*
(a) uitstellen; **the meeting has been put off until next week.**
Let op: **we put the meeting off** *of* **we put off the meeting** *maar alleen* **we put it off**
(b) afleiden; doen walgen, tegenmaken; **don't sing while I'm writing, you're putting me off; he told a story about the hospital which put me off my food; I was going to see that film, but my brother put me off.**

put on, *ww*
(a) aantrekken; **put your coat on; put on your coat if you're going out.**
(b) aandoen; **put the light on, it's getting dark.**
Let op: **put your own coat on** *of* **put on your coat** *maar alleen* **put it on**

put out, *ww*
uitdoen; uitmaken; **don't forget to put out the light when you go to bed.**
Let op: **put the light out** *of* **put out the light** *maar alleen* **put it out**

put up, *ww*
onderbrengen; **can you put me up for the night?**

put up with, *ww*
dulden; **if you live near an airport**

you have to put up with a lot of noise;
how can you put up with all those children?

puzzle ['pʌzl] *zn*
raadsel; puzzel; **it's a puzzle to me why
he doesn't sell his house; she's finished
the crossword puzzle.**

pyjamas [pə'dʒɑ:məz] *zn meervoud*
(*Amer.* = **pajamas**)
pyjama; **I must buy another pair of pyjamas; he ran into the street in his pyjamas.**
Let op: **a pair of pyjamas** *wil zeggen
een jasje en een broek*

Qq

quality ['kwɒlɪtɪ] *zn*
(*a*) kwaliteit; **the cloth is of very high
quality; those tomatoes are of poor
quality.**
(*b*) kwaliteit, goede eigenschap; **he has
many qualities.**
meervoud **qualities**

quantity ['kwɒntɪtɪ] *zn*
hoeveelheid; **a large quantity of rubbish;
there was only a small quantity of milk
left; we have a quantity of waste paper**
= een flinke lading.
meervoud **quantities**

quarrel ['kwɒrəl] **1.** *zn*
ruzie; **they had a quarrel over who should
pay for the meal; we had a quarrel about
the colour of the carpet.**
2. *ww*
ruzie hebben/maken; **they quarrelled
about the colour of the carpet; he
quarrelled with the grocer over the price
of sugar.**
**quarrels—quarrelling—
quarrelled—has quarrelled**

quarter ['kwɔ:tə] *zn*
(*a*) kwart/vierde; **cut the apple into
quarters; the bottle is only a quarter full;
a quarter of our staff are ill; I want a
quarter of a pound of coffee.**
(*b*) **a quarter of an hour** = kwartier;
it's (a) quarter to four = het is kwart
voor vier; **at (a) quarter past seven** =
om kwart over zeven.
Let op: **a quarter** *en* **three quarters** *worden vaak geschreven* ¼ *en* ¾

queen [kwi:n] *zn*
koningin; **the Queen lives in Buckingham Palace; Queen Victoria was
queen for many years.**
Let op: **queen** *wordt met een hoofdletter gespeld als het met een naam
gebruikt wordt of naar een bepaalde
persoon verwijst*

question ['kwestʃn] *zn*
(*a*) vraag; (examen)opgave; **he asked the
teacher a question; the teacher couldn't
answer all our questions; I didn't answer
two of the questions in the exam.**
(*b*) probleem; vraagstuk; **the question
is—do we want to spend a lot of money
on a new car? it is out of the question** =
het is uitgesloten.
question mark, *zn*
vraagteken.

queue [kju:] **1.** *zn*
rij; file; **they stood in a queue for tickets
to the theatre; there were queues of
cars waiting for the ferry; he jumped
the queue** = hij ging voor zijn
beurt.
2. *ww* (*ook* **to queue up**)
in de rij staan. **we had to queue (up) to
get some petrol; they queued (up) for
hours to get into the theatre; I don't like
queuing.**
**queues—queuing—queued—has
queued**

quick [kwɪk] *bn*
vlug; snel; **which is the quickest way to**

get to the post office? I had a quick lunch and then got back to work; she is much quicker at sums than her sister; if you went by air it would be quicker than taking the train.

quick—quicker—quickest

quickly, *bw*
vlug; snel; gauw; he finished his meal very quickly because he wanted to watch a TV programme; the firemen quickly put the fire out.

quiet ['kwaɪət] *bn*
rustig; stil; the children are very quiet—they must be doing something naughty; please keep quiet—I'm trying to work; we had a quiet weekend working in the garden; it's a quiet little town.

quiet—quieter—quietest

quietly, *bw*
stil; zachtjes; geruisloos; the burglar went quietly upstairs; he shut the door quietly.

quite [kwaɪt] *bw*
(*a*) nogal; vrij; it's quite a good film; she's quite a fast typist; the book is quite interesting, but I liked the TV programme best.
(*b*) helemaal; he's quite mad; you're quite right; I quite understand why you want to go to bed; have you finished?—not quite.

quite a few/quite a lot = heel wat; quite a few people were sick; quite a lot of the cars were new; she spent quite a lot of the time lying in bed.

Let op de volgorde: he's quite a good student *maar* he's a fairly good student

Rr

rabbit ['ræbɪt] *zn*
konijn; the rabbit went down its hole.

race [reɪs] **1.** *zn*
(*a*) wedstrijd; he won the 100 metres race; we watched a bicycle race; I like watching horse races on TV.
(*b*) ras; the white races.
2. *ww*
om het hardst lopen etc.; let's race to see who gets to school first; I'll race you to the sweet shop = kijken wie er het eerst bij de snoepwinkel is!

races—racing—raced—has raced

radio ['reɪdɪəʊ] *zn*
radio; he got the message by radio; did you hear the programme on the radio about Germany? switch on the radio—it's time for the news; I was listening to the news on the car radio.

rail [reɪl] *zn*
(*a*) stang; rail; don't step on that rail—

it's electric; the little boy ran across the rails in front of the train.
(*b*) spoor; I go to work by rail; British Rail = de Britse Spoorwegen.

railings, *zn meervoud*
tralies; hek; he looked through the railings at the animals in the zoo.

railway, *zn* (*Amer.* **railroad**)
spoorweg; a railway station; the French railway system.

rain [reɪn] **1.** *zn*
regen; the ground is very dry—we've had no rain for weeks; yesterday London had 3 cm of rain; don't go out in the rain without an umbrella; the rain will help the plants grow.
geen meervoud: some rain; a drop of rain

2. *ww*
regenen; it started to rain as soon as we sat on the grass; you can't go for a picnic

when it's raining; it rained all day yesterday.

rains—raining—rained—has rained
Let op: to rain *wordt alleen met* it *gebruikt*

rainbow, *zn*
regenboog.

raincoat, *zn*
regenjas; put on your raincoat if it's raining; he took off his raincoat and hung it in the hall.

rainstorm, *zn*
(hevige) regenbui; the streets were flooded in the rainstorm last night.

rainy, *bn*
regenachtig; the rainy weather spoilt our holiday.

rainy—rainier—rainiest

raise [reɪz] *ww*
(*a*) (opheffen/(ver)heffen; he raised his arm; don't raise your voice.
(*b*) verhogen; they've raised the bus fares again.

raises—raising—raised—has raised

ran [ræn] *zie* **run**

rang [ræŋ] *zie* **ring**

rapid ['ræpɪd] *bn*
snel; vlug; we heard rapid footsteps on the stairs; the enemy made a rapid attack.

rapidly, *bw*
snel; vlug; he read the names out rapidly.

rare [reə] *bn*
zeldzaam; this is one of the rarest stamps; these animals are getting rarer every year.

rare—rarer—rarest

rarely, *bw*
zelden; he rarely comes to London now.

rat [ræt] *zn*
rat.

rate [reɪt] *zn*
standaard; verhouding; tempo; koers; a high rate of interest; birth rate = geboortecijfer.

at any rate = in elk geval; are you going to the party?—we're going, at any rate.

rather ['rɑːðə] *bw*
(*a*) nogal, vrij; it's rather cold outside; her hat is rather a pretty shade of green
(*b*) *wordt met* would *gebruikt voor iets liever willen;* I'd rather stay at home than go to the party; are you going to pay for everybody?—I'd rather not; she'd rather we stayed with her; they'd rather we went with them.
(*c*) liever/eerder ... dan; rather than wait for a bus, we decided to walk home; rather than have to pay, he said he had no money.

or rather = of beter/liever gezegd; his father is English, or rather Scottish.

raw [rɔː] *bn*
rauw/ongekookt; he eats his meat raw; too much raw fruit can make you ill.

razor ['reɪzə] *zn*
scheermes; scheerapparaat; he was shaving with his electric razor; she used a razor blade to sharpen her pencil.

Rd *zie* **road**

reach [riːtʃ] **1.** *zn*
bereik; afstand; you should keep medicines out of the reach of the children; the house is within easy reach of the station.
2. *ww*
(*a*) (be)reiken; he reached across the table and put a potato on my plate; the little boy is tall enough to reach the cupboard; can you reach me down the box from the top shelf = kun je me de doos aanreiken etc.
(*b*) bereiken; we only reached the hotel at midnight; what time are we supposed to reach London? the letter never reached him; the amount in my bank account has now reached £1000.

reaches—reaching—reached—has reached

read [riːd] *ww*
lezen; I can read Russian but I can't speak it; he was reading the newspaper; I can't read the instructions on the medi-

cine bottle—the letters are too small; he plays the piano by ear, but he can't read music; I'm reading about the American election; the teacher read out all our marks = de onderwijzer(es) heeft ... opgelezen.
reads—reading—read [red]—has read [red]

ready ['redɪ] *bn*
klaar; bereid; **we can't eat yet—the dinner isn't ready; wait for me, I'll be ready in two minutes; are you ready to go to school? the children are ready for bed** = de kinderen staan kant en klaar om etc.; **he's ready for anything** = hij is tot alles bereid.

real [rɪəl] *bn*
(a) echt; werkelijk; **is your watch real gold? this plastic fruit looks very real/look like the real thing.**
(b) heus; echt; **have you ever seen a real live elephant?**
really, *bw*
(a) werkelijk; heus; echt; **is he really American? did she really mean what she said? he really believes that the earth is flat; did the house really belong to your father?**
(b) werkelijk; echt; **you really ought to have your hair cut; he doesn't like chocolate—really, how odd!**

realize ['rɪəlaɪz] *ww*
beseffen; zich realiseren; **he realized that he was becoming deaf; did she realize that ehe car was going too fast? I realize that the holiday will be expensive.**
realizes—realizing—realized—has realized

reason ['riːzn] *zn*
reden; **what was the reason for the train being late? they said the train would be late, but didn't give any reason; the reason he's gone to live in Greece is that it's warmer there than here.**
reasonable, *bn*
redelijk; **the manager was very reasonable when I said I had left all my money at home.**

receipt [rɪ'siːt] *zn*
kwitantie; **keep your receipt—you'll have to show it if you want to change your pullover for another one.**

receive [rɪ'siːv] *ww*
ontvangen; krijgen; **he received a lot of cards on his birthday; did you ever receive the cheque I sent you? he received a gold watch when he retired.**
receives—receiving—received—has received

recent ['riːsnt] *bn*
recent; **his recent film about the war; the Prime Minister's recent speech.**
recently, *bw*
onlangs; kortgeleden; (nog) pas; **have you ever been to Sweden?—I was there quite recently; he's recently joined the tennis club.**

recognize ['rekəgnaɪz] *ww*
herkennen; **the police recognized the writing on the letter; I recognized her by the hat she was wearing; you've had your hair cut—I didn't recognize you!**
recognizes—recognizing—recognized—has recognized

recommend [rekə'mend] *ww*
(a) aanraden/adviseren; **the doctor recommended that he should stay in bed; I wouldn't recommend you to go there; I don't recommend going on a long car ride if you don't like travelling.**
(b) aanbevelen; **this restaurant is recommended in the guide book; I would certainly recommend that dictionary.**

record 1. *zn* ['rekɔːd]
(a) (grammofoon)plaat; **I bought her an Elvis Presley record for her birthday; I don't like his new record—do you? some records are expensive, so I borrow them from the record library; put another Beethoven record on.**
(b) record; **he holds the world record for the 1000 metres; she broke the world record/she set up a new world record in the last Olympics** = ze heeft het wereldrecord gebroken; **they're trying to set a new record for eating sausages.**

2. *ww* [rɪˈkɔ:d]
opnemen; **he recorded the conversation on his pocket tape-recorder; this music has been badly recorded.**
records—recording—recorded— has recorded

recorder, *zie* **tape recorder**
record-player, *zn*
platenspeler; grammofoon; **shall I put my new record on the record-player? switch the record-player off—I want to watch TV.**

red [red] *bn & zn*
rood; **he has red hair; they live in the house with a red door; I'm painting the chair red; he turned red when we asked him what he had done with the money; have you any paint of a darker red than this one? you have to stop when the traffic lights are red.**
red—redder—reddest

Red Cross, *zn*
het Rode Kruis.

reduce [rɪˈdju:s] *ww*
(ver)minderen; verlagen; **you must reduce speed when you come to the traffic lights; we've reduced the temperature in the office.**
reduces—reducing—reduced— has reduced

refer to [rɪˈfɜ:tʊ] *ww*
verwijzen naar; **are you referring to me? he referred to the letter he had just received.**
refers—referring—referred—has referred

referee [refəˈri:] *zn*
scheidsrechter; **the referee blew his whistle; our best player was told off by the referee.**

refrigerator [rɪˈfrɪdʒəreɪtə] *zn*
ijskast/koelkast; **put the milk in the refrigerator; a refrigerator is very useful in hot weather; shut the refrigerator door.** *Let op: wordt vaak* **fridge** [frɪdʒ] *genoemd*

refuse [rɪˈfju:z] *ww*
weigeren; afwijzen; **he came to the party but he refused to talk to anyone; they refused my offer of a lift home; we asked them to come to dinner, but they refused.**
refuses—refusing—refused—has refused

register [ˈredʒɪstə] *ww*
(zich laten) inschrijven; **they registered at the hotel at 6 p.m. and then went out for dinner.**
registers—registering— registered—has registered
registered letter, *zn*
aangetekende brief.
registered mail, *zn*
aangetekende post.

regret [rɪˈgret] *ww*
(*a*) betreuren; spijt hebben van; **he regretted doing it, but he had been told to.**
(*b*) het spijt me etc.; **I regret to have to tell you that your father is ill.**
regrets—regretting—regretted— has regretted

regular [ˈregjʊlə] *bn*
regelmatig, geregeld, vast; **11 o'clock is my regular time for going to bed; if you don't have regular meals you will be ill; regular visits to the dentist are important; is this your regular train?** = de trein die u doorgaans neemt?
regularly, *bw*
regelmatig; **he is regularly late for work; she regularly goes to bed after midnight; you should go to the dentist regularly.**

related [rɪˈleɪtɪd] *bn*
verwant; familie van; **they are related— his mother is her aunt; she is related to the family who run the butcher's shop in the village.**

relation [rɪˈleɪʃn], **relative** [ˈrelətɪv] *zn*
(bloed)verwant; familielid; **all our relations came for grandmother's birthday party; she doesn't speak to any of her relatives; we have relatives in Australia but I've never met them.**
relatively, *bw*
betrekkelijk; **this train is relatively fast; the tickets were relatively cheap.**

religion [rɪˈlɪdʒn] *zn*
godsdienst; religie; **he's a follower of the Christian religion.**
religious, *bn*
godsdienstig; religieus; **they held a religious ceremony to mark the beginning of the school term.**

rely on [rɪˈlaɪ ɒn] *ww*
vertrouwen/rekenen op; **we're relying on you to pay for the tickets; don't rely on the weather being good for your picnic.**
relies—relying—relied—has relied

remain [rɪˈmeɪn] *ww*
(*a*) blijven; **several people remained behind when the speaker left; the weather will remain cold for several days.**
(*b*) overblijven; **two problems remain to be dealt with.**
remains—remaining—remained—has remained

remains, *zn meervoud*
resten; ruïne; overblijfselen; **after the fire the remains of the house had to be pulled down; we'll have the remains of the pie for our supper.**

remark [rɪˈmɑːk] *zn*
opmerking; **he made some rude remarks about the teachers; she passed some remarks about his dirty shoes** = ze maakte een aanmerking op etc.

remember [rɪˈmembə] *ww*
zich herinneren; **do you remember the football game where we lost 20–0? my grandfather can remember seeing the first planes flying; I can't remember where I put my book; I don't remember having been to this restaurant before; I remember her very well; it's odd that she can never remember how to get to their house; remember me to your father** = doe je vader de groeten van me.
remembers—remembering—remembered—has remembered

remind [rɪˈmaɪnd] *ww*
helpen onthouden/herinneren; **remind me to write to my aunt; he reminds me**

of someone I used to know in Africa = hij doet me denken aan iemand etc.
reminds—reminding—reminded—has reminded

remove [rɪˈmuːv] *ww*
verwijderen; **they removed the TV set when we couldn't pay the bill; the police came to remove my car because it was parked in a no parking area.**
removes—removing—removed—has removed

rent [rent] **1.** *zn*
huur; **they had to get out of their flat when they couldn't pay the rent.**
2. *ww*
(*a*) huren; **we rent this office from the government; when I go on holiday I'll rent a car.**
(*b*) verhuren; **when we went to the USA, we rented our house to a Swedish family.**
rents—renting—rented—has rented

repair [rɪˈpeə] *ww*
repareren; maken; **my shoes need repairing; the workmen have repaired the broken gas pipe.**
repairs—repairing—repaired—has repaired

repairs, *zn meervoud*
reparatie; **they have done some repairs to the roof.**

repeat [rɪˈpiːt] *ww*
herhalen; **could you repeat the address so that I can write it down? he kept repeating that he wanted a drink; she keeps repeating herself** = ze valt steeds in herhaling.
repeats—repeating—repeated—has repeated

reply [rɪˈplaɪ] **1.** *zn*
antwoord; **we've had no reply to our letter; I've had so many replies that I can't answer them all.**
meervoud **replies**
2. *ww*
antwoorden; **when I asked him how to get to the post office, he replied that he didn't know; she wrote to the company**

three weeks ago, but they still haven't
replied.
replies—replying—replied—has
replied

report [rɪ'pɔːt] **1.** *zn*
(a) (school)rapport; **she had a very good
report—all the teachers said she did
well.**
(b) rapport; verslag; **they wrote a report
on the problem of crime in large towns.**
2. *ww*
melden; rapporteren; verslag doen; **we
had better report this accident to the
police; you'll get reported if you go on
singing like that—it's after midnight** =
je wordt nog bekeurd als etc.
reports—reporting—reported—
has reported

reporter, *zn*
verslaggever; **a crime reporter/a sports
reporter.**

republic [rɪ'pʌblɪk] *zn*
republiek; **the German republic.**

rescue ['reskjuː] **1.** *zn*
redding; **the rescue of the school children
lost on the mountain; six policemen took
part in the rescue.**
2. *ww*
redden; **the firemen rescued ten people
from the burning house; he tried to rescue
his cat which was up a tree.**
rescues—rescuing—rescued—
has rescued

reserve [rɪ'zɜːv] **1.** *zn*
reserve; voorraad; **our reserves of oil are
low; we're keeping these sandwiches in
reserve in case more people come to the
party.**
2. *ww*
(a) reserveren; vrijhouden; **I'm reserving
the seat next to me for my sister.**
(b) reserveren; bespreken; **I've reserved
a table for six people; can I reserve some
seats by telephone?**
reserves—reserving—reserved—
has reserved

resign [rɪ'zaɪn] *ww*
ontslag nemen; **he has resigned and
gone to work for another company; if**

you don't pay me more I'll resign.
resigns—resigning—resigned—
has resigned

rest [rest] **1.** *zn*
(a) rust; **what you need is a good night's
rest; I had a few minutes' rest and then I
started work again.**
(b) stilstand; **the car came to rest at
the bottom of the hill.**
(c) rest; **here are John and Jim, but
where are the rest of the children? the cat
drank the rest of the milk; he put the rest of
his dinner in the dustbin; she gave away
three apples and ate the rest herself.**
Let op: bij **rest** *wordt het werkwoord
in het enkelvoud gebruikt wanneer het
onderwerp in het enkelvoud staat:*
**here's the rest of the milk;
where's the rest of the string?
the rest of the money has been
stolen;** *bij een meervoudig onderwerp wordt het meervoud gebruikt:*
**here are the rest of the children;
where are the rest of the bricks?
the rest of the books have been
stolen**

2. *ww*
(a) rusten; **don't disturb your mother—
she's resting; they walked for ten miles,
then rested for ten minutes, then walked
again.**
(b) laten rusten/leunen; **he rested his
bike against the wall.**
rests—resting—rested—has
rested

restaurant ['restrɒnt] *zn*
restaurant; **let's not stay at home
tonight—let's go to the restaurant in the
High Street; he's waiting for me at the
restaurant.**

result [rɪ'zʌlt] **1.** *zn*
(a) resultaat; uitslag; **the result of the
game was a draw; I've been told my
maths results—I passed.**
(b) resultaat; gevolg; **he had a cold, with
the result that he had to stay in bed; I
complained that the price was too high,
but with no result; as a result of the accident, six people had to go to hospital;**

Restaurant

1.	bill	*rekening*	
2.	bottle	*fles*	
3.	candle	*kaars*	
4.	chair	*stoel*	
5.	cup	*kopje*	
6.	fork	*vork*	
7.	glass	*glas*	
8.	knife	*mes*	
9.	menu	*menu*	
10.	milk jug	*melkkannetje*	
11.	mustard	*mosterd*	
12.	pepper	*peper*	
13.	plate	*bord*	
14.	salt	*zout*	
15.	saucer	*schoteltje*	
16.	spoon	*lepel*	
17.	table	*tafel*	
18.	tablecloth	*tafelkleed*	
19.	teapot	*theepot*	
20.	waiter	*kelner*	
21.	waitress	*serveerster*	
22.	wine	*wijn*	

the result of all our discussions was that nothing was decided.
2. *ww*
uitlopen op; the accident resulted in a traffic jam; his illness resulted in his being away from work for several weeks.
results—resulting—resulted—has resulted

retire [rɪ'taɪə] *ww*
met pensioen gaan; most men retire at 65, but women only go on working until they are 60; he retired after twenty years in the factory; both my parents are retired.
retires—retiring—retired—has retired

return [rɪ'tɜːn] 1. *zn*
(*a*) terugkeer, terugkomst; on his return to work he was given a present; can you send me your reply by return of post? = per omgaande; many Happy Returns of the Day! = er nog vele jaren!
(*b*) retour(biljet); I want two returns to London; buy a return ticket—it's cheaper than two singles; day return = dagretour.
2. *ww*
(*a*) terugkeren, terugkomen; they returned from holiday last week; he hasn't returned to work since he was ill.
(*b*) terugbrengen, teruggeven; I must return my books to the library; she borrowed my knife and never returned it.
returns—returning—returned—has returned

rhyme [raɪm] 1. *zn*
rijm(pje); don't be silly—'blow' isn't a rhyme for 'cow'; I can't finish my poem because I can't think of a rhyme for 'scissors'.
2. *ww*
rijmen; don't be silly—'blow' doesn't rhyme with 'cow'/'blow' and 'cow' don't rhyme.
rhymes—rhyming—rhymed—has rhymed

rice [raɪs] *zn*
rijst; he was eating a bowl of rice; *zie ook* **pudding**.
geen meervoud: **some rice; a bowl of rice/a spoonful of rice.**

rich [rɪtʃ] *bn*
(*a*) rijk; he's so rich that he doesn't know what to do with his money; if I were a rich man, I'd go to warm places in the winter; she doesn't spend any money and so gets richer and richer.
(*b*) (*van kleur*) rijk; he painted the ceiling a rich chocolate colour.
(*c*) rijk (aan); the country is rich in coal; the town is rich in old churches; the museum has a rich collection of Italian paintings.
(*d*) machtig; this cake's too rich for me.
rich—richer—richest

rid [rɪd] *ww*
to get/to get rid of something = kwijt raken, afkomen van; to be rid of something = af zijn van; I'm trying to get rid of my old car; he can't get rid of his cold—he's had it for weeks; I'm very glad to be rid of my cold.

ride [raɪd] 1. *zn*
rit(je); I'm going for a ride on my bike; do you want to come for a bike ride? can I have a ride on the black horse? we all went for a ride in his new car; the shops are only a short bus ride from our house.
2. *ww*
rijden; I was riding my bike when it started to rain; have you ever ridden (on) an elephant? she's learning to ride a bicycle = ze leert fietsen.
rides—riding—rode [rəʊd]**—has ridden** ['rɪdn]

riding school, *zn*
rijschool/manege.

right [raɪt] 1. *bn*
(*a*) juist; goed; you're right—they didn't win = jij hebt gelijk etc.; he's always right; he gave the right answer every time; I think the answer's 240—quite right! is your watch right? is that the right time? this isn't the right train for London; put the books back in the

right place; **if you don't put the bottle the right way up, all the milk will run out of it; is this right way to get to the post office?** *zie ook* **all right**.
(*b*) rechts/rechter-; **in England, you mustn't drive on the right side of the road; she was holding her bag in her right hand; my right arm is stronger than my left.**
2. *zn*
(*a*) rechterkant; **in England you mustn't drive on the right; in Germany you must keep to the right** = rechts houden; **when you get to the traffic lights, turn to the right** = je moet rechtsaf (gaan/slaan) etc.; **who was that girl sitting on your right?** = aan je rechterhand; **take the second street on the right.**
(*b*) recht; **you've got no right to read my letters; everyone has the right to say what they like about the government.**
3. *bw*
(*a*) recht; rechtaan; regelrecht; **keep right on to the end of the road; instead of turning he went right on into a tree.**
(*b*) (*ook* **right away**) meteen; **he phoned the police right after the accident; the doctor came right away.**
(*c*) helemaal; precies; juist; **his house is right at the end of the road; the TV went wrong right in the middle of the programme; go right along to the end of the corridor; don't stand right in front of the TV—no one can see the picture.**
(*d*) juist; goed; **he guessed right; nothing seems to be going right.**
(*e*) rechts(af); **turn right at the traffic lights; look right and left before you cross the road.**
right-hand, *bn*
rechter/rechts; **look in the right-hand drawer; he lives on the right-hand side of the street.**
right-handed, *bn*
rechts; **he's right-handed.**

ring [rɪŋ] **1.** *zn*
(*a*) ring; **she has a gold ring on her finger.**
(*b*) kring; **we all sat in a ring.**
(*c*) gerinkel; **there was a ring at the door** = er werd gebeld.

(*d*) belletje; **I'll give you a ring tomorrow.**
2. *ww*
(*a*) (aan)bellen; luiden; **he rang at the door; the bells were ringing; ring your bicycle bell and people will get out of the way; is that your phone ringing? that rings a bell** = daar staat me iets van bij.
(*b*) (op)bellen; **he rang me when I was in bed; don't ring tomorrow—I'll be out.**
rings—ringing—rang [ræŋ]—has rung [rʌŋ]
ring back, *ww*
terugbellen; **he said he would ring me back in an hour, but he hasn't.**
ring off, *ww*
ophangen; **when I started to talk he just rang off.**
ring up, *ww*
(op)bellen; **someone rang you up while you were out; she rang up the police to say that her dog was missing.**
Let op: **I rang my father up** *of* **I rang up my father** *maar alleen* **I rang him up.**

ripe [raɪp] *bn*
rijp; **that apple isn't ripe—it will make you ill; are oranges ripe in the winter?**
ripe—riper—ripest

rise [raɪz] *ww*
opgaan; rijzen; stijgen; **the sun rises in the east; the road rises steeply; prices have risen this year.**
rises—rising—rose [rəʊz]—has risen ['rɪzn]

risk [rɪsk] **1.** *zn*
risiko; **is there any risk of being caught by the police? they ran the risk of being caught** = ze liepen het risiko etc.; **there's not much risk of rain** = er is weinig kans op regen.
2. *ww*
riskeren; wagen; **I'll risk going out without a coat; he risked his life to save the little girl.**
risks—risking—risked—has risked

river ['rɪvə] *zn*
rivier; **he's trying to swim across the**

river; don't fall into the river—it's very deep; London is on the River Thames.

Let op: met namen wordt het meestal de River: the River Thames; the River Amazon; the River Nile

road [rəʊd] *zn*
weg; in England, you drive on the left side of the road; be careful—the road's covered with ice; look both ways when you cross the road; where do you live?— 15, London Road.
Let op: wordt vaak in straatnamen gebruikt: London Road, York Road, etc., en wordt vaak geschreven Rd: London Rd, etc.

roast [rəʊst] *ww*
braden; roosteren; the pork is roasting in the oven; I like roast chicken.
roasts—roasting—roasted—has roasted
Let op: gebruik als bijvoeglijk naamwoord roast: roast beef/roast pork, etc.

rob [rɒb] *ww*
beroven; he was robbed of all his money; three men robbed the bank.
robs—robbing—robbed—has robbed
robber, *zn*
rover; dief; they were attacked by robbers.

rock [rɒk] 1. *zn*
(*a*) rots; the house is built on hard rock; the road is cut out of the rock.
(*b*) rots(blok); klip, rots; rocks fell down the mountain; the ship hit some rocks and sank.
2. *ww*
(doen) schommelen; wiegen; deinen; the waves are rocking the boat; he rocked backwards and forwards on his chair.
rocks—rocking—rocked—has rocked
rocking chair, *zn*
schommelstoel.

rode [rəʊd] *zie* **ride**

roll [rəʊl] 1. *zn*
(*a*) rol; a roll of paper; toilet roll = closet-rol; sausage roll = saucijzebroodje.
(*b*) broodje; cheese roll/ham roll = broodje kaas/ham.
2. *ww*
rollen; he rolled the ball across the table; the football rolled down the stairs; the penny rolled under the piano.
rolls—rolling—rolled—has rolled
roll up, *ww*
oprollen; he rolled up the carpet; she rolled the newspaper up.
Let op: she rolled up the carpet of she rolled the carpet up maar alleen she rolled it up

roof [ruːf] *zn*
dak; the cat walked across the roof of the house; the roof needs mending—the rain's coming in; put your suitcases on the roof of the car.

room [ruːm] *zn*
(*a*) kamer; here's the dining room; our flat has five rooms, and a kitchen and bathroom.
(*b*) hotelkamer; I want to book a room for two nights; here's your room—it's just opposite mine.
(*c*) ruimte; this table takes up a lot of room; there isn't enough room for three people; we can't have a piano in our house—there just isn't any room.
geen meervoud voor (c): some room; no room; too much room

root [ruːt] *zn*
wortel; root crops = knolgewassen.

rope [rəʊp] *zn*
touw; they pulled the car out of the river with a rope; he climbed down from the window on a rope.

rose [rəʊz] 1. *zn*
roos; she was picking a bunch of roses; this red rose has a beautiful smell.
2. *ww zie* **rise**

rotten ['rɒtn] *bn*
rot, bedorven; all these apples are rotten; don't eat that potato—it's rotten; a bag of rotten oranges.

rough [rʌf] *bn*
(*a*) oneffen; hobbelig; rul; wild; **a rough road led to the farm; the sea was rough—we were all sick.**
(*b*) ruw; **he made a rough drawing of the scene of the accident; I can only make a rough guess at what happened.**
(*c*) ruw; ruig; **we had a rough game of football.**
rough—rougher—roughest

roughly, *bw*
(*a*) ruw; **they played roughly.**
(*b*) ruwweg; ongeveer; **the cost will be roughly £25; I can't say exactly, but I can tell you roughly how big it is.**

round [raʊnd] **1.** *bn*
rond; **a round carpet; we sat at a round table.**
2. *bw & vz*
(*a*) rond; om(... heen); rondom; **the wheels went round and round; we ran round the house; the wall goes right round the house.**
(*b*) om; **he turned round; don't look round when you're driving.**
(*c*) rond; **they passed round the plate of cakes; there aren't enough cakes to go round** = er zijn niet genoeg taartjes voor iedereen.
(*d*) rond; **we walked round the shops** = de winkels rond.
3. *zn*
(*a*) ronde; **a newspaper round** = krantenwijk.
(*b*) **round of drinks** = rondje; **I'll buy the next round; a round of toast** = een geroosterde boterham.
(*c*) ronde; **if you answer all the questions, you will go on to the next round.**
roundabout, *zn*
(*a*) rotonde/verkeersplein; **turn right at the next roundabout.**
(*b*) draaimolen; **I want a ride on the roundabout.**

row¹ [raʊ] **1.** *zn*
rij; **there were rows of empty seats in the cinema; try and find a seat in the front row; stand in a row facing the camera.**
2. *ww*
roeien; **he's learning to row/he takes**

rowing lessons; **we rowed the boat across the river.**
rows—rowing—rowed—has rowed

rowing boat, *zn*
roeiboot; **let's hire a rowing boat and go on the river.**

row² [raʊ] *zn*
ruzie; herrie; **I had a row with my boss; the engine is making an awful row; stop that row!—I'm trying to work.**

royal ['rɔɪəl] *bn*
koninklijk, vorstelijk; **when we were in Copenhagen we visited the royal gardens; the Royal Family** = de Koninklijke Familie.

rub [rʌb] *ww*
(*a*) boenen; wrijven; **he rubbed the table with a cloth.**
(*b*) wrijven; **she rubbed her knee after she knocked it against the corner of the table; have you hurt your elbow?—come here, and let me rub it for you; he was rubbing his hands with excitement** = hij wreef zich in de handen etc.
rubs—rubbing—rubbed—has rubbed

rub out, *ww*
uitvegen; uitvlakken; **he rubbed out his mistakes; this pencil won't rub out.**
Let op: **he rubbed the word out** *of* **he rubbed out the word** *maar alleen* **he rubbed it out**

rubber ['rʌbə] *zn*
(*a*) rubber; **cars have rubber tyres; they were blowing up a rubber boat; some boots are made of rubber.**
(*b*) vlak(gom)/vlakje; **can you lend me your rubber, I've made a mistake.**
geen meervoud voor (*a*)

rubber band, *zn*
elastiekje; **the cards were held together with a rubber band.**

rubbish ['rʌbɪʃ] *zn*
(*a*) rommel; **put all that rubbish in the dustbin; there is so much rubbish that we will have to burn it.**
(*b*) onzin; **he's talking rubbish; I've never**

heard such rubbish; it's getting cold!—
rubbish! it's hotter than yesterday.
geen meervoud

rude [ru:d] *bn*
onbeleefd; grof; **he was rude to his
customers; you mustn't be rude to your
teachers; she was very rude about my
painting; he's the rudest man I know.**
rude—ruder—rudest

rug [rʌg] *zn*
(vloer)kleedje; **he sat on the rug in front
of the fire.**

rugby [ˈrʌgbɪ] *zn*
rugby; **he's in our rugby team; they both
got hurt playing rugby; we've lost our last
two rugby matches; we had a good game
of rugby on Saturday; did you watch the
rugby game on TV?**
geen meervoud

ruin [ˈruːɪn] *ww*
ruïneren, bederven; **our holiday was
ruined by the bad weather; he is ruining
his chances of getting more money by
being rude to the boss.**
**ruins—ruining—ruined—has
ruined**

ruins, *zn meervoud*
ruïne; puinhoop; **firemen searched the
ruins to see if anyone was still alive; have
you visited the castle ruins/the ruins of
the castle?**

rule [ruːl] **1.** *zn*
regel; **I make it a rule not to smoke
before breakfast; you have to play the
game according to the rules; the referee's
job is to make sure that the players don't
break the rules.**
as a rule = in de regel, normaal; **as a
rule he gets to the office before 9 a.m.**
2. *ww*
regeren; heersen; **a republic is ruled by a
president.**
rules—ruling—ruled—has ruled

ruler [ˈruːlə] *zn*
lineaal; **this line isn't straight—use a
ruler next time.**

run [rʌn] **1.** *zn*
(*a*) rit(je); **he went for a run before**

breakfast = hij ging een stuk hard-
lopen etc.; **I was tired out after that long
run.**
(*b*) rit; **let's go for a run in your new car.**
2. *ww*
(*a*) rennen; deelnemen aan een wedren;
**he ran upstairs; don't run across the road;
he's running in the 100 metres race.**
(*b*) lopen; gaan; **the trains aren't running today because of the fog; the bus is
running late because of the traffic; this
bus doesn't run on Sundays.**
(*c*) draaien; aanstaan; **he left his car
engine running.**
(*d*) lopen; duren; **the main street runs
north and south; the film runs for two
hours.**
(*e*) exploiteren; drijven; leiden; **he runs a
shoe shop; I want someone to run the
sales department for me; he can't afford
to run two cars** = hij kan zich niet permitteren om er twee auto's op na te
houden; **she runs the youth club; the
army is running the country.**
(*f*) rijden; **I'll run you to the station** =
ik breng je in de auto naar het station.
runs—running—ran [ræn]—**has
run**

run away, *ww*
wegrennen; **he's running away from the
police; she threw a stone through the
window and ran away; he ran away from
school when he was 14.**

run in, *ww*
inlopen; inrijden; **I'm running in my new
car.**

run into, *ww*
(op)botsen tegen; **he ran into a tree; the
bus ran into the lamppost.**

runner, *zn*
(hard)loper; atleet; **there are ten runners
in the race.**

run out of, *ww*
opraken; **we've run out of petrol** = onze
benzine is op; **I must go to the shops—
we're running out of jam.**

run over, *ww*
overrijden; **he was run over by a bus; he
drove without looking and ran over a dog.**
Let op: **he ran over a dog** *of* **he ran
a dog over** *maar alleen* **he ran it
over**

runway, *zn*
startbaan/landingsbaan.

rung [rʌŋ] *zie* **ring**

rush [rʌʃ] **1.** *zn*
gedrang; haast; **there was a rush for the door** = er was een stormloop op de deur.
2. *ww*
(binnen)stormen; snel vervoeren; **he** rushed into the room; she was rushed to hospital; why was everyone rushing to the door?
rushes—rushing—rushed—has rushed

rush hour, *zn*
spitsuur; **you can't drive fast in the rush hour traffic; if we leave the office early we'll avoid the rush hour.**

Ss

sack [sæk] **1.** *zn*
(*a*) zak; **we bought a sack of potatoes; I've ordered three sacks of coal.**
(*b*) ontslag; **he got the sack/he was given the sack because he was always late for work.**
2. *ww*
ontslaan; **she was sacked because she was always late.**
sacks—sacking—sacked—has sacked

sad [sæd] *bn*
verdrietig; bedroefd; zielig; treurig; **she's sad because her little cat has died; it was such a sad film that we cried; reading poetry makes me sad.**
sad—sadder—saddest

safe [seif] **1.** *bn*
veilig; **the town is safe from attack** = de stad is beveiligd etc.; **you should keep medicines high up so that they are safe from children; I keep my money in a safe place; even if the school is on fire, all the children are safe; is this snake safe to touch? it isn't safe to touch the bomb; is it safe to go into the house now? don't play with the gas cooker—it isn't safe.**
safe—safer—safest
2. *zn*
kluis/safe; **he puts his gold coins in the safe every night.**

safely, *bw*
veilig; zonder ongelukken; **although the plane was on fire, all the passengers got out safely; he stopped the car safely although the brakes weren't working.**
safety, *zn*
veiligheid; **road safety** = verkeersveiligheid; **safety belt** = veiligheidsgordel; **safety pin** = veiligheidsspeld.
geen meervoud

said [sed] *zie* **say**

sail [seil] **1.** *zn*
(*a*) zeil; **the wind blew so hard it tore our sails; look at those little boats with their blue sails.**
(*b*) zeiltocht(je); **let's go for a sail across the harbour.**
2. *ww*
(laten) varen/zeilen; **hurry up—the ferry sails at 11.30; she was the first woman to sail alone around the world; the children were sailing their little boats in the park; we go sailing every weekend.**
sails—sailing—sailed—has sailed

sailing boat, *zn*
zeilboot.
sailor, *zn*
zeeman; **the sailors and the passengers stood on the deck; he wants to be a sailor, so he's going to join the navy; I'm a bad sailor** = ik heb last van zeeziekte.

sake [seɪk] *zn*
(*a*) **for the sake of** = ter wille van; **for the sake of his health he stopped smoking cigarettes; is it worth working so hard just for the sake of £10 a week?**
(*b*) **for someone's sake** = omwille van mij/jou etc., om mijnentwille etc.; **write her a letter for my sake; you ought to be nicer to your sister for your mother's sake.**

salad ['sæləd] *zn*
salade; **I'll have a chicken salad; we had ham and tomato salad; fruit salad** = fruitslaatje.
geen meervoud

salary ['sæləri] *zn*
salaris; **he has a very good salary; he has applied for a job with a salary of £10,000 a year.**
meervoud **salaries**

sale [seɪl] *zn*
(*a*) verkoop; **this house is for sale** = dit huis staat te koop; **some of these towels are on sale in the market.**
(*b*) uitverkoop; **our store is having a sale of china this week; I bought this hat for 50p in a sale.**
(*c*) **sales** = verkoop; **our sales have gone up this year.**
salesman, *zn*
verkoper; vertegenwoordiger; **ask the salesman to show you the new car.**
meervoud **salesmen**

salt [sɒlt] *zn*
zout; **did you put any salt in this soup? put some more salt on your fish; fish which live in the sea can only live in salt water.**
geen meervoud: **some salt; a spoonful of salt**
salty, *bn*
zout; **sea water is very salty; this soup is very salty—I think you've put too much salt in it.**
salty—saltier—saltiest

same [seɪm] *bn & vnw*
(het)zelfde; gelijk; **you get very bored having to do the same work day after day; she was wearing the same dress as**

she wore last year; **they all live in the same street; everyone else was looking tired—but he stayed the same; these two drinks taste the same; coffee looks the same as tea, but has quite a different taste.**
all the same, *bw*
toch; **I don't like parties, but I shall come to yours all the same.**

sand [sænd] *zn*
zand; **the children were playing in the sand; they raced across the sand on their motorbikes.**
geen meervoud
sandy, *bn*
zanderig, zand-; **a sandy beach.**

sandal ['sændl] *zn*
sandaal; **he's bought a new pair of sandals for his holiday; she was wearing blue sandals.**

sandwich ['sændwɪtʃ] *zn*
sandwich; boterham; **a ham sandwich; two cheese sandwiches; what sort of sandwiches do you want me to make for the picnic? we had a sandwich and some beer in the pub.**
meervoud **sandwiches**

sang [sæŋ] *zie* **sing**

sank [sæŋk] *zie* **sink**

sat [sæt] *zie* **sit**

satisfy ['sætɪsfaɪ] *ww*
tevreden stellen/zijn; **is he satisfied with his new car? they weren't satisfied with the service in the restaurant.**
satisfies—satisfying—satisfied—has satisfied
satisfaction [sætɪs'fækʃn] *zn*
tevredenheid; genoegen; **to his great satisfaction, his daughter married a very rich man.**
satisfactory, *bn*
bevredigend; **his marks in maths are satisfactory, but in English they are bad** = voldoende.

Saturday ['sætədɪ] *zn*
zaterdag; **we go shopping on Saturdays; I saw him at a party last Saturday; today**

is Saturday, September 20th; we'll go to the cinema next Saturday.
Let op: **Saturday** *wordt altijd met een hoofdletter geschreven*

sauce [sɔːs] *zn*
saus; **we eat apple sauce with pork** = appelmoes; **do you want any chocolate sauce on your ice cream? he poured a whole bottle of tomato sauce on his chips.**
saucepan, *zn*
(steel)pan; **put the potatoes in the saucepan; the soup has stuck to the bottom of the saucepan.**

saucer [ˈsɔːsə] *zn*
schoteltje; **he poured so much tea into his cup that it all ran into the saucer; get out another cup and saucer—your uncle is coming to tea.**

sausage [ˈsɒsɪdʒ] *zn*
worst(je); **we had sausages and fried eggs for breakfast; when you go to the butcher's, can you buy me a pound of pork sausages?**

save [seɪv] *ww*
(*a*) redden, behoeden voor; **the policeman saved the little boy from being burnt in the fire; how many people were saved when the ship sank? he saved my life** = hij heeft me het leven gered.
(*b*) besparen/opsparen/uitsparen; **I'm saving to buy a car; they save all the old pieces of bread to give to the birds; if you save £1 each week, you'll have £52 in a year's time.**
(*c*) besparen/uitsparen; **if you walk to work you will save £3 a week on bus fares; he delivered the letter himself so as to save buying a stamp; if you travel by air you'll save a lot of time; if you have your car mended now it will save you a lot of trouble later.**
saves—saving—saved—has saved
save up, *ww*
sparen (voor); **I'm saving up to buy a new car.**
savings, *zn*
spaargeld; **he put all his savings in the**

bank; she spent all her savings on a holiday in Australia.
Let op: **I've saved my money up** *of* **I've saved up my money** *maar alleen* **I've saved it up**

saw¹ [sɔː] **1.** *zn*
zaag; **he cut his hand on the saw; this saw doesn't cut well—it needs to be sharpened; chain saw** = kettingzaag.
2. *ww*
zagen; **he was sawing wood; they sawed the tree into small pieces; he said he was going to saw the piece of wood in half.**
saws—sawing—sawed—has sawn [sɔːn]

saw² *zie* **see**

say [seɪ] *ww*
(*a*) zeggen; **he said he wanted to come with us; don't forget to say 'thank you'; I was just saying that we never hear from Uncle John, when he phoned; can you translate what he said? the TV says it will be fine tomorrow.**
(*b*) luiden; **their letter says that they will arrive on Monday; the timetable says that there are no trains on Sundays** = volgens de dienstregeling etc.
(*c*) zeggen; **choose a number—let's say sixteen; let's meet next week—shall we say Thursday?**
says [sez]—**saying—said** [sed]—**has said**

scales [skeɪlz] *zn meervoud*
weegschaal; **he weighed the sugar on the kitchen scales; the bathroom scales must be wrong—I'm heavier than I was yesterday.**

scarce [skeəs] *bn*
schaars; zeldzaam; **fresh vegetables are getting scarce; when meat is scarce, you should try to eat fish; to make yourself scarce** = je uit de voeten maken; **when father is annoyed, we all make ourselves scarce.**
scarce—scarcer—scarcest
scarcely, *bw*
nauwelijks; **I scarcely know her; she could scarcely speak.**

scarf [skɑ:f] *zn*
das; sjaal; the boys were wearing their school scarves; put a scarf over your hair—it's starting to rain.
meervoud **scarves** [skɑ:vz]

scene [si:n] *zn*
toneel; tafereel; five minutes after the accident, an ambulance arrived on the scene; the police were at the scene of the crime.

scent [sent] *zn*
(*a*) geur; the scent of roses; these flowers have no scent.
(*b*) parfum; she was wearing a new scent; he gave her a bottle of scent.

school [sku:l] *zn*
school; he's four, so he'll be going to school this year; do you like school? what did you do at school today? she ran away from school; he left school and joined the navy; which school do you go to? there are two schools near our house.
primary school = lagere school.
secondary school = middelbare school.
schoolboy, schoolgirl, school-children, *zn' en*
schooljongen, schoolmeisje, school-kinderen.

science [ˈsaɪəns] *zn*
(natuur)wetenschap(pen); he's no good at languages, but very good at science.
scientific [saɪənˈtɪfɪk] *bn*
wetenschappelijk; he carried out scientific experiments.
scientist [ˈsaɪəntɪst] *zn*
geleerde; wetenschapper; wetenschaps-beoefenaar.

scissors [ˈsɪzəz] *zn meervoud*
schaar; the hairdresser was cutting my hair with his scissors; I must buy another pair of scissors; someone has borrowed my scissors and hasn't given them back.
Let op: je kunt **a pair of scissors** *zeggen als je duidelijk wilt maken dat het maar om één schaar gaat*

score [skɔ:] **1.** *zn*
(*a*) stand; the football match ended with a score of 2–0; what's the score in the match so far?
(*b*) scores of = massa's; scores of people caught flu; I've seen that film scores of times.
2. *ww*
(doel)punten maken/'scoren'; he scored three goals; she scored twenty five!
scores—scoring—scored—has scored

Scotland [ˈskɒtlənd] *zn*
Schotland; he went to live in Scotland; are you going to Scotland for your holiday?
Scot, *zn*
Schot(se); he's a Scot; the Scots work hard.
Scotch, *bn*
Schots; **Scotch eggs** = hardgekookt ei in gehakt door paneermeel gerold.
Scottish, *bn*
Schots; the Scottish mountains.
Let op: in Schotland gebruikt men liever, **Scottish** *dan* **Scotch** *en dit laatste wordt nooit voor mensen gebruikt*

scrape [skreɪp] *ww*
(af)schrapen; afkrabben; schaven; he was scraping the paint off the door with a knife; she fell off her bike and scraped her knee.
scrapes—scraping—scraped—has scraped

scratch [skrætʃ] *ww*
krabben; krassen; schrammen; they scratched the top of the table as they were carrying it upstairs; be careful not to scratch yourself on that rose tree; he scratched his name on the wall of the school.
from scratch = van voren af aan; we'll have to start again from scratch.
scratches—scratching—scratched—has scratched

scream [skri:m] **1.** *zn*
schreeuw; gil; you could hear the screams of the people in the burning building.
2. *ww*
schreeuwen; gillen; she screamed when a

man suddenly opened the door; all the children screamed with laughter.
screams—screaming—screamed—has screamed

screw [skru:] **1.** *zn*
schroef; he took out the screws and the car door fell off; the parts of the chair are held together with two screws.
2. *ww*
(*a*) schroeven; the table is screwed down to the deck of the ship; he screwed the lid on to the box.
(*b*) (aan)draaien; don't forget to screw the lid back on to the pot of jam.
screws—screwing—screwed—has screwed

screwdriver, *zn*
schroevedraaier.

sea [si:] *zn*
zee; I like swimming in the sea better than in a river; the sea's rough—I hope I won't be sick; to get to Germany you have to cross the North Sea; send your furniture to Australia by sea—it would be much more expensive by air = per schip/boot.
Let op: in namen wordt **Sea** *meestal met een hoofdletter geschreven.* **Sea** *wordt meestal met* **the** *gebruikt:* **the sea's too cold; the North Sea,** *etc.*
seaman, *zn*
zeeman.
meervoud **seamen**

seasick, *bn*
zeeziek; she didn't enjoy the trip because she was seasick all the time; I'll stay on deck because I'm feeling seasick.

seaside, *zn*
kust; we go to the seaside for our holidays; I like a seaside holiday; this seaside town is empty in the winter = badplaats.

seaweed, *zn*
zeewier; the beach is covered with seaweed.
geen meervoud: **some seaweed; a piece of seaweed**

search [sɜ:tʃ] **1.** *zn*
zoektocht, onderzoek; we went to every shop in search of a German book, but couldn't find it = we gingen in alle winkels op zoek naar etc.; the police sent out search parties to look for people lost in the snow = reddingsploegen/opsporingsploegen; we all joined in the search for his wallet = zochten allemaal mee etc.
2. *ww*
(door)zoeken; we've searched everywhere but can't find mother's watch; they're searching the mountains for people lost in the snow; the customs man searched my suitcase.
searches—searching—searched—has searched

season [ˈsi:zən] *zn*
(*a*) seizoen; jaargetijde; spring, summer, autumn and winter are the four seasons.
(*b*) seizoen; tijd; the cricket season lasts from April to September; the town is very crowded during the holiday season; when are pears in season? apples are out of season just now.
season ticket, *zn*
(seizoen)abonnement.

seat [si:t] *zn*
(zit)plaats; zitting; sit in the front seat of the car = op de voorbank; I want two seats in the front row; I couldn't find a seat on the bus, so I had to stand; this chair isn't very comfortable—it has a wooden seat; why is your bicycle seat so narrow? = zadel; take a seat, please, the doctor will see you in a few minutes.
seat belt, *zn*
veiligheidsgordel/-riem.

second [ˈsekənd] **1.** *zn*
(*a*) sekonde; the bomb will go off in ten seconds.
(*b*) sekonde; ogenblik(je); I saw him a second ago; wait for me—I'll only take a second to get ready.
(*c*) tweede; the German runner was first, the British runner was second; today is the second of January/January the second (January 2nd); Charles the

Second (Charles II) was king at the time of the fire of London.

Let op: in data wordt **second** *meestal geschreven* **2nd**: April 2nd, 1973; November 2nd, 1980; *bij de namen van koningen en koninginnen wordt* **second** *meestal geschreven* II: Queen Elizabeth II

2. 2nd *bn*
tweede; February is the second month in the year; it's Mary's second birthday next week; B is the second letter in the alphabet; men's clothes are on the second floor; this is the second tallest building in the world = het op één na hoogste gebouw; she's the second most intelligent girl in the school; that's the second time the telephone has rung while I'm in the bath.

secondary, *bn*
sekundair/ondergeschikt; **secondary school** = middelbare school.

second class, *zn*
tweede klas(se); **a second class ticket to Edinburgh; she travels second class because it is cheaper.**

second hand, *zn*
sekondewijzer.

secondhand, *bn & bw*
tweedehands; **he's just bought a second-hand car; I bought this car secondhand.**

secret [′si:krət] *zn & bn*
geheim; **I won't tell you what your birthday present will be—it's a secret; he hid his money in a secret place; can you keep a secret?** = kun je een geheim bewaren?

secretary [′sekrətərɪ] *zn*
sekretaresse/sekretaris; **my secretary will tell you when you can come to see me.**
meervoud **secretaries**

see [si:] *ww*
(*a*) zien; **can you see that house over there? cats can see in the dark; I can see the bus coming; we saw the car hit the tree.**
(*b*) zien; **have you seen the film at the cinema? I saw the football match on TV.**
(*c*) (ge)leiden; brengen; **the policeman saw the old lady across the road; my secretary will see you to the door; let me see**

you home; **they saw me off at the airport** = ze hebben me weggebracht etc.
(*d*) inzien; begrijpen; **I don't see why you need so much money; don't you see that we have to be at the station by ten o'clock? I see—you want to borrow a lot of money.**
(*e*) zorgen voor; kijken of; **can you see that the children are in bed by nine o'clock? would you see if the post has arrived?**
(*f*) zien; opzoeken; **I see him often, because he lives quite close to me; see you on Thursday!** = tot donderdag! **see you again soon!** = tot gauw! **I saw him last Christmas; you should see a doctor about your cough** = je moet een dokter raadplegen etc.

sees—seeing—saw [sɔː]**—has seen**

see through, *ww*
doorzien; **I saw through his plan.**

see to, *ww*
zorgen voor iets; **can you see to it that the children are in bed by nine o'clock? will you see to the Christmas cards?** = zorg jij voor etc.

seed [si:d] *zn*
zaad; **I'll sow some carrot seeds; these seeds are so small that you can hardly see them.**

seem [si:m] *ww*
schijnen; lijken; **he seems to like his new job; they seem to be having a good time; I seem to have lost my wallet; it seems that they got lost in the snow; they seem very pleasant; it seems strange that no one answered your letter; it seems to me that we ought to buy a new car** = me dunkt etc.

seems—seeming—seemed—has seemed

seldom [′seldəm] *bw*
zelden; **I seldom go to the cinema; we very seldom go out on Saturdays; he's seldom at home when you phone him.**
Let op: **seldom** *wordt meestal vóór het werkwoord geplaatst*

self- [self] *prefix*
self-defence, *zn*
zelfverdediging.

selfish, *bn*
egoïstisch; **don't be selfish—let me have one of your chocolates.**

self-service, *zn & bn*
zelfbediening; **self-service restaurant** = zelfbedieningsrestaurant; **self-service petrol station.**

sell [sel] *ww*
verkopen; **I sold my bike to my brother; we sold our car for £500; they sold him their house; they sell vegetables in that shop, but you can't buy meat there.**
sells—selling—sold [səʊld]**—has sold**

sell out, *ww*
uitverkopen; **we've sold out of potatoes** = de aardappelen zijn uitverkocht.

send [send] *ww*
zenden, sturen; **he sent me to the butcher's to buy some meat; we send 100 cards to our friends every Christmas; I'll send you a card when I get home.**
sends—sending—sent—has sent

send away for, *ww (ook* **send off for)** bestellen via de post; **I sent away for a watch which I saw advertised in the paper.**

send back, *ww*
terugsturen; **if you don't like your present, send it back and I'll buy you something different.**
Let op: **send the present back** *of* **send back the present** *maar alleen* **send it back**

send for, *ww*
laten komen; **we had to send for the doctor; send for the police!**

send off, *ww*
versturen/verzenden; **I sent the letter off without a stamp.**
Let op: **send the letter off** *of* **send off the letter** *maar alleen* **send it off**

send off for *zie* **send away for**

send up, *ww*
laten/doen (op)stijgen; opdrijven; **they sent up a balloon; the cold weather sent up the price of vegetables.**

sensation [sen'seɪʃn] *zn*
(*a*) gevoel, gewaarwording; sensatie; I

had an odd sensation as if I was floating in the air.
(*b*) sensatie; opschudding; **the new film made a sensation.**

sense [sens] *zn*
(*a*) zintuig; zin; **he lost his sense of smell.**
(*b*) gevoel; **he has no sense of humour** = hij heeft geen gevoel voor humor.
(*c*) zin; **this letter doesn't make sense** = deze brief is onbegrijpelijk.
(*d*) zin; verstand; **it makes sense to save money** = het heeft zin om geld te sparen.

sensible ['sensɪbl] *bn*
verstandig; **he made a very sensible suggestion.**

sensitive ['sensɪtɪv] *bn*
(*a*) (over)gevoelig; **don't mention her hair—she's very sensitive about it.**
(*b*) gevoelig; **his arm is still sensitive where he hurt it.**

sent [sent] *zie* **send**

sentence ['sentəns] *zn*
zin; **the second sentence in his letter doesn't mean anything.**

separate 1. *bn* ['seprət]
apart; gescheiden; **keep the water and the oil separate; I am sending you the book in a separate parcel; can we have two separate bills, please?**
2. *ww* ['sepəreɪt]
scheiden; uiteengaan; **you must separate the big stones from the sand; the family got separated in the crowd; let's separate, and meet again in thirty minutes.**
separates—separating—separated—has separated

separately, *bw*
afzonderlijk; **we want to pay for the two meals separately.**

September [sep'tembə] *zn*
september; **my birthday is in September; today is September 21st; we're going on holiday next September.**
Let op: **September 21st:** *zeg* 'the twenty-first of September' *of* 'September the twenty-first'
Let op: **September** *wordt altijd met een hoofdletter geschreven*

series [ˈsɪəriːz] *zn*
reeks; serie; **there has been a series of accidents at this corner; she wrote a series of letters to the police.**

serious [ˈsɪərɪəs] *bn*
(*a*) ernstig; serieus; **I'm being serious.**
(*b*) ernstig; **he's had a serious illness; there was a serious accident on the motorway.**
seriously, *bw*
ernstig; serieus; **he is seriously thinking of going to work in Canada; she is seriously ill.**

serve [sɜːv] *ww*
(*a*) opdienen; opscheppen; serveren; **let me serve the potatoes; have you served the children? serve yourself if you want some more meat.**
(*b*) dienen; **he served in the Police Force for twenty years.**
(*c*) bedienen; **are you being served?** = wordt u al geholpen? **the bus serves the villages in the hills.)**
(*d*) (*van tennis etc.*) serveren.
serves—serving—served—has served

servant, *zn*
bediende.
service, *zn*
(*a*) dienst; **did he enjoy his service in the Police Force? service charge** = bedieningsgeld; **the service is not included in the bill** = bediening niet inbegrepen; **the car has just had its 10,000 kilometre service** = onderhoudsbeurt.
(*b*) dienst; **the health service** = de nationale gezondheidszorg; **the services** = de strijdkrachten.
(*c*) dienst; voorziening; **the bus service is very bad; the main services** = water-, gas-, en elektriciteitsvoorziening.
(*d*) (kerk)dienst; **I'm going to the nine o'clock service on Sunday.**

set [set] **1.** *zn*
(*a*) stel; **a set of tools; a tea set** = theeservies.
(*b*) toestel; **a TV set.**
2. *ww*
(*a*) zetten, leggen; **he set the table** = hij heeft de tafel gedekt.

(*b*) gelijk zetten, (in)stellen/afstellen; **I've set my watch to the correct time; the bomb was set to go off at ten o'clock.**
(*c*) opgeven; **the teacher set us our maths homework; this book has been set for the exam** = is voorgeschreven etc.
(*d*) doen; laten; **the house was set on fire** = het huis werd in brand gestoken; **the prisoner was set free** = de gevangene werd vrijgelaten.
(*e*) ondergaan; **the sun sets in the west.**
(*f*) op muziek zetten; **the poem was set to music.**
sets—setting—set—has set

set about, *ww*
aanpakken; beginnen; **he set about building a boat; I haven't started yet because I don't know how to set about it.**
set back, *ww*
(*a*) doen achterblijven; **the bad weather has set the crops back by three weeks.**
(*b*) achteruit zetten; **the house is set back from the road** = het huis ligt een eindje van de weg af.
set down, *ww*
afzetten; **the bus set down several passengers at the post office.**
set off, *ww*
vertrekken; op reis gaan; **we're setting off for Italy tomorrow; he set off on a long walk over the mountains.**
set out, *ww*
vertrekken; op reis gaan; **they set out into the snow; we're setting out early tomorrow.**
set to, *ww*
(flink) aan de gang gaan; **he set to, and soon built a boat.**

seven [ˈsevn] zeven
there are seven bottles of milk in the fridge; she's seven (years old); the train leaves at seven (o'clock).
seventeen, zeventien
she's seventeen (years old); the train leaves at seventeen sixteen (17.16).
seventeenth 17th, *bn & zn*
zeventiende; **today is the seventeenth of September/September the seventeenth (September 17th); the seventeenth letter of the alphabet; it's my seventeenth birthday next week.**

seventh, 7th, *bn & zn*
zevende; the seventh of June/June the
seventh (June 7th); a seventh of the
bottle; Charles the Seventh (Charles
VII); it's his seventh birthday on Wednesday.
Let op: in data wordt **seventh** *meestal geschreven* **7th:** **August 7th,
1980; May 7th, 1965;** *bij de namen
van koningen en koninginnen wordt*
seventh *meestal geschreven* **VII:**
King Henry VII
seventieth, 70th, *bn & zn*
zeventigste; the seventieth film which I
have seen this year; tomorrow is grandfather's seventieth birthday.
seventy, zeventig
he's seventy (years old); she's in her
seventies = ze is in de zeventig.
Let op: **seventy-one (71), seventy-
two (72),** *etc., maar* **seventy-first
(71st), seventy-second (72nd),** *etc.*

several ['sevrəl] *bn & vnw*
verscheidene; verschillende; I've met him
several times; several of us are going to
the film; several houses were damaged in
the storm.

sew [səʊ] *ww*
naaien; can you sew this button on my
coat? she's sewing some curtains.
**sews—sewing—sewed—has
sewn**
sewing machine, *zn*
naaimachine.

sex [seks] *zn*
geslacht/sekse; please write on the form
your name, age, and sex.
meervoud **sexes**

shade [ʃeɪd] *zn*
(*a*) schaduw; we'll sit in the shade of the
apple tree; the sun's too hot—let's sit in
the shade.
(*b*) nuance/schakering; another shade of
blue; a darker shade of red.

shadow ['ʃædəʊ] *zn*
schaduw(beeld); I can see the shadow of
a man on the pavement; what a strange
shadow the tree makes!

shake [ʃeɪk] **1.** *zn*
(*a*) ruk; schok; (het) schudden; give your
watch a good shake to start it.
(*b*) milkshake; a milk shake; can I
have a chocolate milk shake?
2. *ww*
schudden; he shook his watch to see if it
would go; the buildings shook in the
storm; don't shake the box—you'll break
the glasses; she shook her head = ze
schudde haar hoofd; he shook hands
with me = hij schudde me de hand.
shakes—shaking—shook [ʃʊk]**—
has shaken**

shall [ʃæl] *hulpww*
(*a*) zal, zullen; we shall leave for Italy on
Saturday; I shan't say anything; we
shan't be home until after 9 o'clock.
(*b*) zal, zullen (soms); shall I shut the
door? shall we wait? shall we go to the
cinema tonight?
Ontkennend: **shan't** [ʃɑːnt]
Verleden tijd: **should, should not,**
meestal **shouldn't**
Let op: **shall** *wordt voornamelijk
gebruikt met* **I** *en* **we**

shallow ['ʃæləʊ] *bn*
ondiep; the water was so shallow that
the boat touched the bottom; if you can't
swim, stay in the shallow end of the
swimming pool.
shallow—shallower—shallowest

shame [ʃeɪm] *zn*
(*a*) schaamte; he was full of shame for
what he had done = hij schaamde zich
voor etc.
(*b*) schande; what a shame you can't
come to the party! = wat jammer!; it's a
shame that it rained when we went on
the picnic = het is zonde dat etc.

shan't [ʃɑːnt] *zie* **shall**

shape [ʃeɪp] *zn*
vorm; model; she's got a ring in the
shape of a letter A; my pullover's beginning to lose its shape = mijn pullover
begint zijn model te verliezen.
shaped, *bn*
in/met de vorm van; her hat is shaped
like a beehive.

shapeless, *bn*
vormeloos; she was wearing a shapeless dress.

share [ʃeə] **1.** *zn*
(*a*) deel; don't eat my share of the cake! has he done his share of the work?
(*b*) aandeel; he bought 300 shares in Marks and Spencers.
2. *ww*
(*a*) verdelen; we have to share the cake between seven people; he doesn't want to share his sweets.
(*b*) delen; we share a bathroom with the flat next door; he doesn't want to share his toys with the other children; we only have one room empty in the hotel—do you mind sharing it?
shares—sharing—shared—has shared

sharp [ʃɑːp] *bn*
(*a*) scherp; be careful with that knife—it's very sharp; I cut my foot on the sharp stones.
(*b*) scherp; onverwacht; a sharp corner; the car made a sharp turn across the road.
(*c*) schel; snerpend; he gave a sharp cry.
sharp—sharper—sharpest

sharpen, *ww*
slijpen; he sharpened his pencil with a knife; this knife doesn't cut well—it needs sharpening.
sharpens—sharpening—sharpened—has sharpened

shave [ʃeɪv] **1.** *zn*
(het) scheren; he hasn't had a shave for two days; I need a shave; where's the plug for the razor?—I want a shave.
2. *ww*
(zich) scheren; he cut himself while shaving; he hasn't shaved for two days.
shaves—shaving—shaved—has shaved

she [ʃiː] *vnw*
zij/ze; she's my aunt; she and I are going on holiday together; I'm angry with Anne—she's taken my bike; she's a nice

little cat; get off the ship—she's sinking.
Let op: she *wordt als lijdend voorwerp* her: she hit the ball/the ball hit her; *als* she *het werkwoord* be *volgt, wordt het meestal* her: who's that?—it's her, the girl we met yesterday

sheep [ʃiːp] *zn*
schaap; he's looking after his sheep; the sheep are in the field.
meervoud sheep: one sheep; ten sheep
Let op: het vlees van sheep *heet* lamb, *of soms* mutton

sheet [ʃiːt] *zn*
(*a*) laken; she pulled the sheet over her head and went to sleep.
(*b*) plaat; blad; vel; a sheet of glass; give me two sheets of paper.

shelf [ʃelf] *zn*
plank; put the books back on the shelves; the jam's on the top shelf.
meervoud shelves [ʃelvz]

shell [ʃel] **1.** *zn*
(*a*) schaal; schelp; to eat a boiled egg you have to take off the shell.
(*b*) granaat; the shells were falling near the castle.
2. *ww*
bombarderen; beschieten; the guns shelled the town.
shells—shelling—shelled—has shelled

shelter ['ʃeltə] **1.** *zn*
schuilplaats; bescherming; you should keep your new bike under shelter; he took shelter from the rain = hij schuilde voor de regen; bus shelter = overdekte bushalte; the people stood in the bus shelter out of the rain.
2. *ww*
schuilen; he sheltered from the rain under a big tree; the sheep were sheltering from the snow behind a wall.
shelters—sheltering—sheltered—has sheltered

shine [ʃaɪn] *ww*
schijnen; glimmen; glanzen; the sun's shining so I think it'll be hot today; he

polished his shoes until they shone; the glasses shone in the sunshine; why do cats' eyes shine in the dark?

shines—shining—shone [ʃɒn]—**has shone**

shiny, *bn*
glanzend; glimmend; the table has a shiny surface.

shiny—shinier—shiniest

ship [ʃɪp] *zn*
schip; we went across to the United States by ship; she's a fine passenger ship; the navy has many ships.
Let op: een ship *wordt vaak met* she/her *aangeduid*

shirt [ʃɜːt] *zn*
(over)hemd; he wore a dark suit and a white shirt; when he came home his suitcase was full of dirty shirts; it's so hot that I'm going to take my shirt off.

shock [ʃɒk] **1.** *zn*
(*a*) schok; schrik; he had a shock when the waiter gave him the bill; it was a shock to see how ill she was.
(*b*) electric shock = (elektrische) schok; when she touched the cooker she got a shock; don't touch that wire—it'll give you a shock.
2. *ww*
schokken; I was shocked to hear he was dead.

shocks—shocking—shocked—has shocked

shoe [ʃuː] *zn*
schoen; he's bought a new pair of shoes; she put her shoes on and went out; I must take my shoes off—my feet hurt.

shone [ʃɒn] *zie* **shine**

shook [ʃʊk] *zie* **shake**

shoot [ʃuːt] *ww*
(*a*) (dood)schieten/(neer)schieten; the soldiers were shooting into the houses; he was shot by a policeman as he tried to run away; he shot two rabbits.
(*b*) schieten, vliegen; he shot into the room; she shot up the stairs; the car shot out of the garage.

shoots—shooting—shot [ʃɒt]—**has shot**

shoot down, *ww*
neerhalen; we shot down three aircraft.

shop [ʃɒp] **1.** *zn*
winkel; the furniture shop is opposite the post office; all the shops are shut on Sundays; don't go to that shop—it's much too dear; I buy my food at the shop on the corner.
2. *ww*
boodschappen doen; winkelen; we've been shopping; he's out shopping.

shops—shopping—shopped—has shopped

shop around, *ww*
rondkijken; if you want a cheap radio, you ought to shop around.

shopkeeper, *zn*
winkelier.

shopper, *zn*
klant; koper.

shopping, *zn*
(*a*) inkopen; boodschappen; I do all my shopping on Saturday mornings; she's doing her shopping; have you done any shopping?
(*b*) aankopen; boodschappen; put all your shopping on the table; he slipped and dropped all his shopping.

geen meervoud: some shopping; a lot of shopping

shore [ʃɔː] *zn*
kust; oever; we walked along the shore; these plants grow on the shores of the lake.

short [ʃɔːt] *bn*
(*a*) kort; I need a short piece of string—about 25 centimetres; the shortest way to the station is to go along the High Street.
(*b*) kort; he was here a short time ago; they had a short holiday in Greece; I had a short sleep on the train.
(*c*) kort, klein; John is shorter than his brother.
(*d*) short of = tekort (komen); we're short of sugar; I can't pay as I'm rather short of money = ik zit slecht bij kas.
(*e*) afkorting (voor); Co. is short for Company; his name is Robert, but we call

him Bob for short = kortheidshalve
noemen we hem Bob.

short—shorter—shortest

shortly, *bw*
kort; **he left the house shortly after
breakfast.**

shorts, *zn meervoud*
short; **he was wearing a pair of football
shorts; you can't go into the church in
shorts.**

shot [ʃɒt] *zn*
schot; **the police fired a shot at the car;**
zie ook **shoot.**

should [ʃʊd] *hulpww*
(a) moest(en) eigenlijk; **you shouldn't eat
so many chocolates; he should go to see
the doctor if his cold gets worse; we
shouldn't have come to this party—it's
terrible; they should have arrived by
now** = ze zouden hier nu moeten zijn.
(b) zou(den); **I should like to go to
Greece if I had enough money.**
Ontkennend: **should not,** *meestal*
shouldn't
Let op: **should** *is de verleden tijd van*
**shall: shall we go to the
cinema?—I suggested we should
go to the cinema**

shoulder [ˈʃəʊldə] *zn*
(a) schouder; **he carried his gun over his
shoulder; the policeman touched him on
the shoulder; his shoulders are very wide
because he spends a lot of time rowing;
she looked over her shoulder to see who
was following her.**
(b) schouder(stuk); **the shoulders of this
shirt are too narrow.**

shout [ʃaʊt] **1.** *zn*
kreet, (uit)roep; **I heard a shout for help;
there were shouts of surprise when the
result was announced.**
2. *ww*
(uit)roepen; schreeuwen; **they shouted
for help; shout when you're ready** = geef
een gil etc.

**shouts—shouting—shouted—has
shouted**

show [ʃəʊ] **1.** *zn*
(a) tentoonstelling; **we are going to the**

flower show; a show house = model-
woning.
(b) voorstelling; **'My Fair Lady' is a
wonderful show; we're going to a show
tonight.**
2. *ww*
laten zien, tonen; wijzen; **can I show
you my stamp collection? he showed her
his new car; show me where you fell
down; ask the policeman to show you
the way to the post office; can you show
me how to get to the post office? he
showed me how the camera worked; my
watch shows the date as well as the
time.**

**shows—showing—showed—has
shown**

show in, *ww*
binnenlaten; **is that Mr Smith?—please
show him in.**

show off, *ww*
pronken (met); zich aanstellen; **don't
look at her—she's showing off; he's
showing off his new car.**

show out, *ww*
uitlaten; **I'll show you out.**

show over, show round, *ww*
rondleiden; **the guide showed us over the
castle/showed us round the castle.**

show up, *ww*
(a) opdagen; verschijnen; **we invited
twenty people to the party, but no one
showed up.**
(b) in de schaduw stellen; **she's so clever
that she shows us all up.**
(c) goed afsteken/uitkomen tegen; **this
orange jacket shows up in the dark when
I ride my bike.**

shower [ˈʃaʊə] *zn*
(a) bui; **we often have showers in April;
the TV says that there will be snow
showers tonight.**
(b) douche; **we've fixed a shower over
the bath; each room in the hotel has a
toilet and a shower; shower curtain** =
douchegordijn.
(c) douche; **she has a shower every
morning before breakfast; I don't like
cold showers!**

Shrove [ʃrəʊv] *zie* **pancake**

shut [ʃʌt] **1.** *bn*
dicht; gesloten; **all the shops are shut on Sundays; we tried to go in, but the door was shut.**
2. *ww*
dichtdoen; sluiten; dichtgaan; **please shut the window—it's getting cold; I've brought you a present—shut your eyes and guess what it is; pubs shut at 3 o'clock.**
shuts—shutting—shut—has shut
shut down, *ww*
sluiten; dichtgaan; **the factory shut down for the Christmas holiday.**
shut in, *ww*
insluiten; opsluiten; **the door closed and we were shut in.**
shut off, *ww*
afsluiten; **can you shut off the electricity?**
Let op: **he shut the electricity off** *of* **he shut off the electricity** *maar alleen* **he shut it off**
shut out, *ww*
buitensluiten; **I'm shut out of the car— I left my keys inside.**
shut up, *ww*
(*a*) opsluiten; **shut the dog up in the kitchen.**
(*b*) zijn mond houden; **shut up! I'm trying to listen to the news.**

sick [sɪk] *bn*
(*a*) ziek; **she's sick in bed.**
(*b*) misselijk; **when I got up this morning I felt sick; he ate too many cakes and was sick all over the floor** = hij heeft op de vloer overgegeven.
(*c*) **to be sick of** = iets beu/moe zijn; **I'm sick of hearing all that noise; I'm sick and tired of looking after all these children.**
(*d*) **to make someone sick** = iemand misselijk maken; **the way he spends money makes me sick.**
sickness, *zn*
ziekte; **there is a lot of sickness in the winter.**

side [saɪd] **1.** *zn*
(*a*) zijkant; zij(de); **turn the box on to its side; the garden is by the side of the house.**

(*b*) (blad)zij; kant; **write on one side of the piece of paper.**
(*c*) kant; zijde; **he lives on the other side of the street; she jumped over the wall to get to the other side; in England cars drive on the left-hand side of the road; we live on the south side of London; their house is on the sunny side of the street.**
(*d*) (sport)ploeg; elftal; **our side was beaten 3–0; which side does he play for?**
(*e*) zij; **lie down on your side; she stood by my side; all the soldiers stood side by side** = naast elkaar/zij aan zij.
(*f*) **to be on someone's side** = aan iemand's kant staan; **I'm on your side; whose side are you on?**
2. *bn*
zij-; **if your shoes are dirty, use the side door, not the front door.**
sidewalk, *zn*
(*Amerikaans voor* = **pavement**) stoep/trottoir.
sideways, *bw*
zijwaarts; van opzij; **they all walked sideways; if you look at him sideways you'll see how big his nose is.**

sight [saɪt] *zn*
(*a*) gezicht(svermogen); **he lost his sight in the war** = hij is blind geworden etc.
(*b*) aanblik; gezicht; **she can't stand the sight of blood; I caught sight of the mountain in the distance** = ik kreeg in de verte de berg in het oog; **the mountain came into sight** = de berg kwam in zicht; **they waved until the ship was out of sight** = ..., totdat het schip uit het gezicht verdwenen was.
(*c*) bezienswaardigheid; **the guide took us to see the sights of the town; she looks a sight in that red hat** = ze ziet er met die rode hoed belachelijk uit.
(*d*) (*van geweer*) **sights** = vizier.

sign [saɪn] **1.** *zn*
(*a*) teken; bord(je); **he made a sign with his hand and the cars began to go forward; go straight on until you come to a sign marked 'town centre'; the shop has a big sign outside it saying 'for sale'.**
(*b*) teken; aanwijzing; **is there any sign**

of the snow stopping? there's no sign of
how the burglar got into the house.
2. *ww*
(onder)tekenen; **he's forgotten to sign
the cheque; the manager signed the letter;
sign here, please.**
**signs—signing—signed—has
signed**

signal ['sıgnəl] *zn*
sein; signaal; **he waved a flag which was
the signal for the race to start; the traffic
signals aren't working** = de verkeers-
lichten etc.

signature ['sıgnətʃə] *zn*
handtekening; **I can't read his signature;
her signature is easy to recognize.**

silence ['saıləns] *zn*
stilte; **the crowd waited in silence; the
teacher asked for silence.**
silent, *bn*
stil; zwijgend; **they kept silent for the
whole meeting.**
silently, *bw*
stil; zwijgend; **they walked silently into
the church.**

silk [sılk] *zn*
zij(de); **she was wearing a silk shirt; this
tie is made of silk.**
geen meervoud: **some silk; a piece
of silk**

silly ['sılı] *bn*
dom; **don't be silly—you can't eat raw
potatoes; what a silly question!**
silly—sillier—silliest

silver ['sılvə] *zn*
(*a*) zilver; **a silver teapot; this ring is
silver; the handle of the knife is made of
silver.**
(*b*) zilver(werk); **don't forget to polish
the silver.**
geen meervoud
silver wedding, *zn*
zilveren bruiloft.

similar ['sımılə] *bn*
(soort)gelijk; dergelijk; **the two houses
are quite similar; his job is similar to
mine; have you something similar but not
as expensive?**

similarly, *bw*
eveneens; **he is very fond of sport: similarly his sister plays tennis every day.**

simple ['sımpl] *bn*
(*a*) eenvoudig/simpel; gemakkelijk; **the
answer is quite simple; I didn't think the
exam was very simple.**
(*b*) gewoon/eenvoudig; **we had a simple
meal of bread and soup; it's a very simple
plan.**
simple—simpler—simplest
simply, *bw*
(*a*) eenvoudig; **he described what
happened very simply.**
(*b*) enkel; **he did it simply to see what
you would say.**

since [sıns] **1.** *bw & vz*
sinds(dien); **he was rude to the teacher
and has had bad marks ever since; we've
been working since 2 o'clock; since we
got home, it has rained every day.**
2. *vw*
omdat/aangezien; **he can't come with us
since he's ill; since it's such a fine day,
let's go for a picnic.**

sincere [sın'sıə] *bn*
eerlijk; oprecht; **was he sincere when he
promised he would work better?**
sincerely, *bw*
eerlijk; **Yours sincerely** = met vriendelijke groeten.

sing [sıŋ] *ww*
zingen; **he was singing as he worked; can
you sing that song again? she was singing
a song about roses.**
sings—singing—sang [sæŋ] **—has
sung** [sʌŋ]
singer, *zn*
zanger(es).

single ['sıŋgl] **1.** *bn*
(*a*) enkel; **I haven't seen a single newspaper; I want a single room for one night**
= eenpersoonskamer; **do you want a
double bed or two single beds?** = wil je
een tweepersoonsbed of twee eenper-
soonsbedden?.
(*b*) ongetrouwd; **he's still single.**
(*c*) **single ticket** = enkele reis.

2. *zn*
(*a*) enkele reis; **I want two singles to London.**
(*b*) (*van tennis, etc.*) **singles** = enkelspel; **the men's singles.**

singular ['sɪŋɡjʊlə] *bn & zn*
enkelvoud(ig); **'mouse' is the singular, and 'mice' is the plural; 'is' is the singular of the verb 'to be' and 'are' is the plural; 'he' is a singular pronoun.**

sink [sɪŋk] **1.** *zn*
gootsteen; **put the dirty plates in the sink.**
2. *ww*
(*a*) zinken; tot zinken brengen; **get off the ship—she's sinking; the boat sank because there were too many people in it; they sank the ship with a bomb.**
(*b*) (neer)zinken; ondergaan; **he sank into an armchair; the sun's sinking in the west; my heart sank** = de moed begaf me.
sinks—sinking—sank [sæŋk]—has sunk [sʌŋk]

sir [sɜː] *zn*
(*a*) (*in winkel of restaurant e.d.*) meneer; **would you like to order your lunch, sir? please sit here, sir.**
(*b*) (*als briefaanhef boven 'n brief aan een onbekende heer*) Heer; Meneer; **Dear Sir.**

sister ['sɪstə] *zn*
zuster/zus(je); **she's my sister; he has three sisters; his sister works in a bank.**

sit [sɪt] *ww*
(*a*) zitten; **he was sitting on the floor; you can sit on the table if you like; sit next to me; she was sitting in bed eating her breakfast.**
(*b*) examen doen; **she failed and had to sit the examination again.**
sits—sitting—sat [sæt]—has sat

sit down, *ww*
gaan zitten; **everyone sat down and the film began; don't sit down—that chair's just been painted.**

sitting-room, *zn*
zitkamer; **let's watch TV in the sitting-room; shut the sitting-room door, please.**

sit up, *ww*
(*a*) rechtop (gaan) zitten; **he sat up in bed; sit up straight!**
(*b*) opblijven; **we sat up until 2 a.m.**

situation [sɪtjʊ'eɪʃn] *zn*
situatie; toestand; **we're in an difficult situation; this has made the situation very difficult for us.**

six [sɪks] zes
she's six (years old); come and have a cup of coffee at six (o'clock); there are six chocolates left.
sixteen, zestien
he's sixteen (years old).
sixteenth, 16th, *bn & zn*
zestiende; **he was sixteenth in the race; the sixteenth of August/August the sixteenth (August 16th); his sixteenth birthday is next week.**
sixth, 6th, *bn & zn*
zesde; **they live on the sixth floor; F is the sixth letter of the alphabet; he spent a sixth of the money; ten minutes is a sixth of an hour; the sixth of February/February the sixth (February 6th); Henry the Sixth (Henry VI); tomorrow is my son's sixth birthday.**
Let op: in data wordt **sixth** *meestal geschreven* **6th: April 6th, 1980; December 6th, 1976;** *bij namen van koningen en koninginnen wordt* **sixth** *meestal geschreven* **VI: King Henry VI**

sixty, zestig
he's sixty (years old); I bought sixty books yesterday; she's in her sixties = ze is in de zestig.
Let op: **sixty-one (61), sixty-two (62)** *etc., maar* **sixty-first (61st), sixty-second (62nd),** *etc.*
sixtieth, 60th, *bn & zn*
zestigste; **he was sixtieth out of 120; a minute is a sixtieth of an hour; it's father's sixtieth birthday tomorrow.**

size [saɪz] *zn*
grootte; omvang; (for)maat; **that onion's the size of a tennis ball; he has a garage about the same size as our house; what's the size of a normal swimming pool? she**

takes size 7 in shoes; what size shirts do your wear?

skate [skeɪt] **1.** *zn*
schaats; she was putting on her skates.
2. *ww*
schaatsen; we went skating on the ice; there is a big skating competition next week; she skates very well.
skates—skating—skated—has skated

skeleton [ˈskelɪtən] *zn*
skelet, geraamte.

ski [skiː] **1.** *zn*
ski.
2. *ww*
skiën; he skied down the mountain; we go skiing every weekend.
skis—skiing—skied [skiːd]**—has skied**

skill [skɪl] *zn*
vaardigheid; bekwaamheid; you need special skills to become a doctor.
skilled, *bn*
deskundig; vakkundig; he's a skilled workman.

skin [skɪn] *zn*
huid; schil; his skin turned brown in the sun; the skin of a cow can be used to make leather; a banana skin.

skirt [skɜːt] *zn*
rok; I like wearing jeans better than wearing a skirt; her skirt's so long it touches the ground.

sky [skaɪ] *zn*
lucht; hemel; look at all the clouds in the sky; when the sky's grey it means it'll be wet; the birds are flying high in the sky.
meervoud **skies**

sleep [sliːp] **1.** *zn*
slaap; she needs eight hours' sleep a night; get a good night's sleep—we have a lot of work to do tomorrow; she had a short sleep in the middle of the afternoon; to go to sleep = inslapen; I'm trying to go to sleep; he went to sleep in front of the TV set.
2. *ww*
slapen; he always sleeps for eight hours

each night; she slept for the whole of the TV programme; don't disturb him—he's trying to sleep.
sleeps—sleeping—slept [slept]**— has slept**

sleep in, *ww*
uitslapen.
sleepy, *bn*
slaperig; I'm feeling sleepier and sleepier; the children are very sleepy by ten o'clock.
sleepy—sleepier—sleepiest

sleeve [sliːv] *zn*
mouw; one sleeve of this coat is longer than the other; I often wear shirts with short sleeves in the summer.

slept [slept] *zie* **sleep**

slice [slaɪs] *zn*
plakje; sneetje; cut me another slice of bread; he ate six slices of ham.

slide [slaɪd] **1.** *zn*
(kleuren)dia; turn out the lights—I'll show you my holiday slides.
2. *ww*
glijden; schuiven; the door slid open; the van has sliding doors; let's go sliding on the ice.
slides—sliding—slid [slɪd]**—has slid**

slight [slaɪt] *bn*
licht; gering; there's been a slight frost; he has a slight temperature; she's had a slight accident.
slight—slighter—slightest
slightly, *bw*
enigszins; een beetje; the new box is slightly larger than the old one; I only know him slightly.

slip [slɪp] *ww*
(*a*) uitglijden; he slipped on the ice and fell down.
(*b*) (weg)glippen; she slipped upstairs when no one was watching; I'll just slip out to the shops for a moment.
slips—slipping—slipped—has slipped

slipper, *zn*
pantoffel; slof; slipper; he took off his shoes and put on his slippers.

slippery, *bn*
glad; glibberig; **watch out—the ice is slippery!**

slope [sləʊp] **1.** *zn*
helling; **a steep slope; the house is built on the slope of the mountain.**
2. *ww*
hellen; **the path slopes upwards; the road sloped down to the river.**
slopes—sloping—sloped—has sloped

slow [sləʊ] *bn*
(*a*) langzaam; traag; **the car was going at a slow speed; the train was very slow; he's very slow at answering my letters.**
(*b*) (*van tijd*) achter; **my watch is three minutes slow.**
slow—slower—slowest

slow down, *ww*
inhouden; vaart minderen; ophouden; **the snow slowed down the cars; the bus slowed down as it came to the traffic lights.**

slowly. *bw*
langzaam; traag; **the car was going very slowly when it hit the wall; we walked slowly round the museum; the teacher must speak slowly so that the children can understand.**

small [smɔːl] *bn*
klein; **small cars use less petrol than big ones; I'm selling my house and buying a smaller one; he only paid a small sum of money; she's smaller than her brother, but her mother's the smallest person in the family; this book isn't small enough to put in your pocket; my son's too small to ride a bike** = mijn zoontje is nog te klein om etc.
small—smaller—smallest

smell [smel] **1.** *zn*
reuk; geur; **dogs have a good sense of smell; the smell of roses makes me sneeze; what a lovely smell of roast meat! do you like the smell of onions? what a nasty smell! there's a smell of burning/ there's a burning smell; there's a funny smell in the kitchen.**
wordt meestal in het enkelvoud gebruikt

2. *ww*
(*a*) ruiken; **I can smell smoke; dogs can smell strangers; can you smell cooking? I can't smell anything when I've got a cold; smell these flowers!**
(*b*) geuren; **this cheese smells very strong; the dinner smells good; the air smells fresh; there's something which smells funny in the kitchen; it smells of gas in here.**
smells—smelling—smelled/ smelt [smelt]—has smelled/has smelt

smelly, *bn*
stinkend; **a smelly river; a smelly old dog.**
smelly—smellier—smelliest

smile [smaɪl] **1.** *zn*
glimlach; **she gave me a friendly smile; he gave a big smile when he read his exam results.**
2. *ww*
glimlachen; **she smiled at me; stop smiling—it's very serious; smile please—I'm taking a photo.**
smiles—smiling—smiled—has smiled

smoke [sməʊk] **1.** *zn*
rook; damp; **the room was full of cigarette smoke; can you smell smoke? I like the smell of cigar smoke; clouds of smoke poured out of the burning ship.**
2. *ww*
(*a*) roken; **the ruins of the house are still smoking.**
(*b*) roken; **she was smoking a cigarette; he only smokes a pipe; she doesn't smoke; we always sit in the 'no smoking' area; smoking can make you ill; if you want to play tennis, you shouldn't smoke.**
smokes—smoking—smoked—has smoked

smoker, *zn*
roker.

smoky, *bn*
rokerig; **a smoky room.**

smooth [smuːð] **1.** *bn*
glad; zacht; kalm; **the table is quite**

smooth; we had a very smooth ride in our new car.

smooth—smoother—smoothest

2. *ww*

gladstrijken; **she smoothed down the sheets on the bed; he tried to smooth over the problem** = hij trachtte het probleem uit de weg te ruimen.

smooths—smoothing—smoothed—has smoothed

smoothly, *bw*

vlak; vlot; glad; geleidelijk; **the car came to a stop very smoothly.**

snack [snæk] *zn*

hapje; snack; **let's have a snack at the station; I always have a snack at 11 o'clock in the morning.**

snack bar, *zn*

snackbar; automatiek.

snake [sneɪk] *zn*

slang; **she's afraid of snakes; some snakes can kill you.**

sneeze [sniːz] 1. *zn*

nies; **she gave a loud sneeze; his sneezes woke me up!**

2. *ww*

niezen; **she sneezed three times; the smell of flowers makes me sneeze.**

sneezes—sneezing—sneezed—has sneezed

snore [snɔː] *ww*

snurken; **he snored so much that none of us could get to sleep; can't you stop him snoring?**

snores—snoring—snored—has snored

snow [snəʊ] 1. *zn*

sneeuw; **look at all the snow which has fallen during the night; the mountains are covered with snow; the trains will be late because the lines are covered with snow; ten centimetres of snow had fallen during the night.**

geen meervoud; **some snow; a lot of snow**

2. *ww*

sneeuwen; **it's snowing! it snowed all**

night; **do you think it's going to snow? it never snows here.**

snows—snowing—snowed—has snowed

Let op: **to snow** *wordt altijd met* **it** *gebruikt*

snowball, *zn*

sneeuwbal; **they threw snowballs at the teacher; he broke a window with a snowball.**

snowed up, *bn*

ingesneeuwd; **we were snowed up for six days.**

snowman, *zn*

sneeuwman; **they made a snowman in the school playground; if the sun comes out, your snowmen will melt.**

meervoud **snowmen**

snowstorm, *zn*

sneeuwstorm.

snowy, *bn*

besneeuwd; sneeuwig; **snowy weather; if it's snowy, you should stay indoors; this is the snowiest winter I can remember; they walked through the snowy streets to the shops.**

snowy—snowier—snowiest

so [səʊ] 1. *bw*

(*a*) zo; **it's so cold that the river has frozen; we enjoyed ourselves so much that we're going to the same place for our holiday next year; the pudding was so sweet that it made me feel ill; she's not so intelligent as her sister.**

(*b*) (en . . .) ook; **he was late and so was I; we all caught flu, and so did the teacher; I like fish—so do I; he can cook well—so can his wife.**

(*c*) van wel; **is this the train for London?—I think so; did the burglars steal all your records?—I'm afraid so; are you coming to the party?—I hope so; will you be at the meeting?—I suppose so.**

2. *vw*

(*a*) dus; daarom; **it was raining, so we didn't go for a walk; she caught a cold, so she couldn't come to the party.**

(*b*) **so that** = zodat; **so as to** = om . . . te; **people on bicycles should wear orange coats so that drivers can see them in the**

dark; we ran to the station so as not to miss the train.
so far, *bw*
tot nu toe; tot dusver; he said he would phone me, but so far he hasn't done so; how do you like your new job so far?

soap [səʊp] *zn*
zeep; I must buy some more soap; they went away on holiday and forgot to take any soap with them; I've put a new bar of soap in the bathroom; this soap has a strong smell—it makes me sneeze.
geen meervoud: some soap; a bar of soap/a cake of soap/a piece of soap

society [sə'saɪətɪ] *zn*
(*a*) maatschappij; gemeenschap; samenleving; money is too important in our society; society has to be protected from dangerous criminals.
(*b*) vereniging; genootschap; a local history society; a society for the protection of birds.
meervoud societies

sock [sɒk] *zn*
sok; he's wearing blue socks and a blue tie; I'm almost ready—I only have to put my socks and shoes on; tennis socks/football socks; knee socks = kniekousen; you'll have to pull your socks up = je zult beter je best moeten doen.

sofa ['səʊfə] *zn*
bank/sofa; we sat on the sofa and watched TV.

soft [sɒft] *bn*
(*a*) zacht; week; the seats in this car are too soft; he was sitting in a big soft armchair; do you like soft ice cream?
(*b*) zacht; she talked in such a soft voice that we could hardly hear her.
(*c*) zacht; zwak; the soft lighting made the room look warm.
soft—softer—softest
softly, *bw*
zachtjes; zwak; I touched her hair softly; she speaks very softly; they crept softly up the stairs; the lights were shining softly.

soil [sɔɪl] *zn*
aarde; grond; put some soil in a pot and plant your seeds in it.
geen meervoud: some soil; a bag of soil

sold [səʊld] *zie* **sell**

soldier ['səʊldʒə] *zn*
soldaat; the soldiers attacked the railway station; soldiers wear brown uniforms.

solid ['sɒlɪd] *bn*
(*a*) hard/vast; water turns solid when it freezes.
(*b*) massief; the table is made of solid metal; a solid gold plate.

some [sʌm] *bn & vnw*
(*a*) sommige; bepaalde; some people drive much too fast; some days it was so hot that we had to stay indoors.
(*b*) enige; enkele; een paar; can you cut some slices of bread? some of these apples are green; there are some people waiting in the queue; I've bought some oranges.
(*c*) wat; can you buy some petrol when you go to town? do you want any sugar?—no, I've already taken some.
some *wordt zowel met telbare als met ontelbare zelfstandige naamwoorden gebruikt:* some people; some apples; some bread, *etc.*

somebody ['sʌmbədɪ], **someone** ['sʌmwʌn] *vnw*
iemand; somebody/someone has stolen my car; there's somebody/someone in the telephone box; if somebody/someone phones, say I will be back at 4 o'clock; I know somebody/someone who's a policeman.
somehow, *bw*
op (de) een of andere manier; hoe dan ook; we must get to London by 4 o'clock somehow.
something, *vnw*
iets; wat; there's something at the bottom of the bag; something's wrong with the engine; can I have something to eat?
sometimes, *bw*
soms; sometimes it is cold in the summer; sometimes the car goes well, and some-

times it doesn't go at all; I sometimes go to London on business.

somewhere, *bw*
ergens; I left my keys somewhere in the office; this restaurant is full—let's go somewhere else; he lives somewhere in Scotland.

son [sʌn] *zn*
zoon; they have two sons and one daughter; her son's gone to work in France; my son Simon likes rowing.

song [sɒŋ] *zn*
lied(je); she was singing a song in the bath; have you a record of his latest song?

soon [suːn] *bw*
(*a*) spoedig, gauw; we'll soon be home; it will soon be dinnertime; I want to see you as soon as possible; I'll see you next week—can't you come any sooner? when did the fire start?—soon after 9 o'clock; sooner or later = vroeg of laat; he drives so badly that sooner or later the police will catch him.
(*b*) would sooner = liever willen; I'd sooner stay at home than go to the party; *zie ook* rather.
as soon as = zodra; as soon as he sat down the telephone rang.
soon—sooner—soonest

sorry ['sɒrɪ] **1.** *bn*
bedroefd; I'm sorry it rained when you went on holiday = het spijt me dat etc.; she trod on my toe and didn't say she was sorry; we were all sorry to hear you had been ill; to feel sorry for someone = medelijden hebben met; I feel sorry for her—her husband is so unpleasant.
2. *tw*
sorry; pardon; sorry! I didn't see that you were in the bathroom; sorry! I've got the wrong number; can you give me a cigarette?—sorry! I haven't any left.

sort [sɔːt] *zn*
soort; type; all sorts of people came to the party; what sort of day did you have at the office? there are three sorts of ice cream to choose from—which sort do you like best? I don't like this sort of coffee.

sort of = nogal; min of meer; I'm feeling sort of tired.

sound [saʊnd] **1.** *zn*
geluid; klank; the sound of music came through the open window; can you hear the sound of a train? I don't like the sound of that = dat lijkt me niet goed.
2. *ww*
(doen) klinken/luiden; that sounds strange; he sounded his horn when he came to the corner = hij claxonneerde/toeterde; it sounds like a car = het klinkt alsof er een auto aankomt; that sounds like my father = (i) dat klinkt net als mijn vader; (ii) dat klinkt alsof mijn vader eraan komt.
sounds—sounding—sounded—has sounded

soup [suːp] *zn*
soep; I don't like onion soup; do you want some soup? we had vegetable soup for dinner; open a tin of soup—I'm hungry; soup bowl/soup plate/soup spoon.
geen meervoud: **some soup; a bowl of soup**

sour [saʊə] *bn*
(*a*) zuur; these oranges are as sour as lemons.
(*b*) sour milk = zure melk; you can put sour cream in your soup.
sour—sourer—sourest

south [saʊθ] **1.** *zn*
(het) zuiden; the town is to the south of the mountains; the wind is blowing from the south.
2. *bn*
zuid-, zuiden; the south coast of England; the south side of the river.
3. *bw*
naar/op het zuiden; zuidwaarts; birds fly south in the winter; go due south for ten kilometres.
South America, *zn*
Zuid-Amerika.
southern ['sʌðən] *bn*
zuidelijk; they live in the southern part of the country.
South Pole, *zn*
zuidpool.

souvenir [suːvəˈnɪə] *zn*
souvenir/aandenken; **this is a souvenir of our holiday in Sweden.**

sow [səʊ] *ww*
zaaien; **sow your seeds in spring; he's sown his beans.**
sows—sowing—sowed—has sown

space [speɪs] *zn*
ruimte; **park your car in that space over there; write your name and address in the space at the top of the paper; this table takes up a lot of space.**

spade [speɪd] *zn*
(*a*) spade; schop; schep; **he dug a hole in the ground with his spade.**
(*b*) (*van kaartspel*) schoppen; **the ten of spades.**

spare [speə] **1.** *bn*
extra; reserve; **you need a spare wheel in case one of your tyres is flat; can I spend the night in your spare bedroom?** = logeerkamer; **what do you do in your spare time?** = wat doe je in je vrijetijd?
2. *ww*
missen; afstaan, geven; het stellen zonder; **can you spare the time to go on holiday? can you spare me a cigarette? I want to buy that car, but I can't spare the money.**
spares—sparing—spared—has spared

speak [spiːk] *ww*
spreken; **he walked past me without speaking; she was speaking to the milkman; can he speak English? I must speak to him about his son.**
speaks—speaking—spoke [spəʊk] **—has spoken**

speaker, *zn*
spreker; **he is a funny speaker** = hij spreekt aardig; *zie ook* **loud-speaker.**
speak up, *ww*
hard(er) praten/spreken; **speak up—I can't hear you!**

special [ˈspeʃl] *bn*
speciaal; bijzonder; **this is a very special**

day—it's my birthday; he has a special pair of scissors for cutting his hair; there is nothing very special about his new car** = niets bijzonders.
specially, *bw*
bijzonder; **the weather has been specially good; she is specially good at making cakes;** *zie ook* **especially.**

spectacles [ˈspektəklz] *zn meervoud*
bril; **he has broken his spectacles; she was wearing a pair of spectacles with gold frames.**

sped [sped] *zie* **speed**

speech [spiːtʃ] *zn*
(*a*) toespraak; speech; **she made a funny speech at the dinner; all the speeches were much too long.**
(*b*) taal; spraak; **the parts of speech** = zinsdelen.
meervoud **speeches,** *maar geen meervoud voor* (*b*)

speed [spiːd] **1.** *zn*
snelheid; vaart; **the car was travelling at high speed; if you go at a speed of 30 miles per hour you'll use less petrol; the ship was going at full speed.**
2. *ww*
snellen; (te) hard rijden; **the car sped across the road; he was arrested for speeding** = hij werd aangehouden wegens het overschrijden van de maximumsnelheid.
speeds—speeding—sped [sped]—**has sped**

speed limit, *zn*
maximumsnelheid; **the speed limit in towns is 30 miles per hour.**
speed up, *ww*
versnellen; sneller doen gaan; opvoeren; **can't you speed up your work?**

spell [spel] **1.** *zn*
tijd(je); periode; **we had a spell of cold weather; the cold spell lasted a week.**
2. *ww*
spellen; **how do you spell your name? you've spelt his name wrong; L-A-U-G-H spells 'laugh'; his name is Steven, but I don't**

know if it's spelt **PH** or **V** = of je het met Ph of V spelt.

spells—spelling—spelled/spelt— has spelled/has spelt.

spelling, *zn*
spelling; he writes very well, but his spelling is bad.

spend [spend] *ww*
(*a*) uitgeven, besteden; I spent £6 on a new tie; I don't like spending too much money on food; he has saved up all his pocket money and is going to spend it on Christmas presents.
(*b*) (*van tijd*) doorbrengen/besteden; we spent our holidays in France last year; he spent two hours mending the car; why don't you come to spend the weekend with us? don't spend hours doing your homework.

spends—spending—spent—has spent

spider [′spaɪdə] *zn*
spin; she's afraid of spiders; help! there's a spider in the bath.

spill [spɪl] *ww*
morsen; knoeien; stromen; I spilled my soup down my shirt; the cat knocked over the bottle and the milk spilled all over the table.

spills—spilling—spilled/spilt [spɪlt] **—has spilled/has spilt**

spite [spaɪt] *zn*
in spite of = ondanks; we went for a walk in spite of the snow; he went to the party in spite of the fact that he had a cold.

splash [splæʃ] **1.** *zn*
plons; (het) spatten; he fell into the swimming pool with a big splash; you could hear the the splash of the waves on the rocks.

meervoud **splashes**

2. *ww*
(be)spatten; plassen; the waves splashed against the rocks; the children were splashing about in the pool; the bus splashed me with dirty water; when you're painting the ceiling, be careful not to splash paint on to the carpet.

splashes—splashing—splashed— has splashed

splendid [′splendɪd] *bn*
prachtig; schitterend; we had a splendid holiday in Sweden; what splendid weather for a picnic! you've passed your exams?—splendid!

split [splɪt] **1.** *zn*
spleet; scheur; there is a split in this piece of wood; do you know that you've got a split in the back of your trousers? banana split = dessert van banaan, slagroom, ijs en noten.
2. *ww*
scheuren; (zich) verdelen; if you get any fatter, you'll split your trousers; my trousers split when I bent down; the committee has split into three groups; let's split the money between us.

splits—splitting—split—has split

split up, *ww*
zich verdelen; the tourists split up into two groups; let's split up and meet at the post office in half an hour.

spoil [spɔɪl] *ww*
bederven; the bad weather spoilt our holidays; the film was spoilt by the bad sound; don't spoil my dinner by talking about hospitals.

spoils—spoiling—spoiled/spoilt— has spoiled/spoilt

spoke [spəʊk], **spoken** [′spəʊkn] *zie* **speak**

spoon [spuːn] **1.** *zn*
lepel; eat your pudding with your spoon, not with your knife; have you got a big spoon to serve the peas? soup spoon = soeplepel.
2. *ww*
lepelen; scheppen; he spooned the sugar into his tea; she was spooning out jam on to all the plates.

spoons—spooning—spooned— has spooned

spoonful, *zn*
lepel(vol); lepel(tje); he put two spoonfuls of sugar into his tea.

sport [spɔːt] *zn*
sport; I like watching sport on TV; do you like the sports programmes on TV?

the only sport I play is football; he doesn't play any sport at all.

sports car, *zn*
sportwagen.

sports day, *zn*
sportdag.

sportsfield/sportsground, *zn*
sportveld/sportterrein.

sportsman, *zn*
sportbeoefenaar/sportman;   he's   an Olympic sportsman.
meervoud **sportsmen**

spot [spɒt] **1.** *zn*
(*a*) plek; this is a good spot for a picnic; this is the spot where the accident took place; he was killed on the spot = hij werd op slag gedood.
(*b*) vlek; stip; spikkeltje; he has a blue tie with red spots; you've got spots of mud on your coat; he must be ill—his face is covered with red spots.
(*c*) spat(je); 'tikje'; hapje; spots of rain were falling; would you like a spot of food? we're having a spot of trouble with the car.
2. *ww*
opmerken; in de gaten krijgen; he spotted a mistake in my homework; did you spot the number of the car?
spots—spotting—spotted—has spotted

sprang [spræŋ] *zie* **spring**

spread [spred] *ww*
(*a*) (zich) verspreiden; don't spread the news—it's supposed to be a secret; the soldiers spread out across the fields; the fire spread to the house next door = het vuur sloeg over etc.
(*b*) uitspreiden; (uit)smeren; she spread a cloth over the table; he was spreading jam on his bread; don't spread too much glue on the paper.
spreads—spreading—spread—has spread

spring [sprɪŋ] **1.** *zn*
(*a*) lente; in spring, the trees grow new leaves; we always go on holiday in the spring; they started work last spring/in the spring of last year; what beautiful spring flowers!

(*b*) (metalen) veer; vering; there are no springs in this bed; there's a spring to keep the door shut; my car needs new springs.
2. *ww*
springen; he sprang out of bed; the door sprang open.
springs—springing—sprang [spræŋ]—has sprung [sprʌŋ]

square [skweə] *zn & bn*
(*a*) vierkant; the floor is covered with black and white squares; it's difficult to fit six people round a small square table; this piece of paper isn't square; ten square metres = tien vierkante meter.
(*b*) plein; the tourists were visiting Trafalgar Square; Red Square is in the middle of Moscow.
Let op: **ten square metres** *wordt meestal geschreven* **10m²**

squash [skwɒʃ] **1.** *zn*
kwast; limonade; a glass of orange squash.
2. *ww*
platdrukken; verpletteren; (zich) persen; he sat on my hat and squashed it; don't put the cakes at the bottom of the bag—they'll get squashed; we all squashed into his little car.
squashes—squashing—squashed—has squashed

squeeze [skwiːz] *ww*
(uit)knijpen, (zich) persen; he squeezed the juice out of the lemon; they all squeezed into the little car.
squeezes—squeezing—squeezed—has squeezed

staff [stɑːf] *zn*
staf; we have 25 teaching staff; the firm has a staff of 100; the staff don't like the new offices.
Let op: bij **staff** *als onderwerp wordt een meervoudsvorm van het werkwoord gebruikt;* **a staff of 25** *maar* **the staff work very hard**

stage [steɪdʒ] *zn*
toneel; he came on to the stage and started to sing.

stairs [steəz] *zn meervoud*
trap; trede/tree; he ran up the stairs to

his bedroom; **she fell down the stairs and broke her leg;** *zie ook* **downstairs, upstairs.**

Let op: het enkelvoud **stair** *wordt soms gebruikt voor één tree:* **she was sitting on the bottom stair**

staircase, *zn*
trap; **he fell down the staircase; this staircase goes down to the ground floor.**

stamp [stæmp] **1.** *zn*
(*a*) postzegel; **you need a 14p stamp for that letter; did you remember to put a stamp on my letter before you posted it? he collects stamps and old coins.**
(*b*) stempel; **he has a stamp for marking the date on letters; the customs put their stamp on the parcel.**
2. *ww*
(*a*) (af)stempelen; frankeren; **did they stamp your passport when you entered the country? send a stamped addressed envelope for a reply** = een gefrankeerde en aan jezelf geadresseerde envelop.
(*b*) stampen; **they stamped on the floor and shouted; he stamped out of the room; the soldiers stamped across the square.**
stamps—stamping—stamped—has stamped

stand [stænd] **1.** *zn*
(*a*) standaard; houder; **put the pot back on the stand.**
(*b*) tribune; **the stands were crowded.**
2. *ww*
(*a*) staan; zetten; **stand the ladder against the wall; the box was standing in the middle of the room; she stood the clock on the table.**
(*b*) (blijven/gaan) staan; **I'm so tired I can hardly keep standing; there are no seats left, so we'll have to stand; don't just stand there—come and help; stand on a chair if you want to reach the top of the cupboard.**
(*c*) uitstaan; verdragen; **I can't stand all this noise; what a dirty office—I don't know how you can stand it; she stopped going to her German class because she couldn't stand the teacher.**
stands—standing—stood [stʊd]**—has stood**

stand around, *ww*
werkloos/lijdelijk toezien; **they just stood around and watched.**
stand back, *ww*
achteruit gaan/wijken; **the police told the crowd to stand back as the cyclists were passing.**
stand for, *ww*
betekenen; **what do the letters GPO stand for?**
stand in for, *ww*
vervangen; **I'm standing in for Mr Smith because he's ill.**
stand out, *ww*
zich aftekenen; uitkomen; **the blue picture stands out very well against the white wall.**
stand up, *ww*
(*a*) opstaan; **when the teacher came into the room all the children stood up; please don't stand up!**
(*b*) rechtop staan; **stand up straight.**
(*c*) rechtop zetten; **stand all those books up; he stood his umbrella up in the corner of the room.**
stand up for, *ww*
opkomen voor; **you must stand up for your rights.**

star [stɑ:] *zn*
(*a*) ster; **look at all those stars—the weather will be fine tomorrow.**
(*b*) ster; **she's the star of the new film; a film star.**

stare [steə] *ww*
staren; **he stared at his plate; it's rude to stare at people; she kept staring at me.**
stares—staring—stared—has stared

start [stɑ:t] **1.** *zn*
begin; **it took 3 hours from start to finish; we must make an early start** = we moeten vroeg van start gaan.
2. *ww*
(*a*) beginnen; **he started eating his sandwiches; it's starting to rain; have you started your new job yet? we'll start by learning the alphabet; we must start to get ready or we'll miss the train; when does the film start?**
(*b*) vertrekken; **let's start at 8 o'clock.**

(c) starten; aanslaan; **I can't start the car/the car won't start.**

starts—starting—started—has started

start off, ww
beginnen; **you start off and I'll follow; we'll start off with soup and then have some fish.**

start out, ww
vertrekken; op pad gaan; **he started out two hours ago.**

start up, ww
(een zaak) beginnen; **he's starting up a restaurant.**

state [steɪt] **1.** zn
(a) staat, conditie, toestand; **the house isn't in a very good state; his state of health is getting worse.**
(b) staat; **the African states; the United States of America; the State of California; the electricity industry is owned by the State; state schools** = openbare scholen.
2. ww
verklaren; mededelen; vermelden; **she stated that she had never been to Paris; the form states the details of the job.**

states—stating—stated—has stated

statement, zn
verklaring; **he made a statement to the police; the government made a statement about prices; bank statement** = afrekening van de bank.
States, zn meervoud
de Verenigde Staten; **we're going to the States for Christmas; I was in the States last year.**

station [ˈsteɪʃn] zn
(a) station; **can you tell me the way to the station? the train doesn't stop at the next station; there's an underground station at the corner of the street; I'll try and have something to eat at the station bar.**
(b) **bus station/coach station** = busstation; **we had to wait at the coach station for an hour.**
(c) bureau, post; **fire station/police station** = brandweerkazerne/politie-

bureau; **power station** = elektriciteitscentrale; **service station** = garagebedrijf; **TV station/radio station** = televisiezender/radiozender.

stay [steɪ] **1.** zn
verblijf; **I'm only here for a short stay.**
2. ww
blijven; logeren; **I'll stay at home tomorrow; we'll stay in Edinburgh on our way to the north of Scotland; how long will you be staying in New York? she's ill and has to stay in bed; they came for tea and stayed until ten o'clock.**

stays—staying—stayed—has stayed

stay away, ww
wegblijven; **he doesn't like big parties, so he stayed away.**

stay in, ww
binnenblijven; **I won't come to the party—I'm staying in tonight.**

stay out, ww
wegblijven; uitblijven; **don't stay out after ten o'clock.**

stay up, ww
opblijven; **we stayed up very late last night; little children shouldn't stay up watching TV; I'm staying up to watch the late football match on TV.**

steal [stiːl] ww
stelen; **the burglar stole all the jewellery; someone has stolen my car.**

steals—stealing—stole [stəʊl]**—has stolen**

steam [stiːm] zn
stoom; **steam was coming out of the kettle; the train was pulled by an old steam engine.**

steel [stiːl] zn
staal; **he has glasses with steel frames; you need a pair of steel scissors—those plastic ones won't cut paper!**
geen meervoud

steep [stiːp] bn
steil; sterk; **the car had difficulty in going up the steep hill; there's been a steep increase in prices.**

steep—steeper—steepest

steer [stɪə] *ww*

sturen; **he steered the boat into the harbour; steer towards that rock.**

steers—steering—steered—has steered

steering wheel, *zn*
stuur.

step [step] **1.** *zn*

(*a*) stap; **he took two steps forward; she took a big step sideways; step by step** = stapje voor stapje.

(*b*) pas; tred; **out of step/in step** = uit/ in de pas; **try to keep in step; wages are out of step with the rise in prices** = lonen en prijzen hebben geen gelijke tred gehouden.

(*c*) afstapje; **there is a step down into the kitchen; be careful, there are two steps up into the bathroom; to go from the house into the garden you have to go down several stone steps.**

(*d*) stap; maatregel; **we must take steps to make sure that we do not lose money; the first step is to find out how much money we spend** = om te beginnen moeten we etc.

2. *ww*

stappen; **he stepped out into the street; she stepped off the bus; step over that heap of rubbish.**

steps—stepping—stepped—has stepped

step in, *ww*
tussenbeide komen; **everything was working very well until the government stepped in.**

step up, *ww*
opvoeren; **we are trying to step up production.**

stick [stɪk] **1.** *zn*

(*a*) stok; tak; **collect some dry sticks to light a fire.**

(*b*) **walking stick** = (wandel)stok; **the blind man had a white stick; he has to walk with two sticks.**

2. *ww*

(*a*) steken; **he stuck a pin into me; the nurse stuck a needle into my arm.**

(*b*) plakken; **he stuck the stamp on the envelope; she tried to stick the handle on to the cup with glue.**

(*c*) klemmen; blijven steken; **stick close to me and you won't get lost** = blijf vlak bij me in de buurt etc.; **the car got stuck in the mud; the door's stuck and we can't open it.**

(*d*) steken, doen; **he stuck the letter in his pocket; stick all those books in the back of the car.**

(*e*) uitstaan; **I can't stick people who make a lot of noise;** *zie ook* **stand**

sticks—sticking—stuck [stʌk]— **has stuck**

sticking plaster, *zn*
pleister; **put a piece of sticking plaster on your cut.**

geen meervoud: **some sticking plaster; a piece of sticking plaster**

stick out, *ww*
uitsteken; **the doctor asked him to stick out his tongue/to stick his tongue out; his wallet was sticking out of his pocket.**

Let op: **he stuck his tongue out** *of* **he stuck out his tongue** *maar alleen* **he stuck it out**

stick up, *ww*

(*a*) opprikken; aanplakken; **he stuck up a notice on the wall.**

(*b*) uitsteken; **the guns were sticking up out of a box.**

stick up for, *ww*
opkomen voor; **he stuck up for her when the head teacher wanted to sack her;** *zie ook* **stand up for.**

sticky, *bn*
plakkerig, kleverig; **there's something sticky on the table; don't sit on that chair—the paint's still sticky.**

sticky—stickier—stickiest

stiff [stɪf] *bn*

(*a*) stijf; **my knee is stiff after playing football; can you open this pot of jam?— the lid's very stiff; brush your coat with a stiff brush; he's frozen stiff** = stijfbevroren.

(*b*) moeilijk, zwaar; **you have to take a stiff driving test.**

stiff—stiffer—stiffest

still [stɪl] **1.** *bn*
stil; **stand still while I take your photo-**

graph; the surface of the water was completely still.

2. *bw*

(*a*) nog (steeds); **they came for tea and they were still here at ten o'clock; I've still got some money left; they're still talking about the election.**

(*b*) nog; **there were fifty people in the room and still more tried to get in; it has been cold all day, and it will be still colder tonight.**

(*c*) toch; in elk geval; **it wasn't very fine—still, it didn't rain; he still went on holiday although he had no money.**

stir [stɜ:] *ww*
roeren; **he stirred his cup of tea; she was stirring the soup.**
stirs—stirring—stirred—has stirred

stir up, *ww*
(onrust) stoken; **she's always stirring up trouble in the office.**

stocking ['stɒkɪŋ] *zn*
kous; **she was wearing blue stockings and white shoes.**

stole [stəʊl], **stolen** ['stəʊln] *zie* **steal**

stomach ['stʌmək] *zn*
maag; buik; **he hit him in the stomach; he crept across the room on his stomach; stomach ache** = maagpijn.

stone [stəʊn] *zn*
(*a*) steen; **a big stone bridge; the houses in the town are all built of stone; these stone floors are very cold.**

(*b*) steentje; **don't throw stones at the cars; she's got a stone in her shoe; the beach is covered with sharp stones.**

(*c*) gewicht (= 14 Engelse ponden = 6.35 kg); **he tried to lose weight and lost three stone; she weighs eight stone.**

Let op: geen meervoud voor (*a*): **some stone; a piece of stone; a block of stone**
geen meervoud voor (*c*): **she weighs ten stone**

stony, *bn*
steen-; steenhard; **a stony beach.**
stony—stonier—stoniest

stood [stʊd] *zie* **stand**

stop [stɒp] **1.** *zn*
(*a*) stilstand; (het) stoppen, eind; **the car came to a stop at the bottom of the hill; we must put a stop to crime; all work came to a stop when the firm couldn't pay any wages.**

(*b*) halte; **we waited for twenty minutes at the bus stop; the bus stop is just in front of the post office; I must get off at the next stop.**

(*c*) **full stop** = punt (.).

2. *ww*
(*a*) (laten) stoppen, stilhouden; **the policeman stopped the traffic to let the children cross the road; the car didn't stop at the red lights; fast trains don't stop at this station; the bus just went past without stopping; stop him! he's stolen my watch!** = houd hem!

(*b*) ophouden/stoppen met; **can't you stop that noise? the clock has stopped at 3.30; it's stopped raining; last week it rained for three days without stopping; he stopped work and went home.**

(*c*) overblijven; logeren; **we stopped for a few days in Stockholm; we'll be stopping in Rome for the weekend; can you stop at the butcher's on your way home and buy some meat for dinner?** = kun je bij de slager langsgaan etc.

(*d*) **to stop someone/something (from) doing something** = verhinderen; weerhouden (van); **the weather stopped us from playing cricket; can the police stop the children from stealing sweets? can't you stop your watch making such a loud noise?**
stops—stopping—stopped—has stopped

stop over, *ww*
een reis onderbreken; **we'll stop over in Amsterdam on the way to Moscow.**

stop up, *ww*
(*a*) opblijven; **are you going to stop up to watch the late football match?**

(*b*) dichtstoppen; **you can stop up the hole with a piece of wood.**
Let op: **stop the hole up** *of* **stop up the hole** *maar alleen* **stop it up**

store [stɔː] 1. *zn*
(*a*) warenhuis; winkel; **you can buy shoes in the big stores in town; does this store have a restaurant?**
(*b*) voorraad; **we have a big store of wood for the winter; we have bought stores for the long journey.**
2. *ww*
opslaan; wegbergen, **we'll store all our apples in that cupboard.**
stores—storing—stored—has stored

storm [stɔːm] *zn*
storm; **two ships sank in the storm; the storm blew down two trees; we often have storms in March.**
stormy, *bn*
stormachtig; **a period of stormy weather.**
stormy—stormier—stormiest

story ['stɔːrɪ] *zn*
(*a*) verhaal; **tell the policeman your story; it's a long story** = een lange geschiedenis; **the film is the story of two children and a little white dog; he writes stories about the war.**
(*b*) verzinsel; verhaaltje; **don't tell stories.**
meervoud **stories**

stove [stəʊv] *zn*
fornuis; **we have a gas stove in the kitchen.**

straight [streɪt] 1. *bn*
(*a*) recht; sluik; **a straight road; draw a straight line; he has long straight hair.**
(*b*) netjes, recht; **your tie isn't straight; we'll try to put the room straight after the party; let's get it straight** = laten we het goed begrijpen.
straight—straighter—straightest
2. *bw*
(*a*) rechtdoor; rechtuit; **keep straight on until you come to the traffic lights; the road goes straight for three miles.**
(*b*) regelrecht; **I'll come straight back; he went straight to the police.**
(*c*) recht, pal; **he drank the milk straight out of the bottle; he ran straight across the road without looking; she looked him straight in the face.**

straight away, *bw*
meteen, onmiddellijk; **I need the money straight away.**

strange [streɪndʒ] *bn*
(*a*) raar; vreemd; **the car engine is making a strange sound; he said some very strange things about his boss.**
(*b*) ongewoon; vreemd; **it's difficult to get to sleep in a strange room; we went to Hong Kong and had lots of strange food to eat.**
strange—stranger—strangest

stranger, *zn* ·
vreemdeling; vreemde; **he's a complete stranger; don't accept presents from strangers; I'm a stranger here—I'm afraid I don't know where the post office is.**

stream [striːm] *zn*
(*a*) stroom(pje); **he jumped over the mountain stream.**
(*b*) stroom; **streams of cars were going towards the coast; you can't cross the stream of traffic.**

street [striːt] *zn*
straat; **the main street is very busy on Saturday mornings; go down the street to the traffic lights; the post office is on the opposite side of the street; where do you live?—16 Oxford Street; High Street** = Hoofdstraat; **his shop is in the High Street.**
Let op: wordt vaak in namen gebruikt: **Oxford Street, High Street,** *etc., en meestal geschreven* **St: Oxford St**

strength [streŋθ] *zn*
kracht; macht; sterkte; **he kicked the ball with all his strength; he doesn't know his own strength.**
geen meervoud

stretch [stretʃ] *ww*
(*a*) (uit)rekken; **the wire was stretched between two poles; you've stretched your pullover by pulling it over your head** = je hebt je pullover uitgerekt etc.
(*b*) zich uitrekken; (zich) uitstrekken; **he stretched out his hand and took a book from the shelf; the cat got up from the**

chair and stretched; she lay stretched out on the floor.
(*c*) zich uitstrekken; **the sea stretched all round us; the road stretches for miles.**
stretches—stretching—stretched—has stretched

strike [straɪk] **1.** *zn*
staking; **the office staff are on strike; the strike by the bus drivers lasted two weeks.**
2. *ww*
(*a*) slaan; botsen (tegen); **he struck a policeman with a bottle; the car went down the hill and struck a tree.**
(*b*) treffen; **I was struck by what she said; it strikes me that she was telling a lie** = mij lijkt etc.
(*c*) staken; **the staff are striking for more money.**
(*d*) (*van klok*) slaan; **Big Ben struck ten.**
(*e*) (*van lucifer*) aanstrijken; aansteken.
strikes—striking—struck [strʌk]—**has struck**

string [strɪŋ] *zn*
(*a*) touw; **tie the parcel up with a piece of string; I bought a ball of string; this string isn't strong enough; have you any more string?**
(*b*) snaar; **a guitar has six strings.**
geen meervoud voor (*a*): **some string; a piece of string**

strong [strɒŋ] *bn*
(*a*) sterk; krachtig; **is he strong enough to pick up that box? the rope's broken—we need something stronger; the strong wind blew all the leaves off the trees.**
(*b*) sterk, zwaar; **this cheese is too strong; this tea is too strong—put some water in it; what I want is a cup of strong black coffee; there was a strong smell of onions; strong drink is bad for you** = sterke drank etc.
strong—stronger—strongest

struck [strʌk] *zie* **strike**

stuck [stʌk] *zie* **stick**

student [ˈstjuːdnt] *zn*
student; **all the science students are working for their exams.**

study [ˈstʌdɪ] **1.** *zn*
studie; **she's finished her studies** = ze is afgestudeerd; **he's making a study of diseases of fish.**
meervoud **studies**
2. *ww*
studeren; **he's studying maths; don't make any noise—we're all studying for our exams.**
studies—studying—studied—has studied

stuff [stʌf] **1.** *zn*
spul; goedje; **put some dry stuff in the bottom of the box; there's some green stuff on the table—I don't know what it is; there's still some stuff left in the car.**
2. *ww*
proppen; **he stuffed the papers into his pocket; she was stuffing her clothes into a suitcase.**
stuffs—stuffing—stuffed—has stuffed

stupid [ˈstjuːpɪd] *bn*
dom; stom; **don't be stupid—you can't drive a car if you haven't passed your test; he's a stupid boy—he spends all his time watching TV instead of doing his homework.**

subject [ˈsʌbdʒekt] *zn*
(*a*) onderwerp; **in the sentence 'the dog fell into the water' the word 'dog' is the subject.**
(*b*) onderwerp; vak; **I have to study three subjects—English, maths and science; what subject does Mr Smith teach?—he teaches English; the subject of his book is English history; she's talking on the subject 'the place of women in Parliament'; let's change the subject** = laten we van onderwerp veranderen.

subtract [səbˈtrækt] *ww*
aftrekken; **subtract 24 from 86 and the answer is 62.**
subtracts—subtracting—subtracted—has subtracted
subtraction [səbˈtrækʃn] *zn*
aftrekking; aftreksom; **I'm good at subtraction, but I can't do division.**

Streets   *Straten*

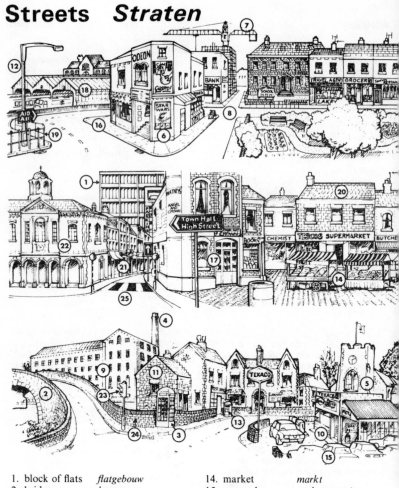

1. block of flats	*flatgebouw*	14. market	*markt*
2. bridge	*brug*	15. car park	*parkeerterrein*
3. call box	*telefooncel*	16. pavement	*stoep*
4. chimney	*schoorsteen*	17. pub	*café*
5. church	*kerk*	18. railway station	*station*
6. cinema	*bioskoop*	19. railings	*hek*
7. crane	*hijskraan*	20. roof	*dak*
8. crossroads	*kruispunt*	21. shops	*winkels*
9. factory	*fabriek*	22. town hall	*stadhuis*
10. garage	*garage*	23. traffic lights	*verkeerslichten*
11. house	*huis*	24. wall	*muur*
12. lamppost	*lantaarnpaal*	25. zebra crossing	*zebrapad*
13. letterbox	*brievenbus*		

succeed [sək'si:d] *ww*
slagen; **he tried to climb up the tree but didn't succeed; she succeeded in opening the box; this book tells you how to succeed in business.**

succeeds—succeeding—succeeded—has succeeded

success [sək'ses] *zn*
(*a*) succes; resultaat; **I've been trying to get a job, but with no success.**
(*b*) succes; **the party was not a success; this new film is a great success.**

meervoud **successes**

successful, *bn*
geslaagd; voorspoedig; **a successful party; he's a successful businessman.**

successfully, *bw*
voorspoedig, met succes; **he successfully finished his studies.**

such [sʌtʃ] *bn*
(*a*) dergelijke; zulk(e); **people such as doctors need to study for many years** = mensen zoals (bijvoorbeeld) doktoren etc.; **there is no such thing as a plastic frying pan** = zoiets als een plastic koekepan bestaat niet; **the customs are looking for such things as drugs or alcohol; there is no such day as February 30th; he was asking for Miss Jones, but there is no such person working here** = zo iemand werkt hier niet.
(*b*) zo'n; zulke; **there was such a crowd of people that there were not enough chairs; he's such a slow worker; people can't afford to drive such large cars.**

suck [sʌk] *ww*
zuigen; **he sucked all the juice out of the orange; she was sucking a big sweet; the baby's sucking its thumb.**

sucks—sucking—sucked—has sucked

sudden ['sʌdn] *bn*
plotseling; onverwacht; scherp; **there was a sudden bang and smoke poured out of the engine; don't drive too fast—there's a sudden bend in the road.**
all of a sudden = plotseling; **all of a sudden the lights went out.**
suddenly, *bw*
plotseling; opeens; onverwacht; **the car stopped suddenly; he suddenly sneezed.**

suffer ['sʌfə] *ww*
lijden; **she suffers from headaches; he suffers from not being able to hear well; if you watch too much TV, your homework will suffer** = je huiswerk gaat eronder lijden etc.

suffers—suffering—suffered—has suffered

sugar ['ʃʊgə] *zn*
suiker; **do you take sugar in your coffee? there's too much sugar in this pudding; can you buy a bag of sugar—we have none left.**

geen meervoud: **some sugar; a bag of sugar; a lump of sugar**

suggest [sə'dʒest] *ww*
voorstellen; suggereren; **I suggest we stop for a cup of coffee; she suggested that we should ask John to the party; we've suggested to the headmaster that he should talk to the parents.**

suggests—suggesting—suggested—has suggested

suggestion, *zn*
voorstel; suggestie; **I don't agree with your suggestion that we should stop for coffee; can I make a suggestion? it was my suggestion that we should all go for a walk.**

suit [su:t] **1.** *zn*
(*a*) pak; kostuum; **he had a dark grey suit on; she was wearing a blue suit.**
(*b*) (*van kaartspel*) kleur; **hearts and diamonds are the two red suits; to follow suit** = een voorbeeld volgen; **he jumped on to the bus and we all followed suit.**
2. *ww*
(*a*) passen bij; goed staan; **green suits you; that hat suits her.**
(*b*) uitkomen; gelegen komen; schikken; **I'll do it when it suits me** = als het me uitkomt; **that suits me fine** = dat schikt me uitstekend.

suits—suiting—suited—has suited

suitable, *bn*
geschikt; **the most suitable date for the meeting would be October 18th.**

suitcase, *zn*
koffer; **she was putting her clothes into a suitcase; your suitcase is very heavy.**

sum [sʌm] *zn*
(*a*) som; **he's no good at sums; I can't do this sum; she tried to do the sum in her head** = ze probeerde de som uit haar hoofd uit te rekenen.
(*b*) som(ma); bedrag; **she received the sum of £25.**

summer ['sʌmə] *zn*
zomer; **most people go on holiday in the summer; last summer we went to Greece; summer is the hottest part of the year; I haven't any summer clothes—it is never very warm here.**

sun [sʌn] *zn*
zon; **we can go for a walk now that the sun's shining again; the sun's so hot that we'll have to sit in the shade; you can't spend all day just sitting in the sun; the sun rises in the east.**
sunglasses, *zn meervoud*
zonnebril; **he kept bumping into the chairs because he wore his sunglasses in the house.**
sunny, *bn*
zonnig; **a sunny day; the sunny side of the street.**
sunny—sunnier—sunniest
sunrise, *zn*
zonsopgang.
sunset, *zn*
zonsondergang.
sunshine, *zn*
zonneschijn; **the sunshine hurts my eyes.**

Sunday ['sʌndɪ] *zn*
zondag; **last Sunday we went on a picnic; the shops are closed on Sundays; shall we meet next Sunday? today is Sunday, October 18th.**
Let op: **Sunday** *wordt altijd met een hoofdletter geschreven*

sung [sʌŋ] *zie* **sing**

sunk [sʌŋk] *zie* **sink**

superlative [suːˈpɜːlətɪv] *zn*
overtreffende trap; **'fattest' is the superlative of 'fat'; 'fastest' is the superlative of 'fast'.**

supermarket ['suːpəmɑːkɪt] *zn*
supermarkt; **go to the supermarket and**

get me some coffee; the supermarket stays open late on Friday evenings.

supper ['sʌpə] *zn*
avondeten; **what did you eat for supper? we have supper at about seven o'clock; come and have supper with us tomorrow.**
zie opmerking bij **dinner**

supply [səˈplaɪ] **1.** *zn*
(*a*) voorziening; proviand; **the electricity supply has broken down; the army dropped supplies to the farms which were cut off by the snow.**
(*b*) voorraad; **we have a good supply of wood for the winter; eggs are in short supply at the moment.**
meervoud **supplies**
2. *ww*
voorzien; verschaffen; **the army is supplying the farms with food; bread is supplied by the local baker; the town is supplied with water from the river; can you supply me with information about the accident? he couldn't supply any information about holidays in Russia.**
supplies—supplying—supplied—
has supplied

suppose [səˈpəʊz] *ww*
(*a*) veronderstellen; aannemen; **I suppose she will be late as usual; I supposed everyone knew about the party; are you going to the party tonight?—I suppose so** = ik veronderstel van wel; **I don't suppose anyone will come; he's supposed to be a good doctor** = men zegt dat hij etc.
(*b*) **to be supposed to** = verondersteld worden; **you're supposed to be in bed.**
(*c*) **suppose/supposing** = indien; **suppose/supposing it rains tomorrow, shall we still go on the picnic?** = stel je voor dat etc.; **suppose/supposing he's had an accident?**
supposes—supposing—
supposed—has supposed

sure [ʃʊə] *bn*
zeker; **I'm sure he'll come to the party; are you sure she'll lend you her car? are you sure you haven't lost the key? it's sure to be cold in Canada in January;**

make sure/be sure you lock all the doors.
= denk eraan/vergeet niet etc.

surely, *bw*
natuurlijk; (toch) zeker; **surely you don't
expect him to go out in the rain? surely
his name is John not James?**

surface [ˈsɜːfis] *zn*
oppervlak(te); **the fish came to the surface of the water to breathe; the table
has a shiny surface.**

surname [ˈsɜːneɪm] *zn*
achternaam; **I know he's called John, but
what's his surname? write your first name
and surname on the form.**

surprise [səˈpraɪz] **1.** *zn*
verrassing; verbazing; **let's hide behind
the door and give him a surprise; they
made her a big birthday cake as a surprise; what a surprise to meet him in the
supermarket.**
2. *ww*
verbazen; verrassen; **I'm surprised to
hear that he is in prison; I shouldn't be
surprised if it snows.**
**surprises—surprising—sur-
prised—has surprised**

surround [səˈraʊnd] *ww*
omringen; **an island is a piece of land
surrounded by water; the garden is surrounded by a high wall; she's always surrounded by young men.**
**surrounds—surrounding—sur-
rounded—has surrounded**

suspect [səˈspekt] *ww*
verdenken; vermoeden; **the police suspect that he was lying; she is suspected
of having killed her brother.**
**suspects—suspecting—suspec-
ted—has suspected**

suspicious [səˈspɪʃəs] *bn*
achterdochtig; **don't mention money —
we don't want to make him suspicious;
I'm suspicious about why she had to go
to Germany quickly.**

swallow [ˈswɒləʊ] *ww*
slikken; **chew your food well or you won't
be able to swallow it; give him a glass of
water—he's swallowed a fly; he swal-**

lowed his dinner and went out = hij
schrokte zijn eten naar binnen etc.
**swallows—swallowing—swal-
lowed—has swallowed**

swam [swæm] *zie* **swim**

sweep [swiːp] *ww*
(*a*) vegen; **he swept the dead leaves into
a pile; don't forget to sweep the kitchen
floor.**
(*b*) voorbijschieten/voorbijvliegen; **the
traffic swept past our house; the crowd
swept into the street.**
**sweeps—sweeping—swept—has
swept**

sweet [swiːt] **1.** *bn*
zoet; **my tea's too sweet—I put sugar in
it twice; do you like sweet food? oranges
are sweeter than lemons; he's got a sweet
tooth** = hij is een zoetekauw.
sweet—sweeter—sweetest
2. *zn*
(*a*) (*Amer.* **candy**) snoepje; **he brought
a bag of sweets to suck in the car; eating
sweets is bad for your teeth.**
(*b*) dessert, toetje; **what's for sweet? I
want ice cream for sweet; I haven't eaten
my sweet yet.**

swept [swept] *zie* **sweep**

swim [swɪm] **1.** *zn*
(het) zwemmen; **we went for a swim
before breakfast; it's too cold to have a
swim; I went for three swims yesterday.**
2. *ww*
zwemmen; **he can't swim; she's learning
to swim; I swam across the river twice;
can you swim under the water? let's go
swimming this afternoon.**
swims—swimming—swam
[swæm]—**has swum** [swʌm]

swimmer, *zn*
zwemmer.

swimming pool, *zn*
zwembad; **our school has an indoor
swimming pool; we have a little swimming pool in the garden; he swam two
lengths of the swimming pool.**

swing [swɪŋ] *ww*
(*a*) zwaaien; schommelen; slingeren; **he**

switch   **take**

was swinging on a rope; the door swung
open.
(*b*) draaien; zwenken; he swung round
and shouted something; the car swung
across the road and hit a tree.
swings—swinging—swung [swʌŋ]
—has swung

switch [swɪtʃ] **1.** *zn*
knop(je); push the red switch to start the
engine; the light switch is behind the
door.
meervoud **switches**
2. *ww*
to switch on/off = aandraaien/uit-
draaien; can you switch the TV off when
you go to bed? he forgot to switch off his

car lights/to switch his car lights off;
switch on the radio/switch the radio on—
it's time for the news.
switches—switching—
switched—has switched
Let op: he switched the radio off
of he switched off the radio *maar*
alleen he switched it off

swum [swʌm] *zie* **swim**

swung [swʌŋ] *zie* **swing**

system [ˈsɪstəm] *zn*
systeem; stelsel; the country's railway
system; I don't understand the education
system; he has a funny system of bells to
wake himself up in the morning.

Tt

table [ˈteɪbl] *zn*
tafel; a dining room table; a kitchen
table; can you set the table please? =
kunt u (de) tafel dekken alstublieft? let
me help you clear the table = laat mij je
helpen (met) afruimen.
tablecloth, *zn*
tafelkleed.

tail [teɪl] *zn*
(*a*) staart; the cat was moving its tail
from side to side; some birds have very
long tails; a fish swims with its tail.
(*b*) (*van munt*) kruis; let's play heads
or tails = laten we kruis of munt
spelen.

take [teɪk] *ww*
(*a*) nemen; pakken; he took the book
from the shelf; she took the newspaper
off the table.
(*b*) meenemen; brengen; can you take
this letter to the post office? she was
taking her children to school; he's taken
the car to the garage.
(*c*) wegnemen; who's taken my pen?
someone has taken my car.

(*d*) bezetten; plaats nemen; this seat is
taken; please take a seat.
(*e*) (*van examen*) afleggen/doen; he's
taking his exams tomorrow so he has to
go to bed early; she took her driving test
three times before she passed.
(*f*) (in)nemen; gebruiken; do you take
sugar in your coffee? he has to take the
medicine three times a day.
(*g*) aannemen/aanvaarden; if he offers
you the job, take it.
(*h*) nemen; I'm going to take a holiday; has he taken his bath yet? he took a
picture of the Houses of Parliament =
hij maakte een foto etc.; hurry up and
take the photo, it's starting to rain; you
should go and take a rest.
(*i*) nodig zijn; (*van tijd*) kosten; it took
three men to lift the car; we took three
days/it took us three days to walk to
Edinburgh; how long does it take to get
to school by bus? he must have been
hungry—it didn't take him long to eat
all his dinner.
(*j*) accepteren; this machine only takes
10p coins; his car can take four passen-

gers = zijn auto biedt plaats aan vier passagiers.

takes—taking—took [tʊk]—has taken

take after, *ww*
aarden naar; he takes after his father.

take away, *ww*
(*a*) afnemen/afpakken; weghalen; take that knife away from him; the police came and took him away.
(*b*) (*bij rekenen*) aftrekken; if you take six away from ten, you have four.
Let op: take away *wordt meestal met het minteken − aangegeven;* **10 − 4 = 6** (*zeg 'ten take away four equals six' tien min vier is/maakt zes*)

take back, *ww*
(*a*) terugbrengen; this shirt is too small—I'll take it back to the shop.
(*b*) terugnemen; I went to the shop with the shirt which I had just bought, but they wouldn't take it back.

take in, *ww*
(*a*) begrijpen; he didn't take in what I said.
(*b*) bedriegen, beetnemen; don't be taken in by what he says.

take off, *ww*
(*a*) uittrekken/uitdoen; he took off all his clothes/he took all his clothes off; take your shoes off before you come into the house.
(*b*) opstijgen; the plane took off at 4.30.

take on, *ww*
aannemen; he's taken on two more jobs; the company has taken on three secretaries.

take over, *ww*
(*a*) overnemen; the firm was taken over last year.
(*b*) (het) overnemen; I'll take over from you now; when the maths teacher was ill, the history teacher had to take over his class.

take up, *ww*
(*a*) innemen, in beslag nemen; this table takes up a lot of room; playing football takes up too much time.

(*b*) (*van sport*) gaan beoefenen; he's taken up tennis.
Let op: he took his shoes off *of* he took off his shoes; she took the shirt back *of* took back the shirt *maar alleen* took them off, took it back, etc.

talk [tɔːk] *ww*
praten; the tourists were talking German; I don't understand what they're talking about; I must talk to the man at the garage about the car engine; he's talking of going to the USA on holiday.
talks—talking—talked—has talked

talk over, *ww*
bepraten/bespreken; go and talk things over with the bank manager.

talk round, *ww*
iemand bepraten; I talked him round.

tall [tɔːl] *bn*
hoog; lang; a tall building; can you see that tall tree over there? he's the tallest in his class—he's taller than all the others; how tall are you? I'm 5 foot 7 (5'7") tall.
tall—taller—tallest
Let op: tall *wordt ook met cijfers gebruikt:* the tree is 10 metres tall; he's 6 foot tall

tap [tæp] *zn* (*Amer.* faucet)
kraan; turn the cold water tap off—my bath's too cold; have you turned the gas taps off?

tape [teɪp] *zn*
(*a*) band; lint; tape measure/measuring tape = centimeter.
(*b*) geluidsband; have you heard his latest tape? let me play you the tape I bought today.
tape recorder, *zn*
bandrecorder; he recorded the conversation on his tape recorder.

taste [teɪst] **1.** *zn*
smaak; I don't like the taste of onions; this ice cream has no taste at all.
2. *ww*
smaken; proeven; can you taste the salt in this soup? this cake tastes of salt

= deze taart smaakt zout; **I have a cold so I can't taste anything; what is it?—it tastes like jam.**

tastes—tasting—tasted—has tasted

taught [tɔːt] *zie* **teach**

tax [tæks] *zn*
belasting; **there's a 10% tax on petrol; you always have to pay tax on the money you earn; no one likes paying tax.**

meervoud **taxes**

taxi ['tæksɪ] *zn*
taxi; **I must call a taxi; why are there no taxis at the station today? there are no buses after 10 o'clock, so we had to take a taxi to the airport.**

taxi driver, *zn*
taxichauffeur.

tea [tiː] *zn*
(*a*) thee; **we've got no tea left—can you buy some at the supermarket? put some tea into the pot and add boiling water; would you like another cup of tea/some more tea? I don't like tea—can I have coffee instead?**
(*b*) kop(je) thee; **two teas, please, and two pieces of cake.**
(*c*) (de) thee; **come and have tea with us tomorrow** = kom morgen bij ons op de thee; **have you had your tea yet? they've asked us to tea; we always have tea at four o'clock.**

geen meervoud voor (a); **teas** *betekent* **cups of tea**

tea-bag, *zn*
theezakje.

teacloth, *zn*
theedoek.

teacup, *zn*
theekop(je).

teapot, *zn*
theepot; **put some tea into the teapot and add boiling water.**

teaspoon, *zn*
theelepeltje.

teatime, *zn*
theetijd (d.w.z. tussen 4 en 5 uur 's middags); **come on, it's teatime! there is an interesting TV programme which is on at teatime.**

teach [tiːtʃ] *ww*
onderwijzen; lesgeven; leren; **he taught me how to drive; she teaches French in our school; she taught herself typing; who taught you to swim?**

teaches—teaching—taught [tɔːt] **—has taught**

teacher, *zn*
onderwijzer(es), leraar/lerares; **Mr Smith is our English teacher; the music teacher is ill today.**

team [tiːm] *zn*
ploeg; 'team'; **there are eleven people in a cricket team; she plays for the school team; which football team is your favourite?; our team played badly last Saturday.**

tear¹ [tɪə] *zn*
traan; **tears ran down her face; he burst into tears** = hij barstte in tranen uit; **she ran out of the room in tears** = in tranen.

tear² [teə] *ww*
(*a*) scheuren; rukken; **he tore a hole in his trousers/he tore his trousers.**
(*b*) scheuren; **I tore the letter into little bits.**
(*c*) vliegen; stormen; **he tore across the room; the cars were tearing past.**

tears—tearing—tore [tɔː]**—has torn** [tɔːn]

tear off, *ww*
afscheuren/uitscheuren; **he tore off the next page in his notebook.**

tear out, *ww*
scheuren uit; **he tore a page out of his notebook.**

tear up, *ww*
verscheuren; **she tore up the letter; they tore up the old newspapers; they used torn up newspapers to pack the cups into the box.**

Let op: **he tore a page out** *of* **he tore out a page; she tore up the letter** *of* **she tore the letter up,** *etc. maar alleen* **he tore it out, she tore it up,** *etc.*

teeth [tiːθ] *zie* **tooth**

telegram ['telɪgræm] *zn*
telegram; **we've had a telegram to say**

he's coming; send a telegram to your mother.

telephone ['telɪfəʊn] 1. *zn*
telefoon; the telephone's ringing; can you answer the telephone for me—I'm in the bath; he lifted the telephone and called the police.
on the telephone = (*a*) aan de lijn/telefoon; **don't make a noise—Daddy's on the telephone; there's someone on the telephone who wants to speak to you.**
(*b*) met telefoon; **are you on the telephone?** = hebt u telefoon? **they're not on the telephone.**
2. *ww*
telefoneren, (op)bellen; **your sister telephoned yesterday; telephone the doctor—the baby's ill; can you telephone New York from here?**
telephones—telephoning—telephoned—has telephoned
Let op: in plaats van **telephone** *wordt vrijwel altijd* **phone** *gebruikt*

telephone book, *zn*
telefoonboek; **this restaurant isn't in the telephone book.**
telephone box, *zn*
telefooncel; **I'm phoning from the telephone box outside the post office.**
meervoud **telephone boxes**

telephone number, *zn*
telefoonnummer; **what's your telephone number? his telephone number's 405 9935.**

television [telɪ'vɪʒn] *zn*
(*a*) televisie; **we watch television every night; is there any sport on television tonight? television programmes are never interesting on Saturdays.**
(*b*) televisie(toestel); **I've bought a colour television; the television has broken down; turn off the television—that programme's awful! when he comes home in the evening he just turns on the television and goes to sleep.**
Let op: **television** *wordt vaak geschreven en uitgesproken als*
TV ['tiː'viː]

television set, *zn*
televisietoestel; **we've bought a new television set.**

tell [tel] *ww*
(*a*) vertellen; zeggen; **he told me a long story; she told the police she had seen the accident; do you think he is telling the truth? don't tell your mother you've been to the pub!**
(*b*) zeggen; vertellen; **can you tell me how to get to the post office? the teacher told the children to sit down; tell me when to start; nobody told me about the picnic.**
(*c*) onderscheiden; zien; **can you tell the difference between butter and margarine? you can tell he's annoyed by the way his ears go red.**
tells—telling—told [təʊld]—**has told**

tell off, *ww*
iemand op zijn kop geven; **he was told off for being late; the teacher will tell us off if we don't do our homework.**
Let op: **she told the boys off** *of* **she told off the boys** *maar alleen* **told them off**

temper ['tempə] *zn*
humeur; **he's in a (bad) temper** = hij heeft een boze bui; **he lost his temper** = hij werd woedend; *zie ook* **bad-tempered.**

temperature ['temprətʃə] *zn*
(*a*) temperatuur; **what's the temperature of boiling water? the temperature in the desert is very hot; the car won't start when the temperature's very low; put the thermometer in your mouth—I want to take your temperature** = ik wil je temperatuur opnemen.
(*b*) verhoging; temperatuur; koorts; **he's in bed with a temperature; the doctor says she's got a temperature.**

ten [ten] tien
he bought ten oranges for £1; he's ten (years old); the train leaves at ten (o'clock).
tenth [tenθ] **10th** *bn & zn*
tiende; **the tenth of June/June the tenth (June 10th); that's the tenth letter I've written today; he spends a tenth of his**

money on food; her tenth birthday is on Wednesday.

tennis [ˈtenɪs] *zn*
tennis; (het) tennissen; **would you like a game of tennis? I'm no good at tennis; he's having tennis lessons; let's play with this tennis ball.**
geen meervoud

tense [tens] *zn*
(*van werkwoord*) tijd; **the past tense of 'go' is 'went'.**

tent [tent] *zn*
tent; **when we go camping we take our tent in the back of our car; his tent was blown down by the wind.**

term [tɜ:m] *zn*
(*a*) termijn; periode; **during his term as President; he was sent to prison for a term of five years.**
(*b*) trimester; **there are three terms in the school year; we play cricket during the summer term and football in the autumn and spring terms; term ends on July 27th; next term, I'm starting to learn German; half term** = krokusvakantie/herfstvakantie.
(*c*) voorwaarde; **what are the terms of the agreement?**
(*d*) verstandhouding; **we're on good terms with the people next door; he's on bad terms with everyone.**

terrible [ˈterɪbl] *bn*
verschrikkelijk; vreselijk; **he had a terrible accident; the last meal I had in that restaurant was terrible.**

terribly, *bw*
verschrikkelijk; vreselijk; **he's terribly kind; these chocolates are terribly expensive.**

test [test] **1.** *zn*
toets; proef(werk); test; **we've had a maths test this morning; he's passed his driving test; the doctor's going to do a blood test.**
2. *ww*
toetsen, testen; **I must have my eyes tested; the teacher tested his French; have you tested your new car in the snow?**
tests—testing—tested—has tested

textbook [ˈteksbʊk] *zn*
leerboek/studieboek.

than [ðæn *of* ðən] *vw*
dan; **my house is bigger than yours; it's colder today than it was yesterday; I know London better than Edinburgh; more than thirty people were waiting for the bus.**

thank [θæŋk] *ww*
(be)danken; **he thanked me for having helped him; she thanked them for coming to see her; I must thank him for his present.**
thanks—thanking—thanked—has thanked

thanks, *zn meervoud & tw*
dank; bedankt; **please give him my thanks for his present** = wil je hem namens mij voor zijn cadeau bedanken; **we got no thanks for all our help; do you want some more coffee?—no thanks, I've had plenty; do you want lift to the station?—thanks, it's a long way to walk.**

thanks to, *bw*
dankzij; **thanks to your father's map, we found our way to the post office; thanks to the rain, we couldn't have the picnic.**

thank you, *tw*
dankjewel/dankuwel; **thank you for the present; did you say thank you to your mother for the book? do you want some more coffee?—no thank you, I've had plenty; do you want a lift to the station?—thank you, it's a long way to walk.**

that [ðæt *of* ðət] **1.** *bn & vnw*
(*a*) dat/die; **that book is the one I was talking about, not this one; can you see that tall man standing by the door? what's the name of that restaurant where we had dinner yesterday? who's that sitting at the next table?**
meervoud those

(*b*) dat/die; **where is the letter that he sent you? they live in a house that has** red windows; here's the box that you left in the bedroom.

Let op: bij een lijdend voorwerp kan that weggelaten worden: where's the letter he sent you? here's the box you left in the bedroom
Bij een onderwerp kan that *veranderen in* which *(voor zaken en dieren) of* who *(voor mensen);* a house that has red windows/a house which has red windows; the man that stole the car/the man who stole the car

2. *vw*
(*a*) dat; (*na werkwoorden als* hope, know, tell, say *en bijvoeglijke naamwoorden als* glad, sorry, happy) he told me that she was out; she said that she was tired; he didn't know that we were coming; I'm glad that you were able to come.
(*b*) (*na* so/such + *bijvoeglijk of zelfstandig naamwoord*) dat; it's so hot here that it makes me thirsty; the meat was so good that I ate all of it; it was raining so hard that we couldn't have our picnic; we had such bad weather that our holiday was spoilt; there was such a crowd that we couldn't get into the cinema.

Let op: that *wordt vaak weggelaten: he didn't know we were coming; it's so hot here it makes me thirsty*

the [ðə; ðɪ *voor een klinker*] *lw*
(*a*) de/het; where's the parcel which came today? there's the dog from next door.
(*b*) (*uniek*) de/het; the sun was shining; men have walked on the moon.
(*c*) (*algemeen*) de/het; do you like listening to the radio? I never use the telephone; the streets are crowded at Christmas.
(*d*) [ðiː] jè (van het); de/het ... bij uitstek; that's the shop for men's clothes = dè winkel; he's the doctor for children; that's not the Charlie Chaplin is it? = dè Charlie Chaplin?
(*e*) (*gebruikt om te vergelijken en voor de overtreffende trap*) hoe ... des te; de/het ... -ste; the less you work the fatter you get; the sooner you do it the better;

that's the best way to do it; he's the tallest boy in our school.

theatre ['θɪətə] *zn* (*Amer.* theater)
theater; schouwburg; we're going to the theatre tonight; is there a good play at the theatre this week?

their [ðeə] *bn*
hun; here's their house; they were eating their dinner.
theirs, *vnw*
van hen; de/het hunne; which house is theirs? he's a friend of theirs; they want to borrow my car—theirs won't start.

them [ðem *of* ðəm] *vnw meervoud*
(*lijdende vorm*) hen/ze; hun; do you like chocolates?—no, I don't like them very much; the children are waiting outside—tell them to come in; if you are going to visit your parents can you take them this present?
themselves, *vnw meervoud*
zich(zelf); zelf; cats clean themselves very carefully; the old ladies were all by themselves in the house = helemaal alleen; they did it all by themselves = helemaal zelf; the doctors were all ill themselves.

then [ðen] 1. *bw*
(*a*) toen/dan; the police said he killed his sister in London on April 23rd, but he was in Scotland then; can you come to a party next week?—no, I shall be on holiday then.
(*b*) toen/daarna; he sat down and then they brought cups of coffee; we had a busy holiday—we went to France, and then to Italy and then to Germany.
2. *vw*
dan; if you don't like fish then you'll have to eat meat; then you already knew that he had died?

there [ðeə] 1. *bw.*
daar(heen), er(heen); we'll go there at 10 o'clock; is the car still there? where's the tea?—there, on the top shelf; have you ever been to Canada?—yes, I went there three years ago.
2. *tw*
(*a*) (*medelijdend*) stil maar; kom, kom!

there, there, don't cry; there, if you sit down, you'll soon feel better.
(*b*) (*het gelijk van de spreker bevestigend*) nu; nou; zie je wel; **there, what did I tell you, we've missed the train.**
(*c*) (*vastbesloten*) zo, nu weet je het! **I'll go to the party all by myself, so there!**
(*d*) (*iets aanbiedend*) **there you are!** = alstublieft!
3. *vnw*
er; (*als onderwerp bij werkwoorden* (*gewoonlijk het werkwoord* to be), *wanneer het werkelijke onderwerp na het werkwoord volgt*) **there's a big dog in the garden; there's a page missing in this book; were there many people at the meeting? is there anything to drink? there seems to have been an accident; there isn't any sugar left.**

therefore ['ðeəfɔː] *bw*
daarom, dus; **there's a lot of snow, therefore the trains will be late; the children are growing up and therefore can look after themselves.**

thermometer [θə'mɔmitə] *zn*
thermometer; **the thermometer showed only 2°—it was very cold.**

these [ðiːz] *zie* **this**

they [ðeɪ] *vnw meervoud*
(*a*) (*onderwerpsvorm*) zij/ze; **where are the cups and saucers?—they're in the cupboard; who are those people in uniform? — they're army officers** = dat zijn legerofficieren; **the children went out in the snow with no coats on, so they all caught colds.**
(*b*) (*algemeen*) ze/men; **they say it's going to be hot; they tell me that you've got married.**
Let op: **they** *wordt* **them** *als lijdend voorwerp:* **we gave it to them;** *als* **they** *het werkwoord* be *volgt, wordt het meestal* **them**

thick [θɪk] *bn*
(*a*) dik; **a thick slice of cake; the walls are two metres thick; this orange has a very thick skin; a thick piece of string; he was carrying a thick pile of papers.**
(*b*) dicht (begroeid); **a thick forest of**

trees; **the lawn was covered with thick grass.**
(*c*) dik; **this paint is too thick—add some water to it; a bowl of good thick soup.**
(*d*) dicht; **the plane couldn't land because of thick fog.**
thick—thicker—thickest

thief [θiːf] *zn*
dief; **thieves broke into the shop and stole 100 watches.**
meervoud **thieves** [θiːvz]

thin [θɪn] *bn*
(*a*) dun; mager; **his legs are very thin; she's getting too thin—she should eat more.**
(*b*) dun; **a thin slice of bread; a thin sheet of paper; a thin piece of string.**
(*c*) dun(begroeid); **the ground was covered with thin grass.**
(*d*) dun verdund; **thin soup; add water until the paint is thin.**
(*e*) doorzichtig; **thin curtains.**
thin—thinner—thinnest

thing [θɪŋ] *zn*
(*a*) zaak; ding; **what's that black thing in the garden? what's that green thing for?**
(*b*) ding; schepsel; **his mother's such a nice old thing; you silly thing!—why did you do that?**
(*c*) **things** = dingen; spullen; **have you brought your football things? I left my painting things in the car.**
(*d*) de zaak/zaken; **how are things going? don't take things so seriously; it was a good thing the train was late** = het was maar goed dat de trein vertraging had; **she just sat there and didn't say a thing; the first thing to do is phone the police; what a silly thing to do!**

think [θɪŋk] *ww*
(*a*) (na)denken; **think before you say anything; he never thinks about what people might say.**
(*b*) denken; menen; geloven; achten; vinden; **I think she is prettier than her sister; what do you think we ought to do now? everyone thought he was mad; what do you think of the film? he's thought to be in Canada** = men denkt dat hij in

Canada is; **he's in Canada, isn't he?—I
don't think so.**
(c) verwachten; **I think it's going to rain;
I didn't think the train would be late.**
(d) van plan zijn; **he's thinking of going
to work in Canada; have you thought
about going to work in Canada?**
thinks—thinking—thought [θɔ:t]—
has thought

think over, ww
overdenken; erover denken; **think it
over, and give me your answer tomorrow.**

think up, ww
bedenken; **he thought up a plan for
making money.**

third [θɜ:d] **3rd,** zn & bn
derde; **my birthday is on the third of Sep-
tember/September the third (September
3rd); he was third in the race; they live in
the third house on the left; King James
the Third (James III); it's his third birthday on Friday.**
Let op: met data wordt **third** *meestal
geschreven* **3rd: September 3rd,
1974; March 3rd, 1981;** *bij de
namen van koningen en koninginnen
wordt* **third** *meestal geschreven* **III:
King Charles III**

thirst [θɜ:st] zn
dorst.
thirsty, bn
dorstig; **I'm thirsty, give me a drink of
water** = ik heb dorst etc.; **if you're
thirsty, have some orange juice.**
thirsty—thirstier—thirstiest

thirteen [θɜ:'ti:n] dertien
she's thirteen (years old).
thirteenth, 13th, bn and zn
dertiende; **she came thirteenth in the
race; the thirteenth of August/August the
thirteenth (August 13th); it's his thirteenth birthday on Monday.**

thirty ['θɜ:tɪ] dertig
**he's thirty (years old); she has thirty
pairs of shoes; he's in his thirties** = in
de dertig.
Let op: **thirty-one** (31), **thirty-two**
(32), *etc., maar* **thirty-first** (31st),
thirty-second (32nd), *etc.*

thirtieth, 30th, bn & zn
dertigste; **he was thirtieth in the race; the
thirtieth of June/June the thirtieth (June
30th); it was her thirtieth birthday last
week.**

this [ðɪs] bn & vnw
(a) dit/deze; **this is the book I was talking
about; this little girl is my sister's daughter; I think I have been to this restaurant
before; this is Mr Martin; these apples
are bad.**
(b) (van tijd) van-; dit/deze; **I saw him
this morning; they are coming to have tea
with us this afternoon; I'll be seeing him
this week; she's retiring this year; we're
going to Greece this summer.**
meervoud **these**

those [ðəʊz] zie **that**

though [ðəʊ] vw
(al)hoewel; **though he's small, he can hit
very hard; though it was snowing, it
wasn't very cold outside;** zie ook
although.
as though = alsof; **it looks as though
it will rain.**

thought [θɔ:t] zie **think**

thousand ['θaʊznd] duizend
**I paid two thousand pounds for it
(£2,000); thousands of people escaped
from the fire** = duizenden mensen etc.
Let op: na getallen krijgt **thousand**
geen **-s: two thousand; ten thousand**

thread [θred] **1.** zn
garen; draad; **I need some strong thread
to sew on my button.**
2. ww
aanrijgen; een draad steken in; **can you
thread this needle for me?**
**threads—threading—threaded—
has threaded**

threaten ['θretn] ww
(be)dreigen; **he threatened to call the
police; the burglar threatened her with a
gun.**
**threatens—threatening—
threatened—has threatened**

three [θri:] drie
she's three (years old); can you see me at three (o'clock)? three men stole my car.
Let op: **three** (3) *maar* **third** (3rd)

threw [θru:] *zie* **throw**

throat [θrəʊt] *zn*
keel; he held her by the throat; a piece of meat got stuck in his throat; he cleared his throat = hij kuchte.

through [θru:] *bw & vz*
(*a*) door (. . . heen); he went through the door; she looked through the window; the water runs through the pipe; the air comes in through the hole in the wall; the road goes straight through the centre of the town; she pushed the needle through the ball of wool.
(*b*) de/het hele . . . door; she went on talking all through the film.
(*c*) via; I sent the letter through the post; we heard of it through my sister.
(*d*) door; I'm trying to get through to Germany = ik probeer verbinding te krijgen met Duitsland; can you put me through to the manager? = kunt u mij met de manager verbinden?
Let op: **through** *wordt vaak na werkwoorden gebruikt:* **to go through; to fall through; to see through,** *etc.*

throughout, *vz & bw*
(helemaal) door; (in/over) de/het hele . . .; roads are blocked by snow throughout the country; heavy rain fell throughout the night.

throw [θrəʊ] *ww*
gooien; werpen; how far can you throw this ball? she threw the stone through the window; he threw the letter into the dustbin; he threw the cushion at his sister.
throws—throwing—threw [θru:] **—has thrown**

throw away, *ww*
weggooien; don't throw away that old bike—we can mend it; she threw away all her old clothes.
Let op: **throw that paper away** *of* **throw away that paper** *maar alleen* **throw it away**

throw off, *ww*
kwijtraken; I've had a cold for weeks, and I can't throw it off.
throw out, *ww*
(*a*) (er)uitgooien; when he couldn't pay the bill, he was thrown out of the restaurant.
(*b*) weggooien/wegdoen; we're throwing out this old carpet.
throw up, *ww*
(*a*) overgeven; the dog has thrown up all over the kitchen floor.
(*b*) opgeven/eraangeven; she threw up her job and went to live in the country.

thumb [θʌm] *zn*
duim; he hit his thumb with the hammer; the baby was sucking its thumb.

thunder ['θʌndə] *zn*
donder(slag); onweer; listen to the thunder! when there's thunder, the cat hides under the bed.
thunderstorm, *zn*
onweersbui; we were caught on the mountain by a thunderstorm.

Thursday ['θɜːzdɪ] *zn*
donderdag; she was ill last Thursday; I go to my evening class on Thursdays; shall we meet next Thursday? today is Thursday, October 27th.
Let op: **Thursday** *wordt altijd met een hoofdletter gesaneven*

tick [tɪk] **1.** *zn*
(*a*) tekentje; 'kruisje'; stip; he put a tick next to each name on the list; put a tick if you want breakfast in your room.
(*b*) het tikken; getik; the room was very quiet—I could only hear the tick of the clock.
2. *ww*
(*a*) aanstippen; he ticked the names of the children who were present; please tick if you want breakfast in your room.
(*b*) tikken; the room was so quiet—all we could hear was the clock ticking; run away—the bomb's ticking!
ticks—ticking—ticked—has ticked

tick off, *ww*
op de vingers tikken; berispen; een

standje geven; **he was ticked off by the police for parking on the yellow line.**

ticket ['tɪkɪt] *zn*
(*a*) kaartje; biljet; **you can't get on the train without a ticket; I've lost my plane tickets—how can I get to New York?**
(*b*) kaartje; plaatsbewijs; **two tickets for the 6.30 show please; I went to several theatres but there were no tickets left anywhere.**
(*c*) bon; bekeuring; **don't leave your car on the yellow line—you'll get a ticket!**

tide [taɪd] *zn*
(ge)tij; **high tide is at four o'clock** = vloed/hoog water; **at low tide/when the tide is out you can walk for miles on the sand** = bij eb/laag water.

tidy ['taɪdɪ] **1.** *bn*
netjes; aan kant; opgeruimd; **you must keep your room tidy.**
tidy—tidier—tidiest
2. *ww*
opruimen; **she was tidying her room.**
tidies—tidying—tidied—has tidied

tidy away, *ww*
opbergen/wegbergen; **he tidied away all the books on the desk.**
tidy up, *ww*
opruimen; **can't you tidy up all those papers? you must tidy up your room before your parents come back.**

tie [taɪ] **1.** *zn*
(strop)das; **he wore a blue tie with white spots; you can't come into the restaurant if you haven't got a tie on.**
2. *ww*
(vast)binden/-knopen; **the parcel is tied with string; he was tying his horse to the fence; the burglars tied her hands behind her back.**
ties—tying—tied—has tied

tie up, *ww*
(*a*) dichtbinden/vastbinden; **the parcel is tied up with string; that dog ought to be tied up or it will bite someone.**
(*b*) **to be tied up** = bezet zijn; het druk hebben; **I'm rather tied up at the moment—can I phone you tomorrow?**

tight [taɪt] **1.** *bn*
dicht; vast; stevig; nauw; strak; **the lid is so tight I can't open it; my trousers are so tight I can't fasten the top button; her dress is so tight that she can't bend down.**
2. *bw*
stevig; strak; **shut the door tight; hold (on) tight!**
tight—tighter—tightest

tighten, *ww*
aandraaien; strak(ker) maken; **can you tighten this screw? the lid needs tightening.**
tightens—tightening—tightened—has tightened

tightly, *bw*
stevig; **he put the lid on tightly; hold on to the handle tightly.**

till [tɪl] *vz*
tot(dat); **I won't be home till nine o'clock; he worked from morning till night.**

time [taɪm] **1.** *zn*
(*a*) tijd; **you don't need to hurry—you've plenty of time; have you got time for a cup of tea? he spends all his time reading the newspaper; don't waste time putting your shoes on—jump out of the window now.**
(*b*) tijd, periode; **I haven't seen him for a long time; it didn't take him much time to get here** = hij heeft er niet lang over gedaan om hier te komen; **it took her a long time to get better; we had a letter from her a short time ago; we're going on holiday in three weeks' time** = over drie weken.
(*c*) tijd(stip); **what time is it?/what's the time?** = hoe laat is het? **the time is exactly 6.35; can you tell me the time please?** = kunt u mij zeggen hoe laat het is? **he's only four—he can't tell the time yet** = hij kan nog niet klokkijken.
(*d*) ogenblik; tijdstip; **I didn't hear the bang as I was asleep at the time; by the time the police arrived the burglars had run away; you can't sing and drink at the same time** = tegelijkertijd.
(*e*) (*geregelde*) tijd; **closing time is 10.30**

= sluitingstijd; **it's dinner time—I'm hungry; is it time to go to bed?** *zie ook* **bedtime, dinnertime, lunchtime, teatime.**

(*f*) (goede/slechte) ervaring; **we had a good time at the party** = we hebben veel plezier gehad.

(*g*) keer/maal; **I've seen that film three times; that's the last time I'll ask you to sing a song; next time you come, bring your football.**

(*h*) **times** = keer/maal; **six times four is twenty four; this box is ten times as heavy as that one; she's a hundred times prettier than her sister.**

in time = op tijd; **we ran fast and got to the station in time to catch the train; hurry if you want to be in time for the train; we were just in time to see the soldiers march past.**

on time = precies/stipt op tijd; **the train arrived on time; he's never on time.**
2. *ww*
de tijd opnemen; op de tijd letten; **if you run round the football pitch, I'll time you; can you time these eggs?—they have to cook for three minutes; the police timed the car—it was going at 70 miles an hour.**

times—timing—timed—has timed

timetable, *zn*
(les)rooster; tabel; dienstregeling; **look up the trains to London in the timetable; we have three English lessons on the timetable today.**

tin [tɪn] *zn*
(*a*) blik(je); **let's open a tin of soup; I bought three tins of food for the cat.**
(*b*) (*voor koekjes etc.*) trommel; **put the cakes into that tin; I gave her a tin of biscuits for her birthday.**

tinned, *bn*
ingeblikt/in blik; **do you like tinned fruit better than fresh fruit?**

tin opener, *zn*
blikopener; **we took a tin of fruit for the picnic, but we forgot the tin opener!**

tiny [ˈtaɪnɪ] *bn*
heel klein/piepklein; **a tiny baby; this plant has tiny blue flowers.**

tiny—tinier—tiniest

tip [tɪp] 1. *zn*
(*a*) punt(je); top(je); **she touched it with the tips of her fingers; he has a stick with a metal tip.**
(*b*) fooi; **I gave the taxi driver a £1 tip; should I give the waiter a tip? is a tip included in the bill?**
2. *ww*
(*a*) laten omvallen/-rollen; legen; **he picked up the bucket and tipped the apples on to the floor; she tipped the money out of her bag.**
(*b*) een fooi geven (aan); **I tipped the waiter £1; shall I tip the driver?**

tips—tipping—tipped—has tipped

tip over/tip up, *ww*
omvallen; om(ver)gooien; **he tipped over the bottle; the lorry tipped over; my cup tipped over and all my tea spilled on to the table.**

tire [ˈtaɪə] *zn*
(*Amerikaans voor* **tyre**) band.

tired [ˈtaɪəd] *bn*
(*a*) moe; vermoeid; **I'm tired—I'll go to bed; if you feel tired, lie down on my bed; I'm tired after that long walk.**
(*b*) **to be tired of something** = genoeg hebben van iets; **I'm tired of hearing the baby cry; she's tired of having to do all the work; can't we play another game— I'm tired of this one.**

tired out, *bn*
doodop; **I'm tired out after that long walk; let her sit down—she's tired out.**

title [ˈtaɪtl] *zn*
titel; opschrift, naam; **the title of his next film was 'The Third Man'; what's the title of that book you're reading?**

to [tuː *of* tə] 1. *vz*
(*a*) naar; **he went to the station; I'm going to the butcher's; is this the way to the post office? the church is to the east of the town; take one step to the left.**
(*b*) tot; voor; **from Monday to Saturday; he slept from ten to eight o'clock; it's ten to six; the time is a quarter to seven.**
(*c*) aan; tegen; **give the book to the**

teacher; pass the sugar to your father; you must be kind to old people.

(*d*) tegen; per; op; voor; **they lost by six goals to four; there are two dollars to the pound; there are three keys to the front door; in this class there are 35 children to one teacher.**

(*e*) boven; met; **I prefer butter to margarine** = ik vind boter lekkerder dan margarine; **you can't compare tinned fruit to fresh fruit.**

2. (*vóór werkwoord*)

(*a*) (om . . .) te; **he remembered to switch off the light; they tried to run away; she agreed to come with us; we decided to leave the office early.**

(*b*) om . . . te; **they came to help us; the doctor left to go to the hospital.**

(*c*) om te; **she was too tired to walk; are these apples good to eat? I'm sorry to be late** = het spijt me dat ik (te) laat ben.

Let op: **to** *wordt gebruikt voor tijdstippen tussen* **half past** *en* **o'clock. 4.35 = twenty-five to five; 4.45 = a quarter to five; 4.50 = ten to five**

toast [təʊst] *zn*
geroosterd brood; **do you want toast and honey for your breakfast? I want some more toast; can you make another piece of toast?**
geen meervoud: **some toast; a piece of toast**

tobacco [təˈbækəʊ] *zn*
tabak; **these cigarettes are made of American tobacco; I must buy a packet of tobacco.**
geen meervoud: **some tobacco**

today [təˈdeɪ] *bw & zn*
vandaag; **he said he was coming to see me today, but he hasn't come yet; today's my birthday; what's the date today? have you read today's newspaper?**
geen meervoud
Let op: om over de ochtend/middag etc. van **today**, *te praten, zeg je* **this morning/this afternoon,** *etc.*

toe [təʊ] *zn*
teen; **he trod on my toe; big toe/little toe** = grote/kleine teen.

toenail, *zn*
teennagel.

together [təˈgeðə] *bw*
(*a*) bij/met elkaar, samen; **we must stay together or we'll get lost; let's go to the cinema together.**
(*b*) aan/bij/tegen elkaar; **tie the two chairs together; can you stick the pieces of the cup together again? add all these numbers together; we've had three lunches and three beers—how much is it all together?**

toilet [ˈtɔɪlət] *zn*
toilet/w.c.; **where's the men's toilet? I want to go to the toilet.**
toilet paper, *zn*
closetpapier.
toilet roll, *zn*
closetrol.

told [təʊld] *zie* **tell**

tomato [təˈmɑːtəʊ] *zn*
tomaat; **have another tomato; a bowl of tomato salad; tomato sauce** = ketchup; **put some tomato sauce on your chips.**
meervoud **tomatoes**

tomorrow [təˈmɒrəʊ] *bw & zn*
morgen; **today's Tuesday, so tomorrow must be Wednesday; can you meet me tomorrow morning? tomorrow is my birthday; we are going to the cinema tomorrow evening.**

ton [tʌn] *zn*
ton (= ± 1016 kg); **that piece of metal weighs three tons.**

tongue [tʌŋ] *zn*
(*a*) tong; **don't stick your tongue out at the teacher; he said it with his tongue in his cheek** = ironisch.
(*b*) taal; **his mother tongue is English** = moedertaal.

tonight [təˈnaɪt] *bw & zn*
vanavond/vannacht; **we're having a party tonight; can you phone me at 11.30 tonight? is there anything interesting on TV tonight? tonight's programmes are very boring.**

too [tu:] *bw*

(*a*) te; **he has too much money; it's too cold for you to play outside; these shoes are too small.**

(*b*) ook; **he had some cake and I had some too; she, too, has a cold/she has a cold too.**

took [tʊk] *zie* **take**

tool [tu:l] *zn*

(stuk) gereedschap; werktuig; **I keep my hammer in the tool box; have you got a tool for taking the wheels off a car?**

tooth [tu:θ] *zn*

(*a*) tand; kies; **don't forget to clean your teeth after breakfast; I must see the dentist—one of my teeth hurts; he had to have a tooth out** = hij moest een tand/kies laten trekken; **he has a sweet tooth** = hij is een zoetekauw.

(*b*) (zaag)tand.

meervoud **teeth** [ti:θ]

toothache, *zn*

kiespijn; **I must see the dentist—I've got toothache.**

geen meervoud

toothbrush, *zn*

tandenborstel.

meervoud **toothbrushes**

toothpaste, *zn*

tandpasta; **I must buy some toothpaste; here's a tube of toothpaste.**

geen meervoud: **some toothpaste; a tube of toothpaste**

top [tɒp] **1.** *zn*

(*a*) top; spits; **he climbed to the top of the mountain; the bird is sitting on the top of the tree.**

(*b*) bovenkant/bovenzijde; deksel; **he sat on the top of his car; take the top off the box; the table has a black top; the cake has sugar and fruit on top; on top of** = bovenop; **put the book on top of the others.**

(*c*) de/het hoogste; bovenaan; **look at the top of the next page; our team is at the top in the competition.**

2. *bn*

hoogste; bovenste; **my office is on the top floor of the building; the jam is on the top shelf; he's the top boy in the class** = hij is de beste/eerste van zijn klas; **he's one of the top players in the world** = één van de topspelers.

torch [tɔ:tʃ] *zn*

(zak)lantaarn; **the policeman shone his torch into the room; I can't see anything in the dark—have you got a torch?**

meervoud **torches**

tore [tɔ:] **torn** [tɔ:n] *zie* **tear**

total [təʊtl] *bn & zn*

totaal; geheel; **what's the total cost? the total which you have to pay is at the bottom of the bill.**

totally, *bw*

totaal; helemaal; **the house was totally destroyed.**

touch [tʌtʃ] **1.** *zn*

(*a*) contact; **I'll be in touch with you next week** = ik neem volgende week contact met je op; **we've lost touch with him now that he's gone to live in the States.**

(*b*) aanraking; **I felt a touch on my arm.**

(*c*) tikje, tikkeltje; (*van penseel*) streek; **add a few touches of green to the picture; there's a touch of frost in the air.**

meervoud **touches,** *maar geen meervoud voor* (*a*)

2. *ww*

(*a*) (aan)raken, aankomen; **the policeman touched me on the shoulder; don't touch that door—the paint isn't dry yet; he's so small that his feet don't touch the floor when he sits on a chair; there is a mark on the wall where the chair has touched it.**

(*b*) **I never touch coffee** = ik drink nooit koffie.

touches—touching—touched—has touched

touch down, *ww*

landen; **the plane touched down at 3.15.**

touch up, *ww*

(verf/lak) bijwerken; **I must touch up the car where it has been scratched.**

tour [tʊə] *zn*

toer; rondreis; **we're going on a coach tour to Germany; he took us on a tour of the old castle.**

tourist ['tʊərɪst] *zn*
toerist; **the town is full of tourists in the summer; tourist office** = V V V kantoor.

towards [tə'wɔːdz] *vz*
(*a*) op. . . af; in de richting van; naar; **he ran towards the policeman; the car was going towards London; the ship is sailing towards the rocks.**
(*b*) tegen; **can we meet towards the end of next week? we went on holiday towards the middle of August.**
(*c*) als bijdrage in de kosten; **they gave me £5 a week towards the cost of food.**
(*d*) tegen; jegens; ten opzichte van; **he behaved very kindly towards me.**

towel ['taʊəl] *zn*
handdoek; **she rubbed her hair with a towel; I can't dry myself—my towel fell into the water.**

tower ['taʊə] *zn*
toren; **let's climb to the top of the church tower; control tower** = verkeerstoren.

town [taʊn] *zn*
stad; **we go to do our shopping in the next town; which is the nearest town to your farm? this town is important for its car factories; let's go to town for an evening meal; his office is in town.**
Let op: **to town** *en* **in town** *hebben geen* **the** *nodig*

town council, *zn*
gemeenteraad.
town hall, *zn*
stadhuis.

toy [tɔɪ] *zn*
(stuk) speelgoed; **he's playing with his toy soldiers; put all your toys away before you go to bed; our children love going to the toy shop.**

trace [treɪs] **1.** *zn*
(*a*) spoor(tje); **there's a trace of onion in the soup; the police found traces of blood in the shop.**
(*b*) **there's no trace of** = er is geen spoor van; **there's no trace of a car having been past here; there's no trace of your letter—it must have been lost by the Post Office.**

2. *ww*
nasporen/opsporen; nagaan; **the police have traced her to New York; I can't trace your letter.**
traces—tracing—traced—has traced

track [træk] *zn*
(*a*) (*van voet etc.*) spoor; (voet)afdruk; **look—there's a track of a bicycle in the sand; I'm trying to keep track of the money we're spending** = ik probeer onze uitgaven in de gaten/in het oog te houden; **I've lost track of how many times I've seen that film** = ik ben de tel kwijt geraakt wat betreft het aantal keren etc.
(*b*) baan; **he's running round the track.**
(*c*) rails; spoorlijn; **the engine went off the track.**
track suit, *zn*
trainingspak.

tractor ['træktə] *zn*
traktor; **he drove his tractor across the field.**

traffic ['træfɪk] *zn*
verkeer; **there's a lot of traffic on Friday nights; the lights turned red, and the traffic stopped; there's so much traffic that it's quicker to take the underground.**
geen meervoud: **some traffic; a lot of traffic**
traffic jam, *zn*
verkeersopstopping; file; **the accident caused a big traffic jam; there are traffic jams every Friday evening.**
traffic lights, *zn meervoud*
verkeerslichten/stoplichten; **turn right at the next traffic lights; he went across the crossroads when the traffic lights were red.**

train [treɪn] **1.** *zn*
trein; **the train to Edinburgh leaves from platform 3; I go to work every day by train; hurry up if you want to catch the next train; we missed the last train and had to take a taxi.**
2. *ww*
(*a*) opleiden; africhten; trainen; **he's**

trained his dog to carry the newspaper from the shop; he's training to be a pilot.
(b) trainen; (zich) oefenen; she's training for the 100 metres race.
trains—training—trained—has trained

translate [træns'leɪt] *ww*
vertalen; he asked me to translate the letter into German; this book is translated from the Chinese.
translates—translating—translated—has translated

translation, *zn*
vertaling; here's the translation of the letter from your Japanese friend.

transport ['trænspɔːt] *zn*
vervoer; transport; the car is the commonest means of transport; does the city have an underground transport system?

trap [træp] **1.** *zn*
val(strik); hinderlaag; we caught the wild cat in a trap; the burglars were caught in a police trap.
2. *ww*
in de val (laten) lopen; vangen; opgesloten zitten; we were trapped in the lift for two hours; the police trapped the burglars inside the bank.
traps—trapping—trapped—has trapped

trap door, *zn*
valluik.

travel ['trævl] *ww*
reizen; he travels to work by car; they're travelling to India by bus; they travelled across the States by bicycle.
travels—travelling—travelled—has travelled

travel agent, *zn*
reisbureau/verkeersbureau; I bought my plane tickets at the travel agent's.
traveller, *zn* (*Amer.* **traveler**)
reiziger.
traveller's cheque, *zn* (*Amer.* **traveler's check**)
reischeque.

treasure ['treʒə] *zn*
schat; they found some treasure when

they were digging a hole in the garden; the burglars hid the treasure in a garage.
geen meervoud: **some treasure; a piece of treasure; treasures** *betekent* **valuable things**

treat [triːt] *ww*
(a) behandelen; bejegenen; he was badly treated by the police; she treats her dogs very kindly.
(b) behandelen; after the accident the passengers were treated in hospital for cuts; he's being treated by his doctor for heart disease.
(c) trakteren; I'll treat you all to an ice cream; he treated himself to a long holiday in Africa.
treats—treating—treated—has treated

treatment, *zn*
(a) behandeling; bejegening; the treatment of prisoners by the police.
(b) behandeling; this is a new treatment for heart disease; she's in hospital for treatment to her back.

tree [triː] *zn*
boom; he climbed up a tree; birds make their nests in trees; we have six apple trees in the garden; let's have our picnic under this tree.

trick [trɪk] **1.** *zn*
truc(je); list; grap; streek; he did some card tricks; she did a trick and made a handkerchief come out of his ear; they played a trick on the teacher = ze hebben de docent een poets gebakken.
2. *ww*
bedriegen; door list overhalen; he was tricked into signing the paper; she was tricked out of her money = haar is listig haar geld afhandig gemaakt.
tricks—tricking—tricked—has tricked

tried [traɪd], **tries** [traɪz] *zie* **try**

trip [trɪp] **1.** *zn*
reis(je); tocht(je); we went on a boat trip down the Thames; he's on a business trip to Canada; a day trip to Stratford costs £25 = dagtocht.

Transport *Vervoer*

1.	airport	*vliegveld*	14.	headlight	*koplamp*
2.	bicycle	*fiets*	15.	helicopter	*helikopter*
3.	bus	*bus*	16.	lorry	*vrachtwagen*
4.	car	*auto*	17.	motorbike	*motorfiets*
5.	carriage	*wagon*	18.	mudguard	*spatbord*
6.	coach	*touringcar*	19.	passenger	*passagier*
7.	control tower	*verkeerstoren*	20.	plane	*vliegtuig*
8.	cyclist	*fietser*	21.	roof	*dak*
9.	door	*deur*	22.	seat	*bank*
10.	driver	*chauffeur*	23.	tyre	*band*
11.	engine (of a train)	*locomotief*	24.	van	*bestelwagen*
12.	engine (of a car)	*motor*	25.	wheel	*wiel*
13.	handlebars	*stuur*	26.	window	*raam(pje)*

2. *ww*
(doen) struikelen; beentje lichten; **he
tripped over the piece of wood; she
tripped and sat down in the mud.**
**trips—tripping—tripped—has
tripped**
trip up, *ww*
om (ver)gooien; omvallen; **they put a
piece of string across the path and
tripped up the postman/tripped the
postman up; he tripped up and fell on his
face.**

tropics [ˈtrɒpɪks] *zn meervoud*
de tropen; **he lives in the tropics; this
fruit comes from the tropics.**
tropical, *bn*
tropisch; **a tropical plant; do you like
tropical fruit such as bananas?**

trouble [ˈtrʌbl] *zn*
(*a*) moeite; last; probleem; **the trouble is
that this old car won't start; it's no
trouble—I can do it easily; the children
are no trouble at all; he has money
troubles; they got into trouble with the
police; it's asking for trouble** = dat is
vragen om moeilijkheden; **he got his
friend into trouble** = hij heeft zijn vriend
in moeilijkheden gebracht.
(*b*) **he took the trouble to write** = hij
nam de moeite om te schrijven.

trousers [ˈtraʊzəz] *zn meervoud*
broek; **he tore his trousers; he was
wearing a blue jacket and brown
trousers; I've bought two pairs of
trousers.**
*Let op: om aan te geven dat het om
één broek gaat, zeg je* **a pair of
trousers**

truck [trʌk] *zn*
vrachtwagen.

true [truː] *bn*
waar; juist; **what he says is true; it's
true that she is married; is it true that
you went to Scotland on holiday?**

trunk [trʌŋk] *zn*
(*a*) stam; **the tree trunk is 3 metres
round; can you jump over that tree
trunk?**

(*b*) slurf; **the elephant picked up the
banana with its trunk.**
(*c*) kist; **I have two suitcases and a trunk.**

try [traɪ] **1.** *zn*
(*a*) poging; **she's going to have a try at
flying a plane; he had two tries before he
passed his driving test.**
(*b*) (*rugby*) doelpunt; **they scored two
tries.**
meervoud **tries**
2. *ww*
(*a*) proberen; pogen; **he tried to climb
up the tree; don't try to drive if you've
never driven before; let me try to start
the car.**
(*b*) proberen; **try one of my cakes; have
you tried this new toothpaste? have you
tried eating fish with jam?**
tries [traɪz]—**trying**—**tried** [traɪd]—
has tried
try on, *ww*
(aan)passen; **try the shoes on before you
buy them; did you try on the shirt?**
try out, *ww*
(uit)proberen; testen; **try out the car
before you buy it.**
Let op: **try this hat on** *of* **try on this
hat; try out the car** *of* **try the car
out,** *maar alleen* **try it on, try it out**

tube [tjuːb] *zn*
(*a*) buis, koker, pijp; **a plastic tube
takes the petrol from the tank to the
engine.**
(*b*) tube; **a tube of toothpaste; a tube of
glue.**
(*c*) Londense ondergrondse; **I go to
work by tube; I met her on the tube yesterday morning; take the tube to the
Tower of London.**

Tuesday [ˈtjuːzdɪ] *zn*
dinsdag; **he came to see me last Tuesday;
I go to the library on Tuesdays** = dins-
dags ga ik (altijd) naar de bibliotheek;
**shall we meet next Tuesday? today is
Tuesday, October 28th.**
Let op: **Tuesday** *wordt altijd met een
hoofdletter geschreven*

tune [tjuːn] *zn*
melodie, wijs(je); **he was whistling a tune**

which he'd heard on TV; play a tune on the piano.

turn [tɜːn] **1.** *zn*
(*a*) draai, slag; he gave the screw two turns.
(*b*) draai, wending; the car made a sudden turn to the right; take the next turn to the left = afslag; the car did a U-turn = de auto keerde.
(*c*) beurt; wait for your turn to see the doctor; it's your turn to play now; let me go first—it's my turn, not yours; don't go out of turn = ga niet voor je beurt; they took it in turns to carry the box/ they took turns to carry the box = ze droegen de doos om de beurt/om beurten.

2. *ww*
(*a*) (om)draaien; omslaan; the wheels are turning slowly; turn the key to the left to open the door; the hands of the clock turned slowly to ten o'clock; the boat turned upside down.
(*b*) afslaan; (*van hoek*) omslaan; turn right at the next traffic lights; he turned the corner; the road turns to the left; the tide has turned = het tij is gekeerd.
(*c*) zich (om)draaien; he turned to look at the camera.
(*d*) veranderen; worden; the leaves turn brown in the autumn; his hair's turned grey; we are turning this field into a football ground.
(*e*) (*van tijd*) overschrijden; it's turned eight, and he still hasn't come home= het is over/na achten etc.; he's turned fifty = hij is boven de vijftig.

turns—turning—turned—has turned

turn away, *ww*
(*a*) wegsturen; the cinema is full, so we have to turn people away.
(*b*) zich afwenden; she turned away because she didn't want to be photographed.

turn back, *ww*
omkeren; the weather was so bad that we had to turn back and go home.

turn down, *ww*
(*a*) weigeren, afwijzen; he was offered a job, but he turned it down; she turned

down a job/turned a job down in the library.
(*b*) lager zetten; turn down the radio— it's too loud; turn down the gas/turn the gas down—it's too hot.

turn in, *ww*
naar bed gaan; it's time to turn in.

turning, *zn*
afslag, zijstraat; take the next turning to the left.

turn off, *ww*
(*a*) afzetten; uitdraaien/uitdoen; don't forget to turn the TV off; turn off the lights/turn the lights off—I'm going to show my film.
(*b*) afslaan; he turned off the High Street into a car park; turn off the main road at the next crossroads.

turn on, *ww*
aandraaien/aandoen; turn the lights on/ turn on the lights—it's getting dark; can you turn on the TV/turn the TV on—it's time for the news.

turn out, *ww*
(*a*) eruit zetten; they were turned out of their house.
(*b*) produceren/afleveren; the factory turns out 2,000 cars a week.
(*c*) afdraaien/uitdraaien/uitdoen; turn out the lights/turn the lights out—I'm going to show a film.
(*d*) blijken; (goed/slecht) aflopen; it turned out that he knew my sister; everything turned out all right.
(*e*) opdagen; the whole school turned out to see the race.

turn over, *ww*
(*a*) omslaan, kantelen; the lorry turned over; the boat turned over.
(*b*) omslaan; turn over the page/turn the page over; you turned over two pages together.

turn round, *ww*
(zich) omkeren/omdraaien; he turned round to look at the camera; she turned round to see who was following her.

turn up, *ww*
(*a*) verschijnen, opdagen; half the people didn't turn up until nine o'clock; the little boy finally turned up in Edinburgh; my pen turned up in my coat pocket.
(*b*) luider zetten; open draaien; can you

turn up the radio/turn the radio up—I can't hear it; turn up the gas/turn the gas up, the kettle hasn't boiled yet.
Let op: **turn the radio down** *of* **turn down the radio; turn the light off** *of* **turn off the light,** *etc., maar alleen* **turn it down, turn it off,** *etc.*

TV ['ti:'vi:] *zn*
(*afkorting voor* **television**) televisie; do you watch TV every night? is there any sport on TV tonight? he's bought a colour TV; our TV set has broken down; some TV programmes make me go to sleep.

twelve [twelv] twaalf
he's twelve (years old); come for a cup of coffee at twelve o'clock; there are twelve months in a year.
Let op: **twelve o'clock** *wordt ook* **midday** *of* **midnight** *genoemd*

twelfth [twelfθ] **12th,** *bn & zn*
twaalfde
he came twelfth in the race; today is the twelfth of November/November the twelfth (November 12th); it's her twelfth birthday next week.

twenty ['twentı] twintig
she's twenty (years old); he's in his twenties = in de twintig.
Let op: **twenty-one** (21), **twenty-two** (22), *etc., maar* **twenty-first** (21st), **twenty-second** (22nd), *etc.*

twentieth, 20th, *bn & zn*
twintigste; she was twentieth in her class; today is the twentieth of December/December the twentieth (December 20th); it's her twentieth birthday on Tuesday.

twice [twaıs] *bw*
twee keer; I've already seen that film

twice; twice two is four; he's twice as old as I am; she earns twice as much money as her sister; this book is twice as big as that one/is twice the size of that one.

twist [twıst] *ww*
(*a*) draaien; (zich) kronkelen; vlechten; the road twisted round the mountain; he twisted the metal bar into the shape of an S; threads are twisted together to make string.
(*b*) verwringen/verdraaien; the fire twisted the metal roof; he twisted his ankle = hij heeft zijn enkel verstuikt.
twists—twisting—twisted—has twisted

two [tu:] twee
there are only two chocolates left in the box; his son's two (years old); they didn't come home until two (o'clock).
one or two = een paar, enkele; there were only one or two people in the shop.
Let op: **two** (2), *maar* **second** (2nd)

tying ['taıŋ] *zie* **tie**

type [taıp] **1.** *zn*
type, soort; you can have two types of cloth for your chairs; this is a new type of apple.
2. *ww*
tikken, typen; he's learning to type; I can only type with two fingers; she's typing all day long.
types—typing—typed—has typed

typewriter, *zn*
schrijfmachine; she has a new electric typewriter; a typewriter's no use to me—I can't type.
typist, *zn*
typist(e).

tyre ['taıə] *zn* (*Amer.* **tire**)
band; my bike's got a flat tyre.

Uu

ugly [ˈʌgli] *bn*
lelijk; she was wearing an ugly hat; they live in an ugly little house.
ugly—uglier—ugliest

UK [juːˈkeɪ] *zie* **unite**

umbrella [ʌmˈbrelə] *zn*
paraplu; can I come under your umbrella? he has an umbrella with red, white and blue stripes; the wind tore my umbrella.

unable [ʌnˈeɪbl] *bn*
niet in staat; onbekwaam; he was unable to come to the meeting; after her accident, she was unable to walk.

uncle [ˈʌŋkl] *zn*
oom; look, here's Uncle John.

under [ˈʌndə] *vz*
(a) onder; he hid under the table; my pencil's rolled under the piano; can you swim under water?
(b) beneden; lager/minder dan; she's under thirty = ze is onder de dertig; the car was sold for under £100; he ran the race in under six minutes.
Let op: **under** *wordt vaak met werkwoorden gebruikt:* **to look under; to go under,** *etc.*

underground 1. *bw & bn*
ondergronds; onder de grond; the railway line goes underground for a short distance; he took an underground corridor to the next building.
2. *zn*
ondergrondse/metro; he goes to work by underground; she took the underground to go to the centre of the town.
underneath, *vz & bw*
onder; beneden; he wore a long green pullover underneath his coat; look and see if my pencil is underneath the piano.

understand [ʌndəˈstænd] *ww*
(a) begrijpen; verstaan; do you understand how this machine works? he doesn't understand English, so don't try to talk to him; I hardly speak any Chinese, but I made myself understood = ik heb me(zelf) verstaanbaar gemaakt.
(b) begrijpen; vernemen; I understood you were going to be late? we understand he's getting married next week.
understands—understanding—understood—has understood

undress [ʌnˈdres] *ww*
(zich) uitkleden; he undressed and got into bed; before you get undressed, can you see if the garage door is shut?
undresses—undressing—undressed—has undressed

unhappy [ʌnˈhæpɪ] *bn*
ongelukkig; bedroefd; she's unhappy because her cat's ill; he looked very unhappy when he came out of the headmaster's room.
unhappy—unhappier—unhappiest

unhappily, *bw*
ongelukkig; bedroefd; she stared unhappily out of the window.

uniform [ˈjuːnɪfɔːm] *zn*
uniform; the policemen were in uniform; was he wearing uniform? the children all have to wear school uniform.

unite [juːˈnaɪt] *ww*
verenigen; verbinden; the United States (of America) = de Verenigde Staten

(van Amerika); **the United Kingdom** =
het Verenigd Koninkrijk.

**unites—uniting—united—has
united**
Let op: **the United States of
America** *wordt meestal* **the US**
genoemd of **the USA; the United
Kingdom** *wordt meestal* **the UK**
genoemd

university [juːnɪˈvɜːsɪtɪ] *zn*
universiteit; **the university is on the
south side of the town; he's studying history at university; are you going to university when you leave school?**
meervoud **universities**
Let op: gebruik **the** *alleen als je het
over één bepaalde universiteit hebt*

unless [ʌnˈles] *vw*
tenzij; **unless you start at once, you'll be
late; don't telephone unless the message is
important; we'll have our picnic in the
field, unless it rains; don't come unless
you want to.**

unload [ʌnˈləʊd] *ww*
uitladen; *(van schip)* lossen; **the ship is
unloading her cargo in the dock; can you
help me unload the bricks from the lorry?**
**unloads—unloading—unloaded—
has unloaded**

unlucky [ʌnˈlʌkɪ] *bn*
ongelukkig; **Friday 13th is my unlucky
day; it's unlucky to walk under a ladder**
= onder een ladder doorlopen brengt
ongeluk.
unlucky—unluckier—unluckiest

unpleasant [ʌnˈplezənt] *bn*
onprettig/onplezierig; naar; onaardig;
**what an unpleasant smell! our teacher
was unpleasant when I told him I couldn't
go to school.**

untidy [ʌnˈtaɪdɪ] *bn*
rommelig; slordig; **your room is so
untidy that you can't find anything in
it.**

until [ʌnˈtɪl] *vz*
tot(dat); **I won't be home until after
eleven o'clock** = pas na elven; **until yesterday, I was very well.**

up [ʌp] *bw & vz*
(*a*) op; (naar) boven; **he climbed up the
stairs; she was going up a ladder; lift your
hands up; why is the cat up there on the
cupboard?**
(*b*) omhoog; **the temperature has gone
up; prices seem to go up every day.**
(*c*) ... langs/ ... op; **go up the street to
the traffic lights and then turn left.**
(*d*) op; wakker; **he's still up—he should
be in bed; she stayed up all night.**
(*e*) naar (het noorden); **I'll be going up
to Scotland next week (from London).**
(*f*) **what's up?** = wat is er aan de hand?
**what's up with the car?—it's making a
strange noise.**
(*g*) **your time's up** = je tijd is om.
Let op: **up** *wordt vaak na werkwoorden gebruikt:* **to keep up; to
look up; to turn up,** *etc.*

up to, *vz*
(*a*) tot (aan); **the bus will hold up to sixty
passengers.**
(*b*) **what are you up to?** = wat voer je
uit/in je schild?
up to date, *bn & bw*
modern; op de hoogte; 'up to date'; **is
this railway timetable up to date? I keep
myself up to date by reading the newspaper every day.**

upper [ˈʌpə] *bn*
boven(ste); hoogste; **the upper part of
the house was destroyed by fire; the
upper forms in the school are taking their
exams this year.**

upright [ˈʌpraɪt] *bn & bw*
recht(op); (recht) overeind; **hold the
stick upright; he kept himself upright by
holding on to the wall.**

upside down [ˈʌpsaɪdˈdaʊn] *bw*
ondersteboven; op z'n kop; **don't hold
the box upside down—everything will fall
out; the car ran off the road and ended
up upside down in a field; the boys were
hanging upside down from a tree; he's not
reading that book—he's holding it upside
down.**

upstairs [ʌpˈsteəz] *bw & zn*
(naar) boven; bovenverdieping; **my**

father's upstairs—I'll ask him to come down; can you go upstairs and get my coat from the bedroom? the upstairs of the house is smaller than the downstairs.

upwards *bw*
omhoog, naar boven; **the path slopes upwards.**

urgent ['ɜːdʒənt] *bn*
urgent; dringend; **he had an urgent message to go to the hospital.**

us [ʌs] *vnw*
ons; **he gave us £1 to buy ourselves some ice cream; who is it?—it's us!** = wij zijn het!; **our class is very happy—the teacher has given us a holiday.**

US [juː'es], **USA** [juːes'eɪ] *zie* **unite**

use¹ [juːs] *zn*
(*a*) gebruik; **can you find a use for this piece of wood?** = heb jij iets aan dit stuk hout? **the cooker has been in daily use for ten years; our flat has no kitchen, but we have the use of the kitchen in the flat downstairs; to make use of something** = gebruiken; **you should make more use of your dictionary** = je moet je woordenboek vaker gebruiken.
(*b*) zin; nut; **what's the use of telling her what to do, when she never does what you want? it's no use sitting here and saying the car needs washing, let's go out and wash it.**

use² [juːz] *ww*
(*a*) gebruiken; **someone's used my knife to open a tin of fruit; he used the money to buy a car; did you use a sewing machine to make your dress? can I use these scissors for cutting flowers? he was using the electric saw when it slipped.**
(*b*) verbruiken; **this car uses a lot of petrol; we're using too much gas and electricity.**
uses—using—used [juːzd]—**has used**

used [juːzd] *bn*
gebruikt; tweedehands; **a used car; this**

typewriter's worth a lot of money—it's hardly used.

used to ['juːsttʊ]
(*a*) to be used to something/to doing something = gewend (zijn) (om te/aan); **he's used to getting up early; she's used to hard work; we're not used to eating so much.**
(*b*) to get used to something/to doing something = wennen (aan); **you'll soon get used to your new job; he never got used to getting up early.**
(*c*) placht(en); **there used to be a baker's shop in the village; when I was a boy, we used to go to the seaside every year for our holidays; she used to teach history at our school; didn't he use to go to work on his bike?**
Let op: de ontkennende en vragende vorm zijn als volgt: **he used to go by bike; he didn't use to go by bike/ he used not to go by bike; didn't he use to go by bike?**

useful, *bn*
nuttig; waardevol; **I find this knife very useful in the garden; he's a very useful man in the office.**

useless, *bn*
waardeloos; nutteloos; **this knife is useless—it isn't sharp; she's useless at numbers** = ze is slecht in rekenen.

use up, *ww*
opmaken; **we've used up all our sugar; he's used up all my cigarettes.**
Let op: **we've used all the sugar up** *of* **we've used up all the sugar** *maar alleen* **we've used it up**

usual ['juːʒʊəl] *bn*
gebruikelijk; normaal; gewoonlijk; **I'll take my usual train this morning; the postman was late, as usual; let's meet at the usual time; as usual, it rained on my birthday.**

usually, *bw*
gewoonlijk; meestal; **he usually gets to work at 9 o'clock; she usually has an apple for lunch.**

U-turn, *zie* **turn**

Vv

vacation [vəˈkeɪʃn] *zn*
(*Amerikaans voor* **holiday**) vakantie.

vain [veɪn] *bn*
in vain = tevergeefs; **we waited in vain for a bus; they tried in vain to start the car.**

valley [ˈvælɪ] *zn*
vallei; dal; **the valley of the Thames/the Thames valley; the town is in the bottom of the valley.**

value [ˈvæljuː] *zn*
waarde; **what's the value of this house? this is very good value** = dit is het geld dubbel en dwars waard.
valuable, *bn*
waardevol; kostbaar; **the burglar stole some valuable books.**

van [væn] *zn*
bestelwagen; **here comes the bread van; the furniture shop delivered the chairs by van; guard's van** = conducteurswagen.

various [ˈveərɪəs] *bn*
verscheiden; verschillend; **we've met on various occasions; there are various ways of getting to London from here; he has written various books on birds.**

vegetable [ˈvedʒtəbl] *zn*
groente; **we have potatoes, cabbages and other sorts of vegetables in the garden; what vegetables do you want with your meat?—peas and carrots, please; I'll have a bowl of vegetable soup.**

vehicle [ˈvɪəkl] *zn*
voertuig; **motor vehicles are not allowed on this path; goods vehicles can park here for 30 minutes.**

verb [vɜːb] *zn*
werkwoord; **in the sentence 'he kicked the ball', the word 'kicked' is a verb.**

vertical [ˈvɜːtɪkl] *bn*
verticaal; loodrecht; **a vertical line.**

very [ˈverɪ] **1.** *bw*
heel/erg/zeer; **it's very hot in here—let's open the window; she's very tall; this meat isn't very good.**
2. *bn*
juist; precies; **he's the very man you want; it happens at the very beginning of the film** = helemaal in het begin.
very many, *bn*
erg/heel veel; **there weren't very many people at the party; we went swimming very many times.**
Let op: **very many** *wordt bij telbare zelfstandige naamwoorden gebruikt:* **very many cars**
very much 1. *bw*
heel/erg veel; **I like ice cream very much; thank you very much for your present; it's very much colder today; she's very much better.**
2. *bn*
heel/erg veel; **he doesn't do very much work; she hasn't got very much money.**
Let op: **very much** *wordt bij niet-telbare zelfstandige naamwoorden gebruikt:* **very much money**

victory [ˈvɪktrɪ] *zn*
overwinning; **the victory of the Scottish team over the English.**
meervoud **victories**

view [vjuː] *zn*
(*a*) uitzicht; blik; **from my window there's a wonderful view over London; you get a good view of the sea from the top of the hill; this photograph is a side view of our house** = zijaanzicht.
(*b*) mening; opvatting; **in my view, the government ought to do something to help poor people; I try to see the headmaster's point of view** = standpunt.

(c) in view of = met het oog op/gezien; vanwege; in view of the weather, we had the party indoors.

village ['vɪlɪdʒ] zn
dorp; we live in a little mountain village; go to the village baker's to get some bread; there aren't many children in the village school.

violence ['vaɪələns] zn
geweld; the game was spoilt by violence.
violent, bn
hevig; geweldig; gewelddadig; there was a violent storm during the night; the game of football was very violent— several players were hurt.

visit ['vɪzɪt] 1. zn
bezoek; visite; he's on a visit to China; let's pay a visit to your mother; they had a visit from the doctor.
2. ww
bezoeken/opzoeken; I must visit my brother in hospital; we are going to visit the factory; he's visiting friends in France.
visits—visiting—visited—has visited

visitor, zn
bezoeker; gast; logé; bezoek; how many

visitors are staying in the hotel this weekend? we had a visitor last night— old Uncle Charles.

voice [vɔɪs] zn
stem; I didn't recognize your voice over the phone; he's got a cold and has lost his voice = hij is zijn stem kwijt; she spoke for a few minutes in a low voice = heel zachtjes.

vote [vəʊt] 1. zn
stem; stemming; there were 10 votes for Mr Smith and only 2 for Mr Jones, so Mr Smith was elected; my vote goes to Mr Smith's plan; if we can't agree, let's have/take a vote.
2. ww
stemmen; we all voted for Mr Smith; only people over 18 can vote in the election; I vote that we have the picnic in the woods = ik stel voor om in het bos te picknicken.
votes—voting—voted—has voted
voter, zn
kiezer.

voyage ['vɔɪɪdʒ] zn
(zee)reis; he went on a voyage round the world.

Ww

wage [weɪdʒ] zn
loon; he gets a good wage at the factory; wages have gone up a lot this year; I'm going to collect my wages.
Let op: meestal wordt het meervoud gebruikt

wagon ['wægn] zn
wagon; a goods wagon; a coal wagon.

waist [weɪst] zn
middel/taille; he measures 85 centimetres round the waist.

wait [weɪt] ww
wachten; wait here while I fetch a policeman; he waited for the bus for half an hour; he gets annoyed if you keep him waiting = als je hem laat wachten; wait a minute, I've got a stone in my shoe; sorry to have kept you waiting!
waits—waiting—waited—has waited

waiter, zn
kelner; the waiter brought us the soup;

how much shall we give the waiter as a tip? *zie ook* **waitress.**

waiting room, *zn*
wachtkamer; go into the waiting room—the doctor will see you in ten minutes.

waitress, *zn*
kelnerin/serveerster; the waitress brought us the soup; shall we give the waitress a tip? *zie ook* **waiter.**
meervoud **waitresses**

wake [weɪk] **1.** *zn*
zog/kielwater; the little boat rocked in the wake of the ferry.
2. *ww*
wekken; wakker maken/worden; the telephone woke me/I was woken by the telephone; can't you wake her?—no, she's fast asleep.
wakes—waking—woke [wəʊk]—**has woken**

wake up, *ww*
wekken; wakker maken/worden; he woke up in the middle of the night; he was woken up by the sound of the telephone; wake up! it's past nine o'clock.
Let op: **I woke up my mother up** *of* **I woke up my mother** *maar alleen* **I woke her up**

Wales [weɪlz] *zn*
Wales; we're going to Wales for our holiday; he's gone to live in Wales.
Welsh [welʃ] **1.** *bn*
in/uit/van Wales; the Welsh mountains are very beautiful.
2. *zn*
(*a*) the Welsh = de bewoners van Wales; the Welsh are very good singers.
(*b*) de taal van Wales; he speaks Welsh; Welsh words are very difficult to pronounce.

walk [wɔːk] **1.** *zn*
wandeling; we all went for a walk in the park; the post office is only five minutes' walk from here = vijf minuten lopen hiervandaan; he's taking the dog for a walk; does anyone want to come for a walk?
2. *ww*
lopen; I'll walk to the bus stop with you; she walked across the room; he was walking along the street; can you walk

to school, or do you have to take the bus? they all walked up the hill.
walks—walking—walked—has walked

walk about, *ww*
rondlopen; they spent hours walking about the town, looking for a restaurant.
walk off with, *ww*
ervandoor gaan (met); the burglar walked off with all our jewellery; she walked off with the prize = ze ging met de prijs strijken.

wall [wɔːl] *zn*
muur; he's building a wall all round his garden; we have a lot of photographs on the walls of the dining room; there's a clock on the wall over his desk; the car went into the wall; can you climb over the garden wall?

wallet [ˈwɒlɪt] *zn*
portefeuille; someone's stolen my wallet from my back pocket.

want [wɒnt] *ww*
(*a*) willen, wensen; he wants a bicycle for his birthday; they want to go to Africa on holiday; she wants to be an air hostess; he wants me to go to see him.
(*b*) nodig hebben, moeten (hebben); we haven't enough space for all the furniture—we want a bigger house; your hair wants cutting = je haar moet (nodig) geknipt worden; the house wants painting.
(*c*) zoeken/op zoek zijn; he's wanted by the police.
wants—wanting—wanted—has wanted

war [wɔː] *zn*
oorlog; in 1814 Britain was at war with France/Britain and France were at war; millions of people were killed in the Second World War.
warship, *zn*
oorlogsschip; slagschip.

wardrobe [ˈwɔːdrəʊb] *zn*
hangkast/klerenkast; put your coat in the wardrobe; the wardrobe's full of her old dresses.

warm [wɔ:m] **1.** *bn*
warm; **it's cold outside in the snow, but it's nice and warm in the house; they tried to keep warm by jumping up and down** = ze probeerden warm te blijven etc.; **are you warm enough, or do you want another blanket?** = hebt u het warm genoeg?
warm—warmer—warmest

2. *ww*
(ver)warmen; warm worden/maken; **warm yourself by the fire; he was warming his hands over the fire; sit down while I warm some soup.**
warms—warming—warmed—has warmed

warm up, *ww*
opwarmen; **this soup will warm you up; I'll warm up some milk to make cocoa.**

warn [wɔ:n] *ww*
waarschuwen; **the children were warned not to go too near the fire; I warned you about that electric wire; the police warned us against playing near the railway line.**
warns—warning—warned—has warned

warning, *zn*
waarschuwing; **the police gave a warning about a dangerous criminal; did you read the warning notice? there's a warning on the bottle of medicine; every packet of cigarettes has a health warning printed on it.**
without warning = onverwachts; **without warning the car ran off the road into a wall.**

was [wɒz] *zie* **be**

wash [wɒʃ] **1.** *zn*
(het) wassen; **he went to the bathroom to have a wash** = om zich te wassen; **I need a wash—where's the bathroom?**

2. *ww*
wassen; **wash your hands before dinner! we must wash the car before we go on holiday; they were washing the windows when it started to rain; your hair needs washing; can you wash this raincoat? —no, you have to take it to the cleaner's.**
washes—washing—washed—has washed

wash down, *ww*
afwassen/afspoelen; **let's wash down the van; the sailors were washing down the deck of the ship.**

washing, *zn*
was; **look at that pile of washing; put the washing in the washing machine; the washing's drying in the wind.**
geen meervoud

washing machine, *zn*
wasmachine.

washing up, *zn*
afwas; **can you help me do the washing up? there was so much washing up after the party, that it took us hours to do it.**

wash off, *ww*
afspoelen; **I'll wash the mud off my boots.**

wash up, *ww*
afwassen; **let's wash up these plates; Daddy's washing up, while I'm watching the TV.**
Let op: **wash the plates up** *of* **wash up the plates** *maar alleen* **wash them up**

wasn't ['wɒznt] *zie* **be**

waste [weɪst] **1.** *zn*
(*a*) afval; **put all the waste in the dustbin.**
(*b*) verkwisting; verspilling; **it's a waste of time trying to telephone—she's not in** = tijdverspilling; **that car's a waste of money—it keeps going wrong** = geldverspilling.
2. *bn*
overtollig; waardeloos; **throw all your waste paper into the dustbin.**
3. *ww*
(*a*) verspillen; **I've wasted three sheets of paper; they waste a lot of food.**
(*b*) verkwisten; verdoen; verknoeien; **she wasted several hours waiting for him to come to fetch her; he wastes his pocket money on sweets.**
wastes—wasting—wasted—has wasted

wasteful, *bn*
verkwistend; **it's wasteful of electricity to leave the lights on all day** = het is elektriciteit verspillen als je de lampen de hele dag aan laat.

watch [wɒtʃ] **1.** *zn*

(*a*) horloge; **he looked at his watch; what time is it by your watch?**

(*b*) wacht; **the police are on the watch for burglars** = is op de uitkijk naar; **she was keeping a watch on the saucepan of milk to make sure it didn't boil over** = ze lette goed op dat de melk niet overkookte.

meervoud **watches;** *geen meervoud voor* (b)

2. *ww*

(*a*) kijken; **did you watch TV last night? I watched a programme on sport; we'll watch him play football; she was watching the children playing.**

(*b*) in de gaten/in het oog houden, letten op; **watch the saucepan—I don't want the milk to boil over; will you watch the baby while I go shopping?**

watches—watching—watched— has watched

watch out, *ww*

oppassen; uitkijken; **watch out! the paint is still wet; you have to watch out for ice on the roads in winter.**

water ['wɔːtə] **1.** *zn*

water; **can I have a glass of water, please? the hotel has hot and cold water in each bedroom; he dived and swam across the pool under water; boil the potatoes in a pan of water.**

geen meervoud; **some water; a drop of water**

2. *ww*

water geven; begieten/besproeien; **the weather's very dry—we'll have to water the garden; he was watering the flowers.**

waters—watering—watered— has watered

waterfall, *zn*

waterval; **let's have our picnic by the waterfall; which is the biggest waterfall in the world—is it Niagara?**

waterproof, *bn*

waterdicht; waterproef; **is your raincoat really waterproof? if your watch is waterproof you can wear it when you go swimming.**

wave [weɪv] **1.** *zn*

golf; **can you hear the noise of the waves on the beach? the ship was sunk by the waves.**

2. *ww*

zwaaien (met); door een handbeweging te kennen geven; wapperen; **the children were waving flags; she waved her handkerchief as the train left; wave to your mother—she's on the other side of the street; I waved to the waiter and asked him to bring the bill; the flags were waving in the wind.**

waves—waving—waved—has waved

way [weɪ] *zn*

(*a*) weg; kant; **my friend lives across the way** = aan de overkant.

(*b*) weg; **can you tell me the way to the post office? the policeman showed us the way to the station; he made his way through the crowd** = hij baande zich een weg door de menigte; **we lost our way and had to ask someone; I'm just on my way to school.**

(*c*) richting; **this is a one-way street; which way is the wind blowing?** = uit welke richting waait het? **come this way, please.**

(*d*) manier/wijze (van doen); **grandmother showed me the way to make bread; she spoke in a friendly way; is there another way of doing it? he always does it that way; I wish I knew a way of making money quickly.**

(*e*) weg; afstand; stuk; **the post office is a long way from here; we've a long way to go before we've finished our work; I'll walk part of the way home with you.**

(*f*) weg; **get out of the way—there's a car coming; keep out of father's way— he thinks you broke the window; he's always in the way.**

by the way = tussen twee haakjes; **by the way, did you see the TV programme on cars yesterday?**

way in, *zn*

ingang; **is this the way in? the way in is through the big blue door.**

way out, *zn*

uitgang; **is this the way out? we couldn't find the way out in the dark.**

way up, *zn*
bovenkant; **keep the box the right way up** = met de goede kant boven; **you're holding the book the wrong way up** = ondersteboven.

we [wi:] *vnw*
wij/we; **the policeman said we could go across the road; we came to London by train; our class went to the cinema—we all enjoyed ourselves very much.**
Let op: **we** *wordt* **us** *als lijdend voorwerp:* **we gave it to him/he gave it to us:** *wanneer* **we** *het werkwoord* **be** *volgt, wordt het meestal* **us:** **who is it?—it's us!**

weak [wi:k] *bn*
(*a*) zwak; slap; **after his illness he was very weak; this tea is very weak—you've put too much water in it.**
(*b*) zwak; **he's very weak at maths; maths in his weakest subject.**
weak—weaker—weakest

wealth [welθ] *zn*
rijkdom; **he's famous for his wealth.**
wealthy, *bn*
rijk; **he's a very wealthy man.**
wealthy—wealthier—wealthiest

weapon ['wepn] *zn*
wapen; **the soldiers were carrying guns and other weapons; he used a broken bottle as a weapon.**

wear [weə] *ww*
(*a*) dragen; **I'll wear my brown coat today; the police are looking for a man wearing a blue raincoat; everyone was wearing uniform; she's wearing my watch.**
(*b*) (ver)slijten; **the car tyres are worn; I've worn a hole in my trousers.**
wears—wearing—wore [wɔ:]**—has worn**

wear off, *ww*
(af)slijten; geleidelijk verdwijnen; **the writing on the wall has worn off; the effect of the cough medicine has worn off.**
wear out, *ww*
(*a*) verslijten, afdragen; **he wore out three pairs of shoes; the engine has worn out** = is versleten.

(*b*) **worn out** = afgemat; uitgeput; **after that game of football I am quite worn out; she came home worn out after a day at the office.**

weather ['weðə] *zn*
weer; **what's the weather like today? the TV said the weather was going to be bad; the weather's always cold in the mountains; look at the rain—is this your normal summer weather? if the weather's fine, perhaps we'll have a picnic.**
geen meervoud

web [web] *zn*
(spinne)web.

wedding ['wedɪŋ] *zn*
bruiloft; huwelijk; **I'm going to my brother's wedding; the wedding's next week; was it fine for the wedding?**

Wednesday ['wenzdɪ] *zn*
woensdag; **I saw her last Wednesday; we've got a day off next Wednesday; all the shops are shut on Wednesdays; can you come to tea on Wednesday afternoon?**
Let op: **Wednesday** *wordt altijd met een hoofdletter geschreven*

week [wi:k] *zn*
week; **there are 52 weeks in the year; we have two weeks' holiday at Christmas; my aunt's coming to stay with us next week; what day of the week is it today? we go to the cinema once a week; a week from now I'll be on holiday** = over een week.
weekday, *zn*
weekdag/werkdag; **the office is open on weekdays.**
weekend, *zn*
weekend/weekeinde; **what are you doing at the weekend? we're going away for the weekend; come to spend the weekend with me; I went to London last weekend; we usually go to the country at weekends.**
weekly, *bn & bw*
week-/wekelijks; **we have a weekly paper which tells us all the local information; we pay the milkman weekly.**

weigh [weɪ] *ww*
wegen; **can you weigh these potatoes for me? this piece of fish weighs 500 grams;**

how much do you weigh? I weigh 120
pounds/I weigh 54 kilos.
**weighs—weighing—weighed—
has weighed**
weight [weɪt] *zn*
(*a*) gewicht; what's the weight of this bag
of potatoes? what's your weight? I'm
trying to lose weight = ik probeer af te
vallen; he's put on a lot of weight = hij
is behoorlijk aangekomen.
(*b*) gewicht; druk; if you lift heavy
weights, you may hurt your back; put a
weight on the pile of papers to stop them
blowing away.

welcome ['welkəm] **1.** *zn*
welkom; (vriendelijke) ontvangst; they
gave us a warm welcome = ze hebben
ons een hartelijke ontvangst bereid.
2. *ww*
(*a*) welkom heten; begroeten; verwelkomen; they welcomed us to the office;
we were welcomed by the dogs when we
got home.
(*b*) verwelkomen; op prijs stellen; I
welcome the news that he has passed his
exams; I would welcome any advice on
how to make bread, because I've never
made it before.
**welcomes—welcoming—
welcomed—has welcomed**

well [wel] **1.** *zn*
bron; put; they pulled the water up from
a well; there are many oil wells in the
North Sea.
2. *bw*
(*a*) goed; he can speak Russian quite
well; she did her homework very well; the
shop's small, but it's doing well; does the
manager work well?
(*b*) een heel eind, ver; it's well after 9
o'clock; it's well worth trying to get a
ticket = zeer de moeite waard; he's well
over sixty = ver over de zestig.
as well = ook; I'm bringing my cat,
but can I bring the dogs as well?; you
can't have a piece of cake and ice cream
as well.
as well as = niet alleen . . . maar ook;
zowel . . . als; he's deaf as well as blind;
the shop sells sweets as well as newspapers.

3. *bn*
gezond; in orde; you're looking well! he's
quite well after his flu; he's not very well,
and has had to stay in bed.
4. *tw*
wel! goed! zo! nee maar! well, as I was
saying; well, the washing up's finished,
so what shall we do now?; well, well!
here's old Mr Smith!

Welsh [welʃ] *zie* **Wales**

went [went] *zie* **go**

were [wɜː], **weren't** [wɜːnt] *zie* **be**

west [west] **1.** *zn*
westen; the sun rises in the east and sets
in the west; the town is to the west of the
river.
2. *bn*
west-, westelijk; the west coast of the
United States; he lives in the west end of
the town.
3. *bw*
westwaarts, naar/in het westen; the
ship's sailing west; if you go west for ten
kilometres, you'll come to a little village.
western ['westən] **1.** *bn*
west-; westelijk; Great Britain is in
Western Europe; they live in the western
part of Canada.
2. *zn*
wild-westfilm; I like watching old west-
erns on TV.

wet [wet] *bn*
(*a*) nat; I didn't have an umbrella, so I
got wet waiting for the bus in the rain;
I'm wet through = doornat; the carpet's
all wet where you spilt your tea.
(*b*) regenachtig; February is the wettest
month of the year.
(*c*) nat; vochtig; don't sit there—the
paint on the chair is still wet.
wet—wetter—wettest

what [wɒt] *bn & vnw*
(*a*) wat; I saw what was in the box; did
you see what he gave me for my birthday?
what he likes most is just sitting in the
sun.
(*b*) hoe; wat (voor een) what time is it?
what's the time? what's his name? what

did you say? what's the German for
'table'? what's the matter with Mrs
Smith? what happened to you? what kind
of car do you drive?
(c) wat; **what a lot of potatoes you've
eaten! what a nasty man! what a beautiful
house! what lovely weather!**
Let op: na het vraagwoord what *komt
het werkwoord voor het onderwerp:*
what's the time? *maar* **they don't
know what the time is**

what about = hoe; wat, **what about
stopping here for a picnic?** = wat
zouden jullie ervan zeggen om etc.;
what about something to drink? = hoe
denken jullie over een drankje? **we've
sent cards to everyone we know—what
about old Mrs Smith?** = wat doen we
met de oude mevrouw Smit?

whatever, *bn & vnw*
(a) (*sterke vorm van* **what**) wat (ook)
maar; **you can eat whatever you like; he
does whatever he feels like doing; I'll buy
it whatever the price is** = wat het ook
moge kosten.
(b) (*sterke vorm van* **what** *in vragen*)
wat ... toch? **whatever made you do
that?**

what for
(a) waarom, waarvoor; **what are you
painting the door for? what's he sitting
on the floor for? we're going out—what
for? he's phoning the police—what for?**
(b) **what's that handle for?** = waarvoor?
waartoe dient ...? **what's this little
button for?**

wheel [wi:l] 1. *zn*
(a) wiel; **a bicycle has two wheels—a
front wheel and a back wheel; I had to
change a wheel because I had a flat tyre.**
(b) wiel; rad; **in English cars, the steering
wheel is on the right hand side.**
2. *ww*
een rijwiel duwen; **he wheeled his bike
into the house; she was wheeling her
motorbike down the steps.**
**wheels—wheeling—wheeled—
has wheeled**

wheeled, *bn*
op/met wielen; **a three-wheeled vehicle**
= driewielig voertuig.

when [wen] **1.** *bw*
wanneer; **when does the last train leave?
when did you see the film? when are we
going to have our dinner? since when has
he been in your class?**
Let op: na het vraagwoord **when** *volgt
het werkwoord voor het onderwerp:*
when does the film start? *maar* **he
doesn't know when the film
starts; when is he coming?** *maar*
**they can't tell me when he is
coming**
2. *vw*
(a) toen; als/wanneer; **when I was young,
we were living in London; when you leave
the house, don't forget to lock the door;
do you remember when we all went to
the seaside in your old car? tell me when
you're feeling hungry; we were all singing
when he came in.**
(b) toen; als/wanneer; nadat; **when we
had finished, we sat down; switch off the
TV when the news has finished; when
you've had your breakfast, please do the
washing up.**

whenever, *bw*
wanneer ... (ook) maar; telkens wanneer; **come whenever you like; I go to see
her whenever I can.**

where [weə] *bw*
(a) waar; **where are my glasses? where's
the restaurant? where did you put the
book? where are you going for your
holiday? do you know where the
manager is?**
(b) waar; **stay where you are; he still lives
in the town where he was born; here's
where he hides his money.**
Let op: na het vraagwoord **where**
*volgt het werkwoord voor het onder-
werp:* **where is the bottle?** *maar* **he
doesn't know where the bottle is**

wherever, *bw*
waar ... ook/maar; **wherever I go, I
meet interesting people; I'd like to find
her, wherever she may be.**

whether [ˈweðə] *vw*
of; **I don't know whether it's true; we hope
to go on a picnic, but it depends on
whether the weather's fine; do you know
whether the manager is in or not?**

whether you're tall or short—it doesn't matter.

which [wɪtʃ] *bn & vnw*
(*a*) (*vraagwoord*) welk(e); **which hat shall I wear? in which hand do you hold a pen? which boy is the one you saw?** = wie is het jongetje etc.; **which of you girls wants to help with the washing up?** = wie van jullie meisjes etc.
(*b*) (*niet voor personen*) die/dat, wat; **the house which is opposite the post office; here's the bread which we bought this morning**
Let op: bij een lijdend voorwerp kan which *weggelaten worden:* **here's the bread we bought this morning.**

while [waɪl] **1.** *zn*
(*a*) poos(je), tijd(je); **we had to wait a little while for the bus; he went away a little while ago; it's nice to go to the cinema once in a while** = nu en dan.
(*b*) **to be worth while** = de moeite waard; **it's worth while having two keys to the door, in case you lose one.**
2. *vw*
(*a*) terwijl; **while I was making the breakfast, everyone else was in bed; you can't do your homework while you're watching TV; while he was on holiday he caught flu; I'll lay the table while you have a bath.**
(*b*) terwijl (. . . daarentegen); **he earns £120 a week while I only earn £90.**

whisper ['wɪspə] **1.** *zn*
gefluister; **he spoke in a whisper.**
2. *ww*
fluisteren; **he was whispering to his wife during the whole film; she whispered to me that she felt ill.**
whispers—whispering— whispered—has whispered

whistle ['wɪsl] **1.** *zn*
(*a*) fluitje; **the whistle blew—it was the end of the game; the policeman blew his whistle.**
(*b*) gefluit; **he gave a loud whistle** = hij floot schel.

2. *ww*
fluiten; **he whistled and his dog came running up; she was whistling a tune.**
whistles—whistling—whistled— has whistled

white [waɪt] *bn & zn*
wit; **he was wearing a white shirt; a white car always looks dirty; the snow was so white that it made my eyes hurt; do you like your coffee black or white?** = met of zonder melk.
white—whiter—whitest

who [huː] *vnw*
(*a*) wie; **who's knocking at the door? who threw the stone through the window? who are all those people in uniform? who are you going home with? who was she talking to? who did you see at the party?**
(*b*) die/dat; **the friend who came to see us yesterday works for the post office; people who didn't get tickets early can't get into the cinema; there's the man who I saw at the pub; do you remember the man who helped to push the car?**
Let op: bij een lijdend voorwerp kan who *weggelaten worden:* **there's the man I saw at the pub**
Let op: wanneer who *als lijdend voorwerp gebruikt wordt, wordt het soms geschreven* whom [huːm]: **whom was she talking to? there's the man whom I saw in the pub**

whoever *vnw*
wie ook, al wie; **whoever finds the money can keep it.**

whole [həʊl] **1.** *bn*
heel; **he's eaten the whole cake; she stayed in bed a whole week; the whole country was covered with snow; the whole school caught flu.**
2. *zn*
(ge)heel; de/het hele; **he stayed in bed the whole of the morning; did you see the whole of the film?—no I only saw the first half of it.**

whom [huːm] *zie* who

whose [huːz] *vnw*
(*a*) van wie; wiens; wier; **whose car is that? whose are these books?**

(b) wiens; wier; **the people whose car was stolen; the man whose hat you sat on.**

why [waɪ] *bw*
waarom; **why did you phone me in the middle of the night? why isn't he at work today? why is the sky blue?** she told me **why she didn't go to the party; I asked him why the train was late; why go by train when the bus is cheaper? why not take the car?**
Let op: na het vraagwoord **why** *volgt het werkwoord voor het onderwerp:* **why isn't he at work today?** *maar* **they don't know why he wasn't at work**

wide [waɪd] *bn*
wijd; breed; **how wide is the River Thames? the cupboard's 3 metres wide; the main road is wider than our street.**
wide—wider—widest

width [wɪdθ] *zn*
wijdte; breedte; **what's the width of the river? the carpet is 3 metres in width.**

wife [waɪf] *zn*
(getrouwde) vrouw; echtgenote; **she's the manager's wife; I know Mr Jones but I've never met his wife.**
meervoud **wives** [waɪvz]

wild [waɪld] *bn*
(a) wild; **he was attacked by a wild animal; you can find all sorts of wild flowers in the mountains.**
(b) woest; woedend; **he was wild when he saw that someone had painted white spots on his car; the teacher was wild with me when I threw a book at him.**
(c) **wild about** = dol/gek op; **she's wild about horses.**
wild—wilder—wildest

will [wɪl] *hulpww*
(a) (*van toekomende tijd*) zal/zult/ zullen; **they will be here soon; will you be staying long in Italy? I won't be able to come to tea; if you ask him to sing, he'll say 'no'.**
(b) zal/zult/zullen altijd; **the cat will keep eating the dog's food.**

(c) (*in beleefde vragen*) willen; **will you all please sit down? will someone turn the light off?**
(d) (*toont bereidwilligheid*) zal/zullen, wil(len); **leave the washing up—I'll do it; the car won't start.**
Ontkennend: **will not** *meestal* **won't** [wəʊnt]
Verleden tijd: **would, would not** *meestal* **wouldn't**
Let op: **will** *wordt vaak afgekort tot* **'ll: he'll** = **he will**

willing, *bn*
bereid(willig); **is anyone willing to wash the car? I need two willing boys to move the piano.**

win [wɪn] **1.** *zn*
overwinning; **our team has only had two wins this year.**
2. *ww*
(a) winnen; **our team won their match yesterday; he won the race easily; which team's winning?**
(b) winnen; behalen; **he won first prize in the music competition; I won a holiday in Greece in a competition in the paper.**
wins—winning—won [wʌn]—**has won**

winner, *zn*
winnaar/winnares; **the winner of the 100 metres race; the winner of the music competition.**

wind¹ [wɪnd] *zn*
wind; **the wind blew the leaves off the trees; don't try to put your umbrella up in this wind; there's no wind at all—the smoke from the fire is going straight up; the flags were blowing in the wind; wind instruments** = blaasinstrumenten.

windy, *bn*
winderig; **a windy day; what windy weather!**
windy—windier—windiest

wind² [waɪnd] *ww*
(a) opwinden; **do you need to wind your watch? my watch needs winding every day.**
(b) slingeren; zich kronkelen; wikkelen;

oprollen; **he wound the string into a ball; she wound the towel round her head.**

winds—winding—wound [waʊnd]—has wound

wind up, *ww*
(*a*) oprollen; zich kronkelen; **he was winding the string up into a ball; the road winds up the mountain.**
(*b*) opwinden; **have you wound up the clock/wound the clock up?**
(*c*) eindigen; **he wound up his speech with a story about his father.**
Let op: **wind the clock up** *of* **wind up the clock** *maar alleen* **wind it up**

window ['wɪndəʊ] *zn*
raam; etalage; **look out of the window— you can see the garden; it's dangerous to lean out of the train window; he threw a stone through the car window; the burglar climbed in through the window; I saw a camera in the shop window.**

wine [waɪn] *zn*
wijn; **let's have a bottle of red wine; pour the wine into the glasses; three glasses of red wine, please.**
Let op: meestal enkelvoud: **some wine; a glass of wine;** *het meervoud* **wines** *betekent verschillende soorten wijn*

wing [wɪŋ] *zn*
vleugel; **the butterfly has white spots on its wings; the plane has V-shaped wings.**

winner ['wɪnə] *zie* **win**

winter ['wɪntə] *zn*
winter; **we can't play outside in the winter because it's too cold; last winter there wasn't any snow; if we go on holiday in winter we try to go to a hot country.**

wipe [waɪp] *ww*
afdrogen; (af)vegen; **I've washed the plates—can someone wipe them? you need a handkerchief to wipe your nose; please wipe the mud off your shoes before you come into the kitchen.**
wipes—wiping—wiped—has wiped

wipe out, *ww*
vernietigen; **the whole army was wiped out in the war.**

wire ['waɪə] *zn*
draad; **tie the basket to your bike with a piece of wire; electric wire** = elektrische leiding; **you have to be careful with this iron—the wire's loose.**

wise [waɪz] *bn*
wijs, verstandig; **it was wise of him to take his umbrella/he was wise to take his umbrella because it soon started to rain.**
wisely, *bw*
wijselijk; **he wisely took his umbrella with him.**

wish [wɪʃ] **1.** *zn*
wens; verlangen; **best wishes for a Happy New Year; please give my best wishes to your mother; he has no wish to go to prison** = hij wenst niet in de gevangenis terecht te komen.
meervoud **wishes**

2. *ww*
(*a*) wensen; verlangen; graag willen; **I wish it didn't always rain on my birthday; I wish I could live on an island; I wish you spent more time on your homework; I wish you wouldn't talk so loudly; I wish I hadn't eaten so much; the headmaster wishes to see you.**
(*b*) (toe)wensen; **he wished me good luck; he wished me a happy Christmas.**
wishes—wishing—wished—has wished

with [wɪθ] *vz*
(*a*) met; bij; **he came here with his sister; they're staying with us for the weekend; I like ice cream with my apple pie.**
(*b*) met; **he came in with his hat on; she's the girl with blue eyes; the house with the red door.**
(*c*) met; **he cut the bread with a knife; he has to walk with a stick; she was eating her pudding with a spoon; they were attacking the enemy with bombs; it's pouring with rain** = het giet van de regen.

(d) van/met de/het; my hands were blue with cold; he was sick with flu.

Letop: with wordt met veel bijvoeglijke naamwoorden en werkwoorden gebruikt: to agree with; to be pleased with, etc.

without [wɪ'ðaʊt] vz

(a) zonder; I'll come without my sister; they lived for days without any food; he was stuck in Italy without any money; how can you do your shopping without a car? he was arrested for travelling without a ticket.

(b) zonder te; she sang for two hours without stopping; they lived in the mountains for months without seeing anybody.

wives [waɪvz] zie **wife**

woke [wəʊk], **woken** [wəʊkn] zie **wake**

woman ['wʊmən] zn

vrouw; there were three women at the next table; an old woman asked me the way to the post office; a woman doctor came to see me = een vrouwelijke dokter; are there any women train drivers?

meervoud **women** ['wɪmɪn]

won [wʌn] zie **win**

wonder ['wʌndə] ww

zich afvragen; I wonder why he always wears a green tie? I wonder where the teacher's gone? he's wondering what to do next; we're wondering who'll be the next president.

wonders—wondering—wondered—has wondered

wonderful, bn

prachtig; heerlijk; we had a wonderful holiday in Sweden; the weather was wonderful; you've passed your driving test?—wonderful!

won't [wəʊnt] zie **will not**

wood [wʊd] zn

(a) bos; the road goes straight through the wood; let's look for flowers in that wood.

(b) hout; the chairs are made of wood;

he hit him on the head with a piece of wood; he put some more wood on the fire.

geen meervoud voor (b): some wood; a piece of wood

wooden, bn

houten; a wooden chair; she stirred the soup with a wooden spoon.

wool [wʊl] zn

(a) wol; in the summer the wool is sent to the market.

(b) wol; she's used three balls of wool to make my pullover; are these socks made of wool?

(c) watten; put some cotton wool on the cut on your finger; steel wool = staalwol.

geen meervoud: some wool; a piece of wool

woollen, bn (Amer. woolen)

wollen; a woollen pullover; a woollen carpet.

woolly, bn

wollig; a woolly sheep; soft woolly clouds in the sky.

word [wɜːd] zn

woord; there are seven words in this sentence; he saw me but didn't say a word; you spelt the word 'through' with two 'g's—that's a mistake; to have a word with = even spreken met; I must have a word with the teacher; in other words = met andere woorden; the manager's ill, in other words I have to do twice as much work.

wore [wɔː] zie **wear**

work [wɜːk] 1. zn

(a) werk; digging holes in the ground is hard work; don't ask me to go out—I've got too much to do; he doesn't do much work—he just sits and watches TV; when you've finished that piece of work, I've got something more for you to do.

(b) werk; baan; I go to work by train every day; we start work at 9 o'clock in the morning; he doesn't come back from work until 7 o'clock at night; he's out of work = werkeloos.

(c) (kunst)werk; a work of art; here are the complete works of Shakespeare = het verzameld werk.

(d) **works** = fabriek; **a car works.**
geen meervoud voor (a) *en* (b): **some work; a piece of work**

2. *ww*
(a) werken; **if you work hard you'll pass your exams; he doesn't work very hard so he doesn't earn much money.**
(b) werken; functioneren; **the clock isn't working; the bell works by electricity; the car didn't work well; he works the biggest machine in the factory** = hij bedient etc.
(c) werken; **he works in a car factory; she used to work in a butcher's shop; he had to stop working because he was so ill; I don't like working in London.**
(d) lukken; **do you think your plan will work? if it doesn't work, try again.**
works—working—worked—has worked

worker, *zn*
(a) werker; **he's a good worker; she's a slow worker.**
(b) arbeider; **the workers left the factory.**
workman, *zn*
werkman; **three workmen came to mend the pipe.**
meervoud **workmen**

work out, *ww*
(a) berekenen/uitrekenen; **I'm trying to work out how much petrol the car uses; she can't work this sum out.**
(b) uitvallen; aflopen; **everything worked out all right in the end.**
workshop, *zn*
werkplaats; atelier; **he's making a table in the workshop behind the house.**

world [wɜːld] *zn*
wereld; **you can fly right round the world; he travels all over the world on business.**

worn [wɔːn] *zie* **wear**

worn out ['wɔːn'aʊt] *zie* **wear out**

worry ['wʌrɪ] *ww*
zich zorg(en) maken; bezorgd zijn; **she's worrying about her exams; I worry when my daughter stays out late; are you worried by the cost of food? they're worried that they won't have enough petrol.**
worries—worrying—worried—has worried

worse [wɜːs] **1.** *bn*
(a) slechter; erger; **the weather is even worse than last week; this TV film is worse than the one I watched last night; I'm worse at English than at geography; that boy is very naughty—but his sister is worse.**
(b) slechter; zieker; **he was feeling quite well yesterday, but is much worse today; she's got worse since she started taking the medicine.**
2. *bw*
slechter; **he drives worse than his sister.**
worse *is de vergrotende trap van* **bad, badly** *en* **ill**

worst [wɜːst] **1.** *bn*
slechtst/ergst; **this is the worst film I've seen this year; she has the worst marks for English; he's the worst swimmer in our team.**
2. *bw*
het slechtst/ergst; **which team played worst? he works worst when he's tired.**
worst *is de overtreffende trap van* **bad** *en* **badly**

worth [wɜːθ] **1.** *bn*
(a) waard; **this house is worth £20,000; that car isn't worth £6,000! what's your car worth?**
(b) de moeite waard; nuttig; **that film is worth seeing; it's worth knowing something about car engines.**
2. *zn*
waarde; nut; **I want £5 worth of petrol** = ik wil graag voor 5 pond benzine; **he bought several pounds' worth of fruit.**

would [wʊd] *hulpww*
(a) (*in beleefde verzoeken*) zou(den) . . . willen; **would someone please turn off the light? would you please sit down? I asked him if he would help us.**
(b) (*verleden tijd van* **will,** *bereidwilligheid tonend*) wou(den)/wilde(n); **he wouldn't come with us, even though we asked him twice; of course the car wouldn't go when we wanted it to; he**

forgot my birthday again this year—he
would! = dat was te verwachten!

(c) placht(en); she would get up at eight
o'clock every morning; he would always
be standing outside the station selling
newspapers, until one day he died; my
uncle would often bring me chocolates.

(d) (*gebruikt voor de verleden tijd van*
will) zou(den); they said they would be
here by nine o'clock; she hoped she would
be able to come.

(e) (*voorwaardelijk*) zou(den); if he could
come he would; if she were still alive, she
would/she'd be a hundred years old
today; if you invited him, he would/he'd
come; if it rained we would/we'd stay at
home.

Ontkennend: **would not** *meestal*
wouldn't
Let op: **would** *is de verleden tijd van*
will; **would** *wordt vaak afgekort tot*
'd: **she'd be a hundred**; **would** *wordt zonder* **to** *en*
alleen met andere werkwoorden ge-
bruikt

would rather, *ww*
liever willen; **I'd rather stay at home than**
go to the party; are you going to pay for
everybody?—I'd rather not; they'd rather
we went with them.

wound¹ [waʊnd] *zie* **wind ²**

wound² [wu:nd] **1.** *zn*
wond; **the nurses were bandaging the**
soldiers' wounds.
2. *ww*
(ver)wonden; **he was wounded in the**
war; the police wounded the burglar as
he was trying to escape.

wounds—wounding—
wounded—has wounded

wrap [ræp] *ww* (*meestal* **wrap up**)
(in)pakken; (zich) hullen in; om zich
heen slaan; **he's wrapping up the Christ-**
mas presents; look at this parcel wrapped
up in blue paper; wrap yourself up in your
blanket if you're cold.

wraps—wrapping—wrapped—
has wrapped

wrist [rɪst] *zn*
pols; **wrist watch** = polshorloge.

write [raɪt] *ww*
(a) (op)schrijven; **she wrote a few words**
on the back of an envelope; who wrote
'Teacher go home' on the blackboard? I'll
write my name and address for you on a
piece of paper; can you write your tele-
phone number on the top of the letter?
he's written a book about the police.
(b) (*een brief*) schrijven; **have you written**
to your mother yet? she writes to me
every week; don't forget to write as soon
as you get to Hong Kong.

writes—writing—wrote [rəʊt]—
has written

write back, *ww*
terugschrijven; (be)antwoorden; **he got**
my letter, and wrote back immediately.

write down, *ww*
uitschrijven; **he wrote down the number**
of the car; she wrote down all the in-
formation on the back of an envelope.

write out, *ww*
uitschrijven; **I'll write out a list of the**
things I need.

Let op: **write the list out** *of* **write**
out the list *maar alleen* **write it**
out

writer, *zn*
schrijver, auteur; **do you know who is the**
writer of this letter? he's the writer of six
books.

writing, *zn*
(hand)schrift; geschrevene; **don't phone,**
please answer in writing; I have his
answer here in writing; can't you type
your letters?—your writing's so bad I
can't read it; *zie ook* **handwriting.**

writing paper, *zn*
schrijfpapier.

wrong [rɒŋ] **1.** *bn*
fout, verkeerd; **what's the time?—I don't**
know, my watch is wrong; I'm sorry, I
was wrong—he does live opposite the
post office = ik had ongelijk; **there's no**
one called Smith living here—you've
come to the wrong house; I think we're
on the wrong road—we should be
going to London, not away from it; can I
speak to Mr Smith please—sorry, you've
got the wrong number = u bent verkeerd
verbonden; **what's wrong with the**

soup?—there's nothing wrong with it, I'm just not hungry = wat mankeert er aan de soep?
2. *bw*
fout; verkeerd; **everything has gone wrong today; you've spelt my name wrong; I think you've added up the bill wrong.**
wrongly, *bw*
foutief; verkeerd; **the waiter added up the bill wrongly; she spelt my name wrongly.**

wrote [rəʊt] *zie* **write**

Yy

yard [jɑːd] *zn*
(*a*) yard (= 0,91 meter); el; **the post office is only a hundred yards away; the piece of string is ten yards long; can you move the chairs a couple of yards to the left?**
(*b*) plaats(je).
(*c*) (*Amerikaans vor* **garden**) tuin.

year [jɜː] *zn*
(*a*) (kalender)jaar; **in the year 1492 Columbus discovered America; last year we went to France on holiday; next year I'm going to work in Africa; the weather has been very bad this year; the New Year; I start my new job in the New Year; New Year's Day.**
(*b*) jaar; **he was born two hundred years ago; she's ten years old tomorrow; the school year starts in September; how many years have you been living in this village?**
yearly, *bn & bw*
jaarlijks.

yellow [ˈjeləʊ] *bn & zn*
geel; **he's painted his car bright yellow; she's wearing a yellow hat; look at the field of yellow flowers; do you have any paint of a lighter yellow than this?**
yellow—yellower—yellowest

yellow pages, *zn*
gele gids; beroepengids; **look up 'Restaurants' in the yellow pages.**

yes [jes] *bw*
ja(wel); **we asked him if he wanted to come and he said 'yes'; do you want**

any more coffee?—yes, please; does she like horses?—yes, she does; didn't he go to school in Scotland?—yes, he did.

yesterday [ˈjestədɪ] *bw & zn*
gisteren; **yesterday was November 13th, so today must be the 14th; we went to London yesterday morning; he came for tea yesterday afternoon** = gisterenmiddag; **the day before yesterday** = eergisteren.

yet [jet] **1.** *bw*
al; nog; **has the postman come yet? I haven't seen him yet; he hasn't read the newspaper yet; have you done your homework yet?**
2. *vw*
toch; **she's fat and yet she can run very fast; it was pouring with rain and yet the children went out for their picnic.**

you [juː] *vnw*
(*a*) jij/je/u; jullie/u; **you're taller than me/than I am; I'll give you my phone number and you'll give me yours; you go first; Hello, how are you? are you both well?**
(*b*) je/men; **you never know what will happen; you need to be very clever to go to university.**
Let op: **you** *is zowel enkel- als meervoud*

young [jʌŋ] *bn*
jong; **he's a young man—he's only twenty-one; my sister's younger than me/than I am; he's the youngest boy in the**

class; this is a TV programme for young children = kleine kinderen.
young—younger—youngest

your [jɔː] *bn*
jouw/je/uw; jullie/uw; **have you brought your toothbrush with you? this is a present for your sister; your trousers are dirty.**

yours, *vnw*
van jou/je/u/jullie; **this book is yours, not mine; you said he was a friend of yours** = van je/u/jullie.

yourself, *vnw*
(je-/jou-/u-)zelf; je/jou/u; (je-/u-)zelf; je/u; **you were washing the car yourself; did you cut yourself on the knife? are you all by yourself?** = helemaal alleen; **did you build the house all by yourself?** = helemaal zelf; **did you both hurt yourselves?**

look at yourselves in the mirror? I hope you all enjoy yourselves.
het meervoud **yourselves** *hoort bij* **you** *als meervoudig onderwerp*

youth [juːθ] *zn*
(*a*) jongeman; jongen; (*meervoud*) jongelui; **two youths came towards me; he was attacked by six youths in a pub.**
(*b*) jeugd; **I did a lot of sport in my youth.**
meervoud **youths** [juːðz] *for (a); geen meervoud for (b)*

youth club, *zn*
jeugdhuis; **we're joining the youth club; the youth club's going on a picnic next Saturday.**

youth hostel, *zn*
jeugdherberg.

Zz

zebra [ˈzebrə] *zn*
zebra; **zebra crossing** = zebra(pad).

zero [ˈzɪərəʊ] nul
the answer is zero; the temperature fell to zero (0°); it's very cold—it's below zero.

zip [zɪp] **1.** *zn*
rits(sluiting); **her dress is fastened with a zip at the back; can you do up this zip for me/do this zip up for me?**
2. *ww*
to **zip up** = dichtritsen; een ritssluiting

hebben; **can you zip up this dress for me/zip this dress up for me?; this dress zips up at the back.**
zips—zipping—zipped—has zipped
Let op: **zip the dress up** *of* **zip up the dress** *maar alleen* **zip it up**

zoo [zuː] *zn*
dierentuin; **we went to the zoo on Sunday afternoon; I had a ride on an elephant at the zoo.**

Oefeningen

1. Hulp bij de grammatika

Telbare en niet-telbare zelfstandige naamwoorden

In het Engels wordt het meervoud van zelfstandige naamwoorden meestal gevormd door -s achter de stam te zetten.

enkelvoud	meervoud
car	cars
chair	chairs

Bij onregelmatige zelfstandige naamwoorden staat het meervoud in de grijze strip onderaan bij het trefwoord.

knife [naɪf] *zn*
  mes; **to lay the table, you put a knife, fork and spoon for each person; cut your meat up with your knife; bread knife** = broodmes.
meervoud **knives** [naɪvz]

lady [ˈleɪdɪ] *zn*
  dame; **there's a lady waiting to see you; a lady doctor** = een vrouwelijke dokter.
meervoud **ladies**

Alle zelfstandige naamwoorden met een meervoud worden telbaar genoemd. Dat betekent dat er meerdere exemplaren van de door het woord aangegeven zaak kunnen zijn en dat je die kunt tellen (**one table, two tables**). Er zijn heel wat zelfstandige naamwoorden zonder meervoud. Zoek in je woordenboek het artikel **butter** op. Boter kun je niet tellen, dus noemen we het een niet-telbaar zelfstandig naamwoord.

Als je over een bepaalde hoeveelheid boter wilt spreken, kun je zeggen **some/a piece of/half a kilogram of butter,** maar je kunt niet zeggen **a/one butter, two butters** enzovoort.

Dingen die je kunt eten en drinken worden meestal met niet-telbare zelfstandige naamwoorden benoemd. Zoek in je woordenboek de trefwoorden **bread, milk** en **porridge** op. Andere woorden zoals **information, advice, luggage** en **furniture** zijn eveneens niet-telbaar. Je kunt niet zeggen **an/one information** of **an/one advice,** maar je kunt wel zeggen **a piece of information/advice/luggage/furniture.**

Om je te helpen bepalen of een zelfstandig naamwoord wel of niet telbaar is, moet je de volgende punten onthouden:

(a) **some, no, any, a lot of, plenty of, enough** kunnen zowel met telbare als niet-telbare zelfstandige naamwoorden gebruikt worden.

(b) **a/an, many, how many, not many, too many, several, few, a few, one, two, three** enzovoort kunnen alleen met telbare zelfstandige naamwoorden gebruikt worden.

(c) **much, how much, not much, too much, little, a little** kunnen alleen met niet-telbare zelfstandige naamwoorden gebruikt worden.

Oefening 1

Bepaal of de volgende zelfstandige naamwoorden wel of niet telbaar zijn.

1. knee
2. news
3. glue
4. enemy
5. coal
6. bacon
7. gold
8. opportunity
9. peace
10. electricity

Sommige zelfstandige naamwoorden kunnen zowel in een telbare als niet-telbare vorm gebruikt worden. Bekijk het trefwoord **hair**.

> **hair** [heə] *zw*
> (*a*) haar; **the dog has left hairs all over the armchair; there's a hair in my soup; you're beginning to get some grey hairs.**
> *meervoud* **hairs**
> (*b*) haar, haren; **she's got long black hair; you ought to wash your hair; his hair is too long; he is going to have his hair cut.**
> *geen meervoud*

Onder (*a*) zie je dat **hair** een meervoud **hairs** heeft.
Onder (*b*) zie je dat er voor **hair** geen meervoud bestaat. In (*a*) betekent **hair** een enkele hoofdhaar (telbaar). We kunnen bijvoorbeeld zeggen:
  he's getting old—look, he's already got several grey hairs.

In (*b*) betekent **hair** al het haar op je hoofd bij elkaar (niet-telbaar). We kunnen bijvoorbeeld zeggen:

  She's got red hair.

Oefening 2

Zoek in je woordenboek de volgende woorden op: **country, coffee, glass, change, lamb.** Bekijk zorgvuldig wat onder elk van die woorden staat. Zoek daarin de vertaling die past bij het cursief gedrukte woord in onderstaande zinnen (geef nummer en/of letter).

1. Do you prefer living in the town or in the *country*?
2. Italy used to be a cheap *country* for a holiday.
3. How many *coffees* did you order?
4. Do you like strong *coffee*, or would you prefer it weak?
5. My brother works in a *glass* factory.
6. Would you like a *glass* of wine?
7. I'm afraid I've got no *change* for the ticket machine.
8. I've noticed several *changes* since I was last in London.
9. The farmer found a *lamb* still alive under the snow.
10. I like pork, but I hate *lamb*.

Oefening 3

Zet het/de juiste cursief gedrukte woord(en) voor het zelfstandige naamwoord in onderstaande zinnen.

1. We're having *a/some* good weather this year.
2. Let me give you *a piece of/an* advice.
3. Have you got *many/much* furniture in your new flat?
4. My family eats *too much/too many* rice.
5. I've got *a few/a little* money left over.
6. *How many/How much* paintings are there in this palace?
7. Could you bring *a little/a few* records to the party?
8. You've put far *too much/too many* mustard in my ham sandwich!
9. I've got *a/some* bad news for you.
10. He doesn't grow *as much/as many* cabbages as he used to.

Zelfstandige naamwoorden met een onregelmatig meervoud

In de grijze strip onderaan bij een zelfstandig naamwoord staat het meervoud wanneer dat niet helemaal regelmatig is, (dat wil zeggen als het niet gevormd wordt met -s).

Oefening 4

Zoek in je woordenboek de volgende woorden op en geef de juiste meervoudsvorm. (Het zijn niet allemaal onregelmatige vormen.)

1. lady
2. valley
3. city
4. country
5. key

6. baby
7. journey
8. reply
9. party
10. day

Verdeel deze meervoudsvormen nu in twee groepen. Kun je het patroon onderscheiden dat geldt voor het meervoud van woorden die op **-y** uitgaan?

Oefening 5

Zoek in je woordenboek de volgende woorden op en geef de juiste meervoudsvorm.

1. foot
2. tooth
3. man
4. woman
5. mouse

Oefening 6

Zoek in je woordenboek de volgende woorden op en geef de juiste meervoudsvorm.

1. shelf
2. knife
3. wife
4. loaf
5. thief

Oefening 7

Zoek in je woordenboek de volgende woorden op en geef de juiste meervoudsvorm.

1. box
2. potato
3. bus
4. glass
5. brush

6. watch
7. dress
8. photo
9. match
10. piano

De vergrotende en overtreffende trap van bijvoeglijke naamwoorden

In de grijze strip onderaan bij eenlettergrepige en sommige tweelettergrepige bijvoeglijke naamwoorden wordt aangegeven hoe hiervan de vergrotende en overtreffende trap gevormd worden.

> **fit** [fit] **1.** *bn*
> fit, in goede conditie; geschikt; **he isn't fit enough to work; you'll have to get fit before the football match.**
> **fit—fitter—fittest**

vergrotende trap	overtreffende trap
He's fitter than I am because he runs regularly	He's the fittest player in our team

Oefening 8

Maak onderstaande zinnen af met de vergrotende trap van het cursief gedrukt bijvoeglijke naamwoord.

1. He is a _____ runner than his brother. *fast*
2. He'll soon be _____ than his father. *tall*
3. France is many times _____ than England. *big*
4. He's getting _____ and _____. He'll have to eat less. *fat*
5. You'll have to be _____ than that if you want to finish your homework before 7.00. *quick*

Oefening 9

Maak onderstaande zinnen af met de overtreffende trap van het cursief gedrukt bijvoeglijke naamwoord.

1. Peter is the _____ learner in the class. *slow*
2. August has been the _____ month this year. *dry*
3. It was the _____ night I can remember. *dark*
4. I'm the _____ of the group – I'm certainly not paying for the drinks! *poor*
5. That is the _____ joke I've ever heard. *weak*

Oefening 10

Maak onderstaande zinnen af met de juiste vorm (vergrotende of overtreffende trap) van het cursief gedrukte bijvoeglijke naamwoord.

1. That film was even _____ than the one I saw last week. *silly*
2. She must be _____ than you if she got higher marks in the exam. *clever*
3. Even John, who's the _____ person I know, didn't say thank you. *polite*
4. My younger sister is _____ than my elder sister. *pretty*
5. The _____ thing to do is not to invite him. *simple*

Oefening 11

Maak onderstaande zinnen af met de juiste vorm (vergrotende of overtreffende trap) van het cursief gedrukte bijvoeglijke naamwoord.

1. I'm not good at maths, but my brother's even _____ than me. *bad*
2. The storm last night was the _____ we've had for years. *bad*
3. My friend's _____ at tennis than I am. *good*
4. That Chinese meal was the _____ I've ever had. *good*
5. If you want to get thinner, you'll have to eat _____ chocolate. *little*
6. She does the _____ work of all of us, and she gets top marks. *little*
7. There are _____ people here than last week. *many*
8. Who scored the _____ runs in the cricket team this year? *many*
9. It's _____ to walk to the other pub, but it's much more friendly than this one. *far*
10. Land's End is the _____ point in England west of London. *far*

Als er in het stukje onder een bijvoeglijk naamwoord geen informatie wordt gegeven over het vormen van de trappen van vergelijking, betekent dit dat deze gevormd worden met **more** en **most**. Dit geldt voor alle bijvoeglijke naamwoorden die uit drie of meer lettergrepen bestaan, zoals:

intelligent   more intelligent   most intelligent
expensive   more expensive   most expensive

en het geldt ook voor een groot aantal tweelettergrepige bijvoeglijke naamwoorden (meestal die welke niet uitgaan op **-y, -e** of **-er,** waarvan de vergrotende en overtreffende trap gevormd worden met **-er** en **-est**), zoals:

certain   more certain   most certain
careful   more careful   most careful

Oefening 12

Maak onderstaande zinnen af met de juiste vorm (vergrotende of overtreffende trap) van het cursief gedrukte bijvoeglijke naamwoord.

1. He's not the _____ teacher I've ever had.   *interesting*
2. 'Smith' is one of the _____ names in Britain.   *common*
3. Don't you know any pubs which are _____ than that?   *close*
4. Wouldn't it be _____ to put the money in the bank?   *sensible*
5. That was the _____ dream I've ever had!   *horrible*
6. She's got _____ hair than she used to have.   *curly*
7. You take this suitcase – it's _____ than that one.   *light*
8. That was certainly the _____ book I've read for a long time.   *exciting*
9. Which is _____, cricket or baseball?   *boring*
10. He never cleans his football boots, and they get _____ and _____.   *muddy*

Het gebruik van het bijwoord

Bijwoorden zijn in het woordenboek te vinden onder het bijvoeglijke naamwoord waarvan ze zijn afgeleid.

regular [ˈregjʊlə] *bn*
regelmatig, geregeld, vast; **11 o'clock is my regular time for going to bed; if you don't have regular meals you will be ill; regular visits to the dentist are important; is this your regular train?** = de trein die u normaal neemt?
regularly, *bw*
regelmatig; **he is regularly late for work; she regularly goes to bed after midnight; you should go to the dentist regularly.**

Om van een bijvoeglijk naamwoord een bijwoord te maken, voeg je **-ly** toe aan de vorm van het bijvoeglijke naamwoord.

bijvoeglijk naamwoord	*bijwoord*
slow	slowly
careful	carefully

Op deze regel zijn twee uitzonderingen:

	bijvoeglijk nw	*bijwoord*
(*a*) **-y** verandert in **-ily**	easy	easily
(*b*) **-le** verandert in **-ly**	sensible	sensibly

Bijvoeglijke naamwoorden zeggen iets over zelfstandige naamwoorden:

This is an easy job.
He's a careful driver.

Bijwoorden zeggen iets over werkwoorden:

I can do this job easily.
He drives carefully.

Oefening 13

Maak onderstaande zinnen af met een van het cursief gedrukte bijvoeglijke naamwoord afgeleid bijwoord. Kijk in je woordenboek voor de juiste spelling.

1. He _____ won't come to the party. *probable*
2. This dress is very _____ made. *simple*

3. He shouted at me _____ when I got the answer wrong.   *angry*
4. He's _____ the fastest runner in the country.   *possible*
5. My father can sit _____ in front of the television for hours.
   happy

Oefening 14

Soms verschilt de betekenis van een bijwoord van die van het bijvoeg-lijke naamwoord waarvan het is afgeleid.

Zoek de volgende bijwoorden op (denk eraan ze op te zoeken onder het bijvoeglijk naamwoord waarvan ze zijn afgeleid).

Bekijk zorgvuldig de vertalingen en de voorbeelden en kies daarna het juiste bijwoord voor elk van onderstaande zinnen.

narrowly, lately, hardly, practically, highly

1. The party was _____ over when I got there.
2. We got home just as the storm started, and _____ escaped getting very wet.
3. His teacher spoke very _____ of him.
4. Have you seen Mary _____?
5. I've got _____ any money left.

Oefening 15

Sommige bijwoorden zijn hetzelfde als de bijvoeglijke naamwoorden waarvan ze zijn afgeleid.

Bepaal of de cursief gedrukte woorden in onderstaande zinnen bijvoeglijke naamwoorden of bijwoorden zijn. Bekijk de vertalin-gen en voorbeelden die in het woordenboek gegeven zijn zorgvul-dig.

1. He works too *hard*.
2. I always get an *early* bus to work.
3. Pauline left the office at 4.00 so John arrived too *late* to see her.
4. He drives a very *fast* car.
5. Have we got to walk *far* from the bus stop?

Werkwoordsvormen

In de grijze strip onderaan bij een werkwoord zijn vier dingen aangegeven:

derde persoon enkelvoud **(he/she/it)** van de tegenwoordige tijd

accept [ək'sept] *ww*
   (*a*) aannemen/accepteren; **will you accept this little present?**
   (*b*) toestemmen; **I invited her to the party and she accepted.**
accepts—accepting—accepted—has accepted

tegenwoordig deelwoord

verleden tijd

    voltooid deelwoord in de voltooid tegenwoordige tijd
    (**has** voor **he/she/it, have** voor **I/you/we/they**)

Zowel regelmatige als onregelmatige vormen zijn gegeven.

Oefening 16

Maak onderstaande zinnen af met behulp van de derde persoon enkelvoud van het cursief gedrukte werkwoord. Kijk in je woordenboek voor de juiste spelling.

1. I don't think this argument _____ you. *concern*
2. He always _____ to his piano lesson on Tuesday. *go*
3. I hope she _____ me to her wedding. *invite*
4. A walk in the fresh air _____ you good. *do*
5. My father always _____ about something when we go to a restaurant. *complain*
6. He usually _____ the shopping for her. *carry*
7. Jerry always _____ the sport on television on Saturday afternoon. *watch*
8. Make sure your daughter _____ her teeth every night and morning. *brush*
9. He _____ his shop early on Friday so that he can get home in time for his favourite television programme. *close*
10. When he stops to talk to the postman on his way to work, he always _____ his bus. *miss*

Om de derde persoon enkelvoud van de tegenwoordige tijd te vormen voeg je meestal alleen -s toe aan de stam van het werkwoord. Uitzonderingen, zoals in Oefening 16, zijn:

(a) werkwoorden die uitgaan op -ch, -sh, -ss of -o krijgen -es.
(b) werkwoorden die uitgaan op -y laten de -y vallen en krijgen inplaats daarvan de uitgang -ies.

Oefening 17

Maak onderstaande zinnen af met behulp van het tegenwoordig deelwoord van het cursief gedrukte werkwoord. Kijk in je woordenboek voor de juiste spelling.

1. They're _____ the car for their holiday now. *load*
2. They say it's _____ quite heavily in Scotland. *snow*
3. She's been _____ around too much; she should rest more. *rush*
4. You should be outside in the sun, instead of _____ indoors. *sit*
5. It's _____ really cold now. *get*
6. Paul is _____ the business all by himself at the moment. *run*
7. Why are you _____ your arm? *rub*
8. He's been _____ that cigar all evening. *smoke*
9. Where are you _____ at the moment? *live*
10. My brother's _____ a model railway. *make*

Het tegenwoordig deelwoord kan gevormd worden door -ing aan de stam van het werkwoord toe te voegen. Hierbij moet met twee dingen rekening gehouden worden:

(a) als het meervoud uitgaat op een letter zoals -t, -b, -m, -n of p, wordt deze meestal verdubbeld.
(b) als het werkwoord uitgaat op -e, wordt de -e weggelaten voor -ing. Kijk nu nog eens naar je antwoorden in Oefening 17.

Oefening 18

Maak onderstaande zinnen af met behulp van de verleden tijd van het cursief gedrukte werkwoord. Kijk in je woordenboek voor de juiste spelling.

1. The car _____ just in time. *stop*
2. We _____ to meet outside the cinema. *agree*
3. We _____ to have the party next week, but nobody will be here. *plan*
4. The police _____ him to the police station. *accompany*
5. They _____ Berlin into two parts. *divide*

Oefening 19

Maak onderstaande zinnen af met behulp van de verleden tijd van het cursief gedrukte werkwoord. Kijk in je woordenboek voor de juiste spelling.

1. I _____ a postcard, but forgot to send it. *write*
2. We _____ a great film last night. *see*
3. Dave _____ some very funny jokes in the pub. *tell*
4. I _____ you were going to the cinema. *think*
5. There were no seats, so we _____ all through the football match. *stand*
6. She _____ a beautiful dress for the wedding. *wear*
7. Mum _____ she was feeling much better. *say*
8. We _____ all the way to the south of France last summer. *drive*
9. Years ago my grandfather _____ his own house. *build*
10. When we were young we _____ mice as pets. *keep*

Oefening 20

Maak onderstaande zinnen af met behulp van het voltooid deelwoord van het cursief gedrukte werkwoord.

1. Have you _____ the electricity bill yet? *pay*
2. He's _____ 30 miles in the last three days. *run*
3. I've _____ myself again shaving. *cut*
4. We've _____ each other since we were at school. *know*
5. I've _____ some money for the milkman. *leave*
6. Have you _____ the clocks forward one hour? *put*
7. I haven't _____ properly for weeks. *sleep*
8. Dad has _____ Joan to the station. *take*

9. A fish bone has got _____ in my throat! *stick*
10. Someone has _____ my watch. *steal*

Het gebruik van het juiste voorzetsel

Oefening 21

Er staan in het stukje onder een voorzetsel verschillende gebruiksvoorbeelden.

Zoek de in onderstaande zinnen cursief gedrukte voorzetsels op. Lees de voorbeelden om voor elke zin het juiste voorzetsel te vinden.

1. I'll meet you *on/at* the station.
2. I don't like that picture *on/at* the living room wall.
3. We were travelling *to/at* 50 miles an hour when the accident happened.
4. Is your wife *in/at* home?
5. My grandparents are coming *on/at* Christmas Day.
6. I've been working here *for/since* two years.
7. Jean has only been working here *for/since* 1981.
8. He usually goes to work *with the/by* train.
9. My German friend is coming to stay *with/by* us for three weeks.
10. *In/On* December we're going to Italy.

Oefening 22

Weet je niet zeker welk voorzetsel je moet gebruiken bij een woord als, bijvoorbeeld, **fond**, zoek het dan in je woordenboek op en lees alle voorbeelden.

In onderstaande zinnen ontbreekt het voorzetsel. Zoek in je woordenboek het cursief gedrukte woord op en lees alle voorbeelden die gegeven worden om het juiste voorzetsel te vinden.

1. I'm very *fond* _____ Brahms.
2. My brother's *good* _____ cricket.
3. She isn't very *keen* _____ the idea of a holiday in Germany.
4. Are you *interested* _____ birds?

5. *According* _____ the papers, the Queen will be going to Australia in May.
6. The house is quite *different* _____ what I expected.
7. I'm still *short* _____ money, but I'll manage.
8. My wife's not *used* _____ living in the city.
9. My dog is *afraid* _____ cats.
10. That's a good *method* _____ saving money.

2. Op zoek naar de betekenis

Woorden die vaak verkeerd gebruikt worden

Oefening 23

Zoek de twee cursief gedrukte woorden op die boven elk paar zinnen staan. Lees zorgvuldig de vertalingen en voorbeelden en maak daarna de zinnen af.

1. *well, good*
   They're getting on _____ with the local people at last.
   I saw a _____ play at the theatre last month.
2. *library, bookshop*
   I borrowed three books from the _____, but forgot to return them.
   If you pass a _____ when you're shopping, could you buy me a copy of 'War and Peace'?
3. *foreigner, stranger*
   Are you a _____ to London, or have you been here before?
   He's a _____. I think he's from Cyprus.
4. *amusing, amused*
   I was _____ to see our local football team lost again last Saturday.
   He told me a very _____ joke, but I've forgotten it.
5. *mean, think*
   Do you _____ we should invite Peter?
   'Look at that car!' 'Which one do you _____?'
6. *after, afterwards*
   Let's go for a coffee _____ the lesson.
   I'll meet you _____ outside the classroom.
7. *since, for*
   Have you been here _____ six months already? It seems more like six weeks.
   I've been living her _____ the beginning of the year.
8. *win, beat*
   Jackson will _____ Leonard in the fight tomorrow!
   If he doesn't _____, I'll lose a lot of money.
9. *take, bring*

Could you _____ these books back to the library next time you go?

I hope my father _____ back a present from Scotland.

10. *wait, expect*

My mother _____ two hours in the snow for a bus.

Who can that be? I'm not _____ any visitors.

Woorden met een speciale betekenis

Zoek in je woordenboek het woord **turn** op. Na de vertalingen van **turn** als zelfstandig naamwoord en als werkwoord volgt een rijtje werkwoorden die uit **turn** plus een ander woord bestaan. Dit andere woord, dat 'partikel' wordt genoemd, verandert de betekenis van het hoofdwerkwoord, zoals bijvoorbeeld:

turn away, turn back, turn down, turn in

Bestudeer het rijtje en de voorbeelden zorgvuldig.

Dit zijn werkwoorden die altijd een bijwoordelijk complement hebben, zogenaamde 'phrasal verbs'; in het Nederlands zijn het scheidbare werkwoorden. Lees hierover meer in een grammatika en ook over werkwoorden met een voorzetselvoorwerp, zogenaamde 'prepositional verbs'.

Opmerking over de woordorde

Bij werkwoorden met een bijwoordelijk complement staat in de grijze strip onderaan een opmerking over de woordorde.

> **turn up,** *ww*
> (*a*) verschijnen, opdagen; **half the people didn't turn up until nine o'clock; the little boy finally turned up in Edinburgh; my pen turned up in my coat pocket.**
> (*b*) luider zetten; open draaien; **can you turn up the radio/turn the radio up—I can't hear it; turn up the gas/turn the gas up, the kettle hasn't boiled yet.**
> *Let op:* **turn the radio down** *of* **turn down the radio; turn the light off** *of* **turn off the light,** *etc., maar alleen* **turn it down, turn it off,** *etc.*

Ga voor je zo'n werkwoord gebruikt na of er in je woordenboek een opmerking over de woordorde bij staat.

Als een zelfstandig naamwoord (**radio, light**) in een korte zin gebruikt wordt, kan het partikel (**down, off**) op twee verschillende plaatsen staan:

Turn the radio down.	Turn the light off.
Turn down the radio	Turn off the light.

Maar als er een voornaamwoord gebruikt wordt (in dit geval **it**), kan het partikel maar op één plaats staan:

Turn it down
Turn it off.

Kijk ook naar dit voorbeeld:

bring up, *ww*
grootbrengen; **he was brought up by his uncle; I was brought up in Scotland.**
Let op: **he brought some presents back** *of* **he brought back some presents; she brought the dog in** *of* **she brought in the dog,** *etc.;* *maar alleen* **he brought them back, she brought it in,** *etc.*

Als er in een korte zin met een van deze werkwoorden een zelfstandig naamwoord gebruikt wordt, kan het partikel (**back, in**) op twee verschillende plaatsen staan:

He brought some presents back.
He brought back some presents.

She brought the dog in.
She brought in the dog.

Maar als er een voornaamwoord gebruikt wordt, (in dit geval **them** en **it**), kan het partikel maar op één plaats staan:

He brought them back.
She brought it in.

Oefening 24

Lees onderstaande zinnen en vervang de cursief gedrukte woorden door een woord of woordgroep met dezelfde betekenis, bijvoorbeeld:

I usually *turn in* at about 11 o'clock.
I usually go to bed at about 11 o'clock.

1. *Turn* the heater *off* if you don't need it.
2. This company *turns out* 3,000 steel chairs a day.
3. They offered him a post as salesman, but he *turned* it *down*.
4. He *turned up* at the meeting at about 10 o'clock.
5. The concert was so popular that we had to *turn* people *away*.

Oefening 25

Zoek in je woordenboek het woord **get** op. Doe daarna hetzelfde als in Oefening 24.

1. The thieves managed to *get away* before the police came.
2. My grandfather's *getting on* now; he's nearly 80.
3. When do you think you'll *get back* from France?
4. Could you *get* the milk *out* of the fridge, please?
5. When are you going to *get up*? It's nearly 10 o'clock.

Oefening 26

Zoek in je woordenboek het woord **make** op. Doe daarna hetzelfde als in Oefening 24.

1. The man who came to mend our piano tried to *make off with* the silver spoons.
2. I was late three times this week, and had to *make up* three different excuses.
3. After he escaped, the prisoner *made for* the coast.
4. What do you *make of* this telegram?
5. Can you *make out* what that sign says from here?

Oefening 27

In de volgende zinnen ontbreekt het partikel of voorzetsel dat aan **get** een speciale betekenis verleent. Gebruik je woordenboek om te ontdekken wat het is.

1. Please don't disturb me – I must get _____ with my work.
2. Ask the bus conductor to tell you where to get _____.
3. He seems to be getting _____ with most people in the office.
4. I hope I get _____ my driving test.
5. It's very difficult to get things _____ if no one speaks your language.

Oefening 28

Zoek in je woordenboek het woord **look** op. Doe daarna hetzelfde als in Oefening 27.

1. If you don't know what a word means, look it _____ in the dictionary.
2. Now that my parents are old, I must look _____ them.
3. I've lost my keys. Can you help me look _____ them?
4. Do look _____ if you're in this area.
5. If you're going to the concert, I'll look _____ for you.

Oefening 29

Zoek in je woordenboek het woord **take** op. Doe daarna hetzelfde als in Oefening 27.

1. I think she looks like her mother, but other people think she takes _____ her father more.
2. You should take your hat _____ before you go into church.
3. Bob has taken _____ as the new manager.
4. Our company is taking _____ 200 extra workers.
5. The worst part of flying is when the plane takes _____.

Uitdrukkingen

Als een bepaald hoofdwoord uit je woordenboek gewoonlijk in een uitdrukking gebruikt wordt, dan is die uitdrukking vaak onder dat woord opgenomen.

Oefening 30

Zoek het boven onderstaande zinnen gegeven hoofdwoord op en kies uit de daarbij afgedrukte voorbeelden een uitdrukking waarmee je de cursief gedrukte woorden in deze zinnen vervangt.

1. *eye*
   Please *watch* my beer for me while I go and make a phone call.
2. *foot*
   I *made him angry by mistake* when I asked him when his wedding was.
3. *hand*
   Please *help me* with this heavy suitcase.
4. *finger*
   We're *hoping very much* that he gets the job.
5. *leg*
   Don't worry – she's only *joking* about that urgent message.

Amerikanismen

Het is belangrijk het verschil in gebruik te kennen dat er tussen sommige woorden in het Amerikaanse Engels en Britse Engels bestaat.

Oefening 31

Vervang de cursief gedrukte Amerikanismen in onderstaande zinnen door een woord uit het Britse Engels dat hetzelfde betekent.

1. We're going to Vancouver in the summer *vacation*.
2. Someone left the *faucet* dripping all night.
3. The *railroad* stretches from the west coast to the east coast.
4. The children always play in the *yard* behind the house.
5. We'll take the *elevator* to the fifth floor.

3. Uitspraak en klemtoon

Uitspraak

Van elk hoofdwoord in het woordenboek is de fonetische spelling aangegeven. Het woord fonetisch slaat op de uitspraak van een letter of groep letters. Er zijn in het Engels 44 verschillende spraakklanken.

Hieronder volgen de fonetische tekens die hiervoor in het woordenboek gebruikt worden:

Klinkers

Korte klinkers

ɪ	bit	ɒ	lot
e	best	ʊ	book
æ	bank	ə	another
ʌ	but		

Lange klinkers

iː	beet	uː	do
ɑː	bar	ɜː	learn
ɔː	door		

Tweeklanken (e + ɪ = eɪ bijvoorbeeld)

eɪ	say	aʊ	now
aɪ	buy	ɪə	ear
ɔɪ	boy	eə	air
əʊ	blow	ʊə	sure

Medeklinkers

Van sommige letters verschilt de fonetische spelling niet van de normale.

| p | post | f | fat |
| b | buy | v | very |

t	today	s	some
d	dog	k	kick (*of* catch)
m	man	z	zoo (*of* lose)
n	nice	h	have
l	long	w	wind
r	ride	g	good

Andere zijn totaal verschillend.

tʃ	church	ð	then
dʒ	jump	ʃ	shut
ŋ	bring	ʒ	measure
θ	thin	j	yet

Leer van je onderwijzer(es) of van iemand die Engels als moedertaal heeft hoe je deze 44 sleutelwoorden moet zeggen. Wanneer je de juiste uitspraak en fonetische spelling hiervan eenmaal onder de knie hebt, moet je in staat zijn elk woord in het woordenboek op de goede manier uit te spreken.

Oefening 32

Bekijk onderstaande fonetische tekens. Zoek elk woord in het rijtje op en vind het bijpassende fonetische teken, bijvoorbeeld 1(d) (hit [hɪt]).

1. ɪ	(a) moon	7. ə	(g) let
2. e	(b) thought	8. iː	(h) put
3. æ	(c) polite	9. ɑː	(i) cut
4. ʌ	(d) hit	10. ɔː	(j) cat
5. ɒ	(e) dark	11. uː	(k) knock
6. ʊ	(f) learn	12. ɜː	(l) sheet

Oefening 33

Doe hetzelfde als in Oefening 32.

1. eɪ	(a) load	5. aʊ	(e) annoy
2. aɪ	(b) cure	6. ɪə	(f) lay
3. ɔɪ	(c) cow	7. eə	(g) sky
4. əʊ	(d) care	8. ʊə	(h) beer

Oefening 34

Doe hetzelfde als in Oefening 32.

1. tʃ	(a) guess	6. ʃ	(f) lose
2. dʒ	(b) think	7. ʒ	(g) catch
3. ŋ	(c) pleasure	8. j	(h) shake
4. θ	(d) judge	9. s	(i) there
5. ð	(e) year	10. z	(j) sing

Oefening 35

Zoek in je woordenboek de volgende woorden op en verdeel ze in twee 'klank' groepen (sommige bevatten de klank aʊ en andere de klank əʊ).

cow, slow, know, brown, now, how, low, throw

Oefening 36

Verdeel de volgende woorden in twee 'klank' groepen, op dezelfde manier als in Oefening 35 (sommige bevatten de klank ʊ en andere de klank uː).

foot, moon, spoon, look, food, book, tooth, put

Oefening 37

Verdeel de volgende woorden op dezelfde manier als in Oefening 35 (sommige bevatten de klank ɪə en andere de klank eə).

bear, clear, dear, wear, ear, hear, tear (werkwoord), near

Oefening 38

Voor de letters **th** zijn twee verschillende uitspraken mogelijk. Het teken θ geeft aan dat het om een zachte klank gaat, het teken ð dat het om een harde klank gaat.

Verdeel de volgende woorden in twee groepen onder θ of ð.

these, thick, thank, weather, without, bath, think, they

Oefening 39

De letter **s** kan of zacht (stemloos, **s**) worden uitgesproken, of hard (stemhebbend, **z**). Verdeel de volgende woorden in twee groepen onder **s** of **z**.

mouse, lose, wise, loose, use (*zelfstandig naamwoord*), use (*werkwoord*), please, grease

Oefening 40

Sommige Engelse woorden die hetzelfde gespeld worden, hebben niettemin een verschillende uitspraak en betekenis. In het woordenboek zijn deze hoofdwoorden verschillend genummerd. Zoek in je woordenboek bijvoorbeeld het woord **wind** op. Het zelfstandig naamwoord [1] wordt uitgesproken [wind] en het werkwoord [2] [waind].

Lees zorgvuldig onderstaande zinnen. Zoek de cursief gedrukte woorden op en noteer van elk de fonetische spelling.

1. Are you going to *lead* us round the castle?
2. You shouldn't put the *lead* of your pencil in your mouth.
3. We live very *close* to the police station
4. What time do the shops *close* in London?
5. When you've read this letter, *tear* it up.
6. He burst into *tears* when he cut his finger.
7. You should make more *use* of your dictionary.
8. You should *use* your dictionary more.
9. I had a terrible *row* with my parents last night.
10. We got to the cinema late and had to sit in the front *row*.

Oefen de schuingedrukte woorden hardop en zorg ervoor dat je het betekenisverschil tussen élk paar kent.

Oefening 41

Als je niet zeker weet hoe de groep letters **-ough** in een woord wordt uitgesproken, moet je altijd de uitspraak van dat woord in je woordenboek nazoeken.

Breng de volgende woorden in verschillende groepen onder op basis van de klank van **-ough** in elk woord.

th**ough**t, c**ough**, r**ough**, br**ough**t, pl**ough**, th**ough**, en**ough**, thr**ough**

Hoeveel verschillende klanken zijn er?

Oefening 42

Zeg welke letter in de volgende woorden niet wordt uitgesproken.

1. know	5. knit	9. empty
2. thumb	6. bomb	10. whole
3. autumn	7. duck	
4. knee	8. knock	

Klemtoon

Als er op een bepaald deel van een woord nadruk valt, noemen we dat een klemtoon.

Een woord bestaat uit één of meer lettergrepen. Een lettergreep is een deel van een woord dat je apart kunt uitspreken, bijvoorbeeld:

ci – ne – ma   (drie lettergrepen)
emp – ty   (twee lettergrepen)
thick   (een lettergreep)

Voor de juiste uitspraak van een woord is het leggen van de klemtoon op de juiste lettergreep even belangrijk als het gebruik van de goede klank.

In de fonetische spelling van woorden van twee of meer lettergrepen wordt in het woordenboek de klemtoon aangegeven door middel van een tekentje vóór de beklemtoonde lettergreep. Het klemtoontekentje ziet er zo uit:

luggage [ˈlʌgɪdʒ]

In **luggage** valt de klemtoon op de eerste lettergreep.

In het voorbeeld van een tweelettergrepig woord hieronder, valt de klemtoon op de tweede lettergreep:

forget [fəˈget]

Als je een woord opzoekt dat je nog niet kende, kijk dan steeds goed op welk deel de klemtoon valt.

Oefening 43

Geef in de volgende woorden aan op welke lettergreep de klemtoon valt. Maak daarbij gebruik van je woordenboek, zelfs als je denkt te weten waar de klemtoon hoort. Verdeel de woorden daarna in twee groepen al naar gelang waar de klemtoon valt.

idea, silly, clever, believe, easy, abroad, local, retire, party, prepare

Oefening 44

Doe hetzelfde als in Oefening 43.

instrument, difficult, develop, cinema, eleven, enemy, division, horizon, memory, opinion

Oefening 45

Doe hetzelfde als in Oefening 43.

education, impossible, intelligent, operation, ability, invitation, particular, mathematics, information, industrial

Oefening 46

Veel tweelettergrepige zelfstandige naamwoorden worden ook als werkwoord gebruikt, alleen wordt de klemtoon dan verlegd. Soms is er ook sprake van een andere uitspraak.

Zoek in je woordenboek de volgende woorden op en geef aan waar de klemtoon komt te liggen. In welke woordparen is er ook sprake van een veranderde uitspraak?

zelfstandig naamwoord	werkwoord
1. record	record
2. increase	increase

3. present	present
4. object	object
5. permit	permit

Oefening 47

Lees onderstaande zinnen en geef in elk cursief gedrukte woord aan
op welke lettergreep de klemtoon valt.

1. Have you got any Elvis Presley *records*?
2. I'm going to *record* my daughter's voice and send the tape to our
   relations in Australia.
3. I think they should *increase* our wages.
4. There has been an *increase* in crime in London.
5. We would like to *present* this gift to you.
6. What a lovely Christmas *present*!
7. What is that *object* on the table?
8. Do you think anyone would *object* if I ate this cake?
9. I can't *permit* you to stay out late again.
10. You need a special *permit* to park here.

4. Woordspelletjes en andere aktiviteiten

Maak gebruik van de illustraties in je woordenboek

Oefening 48

1. Bekijk de tekening van de badkamer op bladzij 15 in je woordenboek en schrijf de woorden op die nieuw voor je zijn.
2. Vul deze groep woorden in met behulp van de cijfers onderaan de
tekening.

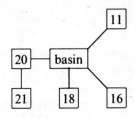

3. Maak onderstaande zinnen af, weer met behulp van de cijfers
onderaan de tekening.

   (a) Have you got a clean (22) I could use?
   (b) My electric (13) is broken – could I borrow yours?
   (c) He spends ten minutes every morning just looking in the (10).
   (d) I've cut myself – have you got a (17)?
   (e) Take your shoes off before you stand on the (4).

4. De voornaamste woorden en uitdrukkingen:

   to have a bath/shower   to comb/brush your hair
   to wash/have a wash   to brush your teeth
   to shave

Oefening 49

1. Bekijk de tekening van de slaapkamer op bladzij 17 in je woordenboek en schrijf de woorden op die nieuw voor je zijn.

2. Vul deze groep woorden in.

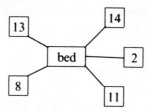

3. Maak onderstaande zinnen af.

    (a) I'm sure I left my jacket in the (16).
    (b) If you want to read in bed, put the (7) on.
    (c) I always sleep with the (17) open and the (4)s drawn.
    (d) Where are my (15)?
    (e) I keep my shirts in the bottom (6).

4. De voornaamste woorden en uitdrukkingen:

to undress/get undressed	to get up
to go to bed	to get dressed
to stay in bed	to make the bed
to lie in	

Oefening 50

1. Bekijk de tekening van het lichaam op bladzij 23 in je woordenboek en schrijf de woorden die nieuw voor je zijn op.
2. Vul de volgende groepen woorden in.

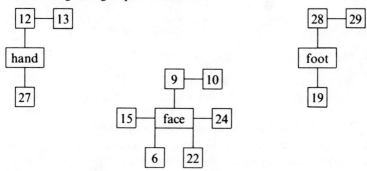

3. Zoek in je woordenboek het woord **joint** op. Welke vijf gewrichten staan er op de tekening?

4. Zoek in je woordenboek het woord **ache** op. Hieronder staan enkele manieren waarop dit woord gebruikt kan worden.

   I slept this morning, and I've had a headache all day.
   You must go to the doctor if your earache doesn't get better.
   She's got stomach ache because she ate too many apples.

5. Kijk nu nog eens naar Oefening 30 op bladzij 268, die laat zien hoe lichaamsdelen gebruikt worden in bepaalde uitdrukkingen.

Oefening 51

1. Bekijk in je woordenboek de tekening van kleren op bladzij 38 en schrijf de woorden die nieuw voor je zijn op.
2. Vul de volgende groepen woorden in.

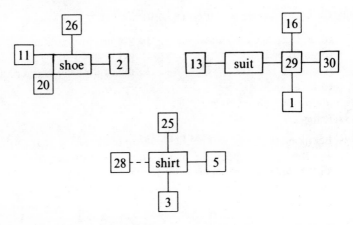

3. Maak onderstaande zinnen af.

   (a) I'm looking for a dark green (17), size 36.
   (b) You should always wear a (12) when you go on a motorbike.
   (c) Have you got a pair of size 8 brown leather (7)s, please?
   (d) You'll need a (19) if you're going to London – it never stops raining there.
   (e) I prefer wearing (23) in the summer.

4. De voornaamste woorden en uitdrukkingen:

to put clothes on
to take clothes off
to do up your coat/buttons/zip
a pair of trousers/jeans/shorts/socks/shoes/gloves

5. Dialoog
Vul samen met een ander de ontbrekende woorden in. De leerling die de rol van de klant speelt kan een kledingstuk op de tekening uitzoeken en in de eerste opengelaten ruimte invullen.

SHOP ASSISTANT: Good morning, sir/madam. Can I help you?
CUSTOMER: I'm looking for _____.
SHOP ASSISTANT: Certainly. What size?
CUSTOMER: _____.
SHOP ASSISTANT: Are you looking for any particular colour?
CUSTOMER: Yes, I'd like _____.
SHOP ASSISTANT: The _____ are over there by the lift.
SHOP ASSISTANT: Would you like to try this one/these?
CUSTOMER: It's/They're too small/big/tight/loose/short/long.
SHOP ASSISTANT: Try a smaller/bigger size.
CUSTOMER: That's fine. I'll take it/them, thank you.

Oefening 52

1. Bekijk de tekening van het landschap op bladzij 45 in je woordenboek en schrijf de woorden die nieuw voor je zijn op.
2. Beantwoord de volgende vragen:

   (a) What types of animal are there in the picture?
   (b) Where would you go if you wanted to swim in the sea?
   (c) What is the line showing the furthest point you can see?
   (d) What is the man in the field driving?
   (e) What is the word for a private area of grass in front of or behind a house?
   (f) What is the word for a small area of trees?
   (g) How do you get from the farmyard into the field?

3. Schrijfoefening:
   Doe alsof je hier je vakantie doorbrengt en beschrijf dit landschap
   zo volledig mogelijk in een brief aan een vriend(in).

Oefening 53

1. Bekijk de tekening van de keuken op bladzij 103 in je woordenboek
   en schrijf de woorden die nieuw voor je zijn op.

2. Beantwoord de volgende vragen:

   (a) Which things in the kitchen would stop working without elec-
       tricity?
   (b) Where is the frying pan?
   (c) Where are the glasses?
   (d) Where is the saucepan?
   (e) Where is the milk?
   (f) Where are the teacloths?

3. De voornaamste woorden en uitdrukkingen:

to wash up	to roast
to cook	to freeze
to boil	frozen food
to fry	tinned food

Oefening 54

1. Bekijk de tekening van de woonkamer op bladzij 112 in je woordenboek en schrijf de woorden die nieuw voor je zijn op.
2. Beantwoord de volgende vragen:

   (a) What four things in the living room can you sit on or in?
   (b) Where is the picture?
   (c) Where is the television?
   (d) Where are the loudspeakers?
   (e) Where is the rug?
   (f) Where is the telephone?

3. De voornaamste woorden en uitdrukkingen:

to watch television	to sit on a chair
to listen to the radio	on a sofa
a programme on television/on the radio	in an armchair

4. Schrijfoefening:
   Beschrijf je eigen huiskamer zo volledig mogelijk en maak daarbij gebruik van de woorden op het plaatje.

Oefening 55

1. Bekijk de tekening van het kantoor op bladzij 137 in je woordenboek en schrijf de woorden die nieuw voor je zijn op.

2. Beantwoord de volgende vragen:

   (a) Can you name five things on the desk where the woman is sitting?
   (b) What is the woman doing?
   (c) What is on the empty chair?
   (d) Where is the noticeboard?
   (e) How is the calendar fixed to the wall?
   (f) Where is the safe?

3. De voornaamste woorden en uitdrukkingen:

to go to work	to arrange a meeting/an
to work for a firm/company	appointment
to phone/ring someone (up)	coffee/tea break
to be on the phone/other line	lunch hour

Oefening 56

1. Bekijk de tekening van het restaurant op bladzij 169 van je woordenboek en schrijf de woorden die nieuw voor je zijn op.

2. Vul de groepen woorden in.

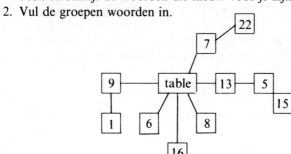

3. Maak onderstaande zinnen af.

   (a) Excuse me, may we have the (1), please?

(b) We'll have to ask the (21) for another (7).
(c) Would you pass the (14) and (12), please?
(d) Do you have a (17) for five?
(e) My brother works as a (20) in the evenings.

Oefening 57

1. Bekijk het menu voor de lunch op bladzij 121 in je woordenboek en schrijf de woorden die nieuw voor je zijn op.
2. Vul samen met een ander de ontbrekende woorden in in onderstaande dialoog. De leerling die de rol van de klant speelt kan gerechten op het menu kiezen om in de opengelaten ruimtes in te vullen.

CUSTOMER: A table for one, please.
WAITER: This way, please.

WAITER: May I take your order, sir/madam?
CUSTOMER: I'll start with _____, and then have _____, please.

WAITER: Any vegetables?
CUSTOMER: Yes, I'd like some _____ and some _____.

WAITER: Anything to drink?
CUSTOMER: _____.

CUSTOMER: Can I see the menu again, please?
WAITER: Certainly. Here you are.

CUSTOMER: I'll have _____, and a cup of coffee. And could I have the bill, please?

De leerling die de rol van de kelner speelt kan uitrekenen hoeveel de maaltijd gekost heeft. Denk erom dat de bediening niet is inbegrepen.

3. De voornaamste woorden en uitdrukkingen:

to eat out (= at a restaurant, not at home)
to book/reserve a table
to order
to tip the waiter/waitress
to leave a tip

service charge
first course
main course
dessert

Oefening 58

1. Bekijk de tekening van de straten op bladzij 204 in je woordenboek en schrijf de woorden die nieuw voor je zijn op.
2. Maak onderstaande zinnen af.

   (a) It's safer to cross the road at the (25).
   (b) The bank is just on the corner, at the (8).
   (c) Could you tell me where the nearest (3) is, please?
   (d) There's a (13) just outside the post office.
   (e) Wait until the (23) are red before you cross the street.

3. Kombineer de boodschappen op het lijstje met de winkel waar je ze kunt krijgen.

bread	milk	(a) butcher's
butter	newspaper	(b) baker's
		(c) post office
cheese	apples	(d) supermarket
cabbage	cakes	(e) grocer's
		(f) greengrocer's
beef	birthday card	(g) newsagent's
potatoes	cough medicine	(h) chemist's
	stamps	

Maak voor iedere winkel een 'woordgroep', waaraan je nieuwe woorden die je leert toevoegt.

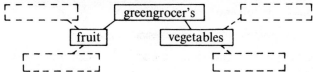

4. Schets een eenvoudige plattegrond van de voornaamste winkelbuurt in een stad of gedeelte van een stad die je goed kent en geef de gebouwen en winkels aan. Welke dingen zijn ook op de tekening in je woordenboek te vinden?

Oefening 59

1. Bekijk de tekening van vervoersmiddelen op bladzij 223 in je woordenboek en schrijf de woorden die nieuw voor je zijn op.
2. Vul de groep woorden in.

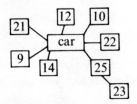

3. Maak onderstaande zinnen af.
   (a) He always goes to work by (17).
   (b) If you want to move house, you'll have to hire a (24).
   (c) Some businessmen go to work by (15).
   (d) The car nearly hit a (8) at the roundabout.
   (e) It's much cheaper to go by (6) than by train.

4. De voornaamste woorden en uitdrukkingen:

   to go by car/train/bus/air   season ticket
   to go on foot   single/return ticket
   to get into/out of a car/taxi   rush hour
   to get on/off a bus/coach/train/bicycle/   traffic
      motorbike   traffic jam
   to catch a bus/train/plane   traffic lights

5. Discussie:
   Hoe ga je naar je werk/school? Hoe lang doe je erover? Hoeveel kost het je per maand?

Spelling

Woorden van 'n woord

Je kunt leren spellen door te kijken hoeveel woorden je kunt maken van de letters in een bepáald woord. Iedere letter van dat woord kan in elk nieuw woord maar één keer gebruikt worden. Bekijk het volgende voorbeeld:

dictionary   ton, air, tin, ran, rain, coat, cat

Maak zoveel woorden als je kunt uit:

opportunities, moustache, development, education, mathematics

Zoek de door jou bedachte woorden en hun spelling in het woordenboek op.

Letter vierkant

Probeer met behulp van het onderstaande vierkant woorden te vormen door een letter naar een ander hokje te verplaatsen in elke gewenste richting.

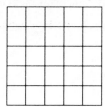

Zoek de woorden die vindt in je woordenboek op.

Het kruiswoord spel

Dit spel wordt in een groep gespeeld.
Elke speler tekent een aantal lege hokjes, bijvoorbeeld 5 bij 5:

De eerste speler noemt een letter en de overige spelers plaatsen deze letter in een van hun hokjes zonder de anderen te laten zien waar.

De tweede speler noemt daarna op zijn beurt een letter, die de overige spelers in hun kruiswoord opschrijven. De letter mag overal geplaatst worden, maar eenmaal opgeschreven mag ze niet meer worden verplaatst. De volgende letter wordt pas gegeven als iedereen de vorige heeft opgeschreven.

Gebruik je woordenboek als hulp bij het vinden en plaatsen van de letters en om mogelijke woorden op te zoeken.

Als alle hokjes vol zijn, moet je zowel horizontaal als vertikaal zo veel mogelijk woorden hebben.

Je krijgt: 3 punten voor een woord van drie letters.
4 punten voor een woord van 4 letters.
5 punten voor een woord van 5 letters.

Degene die aan het eind van het spel de meeste punten verzameld heeft, is de winnaar.

Woorden bouwen

Woorden verzamelen

Dit spel kan in de klas of in een groep gespeeld worden. Het is de bedoeling om een groep woorden samen te stellen die met dezelfde letters beginnen.

De leerkracht of een groepslid leest uit het woordenboek vijf vertalingen voor van woorden die allemaal met **com-** beginnen.

1. commissie   *committee*
2. gewoon   *common*
3. metgezel   *companion*
4. bedrijf   *company*
5. geheel   *complete*

De overige groepsleden proberen het juiste woord te bedenken en op te schrijven (zonder daarbij in hun woordenboek te kijken!).
Doe hetzelfde met onderstaande lettergroepen:

per-, car-, che-, dis-, sha-

Samenstellingen verzamelen

Dit spelletje lijkt op 'woorden verzamelen', maar het gaat hierbij om samenstellingen (een samenstelling bestaat uit twee aaneengevoegde woorden, bijvoorbeeld, **seaside**). Het is geschikt voor in de klas of in een groep.

Er worden door iemand vertalingen voorgelezen van samenstellingen die met een bepaald hoofdwoord beginnen, bijvoorbeeld **sea**. De overige leden van de groep krijgen het hoofdwoord op en moeten zelf de samenstellingen bedenken en opschrijven.

1. zeeman   *seaman*
2. zeeziek   *seasick*
3. zeekust   *seaside*
4. zeewier   *seaweed*

Doe hetzelfde met de volgende woorden:

eye, post, cross, tooth, hand, hair, life

Sleutel voor de Oefeningen

Oefening 1

1. telbaar	6. niet-telbaar
2. niet-telbaar	7. niet-telbaar
3. niet-telbaar	8. telbaar
4. telbaar	9. niet-telbaar
5. niet-telbaar	10. niet-telbaar

Oefening 2

1. (b)	6. (c)
2. (a)	7. **1.** (b)
3. (b)	8. **1.** (a)
4. (a)	9. (a)
5. (a)	10. (b)

Oefening 3

1. some	6. how many
2. a piece of	7. a few
3. much	8. too much
4. too much	9. some
5. a little	10. as many

Oefening 4

1. ladies	6. babies
2. valleys	7. journeys
3. cities	8. replies
4. countries	9. parties
5. keys	10. days

Groep 1: 1, 2, 3, 4, 6, 8 en 9
Groep 2: 2, 5, 7 en 10

Het patroon: aan een zelfstandig naamwoord met een klinker voor de uitgang **-y** in het enkelvoud wordt in het meervoud **-s** toegevoegd; zelfstandige naamwoorden met een medeklinker voor de uitgang **-y** krijgen in het meervoud **-ies** inplaats van **-y**.

Oefening 5
1. feet
2. teeth
3. men
4. women
5. mice

Oefening 6
1. shelves
2. knives
3. wives
4. loaves
5. thieves

Oefening 7

1. boxes	6. watches
2. potatoes	7. dresses
3. buses	8. photos
4. glasses	9. matches
5. brushes	10. pianos

Algemeen geldt de regel dat zelfstandige naamwoorden die uitgaan op **-ch, -sh, -s, -x** en **-o** in het meervoud **-es** krijgen. Let op de uitzonderingen **photos** en **pianos**.

Oefening 8
1. faster
2. taller
3. bigger
4. fatter and fatter
5. quicker

Oefening 9
1. slowest
2. driest
3. darkest
4. poorest
5. weakest

Oefening 10
1. sillier
2. cleverer
3. politest
4. prettier
5. simplest

Oefening 11

1. worse	6. least
2. worst	7. more
3. better	8. most
4. best	9. further
5. less	10. furthest

Oefening 12
1. most interesting
2. commonest
3. closer
4. more sensible
5. most horrible
6. curlier
7. lighter
8. most exciting
9. most boring
10. muddier and muddier

Oefening 13
1. probably
2. simply
3. angrily
4. possibly
5. happily

Oefening 14
1. practically
2. narrowly
3. highly
4. lately
5. hardly

Oefening 15
1. adverb
2. adjective
3. adverb
4. adjective
5. adverb

Oefening 16
1. concerns
2. goes
3. invites
4. does
5. complains
6. carries
7. watches
8. brushes
9. closes
10. misses

Oefening 17
1. loading
2. snowing
3. rushing
4. sitting
5. getting
6. running
7. rubbing
8. smoking
9. living
10. making

Oefening 18
1. stopped
2. agreed
3. planned
4. accompanied
5. divided

Oefening 19
1. wrote
2. saw
3. told
4. thought
5. stood
6. wore
7. said
8. drove
9. built
10. kept

Oefening 20
1. paid
2. run
3. cut
4. known
5. left
6. put
7. slept
8. taken
9. stuck
10. stolen

Oefening 21
1. at
2. on
3. at
4. at
5. on
6. for
7. since
8. by
9. with
10. in

Oefening 22
1. of
2. at
3. on
4. in
5. to
6. from
7. of
8. to
9. of
10. of

Oefening 23
1. well, good
2. library, bookshop
3. stranger, foreigner
4. amused, amusing
5. think, mean
6. after, afterwards
7. for, since
8. beat, win
9. take, brings
10. waited, expecting

Oefening 24
1. switch off
2. produces
3. refused
4. arrived
5. send away

Oefening 25
1. escape
2. becoming old
3. return
4. take out
5. get out of bed

Oefening 26
1. steal
2. invent
3. went towards
4. think about
5. see

Oefening 27
1. on
2. off
3. on
4. through
5. across

Oefening 28
1. up
2. after
3. for
4. in
5. out

Oefening 29
1. after
2. off
3. over
4. on
5. off

Oefening 30
1. keep an eye on
2. put my foot in it
3. give me a hand
4. keeping our fingers crossed
5. pulling your leg

Oefening 31
1. holiday
2. tap
3. railway
4. garden
5. lift

Oefening 32
1. (d)   7. (c)
2. (g)   8. (l)
3. (j)   9. (e)
4. (i)   10. (b)
5. (k)   11. (a)
6. (h)   12. (f)

Oefening 33
1. (f)   5. (c)
2. (g)   6. (h)
3. (e)   7. (d)
4. (a)   8. (b)

Oefening 34
1. (g)   6. (h)
2. (d)   7. (c)
3. (j)   8. (e)
4. (b)   9. (a)
5. (i)   10. (f)

Oefening 35

aʊ	əʊ
cow	slow
brown	know
now	low
how	throw

Oefening 36

ʊ	uː
foot	moon
look	spoon
book	food
put	tooth

Oefening 37

ɪə	eə
clear	bear
dear	wear
ear	tear
hear	
near	

Oefening 38

θ	ð
thick	these
thank	weather
bath	without
think	they

Oefening 39

s	z
mouse	lose
loose	wise
use (*zelfstandig naamwoord*)	use (*werkwoord*)
grease	please

Oefening 40
1. li:d
2. led
3. klɔʊs
4. kləʊz
5. teə
6. tɪəz
7. ju:s
8. ju:z
9. raʊ
10. rəʊ

Oefening 41
Groep 1 thought, brought
Groep 2 cough
Groep 3 rough, enough
Groep 4 plough
Groep 5 though
Groep 6 through

Oefening 42
1. k
2. b
3. n
4. k
5. k
6. b
7. b
8. k
9. p
10. w

Oefening 43
Groep 1
i*dea*
be*lieve*
a*broad*
re*tire*
pre*pare*

Groep 2
*si*lly
*cle*ver
*ea*sy
*lo*cal
*par*ty

Oefening 44
Groep 1
*in*strument
*di*fficult
*ci*nema
*e*nemy
*me*mory

Groep 2
de*ve*lop
e*le*ven
di*vi*sion
ho*ri*zon
o*pi*nion

Oefening 45
Groep 1
edu*ca*tion
ope*ra*tion
invi*ta*tion
mathe*ma*tics
infor*ma*tion

Groep 2
im*po*ssible
in*te*lligent
a*bi*lity
par*ti*cular
in*du*strial

Oefening 46
zelfstandig naamwoord
1. *re*cord
2. *in*crease
3. *pre*sent
4. *ob*ject

werkwoord
re*cord*
in*crease*
pre*sent*
ob*ject*

5. *per*mit   per*mit*
In paren 1, 3, 4 en 5 verandert de uitspraak.

Oefening 47
1. *re*cords
2. re*cord*
3. in*crease*
4. *in*crease
5. pre*sent*
6. *pre*sent
7. *ob*ject
8. ob*ject*
9. per*mit*
10. *per*mit

Oefening 48
2.

3. (a) towel
   (b) razor
   (c) mirror
   (d) plaster
   (e) scales

Oefening 49
2.
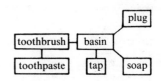

3. (a) wardrobe
   (b) lamp
   (c) window, curtains
   (d) slippers
   (e) drawer

Oefening 50
2.
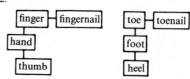

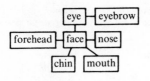

3. ankle, elbow, knee, neck, wrist

Oefening 51

2.

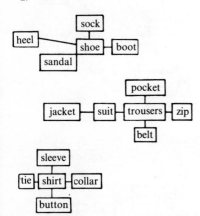

3. (a) pullover
   (b) helmet
   (c) gloves
   (d) raincoat
   (e) shorts

Oefening 52

2. (a) cows, ducks, hens, horses, pigs, sheep
   (b) to the beach
   (c) the horizon
   (d) a tractor
   (e) lawn
   (f) wood
   (g) through the gate

Oefening 53

2. (a) cooker, electric light, fridge, kettle, oven
   (b) on the wall
   (c) in the cupboard
   (d) on the cooker
   (e) in the fridge, in the jug on the table
   (f) on the cupboard door

Oefening 54

2. (a) in the armchair/rocking chair, on the sofa/chair
   (b) on the wall, above the fireplace
   (c) on the cupboard
   (d) on the (top) shelf
   (e) on the floor
   (f) next to the record player

Oefening 55

2. (b) talking on the telephone
   (c) a magazine
   (d) on the wall
   (e) with a drawing pin
   (f) against the wall, under the window

Oefening 56

2.

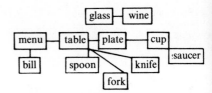

3. (a) bill
   (b) waitress, glass
   (c) salt, pepper
   (d) table
   (e) waiter

Oefening 58

2. (a) zebra crossing
   (b) crossroads
   (c) call box
   (d) letterbox
   (e) traffic lights

3. (a) beef
   (b) bread, cakes
   (c) stamps
   (d) bread, butter, cheese, cabbage,
   beef, potatoes, milk, apples, cakes
   (e) butter, cheese, milk
   (f) cabbage, potatoes, apples
   (g) newspaper, birthday card
   (h) cough medicine

Oefening 59

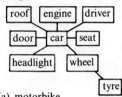

3. (a) motorbike
   (b) van
   (c) helicopter
   (d) cyclist
   (e) coach